D1605874

DAILY LIVES OF

Civilians in Wartime Early America

DAILY LIVES OF

Civilians in Wartime Early America

From the Colonial Era to the Civil War

EDITED BY DAVID S. HEIDLER AND JEANNE T. HEIDLER

The Greenwood Press "Daily Life Through History" Series
Daily Life of Civilians during Wartime
David S. Heidler and Jeanne T. Heidler, Series Editors

GREENWOOD PRESS
Westport, Connecticut • London

Library of Congress Cataloging-in-Publication Data

Daily lives of civilians in wartime early America : from the colonial era to the Civil War / edited by David S. Heidler and Jeanne T. Heidler.
    p. cm. — (The Greenwood Press Daily life through history series : daily lives of civilians during wartime, ISSN 1080–4749)
  Includes bibliographical references and index.
  ISBN 0–313–33526–5 (alk. paper)
  1. United States—History, Military—To 1900. 2. United States—Social conditions—To 1865. 3. War and society—United States—History.
4. Combatants and noncombatants (International law)—History.
5. Civil-military relations—United States—History. I. Heidler, David Stephen, 1955– II. Heidler, Jeanne T.
  E181.D23 2007
  973.5—dc22   2006030403

British Library Cataloguing in Publication Data is available.

Library of Congress Catalog Card Number: 2006030403
ISBN 10: 0–313–33526–5
ISBN 13: 978–0–313–33526–6
ISSN: 1080–4749

First published in 2007

Greenwood Press, 88 Post Road West, Westport, CT 06881
An imprint of Greenwood Publishing Group, Inc.
www.greenwood.com

Printed in the United States of America

The paper used in this book complies with the Permanent Paper Standard issued by the National Information Standards Organization (Z39.48–1984).

10 9 8 7 6 5 4 3 2 1

Contents

Series Foreword

Few scenes are as poignant as that of civilian refugees torn from their homes and put to plodding flight along dusty roads, carrying their possessions in crude bundles and makeshift carts. We have all seen the images. Before photography, paintings and crude drawings told the story, but despite the media, the same sense of the awful emerges from these striking portrayals: the pace of the flight is agonizingly slow; the numbers are sobering and usually arrayed in single file along the edges of byways that stretch to the horizon. The men appear hunched and beaten, the women haggard, the children strangely old, and usually the wide-eyed look of fear has been replaced by one of bone-grinding weariness. They likely stagger through country redolent with the odor of smoke and death as heavy guns mutter in the distance. It always seems to be raining on these people, or snowing, and it is either brutally cold or oppressively hot. In the past, clattering hooves would send them skittering away from the path of cavalry; more recently whirring engines of motorized convoys push them from the road. Aside from becoming casualties, civilians who become refugees experience the most devastating impact of war, for they truly become orphans of the storm, lacking the barest necessities of food and clothing except for what they can carry and eventually what they can steal.

The volumes in this series seek to illuminate that extreme example of the civilian experience in wartime and more, for those on distant home fronts also can make remarkable sacrifices, whether through their labors to support the war effort or by enduring the absence of loved ones far from home and in great peril. And war can impinge on indigenous populations in eccentric ways. Stories of a medieval world in which a farmer fearful about his crops could prevail on armies to fight elsewhere are possibly exaggerated, the product of nostalgia for a chivalric code that most likely did not hold much sway during a coarse and vicious time. In any period and at any place, the fundamental reality of war is that organized violence is no less brutal for its being structured by strategy and tactics. The advent of total war might have been signaled by the famous *levee en masse* of the French Revolution, but that development was more a culmination of a trend than an innovation away from more pacific times. In short, all wars have assailed and will assail civilians in one way or another to a greater or lesser degree. The Thirty Years' War displaced populations just as the American Revolution saw settlements preyed upon, houses razed, and farms pillaged. Modern codes of conduct adopted by both international consent and embraced by the armies of the civilized world have heightened awareness about the sanctity of civilians and have improved vigilance about violations of that sanctity, but in the end such codes will never guarantee immunity from the rage of battle or the rigors of war.

In this series, accomplished scholars have recruited prescient colleagues to write essays that reveal both the universal civilian experience in wartime and aspects of it made unique by time and place. Readers will discover in these pages the other side of warfare, one that is never placid, even if far removed from the scenes of fighting. As these talented authors show, the shifting expectations of governments markedly transformed the civilian wartime experience from virtual non-involvement in early modern times to the twentieth century's expectation of sacrifice, exertion, and contribution. Finally, as the western powers have come full circle by asking virtually no sacrifice from civilians at all, they have stumbled upon the peculiar result that diminishing deprivation during a war can increase civilian dissent against it.

Moreover, the geographical and chronological span of these books is broad and encompassing to reveal the unique perspectives of how war affects people whether they are separated by hemispheres or centuries, people who are distinct by way of different cultures yet similar because of their common humanity. As readers will see, days on a home front far from battle usually become a surreal routine of the ordinary existing in tandem with the extraordinary, a situation in which hours of waiting and expectation become blurred against the backdrop of normal tasks and everyday events. That situation is a constant, whether for a village in Asia or Africa or Europe or the Americas.

Consequently, these books confirm that the human condition always produces the similar as well as the singular, a paradox that war tends to amplify. Every war is much like another, but no war is really the same as any other. All places are much alike, but no place is wholly separable from its matchless identity. The civilian experience in war mirrors these verities. We are certain that readers will find in these books a vivid illumination of those truths.

David S. Heidler and Jeanne T. Heidler, Series Editors

Introduction

David S. Heidler and Jeanne T. Heidler

Archeological evidence shows that before European settlement occurred in North America, Native American noncombatants endured frequent war, and from the outset of Spanish, English, and French colonization in North America, civilians regularly experienced war. Historians such as Russell Weigley and John Grenier have written extensively about an "American Way of War,"[1] yet the American civilian experience in wartime defies a rigid description. The only constant during the two centuries after colonization was that American civilians experienced war, sometimes in their own backyards, and that the lines between civilians and combatants were usually blurred.

Though often accompanied by soldiers who had fought in Europe or Ireland, many colonists who came to North America had never experienced war firsthand. Because soldiers in North America needed help fighting Indians or other Europeans, civilians quickly learned the rudiments of combat. A militia system rapidly emerged in the British colonies that despite its imperfections at least forced civilians to shoulder the burdens of organized self-defense. In fact, they had little choice, for as Armstrong Starkey points out in his essay on civilians during the colonial wars, military discipline was essential for the survival of the Jamestown colony. Savage wars that interrupted periods of relative peace featured frequent attacks on civilian targets by both sides as cycles of retribution targeted women and children and left entire towns in ashes.

European and Native American notions of warfare both justified the killing and terrorizing of civilians, but for different reasons. Protestant Englishmen who had fought Catholic Irishmen viewed new Indian enemies as virtually the same as old Irish foes, and neither, in the British estimation, deserved quarter. Indians saw little distinction between soldier and civilian. In war, all were enemies and treated accordingly. By the late seventeenth century issues of race increasingly justified the killing or enslaving of noncombatants. Indians were swift to retaliate, and any undefended white village or home was fair game, although for English colonists, attacks did not always end in death. Indians often took colonists captive either to take the place of loved ones killed by Europeans or to hold hostages for ransom. Many such captives eventually returned to their families, but others, particularly white children raised by Indians, frequently chose to stay with their captors and live as Indians.

The indiscriminate violence of colonial warfare can create the false impression that in this world knives were always drawn and fighting was a constant state of affairs. Yet, most colonists were never attacked by Indians, and most Indians were not killed directly by colonists. Following the initial stages of settlement, colonists usually lived in relative peace, especially in places such as Pennsylvania. In areas where land and resources were limited, however, colonists could be in life and death struggles with native inhabitants.

Competition for marginal farmlands in New England, for instance, produced one of the bloodiest colonial Indian wars in 1675. As with almost all of these quarrels, land was at the center of the dispute. While natural increase and immigration swelled the English population, European diseases devastated Indians, who were compelled to surrender more and more land until such cessions sparked hostilities. Colonists called it King Philip's War, their name for the Wampanoag headman Metacom.

By the end of the seventeenth century, competition between European colonizing powers for North American lands placed the British and French in the North and the British and Spaniards in the South on collision courses. As these European powers vied for control of North America from the 1690s to 1763, colonists were swept up in astonishingly vicious wars. These imperial conflicts culminated in what American settlers called the French and Indian War (the Seven Years' War in Europe), a war that ended with the conquest of French Canada (New France) by the British and the ceding of Spanish Florida to Great Britain. Without contiguous threats to Britain's possessions, relative peace settled on British colonial frontiers. But Britain's efforts to organize its empire more efficiently gradually alienated the North American colonies and transformed some of the subjects living there into revolutionaries.

Like colonial conflicts, the American Revolution blurred the lines between civilians and combatants. Local militias figured prominently in both American and British forces and hailed from communities deeply divided over the conflict. Understandable frictions resulted. Soldiers away with either the Continental or British armies feared for their families, and with good reason, for at some point in the war virtually every part of the country was invaded by British soldiers or their Tory allies, and few of either camp had any compunction about looting homes for valuables as well as necessities. Officers tried to prevent the worst atrocities, but sometimes they were either absent or simply chose to look the other way as property was destroyed, women were raped, and murders occurred.

In some areas, the American Revolution devolved into civil war. The toll on the civilian population in such cases was much higher as neighbor fought neighbor, entire communities were destroyed, and murders happened with impunity. In areas Revolutionaries controlled, Loyalists were economically persecuted and physically threatened. Loyalists who tried to stay in their homes could be forced to swear allegiance to the Patriot cause and were carefully monitored in any case.

Some historians have estimated that during the early stages of the Revolution, about half the population was neutral. The large number of Quakers and Moravians in America had religious scruples against all war, but all pacifists were suspected by both Revolutionaries and Loyalists. Other colonists simply tried to remain neutral throughout the conflict, although they were usually compelled to swear allegiance to one side or the other. As Wayne Lee demonstrates in his essay on the American Revolution, those who refused often became destitute refugees, looking for safe haven anywhere they could find it.

Both sides expected able bodied men to fight, and as large a percentage of the male population served in some military capacity during the American Revolution as in any other American war. As the war dragged on, increasing manpower needs pressured men to join a military unit, and the spreading conflict scattered even state militias far from their homes. Absent husbands, fathers, and sons left women and children to eke out existence on farms where only labor-intensive planting and harvesting stood between them and starvation. States tried to alleviate these burdens on communities by devising systems that used only part of the militia at any one time, but invasions required all men to take up arms.

In addition to manning the armies, the civilian population also provided supplies to the armies in the field, especially food. Armies that numbered in the thousands sorely taxed local resources, sometimes to the breaking point. Even supporters of the army hid food and livestock to prevent soldiers from stripping their larders and plundering their pastures. Stealing food and supplies presented few moral dilemmas for the British, but Revolutionaries needed to maintain good local relations to have any chance at success. General George Washington, for example, tried to prevent his forces from overly irritating civilians with demands for food, but such efforts could prove futile when men were hungry and desperate.

Excesses against civilians by both sides undoubtedly shaped opinions about the conflict, views that hardened when armies deliberately terrorized local populations. British forces mounted such a campaign in Virginia in 1781 when raiders under Benedict Arnold and soldiers under Lord Cornwallis convinced even the most cautious Virginians to support the Patriot cause.

Many Americans suffered during the war—both rural villages and size-able towns experienced shortages and saw prices rise—but a few prospered, such as merchants who sold goods at inflated prices to both armies. Those who sold to the British saw the greatest short-term gains, but they lost much of this wealth when the British lost the war. Loyalist merchants were not the only ones who suffered at the end of the war. Patriots faced dire challenges as well. Economic devastation and greatly impaired commercial relations with Great Britain meant years of economic depression. And former colonists no longer had the British army to protect frontiers inhabited by Indians, people who increasingly counted land-hungry Americans as enemies.

The end of the American Revolution did not mean an end to warfare on the frontier. Those Native Americans who sided with the British during the Revolution might have suffered a devastating defeat at the close of the war, but they were nonetheless unwilling to relinquish native lands to the United States. During the next two decades, intermittent Indian warfare on the northern and southern frontiers punctuated an uneasy calm with Britons in Canada and Spaniards in Florida and Louisiana. The French Revolutionary and Napoleonic wars, however, threatened that fragile peace and finally destroyed it.

A variety of irritants led to the War of 1812 between the United States and Great Britain. One involved supposed foreign encouragement of Indian unrest on America's frontiers. American expansion into the West increased pressure on Indian populations, and Native Americans first resisted white settlement with warfare in the 1780s and 1790s and then tried to control it with treaties. But white settlers still came. As northern Indians sought help from their former British allies in Canada, their south-ern counterparts asked for Spanish aid from Florida. In addition, nativ-ist movements rejected white culture and urged a return to native ways to combat white encroachment. Some, such as the charismatic Shawnee prophet Tenskwatawa, believed that war was the only solution, an atti-tude that prompted a preemptive strike against Tenskwatawa and his brother Tecumseh when William Henry Harrison led a military expedi-tion against Prophet's Town on Tippecanoe Creek in November 1811. In some respects, the campaign was the opening of the War of 1812, because Harrison's victory drove the survivors of Prophet's Town into the arms of the British in Canada. By 1813, Indian warfare plagued the frontier from New York to the Great Lakes to the Gulf of Mexico

The South was the scene of some especially vicious fighting. Creek Indians were among those Indians alarmed by the encroachments of white settlers, and a faction of nativists called Red Sticks went to war with fellow Creeks who were inclined to accommodate whites. Early in this Creek civil war, Red Sticks attacked a settlement at Fort Mims, which contained whites and mixed white–Creek settlers in August 1813, killing most of the civilians and spurring the U.S. government to muster neighboring state and territorial militias to defeat the Red Sticks. By March 1814, Major General Andrew Jackson had cornered many of the Red Stick warriors as well as their families at a place called the Horseshoe on the Tallapoosa River in modern-day Alabama. In the battle of Horseshoe Bend, Jackson killed most Red Stick warriors and took the women and children prisoner.[2]

By then, the United States had been at war with Britain for almost two years. In an essay of exceptionally broad scope, Richard Barbuto illustrates that the War of 1812, like all wars, exposed American civilians to a variety of experiences. Although the war primarily assailed the country's edges—its frontiers and coastlines—many Americans in the interior felt the war's effects as well. Shortages and high prices beset most people; exporters could not ship products out of the country; and importers could not bring products in.

But for those on the edges who experienced the war firsthand, suffering reminiscent of the worst days of colonial warfare and the Revolution tore at the very heart of civilian lives. The frontier and the border regions of British Canada were the settings for horrific violence. By the second year of the conflict, the British navy was bringing the war to the American seacoast, particularly in lightly defended towns and villages, and by 1814 civilians in Washington, Baltimore, Plattsburgh, and New Orleans saw their cities menaced and, in the case of the capital, occupied and destroyed.

As Barbuto shows, matters did not start or progress well. In Michigan, an old, tired Revolutionary War veteran named William Hull disgraced his command by surrendering Detroit, ostensibly to spare American civilians from an Indian massacre. But surrender did not always mean safety. Indians attacked civilians retreating with soldiers from Fort Dearborn (modern-day Chicago) and killed most of the men, women, and children. On the frontier bracketing the Niagara River, civilians endured a cycle of attack and retaliation that left towns and villages in ashes and forced civilians to wander the countryside in the dead of winter looking for shelter and food. Along the Atlantic coast and in Chesapeake Bay, the situation was no better. British forces bombarded and raided port towns. Defenseless villages along the Maine coast were occupied for much of the war. The worst excesses occurred in Chesapeake Bay, where towns were pillaged and destroyed. In Hampton, Virginia, soldiers preyed on the female population and committed numerous rapes. The British seized Washington, D.C., and burned its public buildings.

And yet there were American successes. In the fall of 1814, the British were repelled at Plattsburgh and Baltimore, and the massive British offensive against New Orleans, the most important port on the Gulf of Mexico, was an utter failure. With New Orleans in near panic, Andrew Jackson systematically prepared the city's defenses, commanded a force made up of militia forces from all over the South, and solicited the aid of New Orleans' civilians (including the free black population there), to crush the British assault on January 8, 1815. The news of Jackson's victory reached Washington, D.C., just as reports were arriving that British and American negotiators had signed a peace treaty in Ghent, Belgium.

The nation erupted in wild celebrations. Although the Treaty of Ghent simply returned the two countries to their prewar status and did not address any American grievances, the United States took pride in holding its own against Great Britain, then the most powerful nation on Earth. Nationalism surged, and a spirit of expansionism beckoned settlers westward. That expansion eventually sparked more Indian conflict and ultimately gave rise to the policy of Indian removal that would exile eastern tribes to lands west of the Mississippi. And expansion also set the United States at odds with its southern neighbor.

War with Mexico broke out in 1846, a direct result of American settlement in Texas that had begun in the 1820s. The Mexican government, desiring a frontier buffer for the more populated parts of Mexico, encouraged settlers to inhabit thinly populated Texas, yet by the early 1830s, these American immigrants were increasingly restive under Mexican rule. In 1836, they staged a revolution that won them their independence. Because Mexico refused to recognize Texas's independence, the new republic embarked on a tense journey of nationhood marked by unceasing vigilance lest Mexico try to reestablish its dominion. In this uncertain atmosphere, Texas lobbied for U.S. annexation, but American arguments over slavery frustrated such efforts for almost a decade. Finally in 1845 a joint resolution for annexation passed Congress, and Texas was admitted to the Union.

The annexation of Texas was a divisive domestic issue, but it was nothing compared to the diplomatic firestorm it raised with Mexico. Livid that its neighbor had annexed its territory, Mexico was further enraged when President James K. Polk supported the Texas claim that its border with Mexico was the Rio Grande rather than the Nueces River, a claim that greatly increased the size of Texas. Mexico broke diplomatic relations with the United States, making it all but impossible to resolve the border dispute and dashing Polk's plans to purchase additional Mexican territory, especially what was called Upper California. Polk sent troops to the disputed area between the Nueces and Rio Grande and dispatched a diplomat to Mexico City, but the Mexican government refused to receive the diplomat and sent soldiers to oust the Americans from the disputed territory. In April 1846 Mexican and American forces clashed in this region, starting the Mexican War.

The American civilian response to hostilities was mixed. The conflict was remote and provided for most civilians what Gregory Hospodor describes in his essay as a vicarious experience; most Americans never experienced this war firsthand. They saw neither combat nor destruction of property nor did they fear invasion. As in previous wars, though, Americans were divided about the worth and legitimacy of this conflict. Some saw the war as simply naked aggression against a weaker neighbor, its exclusive goal the acquisition of territory. In fact, critics feared that the war's real purpose was to expand slavery and enhance the slave states' power in Congress. A large segment of the population, however, believed that it was the Manifest Destiny of the United States to stretch from Atlantic to Pacific, perhaps even to extend dominion over the entire continent.[3] Primarily southerners and westerners, proponents of Manifest Destiny saw the war as necessary, and the South and West provided most of the thousands of civilian volunteers who swelled the army's ranks after the declaration of war.

Most Americans followed the war from a distance, because all fighting took place on Mexican soil. Newspaper reporters sent dispatches from the front—sometimes they were accurate—that Americans read with enthusiasm. Any news from the scene of fighting was treasured by neighbors as well as families. Soldiers' letters home relating life in camp and on the march, describing Mexican scenery, and recounting battles were passed around the community, often returning to original recipients in shreds from being handled by so many readers. The nation celebrated American victories with church services and commemorations, and politicians made speeches proclaiming America's mission.

The volunteer units accounted for about three-fourths of the men who served in Mexico, often commanded by community leaders who hoped that military glory would pave their way to higher political office. Jefferson Davis and Franklin Pierce, for example, became national political figures on the basis of their exploits in Mexico. Yet, the war required a relatively small number of men, meaning that fewer women on the home front bore burdens that they had in past wars and would in future ones. As before, though, women who were left on their own managed farms and plantations, ran shops, and cared for their children with resolve and courage.

Dissent against the war was evident from its start. The greatest number of protests occurred in New England, partly because that section's numerous abolitionists deemed the war as part of a slave power conspiracy. Yet New Englanders were also perennially anxious about their declining influence in an expanding nation. Other northerners, though, including northern Democrats who had originally supported the war, began to weigh the conflict as only benefiting the South. Though unsuccessful, efforts in Congress to prohibit the expansion of slavery into territory acquired from Mexico became a compelling rallying point for antislavery activists of all stripes. Even southerners had reservations about the war. Southern Whigs were troubled by its divisive effect on their party, and prominent South Carolinian John C. Calhoun feared that any debate about slavery could only hurt the South.

In the end, everyone's fears were realized. The United States won the war, but the aftermath revived angry disputes about slavery, at first focusing on whether slavery should be allowed in the new territory acquired from Mexico. Sectional tensions increased in the 1850s until 11 southern states seceded from the Union after the election of Abraham Lincoln, and the government's efforts to suppress a southern rebellion resulted in the American Civil War.

While northern and southern civilian experiences in the Civil War bore some similarities, such as women coping without husbands and fathers, those experiences were very different as well. Most fighting took place in the South, and consequently southerners felt the war's impact more profoundly, especially in the upper South where major fighting occurred early and continued throughout the conflict. From the eastern theater's first major battle at Manassas Junction to Lee's surrender at Appomattox Court House, Virginia experienced the devastating effects of modern war in its most horrible manifestations. At best, Virginians lived under the constant burden of supporting Confederate armies or coping with invading northern ones. They faced the threat of their towns being looted or their homes being destroyed, a menace that much of the South eventually faced as well.

James Marten's essay on southern civilians shows how even those who did not see the early fighting or its consequences felt it in other ways. That women and children would be left to fend for themselves while men marched off to war was both typical and expected in both North and South, but shortages and rampant inflation were hardships few southerners had anticipated. They viewed the destruction of slavery as a major catastrophe. Consequently even areas removed from the war suffered significantly. Food shortages killed some southerners and pushed others to the edge of starvation, and worthless currency impoverished the wealthy and doomed the poor to even greater hopelessness.

The worst misery, however, did not come until the final two years of the war. During its early stages, enthusiastic nationalism and "victory disease" encouraged Confederate civilians to rally to the war effort. Women made uniforms, blankets, and bandages. Some served as nurses, either on the front lines or when the war came to them. Women and children did the back breaking work on farms. They raised money for the war effort. They became indispensable on the home front, proving that in this war, more than any other in the American experience up to that time, everyone would have to contribute to the effort for victory.

Ultimately southern civilians were reduced to fighting for their own survival. Union attacks on cities such as Richmond, Charleston, Columbia, Atlanta, and Vicksburg made the war a violent reality as sieges starved civilians and bombardments terrified those they did not kill. Armies marched first one way and then the other through villages and towns, often taking anything of value with them. Soldiers from both sides descended on isolated farms and plantations to take or "buy" whatever was left to eat. Civilians who had nothing left simply took to the road, becoming forlorn refugees.

By the third year of the war, another sort of civilian refugee took to the roads in search of food and freedom. As northern troops moved deeper into the South, slaves left farms and plantations, sometimes following the Union armies, sometimes heading to a fabled promised land of freedom in the North. Their suffering was immense. They had no families to flee to, and they were looked on with suspicion and hostility by many northern soldiers as well as white southerners. Union armies tried to aid these former slaves, referred to as "contraband," but many perished of starvation and exposure.

By 1865 both white and black southerners realized that the end was near. Most met their fate with resignation born of exhaustion and some measure of relief, accepting northern occupation as a natural consequence of Confederate defeat. Yet for many white southern civilians, surrender was too bitter to contemplate, and they nurtured dreams of a Confederate resurgence. Many would go to their graves expecting the South to rise again.[4]

In contrast to the South, the North endured little fighting on its soil during the Civil War. With the exception of a few border state raids by Confederate forces and Lee's 1863 invasion of Pennsylvania, most northern civilians never saw combat or its grim toll during the war. Yet, as Paul Cimbala points out in his essay on the northern experience in the Civil War, the home front mobilized for the titanic struggle, and the war, no matter how remote, was omnipresent in daily life.

Northern women bade sad farewell to husbands, fathers, and brothers, and took on important roles in both household and commerce. They sewed blankets, made bandages, and sent packages to loved ones and neighbors in the army. Many northern women joined various nurses' organizations and worked at the front or at remote army hospitals. A small number of women on both sides took extraordinary steps to prevent separation from their men folk or to satisfy a longing for adventure or to answer the call of patriotism: these unique people dressed as men and joined the army, some even paying the ultimate sacrifice by dying on the battlefield.[5]

Civilian life in the North became routine, even as it was considerably altered by the war. The government printed paper money, industries transformed to supply the war effort, and transportation changed to support it. Meanwhile, the potential for the death of loved ones in combat or, as was more likely, from disease, was a constant terror. Many men returned home with missing limbs or less obvious but no less tangible scars that would be vivid reminders of their sacrifices and the war's high human cost.

The end of the Civil War marked a closing of the circle in some respects. During the centuries after colonization, America had moved from a time in which all citizens experienced war as either impending or seemingly constant to a time when many Americans, especially in the Confederacy, again felt war in its most horrible rigors. And yet for many Americans war had changed. Never again would most Americans live for protracted periods with the life and death drama of war as their daily diet. Americans encountered danger as they moved to the West to untamed frontiers or traveled to foreign lands where peace could be fragile and fleeting, but at the close of the span of time covered by this volume, it seemed as though war on American soil would never be so intimate, threatening, and frightening again—at least, not for another century and a half.

NOTES

1. Russell Weigley, *The American Way of War: A History of United States Strategy and Policy* (New York: Macmillan, 1973); and John Grenier, *The First Way of War: American War Making on the Frontier* (New York: Cambridge University Press, 2005).

2. See David S. Heidler and Jeanne T. Heidler, *Old Hickory's War: Andrew Jackson and the Quest for Empire* (Baton Rouge: Louisiana State University Press, 2003), pp. 19–22.

3. The phrase "Manifest Destiny" was coined by expansionist journalist John L. O'Sullivan in 1845. See David S. Heidler and Jeanne T. Heidler, *The Mexican War* (Westport, CT: Greenwood Press, 2006), p. 50.

4. See Bertram Wyatt-Brown, *The Shaping of Southern Culture: Honor, Grace, and War, 1760s-1880s* (Chapel Hill: University of North Carolina Press, 2001), chapter 10.

5. For discussions of civilian women taking on nontraditional roles during the Civil War see Elizabeth D. Leonard, *All the Daring of the Soldier: Women of the Civil War Armies* (New York: W. W. Norton, 1999), and Dee Anne Blanton and Lauren Cook, *They Fought Like Demons: Women Soldiers in the American Civil War* (Baton Rouge: Louisiana State University Press, 2002).

Chronology of Principal Events

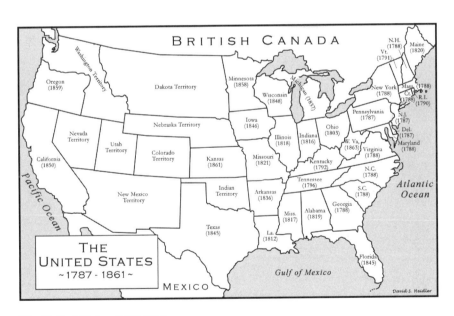

The United States, 1787–1861.

THE COLONIAL PERIOD

May 1607	Jamestown, Virginia, colony settled
December 21, 1620	Plymouth Colony settled by the Pilgrims
March 21, 1621	Treaty of peace between the Plymouth Colony and Wampanoag Indians
March 22, 1622	Indians massacre hundreds of Virginia colonists leading to a series of reprisals
July 1636	Pequot War begins in New England
June 5, 1637	Colonists destroy main Pequot encampment near Stonington, Connecticut, essentially ending the Pequot War
February 1674	Treaty of Westminster transfers Dutch colonies in North America to British control
June 1675	King Philip's War begins in New England
August 2–4, 1675	King Philip's Wampanoag-Nipmuck Indians attack Brookfield, Massachusetts
September 1675	King Philip's forces mount a series of attacks against Deerfield, Hadley, and Northfield, Massachusetts
October 16, 1675	King Philip's forces attack Hatfield, Massachusetts
November 1675	Colonial forces attack Narragansett Indians in Rhode Island
March 1676	Indians mount attacks on Plymouth, Massachusetts, and Providence, Rhode Island
May 1676	North Carolina colonists defeat Susquehannock Indians
August 1676	King Philip's War ends with the defeat of the Indians
May 1702	The War of the Spanish Succession (Queen Anne's War) begins and sparks serious Indian hostilities against British colonists
August 1703	Abenaki Indians attack settlements in the Maine District of Massachusetts Bay Colony
February 1704	Abenaki warriors with French allies attack Deerfield, Massachusetts
July 1704	New England colonists attack French settlements in Nova Scotia
August 1708	As Queen Anne's War continues, French soldiers and Indians massacre the settlement at Haverhill, Massachusetts

December 1708	The French–Indian capture of St. John's, Newfoundland, places significant portions of the North Atlantic coast under French dominion
October 1710	British and colonial forces take Port Royal, Nova Scotia
September 1711	The Tuscarora Indian War begins in North Carolina
January 1712	A force of Tuscarora Indians are defeated on the Neuse River
March 1713	The Tuscarora War ends with the defeat of the Indians
April 1715	Yamassee Indian War begins in the Carolinas
January 1716	South Carolina colonists defeat the Yamassee Indians
February 1727	British and Spanish settlers clash and begin a brief Anglo-Spanish War
October 1739	The War of Jenkins' Ear breaks out between Britain and Spain and will later merge (1740) with the War of the Austrian Succession (King George's War)
June 1745	New England militia in cooperation with the Royal Navy capture Louisbourg, a French stronghold on Cape Breton Island
August 1745	French soldiers and Indians mount raids in the Maine District
November 1745	The French destroy Saratoga, New York
October 1748	King George's War ends
May 1754	The Seven Years' War (French and Indian War) breaks out in the Ohio River Valley
July 1755	British general Edward Braddock's force of regularts and colonial militia is massacred by Indians as it marches on French Fort Duquesne in the Ohio River Valley
August 1756	French forces destroy Oswego and Fort George
August 1757	Fort William Henry is surrendered to the French
May 1758	Cherokee Indians begin attacking settlements on the Virginia frontier
July 1758	British forces take Louisbourg
September 1759	The British capture the seemingly impregnable French stronghold of Quebec
October 1759	Full-scale war breaks out between Cherokees and southern colonists
April 1760	Brutal Indian attacks plague the Virginia and Carolina frontiers

August 1760	The garrison at Fort Loudoun on the Little Tennessee River surrenders to Indians and is massacred
February 1763	The French and Indian War ends
May 1763	Ottawa chief Pontiac commences a war against British settlements on the northwestern frontier
April 1764	Several Indian tribes of Pontiac's alliance make a separate peace with the British
November 1764	Pontiac's War ends; Pontiac will not formally agree to peace until 1766

THE AMERICAN REVOLUTION

April 19, 1775	Colonists clash with the British army at Lexington and Concord, Massachusetts
May 10, 1775	American forces capture Fort Ticonderoga
June 17, 1775	Battle of Breed's Hill (often misidentified as Bunker Hill)
July 3, 1775	George Washington takes command of the Continental Army at Cambridge, Massachusetts
December 31, 1775	American forces are repelled at Quebec
March 1776	British evacuate Boston
May 10, 1776	The Continental Congress directs the colonies to form state governments
June–November 1776	British campaign seizes New York City and its environs
July 4, 1776	The Continental Congress adopts the Declaration of Independence
August 2, 1776	Most members of the Continental Congress sign the Declaration of Independence
September 22, 1776	American captain Nathan Hale is executed for espionage
December 26, 1776	American forces score a surprise victory at Trenton, New Jersey
July 1777	Indian atrocities against civilians by British-allied Indians spur American enlistments
September 9–11, 1777	American forces suffer defeat at Brandywine, Pennsylvania as the British drive toward Philadelphia
September 26, 1777	British forces occupy Philadelphia
October 7, 1777	British forces are defeated in a major battle at Saratoga, New York

November 1777	The Continental Congress approves the Articles of Confederation
December 1777	The Continental Army enters winter quarters at Valley Forge, Pennsylvania
February 1778	The Franco-American alliance secures French assistance against British forces
June 28, 1778	American forces defeat the British at the Battle of Monmouth
July 1778	Loyalists and Indians raid civilian settlements in northern Pennsylvania
December 1778	The British open a southern offensive by capturing Savannah, Georgia
May 10, 1779	British forces destroy Portsmouth and Norfolk, Virginia, in one of the most violent episodes of the war involving civilians
October 1779	The Continental Army goes into winter quarters at Morristown, New Jersey, to suffer its worst winter of the war
May 1780	British forces take Charleston, South Carolina; British cavalry under Banastre Tarleton begin a campaign of destruction and intimidation against civilians in the Carolinas
August 16, 1780	American forces suffer a staggering defeat at Camden, South Carolina
September 1780	Benedict Arnold is exposed as a traitor and flees to British lines
October 7, 1780	A defeat at Kings Mountain causes the British to break off the invasion of North Carolina
January 17, 1781	Americans defeat Tarleton at Cowpens, South Carolina
March 15, 1781	British victory at Guilford Courthouse, North Carolina, is costly enough to end plans for conquering the Carolinas; by April this British army will be campaigning in Virginia
August 1781	British forces encamp at Yorktown, Virginia
September 6, 1781	British forces under Benedict Arnold destroy New Lond, Connecticut
October 19, 1781	The besieged British army at Yorktown surrenders, a loss so serious that it ends British military efforts to suppress the American Revolution
September 3, 1783	The Treaty of Paris secures American independence and ends the Revolutionary War

WAR OF 1812

June 19, 1812 Following congressional approval, President James Madison proclaims a state of war with Great Britain

July–August 1812 Connecticut and Massachusetts governors refuse the service of their militias to the federal government

August 15, 1812 Indians massacre an American garrison as it evacuates Fort Dearborn (Chicago)

August 16, 1812 American forces surrender Detroit

October 13, 1812 American forces are defeated at Queenston Heights, Ontario

January 1813 Following a defeat on the Raisin River (near the western end of Lake Erie), Americans are massacred by British-allied Indians

April 1813 Americans occupy territory between the Pearl and Perdido rivers near Mobile

May 1813 Americans defend Fort Meigs in northwestern Ohio from British forces and Indians under Tecumseh; a British naval blockade provides cover for extensive raids on Chesapeake Bay

May 27, 1813 Americans capture Fort George at the mouth of the Niagara River

May 28–29, 1813 The British assault on Sacketts Harbor fails

August 3, 1813 The Creek War begins in the Mississippi Territory

September 10, 1813 Oliver Hazard Perry defeats a British squadron on Lake Erie

October 5, 1813 The British are defeated at the Battle of the Thames where Tecumseh is killed

December 1813 A series of retaliatory raids mounted by British forces and their Indian allies in upstate New York leaves much of the region in ruins

March 27, 1814 Andrew Jackson decisively defeats hostile Creeks at the Battle of Horseshoe Bend

July 1814 An American campaign on the Niagara frontier leads to victories at Fort Erie and Chippewa but ends with the bloody stalemate at Lundy's Lane near Niagara Falls

August 9, 1814 The Treaty of Fort Jackson cedes two-thirds of Creek lands to the United States

August 24–25, 1814	British forces occupy Washington and burn many public buildings including the Capitol and the Executive Mansion
September 12–14, 1814	The combined British army–navy force that had mounted the campaign against Washington is repulsed at Baltimore
December 15, 1814	Disaffected New England Federalists meet at Hartford, Connecticut, to protest the war. The convention will sit until January 5, 1815.
December 24, 1814	The Treaty of Ghent is signed by American and British peace commissioners
January 8, 1815	Andrew Jackson defeats the British at New Orleans
February 17, 1815	The U.S. Senate ratifies the Treaty of Ghent ending the war

MEXICAN WAR

April 25, 1846	Mexican cavalry attacks part of General Zachary Taylor's army encamped on the north bank of the Rio Grande; at President James K. Polk's request, Congress declares war on Mexico on May 13, 1846
May 8–9, 1846	Taylor defeats Mexican forces at Palo Alto and Resaca de la Palma
May 18, 1846	American forces occupy Matamoros
June 14, 1846	The Bear Flag Republic proclaims California's independence from Mexico
June 17, 1846	James Russell Lowell's "Biglow Papers" are an example of growing opposition to the war
August 8, 1846	The Wilmot Proviso seeks to exclude slavery from any territory acquired from Mexico
August 18, 1846	American forces establish a temporary government at Santa Fe, New Mexico
February 22–23, 1847	Taylor defeats Santa Anna at Buena Vista
March 1, 1847	Missouri volunteers under Alexander Doniphan occupy Chihuahua
April 1847	After taking Vera Cruz, Winfield Scott commences a march on Mexico City that will end with his taking the city in September, collapsing Mexican resistance
September 20–24, 1847	American forces under Taylor take Monterrey, Mexico

December 22, 1847	Freshmen Illinois congressman Abraham Lincoln speaks against the war in his first address to the House of Representatives
February 2, 1848	The Treaty of Guadalupe Hidalgo ends the war

CIVIL WAR

November 1860	The election of Abraham Lincoln to the presidency sparks the secession crisis
December 20, 1860	South Carolina secedes
January 9, 1861	Mississippi secedes
January 10, 1861	Florida secedes
January 11, 1861	Alabama secedes
January 19, 1861	Georgia secedes
January 26, 1861	Louisiana secedes
February 4, 1861	The Confederate States of America is formed
February 1, 1861	Texas secedes
April 12, 1861	Fort Sumter is fired on in Charleston Harbor beginning the Civil War
April 17, 1861	Virginia secedes
May 6, 1861	Arkansas secedes
May 20, 1861	North Carolina secedes
May 21, 1861	Richmond, Virginia, becomes the Confederate capital
July 2, 1861	Lincoln suspends *habeas corpus*
July 21, 1861	Union forces are defeated at Manassas, Virginia
August 5, 1861	The United States institutes an income tax
February 6, 1862	Fort Henry, the Confederate stronghold on the Tennessee River, falls; Fort Donelson on the Cumberland River will surrender 10 days later
June 26–July 2, 1862	A series of battles that stretch over a week, and consequently will be dubbed the Seven Days, end the Union's peninsula campaign against Richmond
August 30, 1862	Union forces are defeated again on the same ground as a year earlier in the second Battle of Manassas
September 17, 1862	The Battle of Sharpsburg on Antietam Creek in western Maryland is the costliest day of the war and turns back the Confederate invasion of the North

December 13, 1862	Union forces are routed at Fredericksburg, Virginia
January 1, 1863	The Emancipation Proclamation goes into effect
May 2–4, 1863	Union forces are defeated at Chancellorsville, Virginia
July 1–3, 1863	Confederate forces are defeated at Gettysburg, Pennsylvania, ending the second and final invasion of the North
July 4, 1863	Vicksburg, Mississippi, falls after more than a month under siege
July 13–16, 1863	Fueled by racial tensions, massive riots break out in New York City in protest over conscription
September 19–20, 1863	Defeat at the Battle of Chickamauga drives Union forces into Chattanooga
November 23–25, 1863	Union forces break the siege at Chattanooga and set the stage for the invasion of Georgia
December 3, 1863	Confederate forces withdraw from Knoxville, Tennessee
January 14, 1864	The Union occupation of Meridian, Mississippi, features the destruction of supplies, buildings, and transportations systems
April 12, 1864	Black Union soldiers at Fort Pillow on the Mississippi River are massacred by Confederate soldiers
June 1864	After a costly campaign in northern Virginia, Union forces lay siege to Petersburg on the outskirts of Richmond
September 2, 1864	Union general William T. Sherman takes Atlanta, Georgia
December 22, 1864	Sherman occupies Savannah, Georgia, concluding his destructive "March to the Sea;" in January his forces will invade the Carolinas and cause even more havoc
February 17, 1864	Columbia, South Carolina, is burned
April 9, 1864	Robert E. Lee surrenders to Ulysses S. Grant at Appomattox Court House, Virginia
April 14, 1864	Abraham Lincoln is mortally wounded and dies the following morning
April 18, 1865	Joseph E. Johnston surrenders the last major Confederate army in the East
May 13, 1865	All Confederate forces west of the Mississippi River are surrendered ending organized resistance to federal authority

ONE

Wartime Colonial America

Armstrong Starkey

What is a civilian? Today, in the West at least, we assume that civilians in wartime are noncombatants who are not part of established military forces. Although its protection has often been breeched, international law has sought to shield civilians from the horrors of war. This view was embodied in the 1868 St. Petersburg Declaration, which declared that "considering that the progress of civilization should have the effect of alleviating as much as possible the calamities of war; That the only legitimate object which States should endeavour to accomplish during war is to weaken the military forces of the enemy...."[1] This statement represented a high point in the tradition of *jus in bello,* which seeks to regulate the conduct of war. The hope of protecting civilians in wartime perhaps appeared most attainable in palmy days of the nineteenth century when the progress of civilization seemed assured.

Even Enlightenment writers were not prepared to make such distinctions. Emmerich von Vattel, a leading eighteenth-century expert on international law, defined war as a conflict between states but warned that all subjects of an enemy state, including women and children, were to be considered enemies. His only qualification was that they should be spared provided that they made no resistance. Furthermore, he observed that "when we are at war with a savage nation, who observe no rules, we may punish them in the person of any of their people whom we take."[2] Vattel's outlook was much closer to the realities of colonial conflict. Indeed, the special status of a civilian seems limited in time and space to Europe.

In the seventeenth century European civilians were victims of the Thirty Years War. Even in the eighteenth century European commanders did not hesitate to act against civilians in what might be considered to have been fringe areas, such as Corsica or the Scottish Highlands. But as one scholar has concluded, these were specific operations aimed at achieving finite goals. In America during the colonial period, settlers were exposed to prolonged and seemingly endless periods of conflict in which the conventions that defined and protected civilians did not apply.[3]

SEVENTEENTH-CENTURY VIRGINIA

From the founding of Jamestown in 1607, colonists were expected to provide for their own defense. In 1609 war erupted with the neighboring confederation of Powhatan Indians. Initially the English were heavily outnumbered, and the colony was almost abandoned before timely reinforcements and experienced soldiers arrived in 1609. As a result the colony may be said to have been militarized. The new governor and his officers were veterans of the Elizabethan Irish wars and campaigns in the Netherlands. They imposed a strict military regime upon the inhabitants. Regulations borrowed from Elizabethan military practice required strict discipline and obedience to a well-defined hierarchy of officers, sergeants, and corporals. The licentious behavior of the settlers was constrained by strict penalties against the crimes of blasphemy, dueling, pillaging, and mutiny. Clean living and religious observance were required of all. One historian concludes that Virginia's military regime was unique in American history. Social status and privilege came largely to depend on military rank rather than English background.[4]

The English strategy to defeat their Indian adversaries seems to have been adapted from their experience in fighting Irish insurgents. That strategy was fourfold: to seek out and destroy the enemy in open battle; to seek aid from among the Irish themselves; to hem in the enemy with fortifications; and, in the last resort, to devastate the countryside so that hostile forces could not live upon it.[5] As applied in Ireland and the Tidewater, English counterinsurgency methods made no distinction between combatants and noncombatants. The Powhatans lived in a region penetrated by numerous waterways. Their enemy exploited this feature by hemming them in with lines of fortifications and sailing into their homelands on heavily armed ships. This enabled the English to burn villages and crops. When the Indians made a stand in open fields to defend their food supplies, in battles referred to by contemporaries as food fights, they were no match for the volley fire of English musketeers. On one occasion in 1610, 70 English militiamen attacked a small Powhatan tribe whose land included Jamestown. They burned the main village, stole the grain, and killed 65 people including children.[6] These attacks against Indian villages were to be a recurring feature of the wars against Indian peoples into the late nineteenth century. On many occasions the majority of Indian casualties appear to have been the elderly, women, and children who lacked the means to defend themselves. From the beginning of these wars, there seems to have been little distinction drawn between combatant and noncombatant.[7]

The end of the first Powhatan war in 1614, led to the end of the military regime that had been imposed upon the English settlers who now became preoccupied with making money from tobacco. After 1619 men were no longer required to drill, train, or carry guns. Nevertheless, relations between the Powhatans remained tense. On March 22, 1622, the Indians launched a carefully planned surprise attack on the scattered English settlements in the Tidewater. Of the 1,240 English colonists, 347 were killed in a single day, women and children included. The Indians failed to follow up this attack, and it led to a war that dragged on until 1632. Continued pressure on Indian lands led to yet another surprise attack on unprotected English settlements on April 18, 1644, which resulted in nearly 500 deaths. Ultimately, however, the English strategies outlined previously, coupled with growing demographic advantages, brought victory against their native opponents. To survive this prolonged period of conflict, the Virginia assembly created a militia that included almost every adult male in the colony. William Shea finds that the militia officers of the 1630s and 1640s were not the veteran soldiers of the earlier era. Most were planters without military training, but they proved adept at fighting an irregular war. He concludes that the qualities that made a man an effective frontier entrepreneur might also make him an effective frontier officer.[8] The colony's victory in the 1640s represented the highpoint of the militia as an institution that required all able-bodied men to serve as citizen soldiers.

By the 1670s, tensions between settlers and Indians on the frontier became complicated by tensions between frontiersmen and the planter elite led by Governor William Berkeley. These tensions erupted in the 1676 incident known as Bacon's Rebellion, named after its leader Nathaniel Bacon. Bacon, a wealthy planter and member of the governor's council, advocated an aggressive "forward" policy against restive Indian tribes on the frontier, thus undermining Berkeley's more prudent approach that relied on a line of nine garrisoned forts. From a military point of view, such forts were seldom effective in preventing Indian raids of frontier communities. Frontiersmen might reasonably conclude that the forts were intended to insure peace by serving as a bridle on their own expansionist activity. Bacon exploited the frontiersmen's unrest by leading militia forces to seize Indian land and captives to be sold into slavery. Declared an outlaw by Berkeley, he turned against royal authority and besieged and captured Jamestown. Bacon's death in October 1676 spelled the end of the rebellion. Berkeley crushed the remnants of Bacon's followers in January 1676, and order was fully restored by royal commissioners who arrived with the backing of regular troops. The rebellion had major consequences for the militia as an institution. The defense of the frontier was henceforth assigned to a force of paid provincial soldiers drawn from poor freedmen within the colony. This force was supplemented by a politically reliable militia, which excluded slaves and servants. Defense of the social order now took precedence over external threats. Fortunately, Virginia would face no serious external threat until the 1750s, and the militia was allowed to decay until it became known as "the worst in the King's Dominions."[9] Bacon's rebellion had other consequences. For decades thereafter the

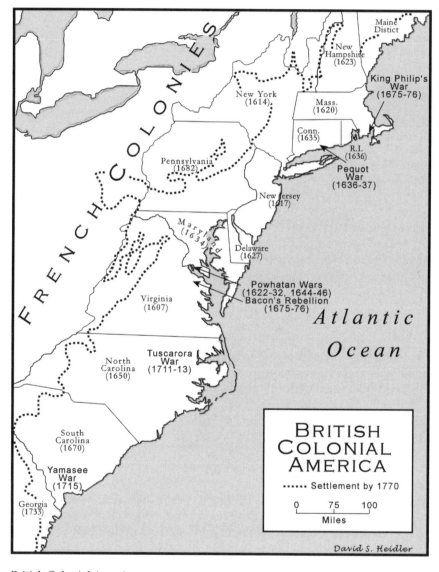

British Colonial America.

planter elite recognized that their power was constrained by the need to mollify frontier opinion.

Early Virginia's experience was not typical of that of other colonies, for many featured unique characteristics from the beginning of their establishment. Not all were forged in war and some possessed good Indian relations. However, when war did come, the patterns of frontier warfare were similar. War between settlers and Indians frequently replicated the conditions in early Virginia where noncombatants, white or Indian, were common targets of military action.

INDIAN ATTITUDES TOWARD WAR

In 1622 and 1644 the Powhatan Indians had demonstrated great organizational and tactical skill in delivering devastating surprise attacks upon the Virginia settlements but failed to gain decisive victories. While this may suggest that the Indians lacked a true strategic plan, it also reflects a very different understanding of war from that possessed by the English settlers. It may be that the Powhatans intended the attacks to serve as lessons that might teach the English to change their behavior or even withdraw from the colony.[10] They had exactly the opposite effect and led to the destruction of the Powhatan confederacy. Nevertheless, the nature of the attacks reveals that the colonists faced opponents who conducted war within a cultural context far different from that which prevailed in Europe. Generalizations about Indian attitudes toward war are complicated by the fact that there was more than one Indian culture. Some of the most blood-chilling practices associated with Indian warfare, such as cannibalism, were not universal. Nevertheless, common Indian attitudes toward war bode ill for the concept of the civilian as a protected noncombatant. Indian warriors did not fight as part of the disciplined field armies that were making their appearance in the Europe of the Thirty Years War. Rather they operated as guerilla or commando style warriors in a manner that has been referred to as "the skulking way of war," emphasizing raiding, surprises, and ambushes.[11] This is a form of warfare that often dissolves the distinction between soldier and civilian. Furthermore, Indian cosmologies and religious rituals provided very different cultural conceptions of war. The Indian way of war paralleled the Indian male's life as a hunter. Not only were the tactics similar, it appears that Indian warriors did not draw a distinction between hunting animals and human opponents. Both practices were governed by ritual, but, as one observer concluded, the Indian warrior "uses the same stratagems and cruelty as against wild beasts."[12] In some cases, Indians did not perceive people who were not members of their tribe as fully human, a flaw that could only be remedied by ritual initiations. This helps explain the brutal treatment of prisoners seized by warriors who, prizing bravery above all things, had little sympathy for those who fell into their hands. Nor did Indians share the European distinction between war and murder. Richard White in his study of the Great Lakes Indians finds that they believed in two kinds of killings: those at the hands of enemies and those at the hands of allies. If the killer belonged to an allied group, his family and community were expected to "cover" the dead with compensation and ritual ceremony or else experience a blood feud. Killings by enemies required blood revenge whether in or out of battle.[13] Thus European settlers would face a culture whose military values did not place war within a separate culture zone that theoretically at least restricted violence to soldiers on the field of battle.

The Indian approach to war thus did not conform to European military values embodied in religious writings, the work of jurists, and military codes that drew a distinction between soldier and civilian. As a consequence civilians suffered heavily from the violence of the frontier wars of the seventeenth and eighteenth centuries. Those who were not attacked lived in fear and terror of the fate that awaited them if they were. On the other hand, English strategies and tactics against the Indians as "savage" peoples fully exposed Indian communities to the brutalities of war. Although American civilians would suffer from the cruelties of war in other conflicts, notably the American Revolution and the Civil War, the colonial wars would surpass all others in their disregard for what may be thought of today as common standards of humanity.

THE CONTEXT OF CIVILIAN LIFE[14]

It would be a mistake, however, to consider war as the permanent condition of Indian–settler relations in the colonial period. About two-thirds of the period under discussion was a time of general peace, and even in periods of war not all colonies were affected. Pennsylvania benefited from the wise Indian policies of its Quaker founder William Penn, who insisted that settlement occur only after Indians were paid fair prices for their land. Indians mistreated by other colonies migrated to Pennsylvania and provided a security screen for colonists' settlements in the Delaware valley. Not until the 1720s, when white settlement began to shift westward, did tensions develop.[15] The example of Pennsylvania confirms that Virginia's experience was not typical of other colonies. It is true that all colonists shared the experience of life in the early modern world. The economy depended upon agriculture, and land was the basic ingredient of wealth throughout the colonial era. Hard physical work was the lot of the overwhelming majority of colonists who sought to extract their living from the land and from the sea. Beginning with tobacco, the export of agricultural products provided colonists with consumer goods, although only wealthy planters and merchants could aspire to luxury. Life expectancies in the colonies, at least after 1650, were higher than those in England, and most white colonists had enough to eat. But the grim facts of early modern life were inescapable. Birth was but the first survival test for mother and child.

Thereafter epidemic diseases such as smallpox, influenza, and measles might take a higher toll on life than any of the wars of the period. Increasing commercial ties and the tumult of war both conspired to spread disease. The example of the great smallpox epidemic of 1775–1782, described by the historian Elizabeth Fenn, is slightly outside our period, but it killed more than 100,000 people and left devastation and despair in areas unvisited by armies.[16] But some colonies were healthier than others. Virginia experienced an annual mortality rate of 25 percent until 1650, and plantations in that colony and in South Carolina were especially vulnerable to mosquito born illnesses such as malaria and yellow fever. New England small farmers lived in healthier environments and many might expect to live to the age of 70 if they survived childbirth.

While colonists shared many conditions, they lived in a more diverse world than they or their ancestors had experienced in their European homelands. The southern colonies, particularly Virginia and South Carolina, had established unique identities by the eighteenth century as plantation economies dependent on slave labor. In many areas African slaves outnumbered whites who resided on dispersed plantations. In the low country of Georgia and South Carolina the margin was two slaves to one free white person, while slaves constituted 40 percent of the population in the Chesapeake region. Slave owners and non–slave owners alike lived in greater fear of slave insurrection than of attack by external enemies. The great planters adopted harsh slave codes to keep their slaves in check and encouraged the sense of a common white identity with smaller landowners upon whom they depended for militia service. The lessons of Bacon's rebellion remained fresh in the minds of the Virginia elite.

By contrast, New England developed as an economy of small family farms where residents struggled to make productive a rocky and marginally fertile land. New Englanders provided for mutual support by centering their life in towns. There was a more equitable distribution of wealth in New England than in the southern colonies, but the harsh terrain and Indian opposition made it difficult to find new farms for everyone. Many young men had to wait their turn to inherit family farms. As we will see, they provided a pool of "temporary poor" from whom soldiers could be drawn. This surplus of free labor coupled with town institutions provided a sounder basis for militia institutions than did conditions in the South. Through hard work and entrepreneurial spirit, New Englanders found their way to modest prosperity by the eighteenth century. They exported a modest agricultural surplus to the colonies of the West Indies, created a thriving ship building industry, and took to the sea in pursuit of fish. When war came they took to the sea against their enemies. During wartime merchants were plagued by attacks upon their trade by enemy warships and privateers, but privateering was an attractive occupation for many colonial seamen in the period.

The Middle Colonies possessed the most diverse white population. New York was colonized by the Dutch who seized land from Indians in the Hudson Valley in a series of bloody encounters. The Dutch regime was thus one of conquest, but the West India Company's merchants at Albany preferred to advance their fur trade through peaceful relations with the powerful Iroquois confederacy. New Amsterdam was not a successful enterprise and was conquered by the English in 1664. Nevertheless, the Hudson retained a Dutch character for decades, and tensions between Dutch and English inhabitants remained a source of political conflict in the eighteenth century.

Pennsylvania was the most diverse of all. Its visionary founder, William Penn, was motivated by profit and a desire to establish a haven for persecuted fellow Quakers. These goals were contradictory and Penn was to die bankrupt. The rights of his descendants, the Proprietors, versus those of the colonists remained a source of tension in the eighteenth century. The Quakers have rightfully earned praise for their enlightened Indian policy, which sheltered the frontier well into the eighteenth century. But that century saw the arrival of other immigrant groups. Most important were German Protestants of a variety of sects who fled the war-ravaged Rhineland and the high taxes imposed by authoritarian princes. These devout, hard-working middling farmers retained their cultural identity (which remains distinct in part of the state to this day), but were otherwise well suited to fit into Pennsylvania's political, economic, and religious environment. They shared many of the values of the colony's original Quaker settlers, particularly their pacifism. The Germans enjoyed prosperous farms in the eastern part of the colony and benefited from peaceful and stable relations with Indian neighbors. They constituted 40 percent of the colony's population by 1750 and combined with the Quakers to oppose the establishment of a militia. Their common experience allows us to consider the strengths and weaknesses of pacifism as a policy. Pacifism worked because neighboring Indian tribes were weak and saw their own best interests served by friendly relations. It worked because there was a consensus between two of the colony's most important ethnic groups that this was the best policy. It failed however when a third immigrant group, Ulster Presbyterians (the so-called Scots-Irish), fleeing the harsh conditions of northern Ireland, pressed upon the frontier in search of new farmland. Their land hunger, abetted by unscrupulous speculators, ultimately destroyed the pacifist policy. Living on the sharp edge of the frontier and without any tradition of pacifism, the Scots-Irish, unlike their eastern neighbors, lived in a Hobbesian world and looked to the government for military protection. This would have explosive consequences by the mid-eighteenth century.

CONFLICT IN SEVENTEENTH-CENTURY NEW ENGLAND

In New England, relations were largely peaceful from the time of the first settlement at Plymouth until the outbreak of King Philip's War in 1675. Rather than suffering the surprise assaults that threatened the existence of the Virginia settlements, the survival of Plymouth colony benefited from the aid of the neighboring Wampanoags. The first half century of relations were characterized by peace and commerce with Indians supplying their neighbors with food, furs, and land in exchange for English trade goods, which included weapons. One historian has portrayed an integrated economy that was symbolized by the appearance of wampum, strings of Indian-produced decorative shells as a fur-backed currency of exchange accepted by all of the peoples of New England.[17] This condition was undermined by the decline in the demand for beaver pelts after 1650, which left land as the sole commodity that Indians might exchange for commercial goods. An expanding English population placed pressure on the lands of Southern New England Indian peoples whose population had been diminished by epidemics from a precontact figure of 144,000 to a stagnant 10,000. Unlike the case of Virginia where the Powhatans do not seem to have suffered such a demographic disaster at the hands of European disease, the high mortality in New England had left abundant land for Indian and settler alike. After 1650, however, this condition began to change.[18]

The one exception to this peaceful pattern was the brief but brutal Pequot War, which erupted in 1637. In this conflict the English demonstrated a consistency with the tactics of the Virginia settlers. The English possessed an overwhelming superiority in firearms and allies in the Narragansett Indians who resented Pequot dominance over the fur trade in the Connecticut River. The ability to move troops by water allowed the English to launch a surprise attack on a Pequot village near Mystic, Connecticut. Despite their resentment of the Peqout, the Narragansetts were nonetheless shocked and appalled when the English surrounded the Pequot village and set it ablaze. When the inhabitants, who consisted mainly of women, children, and the elderly attempted to flee, they were slaughtered by the English militiamen. Many of the Pequot warriors were not present. The massacre of the Pequot village echoed events in the Tidewater wars and offered a grim precedent for the war that broke out in 1675.[19]

PURITANS

In New England the issue of Puritanism complicated relations between settlers and Indians. While competition for land lay at the heart of conflict in both Virginia and New England, religion was not a factor in Virginia, and historians have spent little time exploring the Virginia "mind." However, religion clearly influenced New Englanders' perception of their Indian neighbors, though historians disagree on the nature of that influence. Arriving in New England to found a New Jerusalem, the Puritans encountered non-Christian Indian neighbors with differing social customs. This situation suggested two contradictory responses. Richard Slotkin has offered a psychological interpretation that suggests that violent conflict between the two peoples was inevitable. He concludes that the Puritans sensed in the Indians a dark, threatening presence, a people outside civilization and without religion whose very existence challenged those virtues among the Puritans themselves. The Indians were thus dismissed as agents of the devil, and their religious practices were scorned as magic and witchcraft. Their freedom from the restraints of civilized conduct held out seductive temptation that might lead to barbarism and loss of faith.[20] On the other hand it has been argued that the very nature of the Puritans' religion ensured that they were fair and just in their dealings with the Indians.[21] Jill Lepore has demonstrated that mid-seventeenth-century New Englanders prized their good relations with their Indian neighbors in contrast to the cruelties of the Spanish conquest of Mexico.[22] An alternative to the extermination of the heathen was to convert them to Christianity and to teach them the benefits of civilized life. Many Puritans supported the efforts of missionaries such as John Eliot and Daniel Gookin to civilize and Christianize the Indians as part of the divinely ordained Christian mission in the wilderness. Although less successful than Jesuit missionary activity in Canada, the Puritans did convert 20 percent of the southern New England Indians by 1675.[23]

Although Slotkin and Francis Jennings portray Puritanism as an ideology that promoted and justified violence against the Indians, this argument appears to be overstated. It is true that Eliot demanded that converted Indians surrender their cultural institutions and political independence and that his missions served as agents of English land hunger. It also appears that Rhode Island dissenters such as Roger Williams, John Easton, and Samuel Gorton were more active in seeking peaceful accommodation with the Indians than were the leaders of Plymouth Colony and Massachusetts Bay in 1675. Missionary activity was one of the factors that prompted King Philip (Metacom) to take up arms in 1675. Furthermore, tensions were evident in the period preceding the outbreak of hostilities. About six months before, Massachusetts Indian Superintendent Daniel Gookin wrote of the Indian religious leaders, the "powwows" as "partly wizards and witches holding familiarity with Satan," and also of the pernicious influence of Catholic priests.[24] Once war began, Puritan divines invoked religious justifications for acts as cruel as those inflicted by Spaniards in Mexico. The Puritan portrayal of Indian "savages" as agents of the devil had wide-reaching ramifications in the English community. As Mary Beth Norton has demonstrated, continued Indian attacks against frontier settlements coincided with fear that New England communities were under a spectral assault in 1692.[25] In this regard, the Puritan response to frontier warfare was unique.

KING PHILIP'S WAR

King Philip's War erupted in 1675 and ended the following year, although aftershocks continued for decades.[26] The catalyst was the execution by Plymouth authorities of three Wampanoag Indians for the murder of the

Indian missionary John Sassamon. During the 1660s, John Eliot had hoped to use Sassamon as a means of converting Philip and his followers, but without success. Indeed, Sassamon had been expelled from the tribe for crooked dealings. The execution of his murderers enraged the most war-like of Philip's followers and led to hostile demonstrations and skirmishes around the town of Swansea. As a result, a number of Plymouth and Massachusetts troops, including militiamen, mercenaries, and Christian or praying Indians, were mobilized to capture Philip on the peninsula in which his home at Mount Hope was located. However, Philip's escape exposed New England to a wider conflict. This event was followed by an unfolding war in four phases. First, there was a rising by the Nipmucks, including converts of Eliot's mission, against the western Massachusetts towns in the upper Connecticut valley, in which the colonists suffered a series of defeats and saw towns burned or abandoned. Second, was the December 1675

New England communities rallied to fight in King Philip's War. (Library of Congress)

campaign against the Narragansetts in Rhode Island, which culminated in an assault on their fortified swamp village by a 1,000-man United Colonies army drawn from Plymouth, Massachusetts, and Connecticut. Three hundred Indian warriors and as many women and children were killed in this attack by the colonists, who themselves suffered heavy casualties. Third, an Indian offensive in February–May, 1676, struck a terrifying blow at eastern towns in Massachusetts, Plymouth, and Rhode Island. Finally, there was a reversal of fortune in the summer of 1676 as the colonists adapted to the demands of frontier warfare, and the Indian effort collapsed as a result of disunity and critical shortages of food and ammunition.

Recently James Drake, drawing on the work of English Civil War historian Barbara Donagan, has argued that the horrors of King Philip's War were mitigated by its nature as a civil war. Drake subscribes to the view that the English and the Indian peoples of New England lived in one integrated community rather than in two alien and competitive worlds. Nevertheless, although initially both sides attempted to show restraint, as the conflict developed, Indian hating developed among volunteers, civilians, and combatants who lacked formal military training. Colonial authorities viewed Indians, who had previously subjected themselves to colonial governments, as rebels and traitors. Therefore they did not consider them to be protected by the laws of war. Drake argues that the enslavement rather than the execution of Indian captives might have been regarded as an act of mercy under the circumstances.[27] As we have seen, Native American definitions of war differed from those understood by English settlers. As Jill Lepore points out, some contemporaries such as William Hubbard, shocked by the atrocities that accompanied the conflict, did not believe that it deserved the name of a war. Hubbard referred to it as a time of *troubles*.[28] Living today in a period in which the word war appears to have lost any real meaning and combatants are arbitrarily denied the protection of the laws of war, we can perhaps conclude that defining the conflict as an insurrection or *troubles* was likely to make things worse than better. Participants in *troubles* fall into gray areas and may not be protected by any laws at all.

However merciful the colonists may have thought themselves, King Philip's War was fought without distinction for combatant and noncombatant. Rhode Island dissenter James Eason painted a bleak picture of the behavior of colonial soldiers and their spiritual leaders: "now the English army is out to seeke after the Indians, but it is most lickly that such most abell to do mischif will escape and women and children and impotent mai be destroyed and so the most abell will have les incumbrance to do mischief. . . . I am so perswaded of New England priests thay are so blinded by the spirit of persecution . . . that the law of nations, and the law of arems have bine violated in this war . . ."[29] New England soldiers won little honor in this war in which they often blundered into ambush, killed indiscriminately, and sold surviving prisoners into slavery. The war was a catastrophe for the native peoples. James Axtell has concluded that of 11,600 Indians in southern New England in 1675, the war claimed 7,900 or 68 percent of the population. This included almost 2,000 dead as a result of battle or wounds, 3,000 dead as a result of disease or exposure, 1,000 sold as slaves and transported, and 2,000 permanent refugees.[30] Indian "civilians" thus bore the heaviest burden of the war.

The colonists themselves were submitted to the horrors of war as Indian attacks spread from west to east across southern New England. Unlike Virginia, New England was a town-centered society and, of 90 New England towns, 52 were attacked, with 25 pillaged and 17 destroyed.[31] Drake has concluded that the destruction of property and the cost of conducting the war amounted to 21 pounds per household, more than the annual salary of the secretary or deputy governor of Connecticut.[32] John Canup finds that the war forced a temporary retreat from the prewar frontier of settlement. Surviving frontier settlements found themselves isolated and vulnerable. "Now, through the Indians' attacks, the wilderness was reclaiming its losses and reasserting its old chaos over the superficial overlay of English order."[33] Indian attacks produced a wave of refugees who swamped eastern towns struggling to sustain the burdens of the war. The refugees presented a unique problem for the undamaged towns whose systems of poor relief were designed to support only a few individuals. Indeed, the General Court, ordering residents of communities under attack to stand fast or lose property, forbade poor relief for refugees. Puritan divines seem to have had scant sympathy for these victims, for they blamed the war on the scattered frontier settlements whose inhabitants had begun to live like Indians and, considering their degenerate state, were liable to God's judgment. In reality, families and friends in the safe towns took in refugees by the hundreds. Many found employment as maids, gravediggers, and laborers. Despite the New Englanders' generosity, the presence of the refugees as dependents or as menial laborers contributed to the tensions that would continue to beset the towns in the last quarter of the seventeenth century.[34]

The towns had to cope with this flood of refugees while many ablebodied men were being drafted for military service. This placed a great strain on the agricultural communities dependent on their labor and raised questions of fairness. One petitioner declared that due to his two sons absence for two months "many Inconveniences and great Damages, have been sustained by us for want of my Elder son, who hath house and cattle of his own adjoining Mine being a mile from the Town, and therefore nobody to look after them in his absence." Others in the town had not served, but had declared their willingness to do so and therefore his sons' replacement was only fair. "If [God] should now take them away before I do again see them I know not how I should beare it." In April, 1676, a lieutenant, sergeant, corporal, and 40 men petitioned that they had been in service since August to the great cost of their families and elderly parents. They too asked to be replaced by others.[35]

Colonial troops appeared to be helpless to check the Indians' spring offensive. Fortified garrison houses offered the inhabitants of frontier towns some protection, but residents caught outside or in undefended dwellings were in peril. Columns of troops rushing to the relief of these beleaguered towns were tempting targets for ambush. The desperation of the authorities was evident on March 23 when a council at Boston ordered the construction of a stockade between the Charles and Merrimack rivers, leaving the frontier towns exposed. Even towns included within the proposed defense were unenthusiastic. Marblehead's reply was typical of other towns: it was too poor to contribute to the project, that it was unfair to the towns cut off, that the Merrimack was fordable in many places, and that the expense of maintaining fortifications was too great. It announced that it was too poor to send a representative to discuss the matter.[36]

At the same time anti-Indian hysteria gripped the colonists. Even Christian Indians were regarded as the enemy within, and Massachusetts took steps to disarm them and confine them to their dwellings. They were allowed to travel only in the company of an Englishman and could be shot on sight if found alone. As terrifying reports of Indian military success poured in, anger was turned on those such as Daniel Gookin and John Eliot who tried to defend them. Eliot warned that these actions, which were "worse yn death," would only prolong the war.[37] But popular opinion was better reflected by another writer who referred to the Christian Indians as "preying" Indians: "they have made preys of much English Blood but now they are all much reduced to their Several Confinements; which is much to the general Satisfaction in that respect."[38] Eventually some 500 praying Indians were confined on Deer Island in Boston harbor in conditions of great distress.

CAPTIVITY

King Philip's War stands out in American memory because it was the first to be the subject of extensive literary record. We may also see it as the beginning of a genre that, while not unique to America, was central to the colonial literary experience: the captivity narrative.[39] Throughout the remainder of the period covered in this chapter, Indian raiders carried off hundreds of colonists, sometimes for adoption and sometimes for ransom. These narratives made for chilling reading, tales of terror that might happen to anyone. Perhaps the narratives provide clues to the recurring nightmares of many colonists. They capture the colonists' continued fear of Indian raiders even in times of peace. One historian has found that inhabitants of the Carolinas were never free of such fears throughout the colonial era.[40] Narrators recalled the horrifying details of the surprise attack, the slaughter of family members and neighbors, the forced march through the woods conducted by their savage captors, and their captivity among a strange and barbaric people. Many captives did not survive the harsh conditions to which they were submitted, and others experienced spiritual crises and were left with deep psychological wounds. One of the most famous captives was Mary Rowlandson who was taken in a raid on Lancaster, Massachusetts, on February 16, 1676, at the beginning of the Indians' spring offensive against the New England towns. She was forced to follow her captors through the snow while carrying a wounded child whom the Indians threatened to kill if she did not keep up. The only available food was broth made from a horse's leg. Despite these hardships and the death of her child, she survived the march and was reunited with a daughter and a son. She was taken in by an Indian family who did not treat her badly as long as she did her share of the work. The narrative makes clear the horrors of a war fought with indiscriminate terror, but, as in the case of many captives who survived, Rowlandson recognized the essential humanity of the Indian people among whom she lived. In retrospect, she interpreted her experience as a spiritual test: "*It is good for me that I have been afflicted.* The Lord has shown me the vanity of these outward things."[41]

Rowlandson's narrative is considered by Richard Slotkin to be the archetype of the captivity genre, though that of the Reverend John Williams, *The Redeemed Captive Returning to Zion,* is at least equally famous. Williams and his family were victims of a French and Indian raid on Deerfield, Massachusetts, on February 29, 1704. Frontier communities such as Deerfield remained as vulnerable to such attacks as they had been over a quarter of a century before. On October 22, 1703, the Reverend Solomon Stoddard of Northampton had warned Governor Joseph Dudley of Deerfield's continuing vulnerability. He advocated freeing the residents from taxes in wartime and the use of dogs to track Indians in the woods. "If the Indians were as other people are and did manage their wars fairly after the manner of other nations, it might be looked upon as inhumane to pursue them in such a manner. But they are to be looked upon as thieves and murderers; they do acts of hostility without proclaiming war. They don't appear openly in the field to bid us battle [and] they use most cruelly that fall into their hands. They act like wolves and are to be dealt withal as wolves."[42] Whatever precautions taken were in vain. The raiders killed 40 to 50 inhabitants, burned the town, and carried off 109 prisoners. Twenty prisoners were killed on a march of some 300 miles to Canada. Two of Williams' children and a servant were killed in the attack, and his wife was slain on the march, apparently because she could not keep up. On the other hand, the Indians provided the party with snowshoes and constructed sleds to carry the children and the wounded. Williams' Indian captor carried his pack when he became lame and saved the family from starvation by shooting five moose along the way. Arriving at Chambly near Montreal, he was treated kindly, and eventually he and two of his children were redeemed by Governor Vaudreuil and allowed to return home. But the return to "Zion" was troubled by his son's conversion to Catholicism and the decision of his daughter Eunice to remain in Canada and marry an Indian. Puritan fears that captives might be converted to the devil's ways seem to have been realized in this case.[43] Eunice Williams' experience was not unique, however. Throughout the colonial period many white captives were adopted into Indian families and found Native American life preferable to that which they had experienced at home. Peace negotiations between whites and Indians were often complicated by the issue of captives who did not wish to leave their new families. The return of these captives was often an occasion of mourning in Indian communities.

Puritan captivity narratives emphasize the captive as victim, a sufferer put to the test by God. Most captives were in a state of shock, fear, and exhaustion, but there were exceptions who made good their escape. A hero of King William's War was Hannah Dustin, a 40-year-old Massachusetts woman, who persuaded another woman captive and a boy to surprise and murder their sleeping captors. They killed and scalped 10 Abenaki Indians, including 2 women and 6 children. Dustin cashed in her scalps under Massachusetts's scalp bounty program and was lionized by the assembly and Puritan ministers. One historian remarks that the celebration of Dustin's feat only underlines the futility of the war effort.[44]

Increase Mather believed that the English victory in King Philip's War was the Lord's work: "God has wasted the Heathen by sending the destroying Angell amongst them since this war began. . . ."[45] Yet the victory was strangely inconclusive. Southern New England had been conquered, but as the story of the "Redeemed Captive" demonstrates, residents of frontier communities would have little reason to feel safe from the murderous surprise raid in the night. Coastal settlements in present day New Hampshire and Maine, then part of Massachusetts, had suffered heavily from Indian assaults into 1677. This was followed by a period of truce on the "eastern" frontier and the rebuilding and resettling of coastal towns that lived upon fishing, agriculture, and the fur trade with Indian neighbors. In 1688, however, the war erupted again on a vaster scale as North America became a battleground in a war between England and France that, with the exception of an interlude of three years, would last until 1713. For the settlers in northern New England, an alliance between the neighboring Indians and French Canadians represented a formidable challenge. French soldiers such as Hertel de Rouville, who led the attack on Deerfield, had adapted to the Indian way of war in a manner beyond most New Englanders. A French alliance gave the Indians a level of strategic depth never available to Philip and his followers, furnishing supplies, weapons, ammunition, and sanctuaries. French and Indian raiders could strike and disappear in the vast forested region that defied effective pursuit. Furthermore, an alliance between "satanic savages " and the agents of the papist Antichrist appeared to New England Puritans as a pact forged in hell.

Beginning in 1688 the coastal communities were ravaged once again, and the survivors fled south as a new wave of refugees. They brought with them terrifying tales, including numerous captivity accounts, which Cotton Mather recorded in 1699. During 1689–1691, Pemaquid, Salmon Falls, Casco, Wells, and York were victims of these assaults. In describing the January 25, 1691, raid on York, Mather lamented that the winter of 1691 "must not pass over without a storm of Blood! The Popish Indians. . . . These Blood-Hounds being set on by some Romish Missionaries, has long been wishing, that they might Embrue their Hands in the Blood of some New-England Minister; and in this Action, they had their Diabolical Satisfaction."[46] Unable to defeat the Abenaki Indians in forest warfare, and without any substantial assistance from England, colonial authorities recognized that they must act on their own to defend themselves. They began to develop the strategy that targeted Quebec as the enemy's strategic center. In 1690 Sir William Phips led a successful sea expedition consisting primarily of Massachusetts ships and soldiers that captured Port Royal in Acadia, while at the same time representatives from Massachusetts, Connecticut, Plymouth, and New York met to plan a joint invasion of Canada. The invasion route would become a familiar one in succeeding decades, with one army striking up the Lake George–Lake Champlain corridor while a naval expedition sailed up the Saint Lawrence to Quebec. This strategy would achieve success in the Seven Years' War, but was beyond the means of the colonies in 1690. Only Phips's naval expedition reached its objective, but disease, inept tactical leadership, and the weather forced its withdrawal with nothing gained other than the release of a few prisoners taken in Indian raids. The collapse of the Phips expedition had brought evil consequences for the inhabitants of Massachusetts. The expense of the campaign crippled the economy, and the survivors spread smallpox among communities on their return. To finance the campaign, Massachusetts had issued paper currency for the first time, but its value was suspect, and it depreciated 25 to 50 percent. One merchant wrote that "not many will take it those that will scarce know what to do with it."[47] Colonists found their taxes raised to over 30 times the prewar level even as the government proved incapable of protecting the frontier.

WITCHCRAFT

The connection between the war and the Salem witchcraft trials that resulted in 18 executions and 1 death through torture in 1692 has long been noted. Most recently Mary Beth Norton has argued that the war provided a crucial context for the outbreak of accusations. Some of the young women accusers were refugees from the eastern frontier communities employed as servants in Essex County, Massachusetts. Their allegations of spectral assaults by the Devil's agents reflected their frightening experiences on the frontier at the hands of those raiders who themselves were seen as satanic. Refugees such as the Reverend George Burroughs were also the targets of witchcraft accusations for it was alleged that he had bewitched soldiers and had worked with the Indians. Norton also believes that Massachusetts magistrates were more willing than usual to credit the accusations because the belief in a devilish conspiracy deflected blame from their own inability to defend the colony. Finally, the accusations may have been rooted in the resentment of young women refugees at being reduced to servants and relegated to the bottom of the social ladder. All of these conditions were rooted in the war and led to one of the most disturbing episodes in American history.[48]

NEW YORK

In the period 1675–1713, New England bore the brunt of the Indian wars. Other colonies were further removed from the conflict and their inhabitants less affected. Although a French and Indian raid destroyed Schenectady in February, 1690, Michael Kammen has concluded that "New York's involvement in both King William's War and Queen Anne's War was relatively small, and the reasons are revealing, especially since the province had so much at stake."[49] Albany merchants believed that an intercolonial attack on Quebec could work, but sought to avoid bloody frontier clashes. Here the Indian neighbors were not the warlike Abenakis who retained antagonisms from King Philip's War, but the Iroquois who had adopted a neutral stance between England and France. Thus the French, who did not wish to provoke their long-time Iroquois enemy, for the most part desisted in frontier attacks. Nevertheless New York suffered financially from the war. The Albany fur trade declined and shipping suffered as well. Contributions to unsuccessful expeditions against Quebec in 1709 and 1711 placed a heavy burden on the economy. Specie, as coin money was called, was drained from the colony, and merchants were deeply in debt to London. These conditions were exacerbated by the refusal of the assembly to vote taxes to sustain the war effort. "By 1710, fiscal irresponsibility had just about brought the colony to complete ruin."[50]

THE EIGHTEENTH CENTURY

In the eighteenth century, war and peace in colonial North America depended primarily on decisions taken in London and Paris. The Peace of Utrecht of 1713 and the subsequent Anglo-French entente defused conflict in America. Wars might occur as a result of local tensions, such as the 1715 Yamasse War in South Carolina, or Dummer's War in Vermont in which the western Abenaki leader Grey Lock carried out a guerilla campaign that closed much of the area to white settlement, but the normal condition of the colonies was peace. This had a positive effect on colonial development. For example, Kammen notes that the population of Albany County could now safely expand, and did so, thus causing a real estate boom. The creation of new farms caused grain and lumber to emerge as the dominant factor in the upriver economy, which in turn became a factor in a triangular trade between Amsterdam, Albany, and the Dutch West Indies.[51] This happy period ended with the Anglo-Spanish War of 1739, which became part of a larger European conflict, the War of the Austrian Succession, 1740–1748. Americans participated in this war on a large scale, including the unsuccessful expedition against St Augustine, Florida, in 1740 and Admiral Edward Vernon's massive and unsuccessful amphibious assault on Cartagena in 1741, with his force of about 3,600 Americans. About 4,300 men, chiefly New Englanders, made up the army that achieved the colonists' greatest success in the war, the capture of the French fortress of Louisbourg at the entrance to the Saint Lawrence, a position of little strategic value, but coveted for its cod fishery.[52] The capture of Louisbourg by provincial soldiers (ably assisted by the Royal Navy) was a great morale booster for the public and had more symbolic value than military value. Its return to France at the end of the war thus caused greater consternation in Boston than in London. In Georgia and North Carolina local forces beat off Spanish attacks, but New England and New York experienced new French and Indian attacks that they met with the usual lack of success. While the war between the imperial powers ended in a stalemate, the war on the New England frontier was a French and Indian victory. Vermont had been barred to white settlement, and the colonial military system had again proven unable to defend the frontier.

THE SEVEN YEARS' WAR

At least New England and New York had a military system. These colonies had experienced attacks on their frontiers and taken measures to defend them. Until 1754 Virginia had enjoyed the blessings of almost uninterrupted peace since Bacon's rebellion. Relations between neighboring Indians and frontier settlers moving south into the valley between the Blue Ridge and the Appalachians had been peaceful, and Virginia's militia system had reached a state of advanced decay. The colony was ill prepared for the great conflict that broke upon them beginning in 1754, the Seven Years' War.[53] In America, the origins of the Seven Years' War centered upon disputes between Britain and France over the control of the Ohio Valley. To protect its western trading empire, France had moved aggressively to establish claims to the Ohio country and consolidate them with a chain of forts. The British government opposed this move on strategic grounds, while wealthy Virginia land speculators saw their investments in western lands threatened. Virginia Governor Robert Dinwiddie, himself a member of the Ohio Company, which speculated in western lands, advocated a forward policy in the west on strategic grounds, although financial considerations were probably a strong private motive. It was Dinwiddie who in 1754 dispatched Virginia troops under George Washington to clear the French from the area. The failure of this expedition instead revealed Virginia's lack of preparation for frontier war and set in motion forces that would bring devastation to the frontier communities of Virginia and Pennsylvania.[54]

James Titus has argued that most Virginians were uninterested in events hundreds of miles from their own frontier settlements and did not feel threatened by French moves in the Ohio Valley. Many suspected that Dinwiddie and other wealthy individuals sought to advance their private schemes at public expense. Although Virginia had a large militia based on the historic obligation of every able-bodied man to defend his country, militiamen understood this to be a requirement of local defense of hearth and home, not service in imperial expeditions far from home. Southern militiamen had a special incentive to remain at home for they feared a slave uprising in their absence. Thus Dinwiddie, who unrealistically expected that the French would be easily expelled from the Ohio, led Virginia into a war for which it was unprepared and for which there was little public support. Most colonies found it difficult to utilize their militias for long periods of service far from home and instead raised provincial troops, who for bounties and pay served for periods of up to a year. In 1754 Dinwiddie turned to this expedient by raising the Virginia Regiment, which sought to recruit soldiers motivated by patriotism and the spirit of adventure. The results of this effort, which drew largely on nonnative Virginians, were disappointing, but the arrival of Major General Edward Braddock's regulars in 1755 seemed to offer assurance of a short and victorious war.

Indians set upon soldiers and civilians departing from surrendered Fort William Henry during the Seven Years' War. (Library of Congress)

Braddock's subsequent defeat and the withdrawal of the remainder of the British troops confronted Virginians and Pennsylvanians with the full horrors of war. The British retreat was accompanied by the flight of refugees from the frontier now fully exposed to French and Indian raids.

Matthew Ward views the attack on the frontier as a conscious French strategy aimed at terrorizing the settlers, one that accorded well with traditional Indian warfare. The Governor of Canada, the Marquis de Vaudreuil, directly encouraged attacks on civilians as the only possible strategy against a larger and potentially more powerful opponent. Ward has calculated the cost of the war for the two colonies as nearly one percent of the total population killed or captured, a figure that rose to four percent for the backcountry counties. He concludes that such figures are comparable to those of the Revolutionary and Civil Wars and much higher than those of other Indian wars.[55] Along with loss of life came property damage, with raiders burning crops and farm buildings and destroying live stock. The collapse of frontier economy caused bankruptcies among merchants in coastal communities whose trade was also disrupted by attacks by French privateers. Colonial authorities sought to meet the attacks through a variety of measures: an expanded Virginia regiment drafted from the militia, a chain of frontier forts, and an alliance with the Cherokees on Virginia's southwestern border. Virginia's strategy was to prove a distinct failure.

Jane T. Merritt sees the Seven Years' War as the crucial event that shattered the social and political equilibrium on the Pennsylvania frontier. Indians who had become members of peaceful Moravian communities became victims of this rupture. She finds that close contact between whites and Indians exacerbated rather than reduced the war's violence. Pennsylvania had depended on the peaceful diplomacy of its Quaker leaders to keep the peace with its Indian neighbors, and therefore entered the war with no military system at all. Pacifist Quakers withdrew from public life rather than oppose the creation of a defense force, but political squabbles between the proprietors and the assembly blocked effective measures.[56]

In Virginia the draft was compromised by exemptions for the well-to-do, which produced public support for draft dodging and desertion. The weak fortress chain proved easily permeable by raiders and not always safe havens from assault. The inability of governments to defend the people, many of whom saw the war as unnecessary in the first place, led to a crisis of authority, particularly on the frontier. Nor did the attacks inspire unity. Ward finds that in Pennsylvania, a colony with great ethnic and religious diversity, the war created distrust of immigrant groups such as Germans and Catholic Irish. In both colonies Quakers were seen as undermining effective defense. While some people profited from the war by gaining possession of deserted farms or engaging in war profiteering, civilians were submitted to "hard war," even in counties not on the frontier.

An investigation of the Seven Years' War exposes the myths that have surrounded the colonial militia and the frontier marksman as effective opponents of the Indians in forest warfare. The war was won by conventional means under the leadership of British Prime Minister William Pitt the Elder. Pitt committed major British land and naval forces to the conquest of Canada and, by assuming the financial cost of provincial troops, cleared the way for the establishment of effective local forces. The Virginia Regiment, now assured of regular pay, which made possible effective military discipline, proved its worth in Brigadier General John Forbes's successful campaign against Fort Duquesne in 1758 and later in campaigns against the now hostile Cherokees.

The northern colonies had had much more recent war experience than Virginia or Pennsylvania, but 1758 was a turning point for them as well, as more effective policies overcame initial setbacks and floundering. Fred Anderson has provided a concise picture of the effect of the war on Massachusetts: "Before the Seven Years' War was over, it would draw a third or more of the colony's service eligible men into provincial armies and employ thousands of others in tasks directly related to the military effort. It would drive taxes to the highest levels in the history of the province, create a massive public debt, and bring the government on one occasion to the brink of bankruptcy. The war would also cause a massive influx of British specie and credit, temporarily expanding Massachusetts' hard-money economy. It would transform the scale and nature of provincial politics and create a new sense among Bay colonists of their importance and participation in the British Empire."[57]

In New York war raged across the northern frontier, but here there was a massive presence of regulars as well provincial troops. The problem of quartering these regulars caused tensions with the civilian population. Although the British commander Lord Loudon built barracks for the rank and file, civilians were unenthusiastic about his demand that officers be billeted in private houses. Merchants complained about an embargo on shipping, but others made great profits as privateers and later by carrying supplies to the starving islands of the French West Indies. There was money to be made by supplying the army assembled in the North, and resulting shortages drove up prices. Military operations caused economic dislocations as the war shifted away from New York after 1759, and a serious depression set in. Pitt's promise of reimbursement prodded the assembly in 1759 to agree to raise pay and clothe 2,869 men and to draft men from the militia to make up for any shortage of volunteers. This was a considerable commitment because, by comparison, the Virginia regiment consisted of about 1,000 men at its greatest strength. Assured of reimbursement, the assembly patriotically agreed to lend General Amherst 150,000 pounds. Reimbursement was the great stimulus for colonial action, but did not cover all expenses. Despite reimbursement, New York incurred indebtedness of 291,000 pounds of which 115,000 was still unpaid in 1765.[58]

Fred Anderson's study of the Massachusetts provincial forces offers a contrast to the Virginia Regiment, which was drawn largely from nonnative

Virginians. Rather than being drawn from a marginal proletariat, Massachusetts reflected the social conditions of the colony in which young men waited to inherit the family farm. While they waited they contributed to the farm or worked as wage laborers. They were temporarily poor and available for military service. Provincial military service was attractive to these young men for it provided steady employment, enlistment bounties, and relatively high wages, which, being paid at the expiration of enlistment, came in the form of a sum of cash that could be used for a start in life. The prospect of economic reward coupled by the appeal of adventure was compelling. Ninety percent of New England provincials were volunteers. Provincial enlistment was an attractive alternative to enlistment in the regulars, which meant longer service, lower pay, harsher discipline, and other abuses. In New England, at least, the provincial service mirrored social realities that the regulars never could. Harold Selesky has demonstrated that similar conditions existed in Connecticut.[59] Religious zeal continued to be a motivator in Massachusetts to a greater degree than in the southern colonies. A sermon preached in thanksgiving of the conquest of Quebec placed the event in the context of providential history beginning with the Protestant Reformation and taking it to 1759. "In fine, it was God, the great Ruler of the universe that gave Quebec into our hands."[60]

The Seven Years' War was a great experiment in imperial cooperation. Massachusetts led the way in contributing six times as many men in proportion to its white population as did Virginia, but other colonies made significant efforts. However, war also produced frictions with imperial authorities. There were disputes between regulars and provincials and resistance to the quartering of troops. In King George's War mobs formed to resist press gangs seeking to seize American seamen in Boston. William Pencak finds that in every instance the entire province united behind resistance to imperial authority. It was the first time since the Glorious Revolution of 1688–1689 that crowd violence had been directed against British power.[61]

In the colonial period, civilians experienced long periods of peace. When war came, it did not fall equally upon all of the colonies. One cannot generalize about individual experience. For example, while George Washington won fame as a soldier during the Seven Years' War, his younger contemporary Thomas Jefferson seems to have been untouched by the conflict. Nevertheless, colonial civilians experienced the brutalities of war more directly than those of any other period save the War of American Independence and the Civil War. The colonial wars stand out in the extent to which the killing and capture of noncombatants were essential ingredients in the strategies and tactics of the belligerents. The primary enemies of the colonists were Native Americans whose way of war did not make a distinction between combatant and noncombatant. Colonial settlers exposed to Indian raids lived in fear of death, torture, or captivity. Religious authorities demonized these raiders and their French allies so that war assumed a cosmic aspect in the eyes of many colonists. In return the colonists adopted strategies against Native Americans that committed them to the annihilation of Indian resistance. From a modern perspective, the wars against Native Americans were racist in character. Indian hating was wide spread in the civilian population. As we have seen, New Englanders during King Philip's War usually did not distinguish between friendly and unfriendly Indians. In 1763 a mob of Pennsylvania ruffians known as the Paxton Boys murdered peaceful and defenseless Indians including some who had been placed in jail for their own protection. This violence outraged the British commander Henry Bouquet who wrote "will they not say that they have found it easier to kill Indians in a Goal than to fight them fairly in the woods?"[62] While the Paxton Boys were eventually threatened with cannon and dispersed, no action was taken against them. Americans thus used an early version of lynch law justice against people considered aliens in their midst. On the other hand the Paxton Boys reflected the sense among Scotch-Irish frontiersmen that the government had failed in its fundamental obligation to protect them. Jane Merritt concludes that the Paxton Boys "tied national and racial differences together to create an essentialized Indian enemy whose blood descendants could and would be disinherited from their claims to a 'native' American past and, thereby, to the land they possessed."[63]

The nature of frontier war required colonists to defend themselves. How successful they were is a matter of debate. Militia institutions provided local, part-time defense, but farmers were seldom willing to leave their families, crops, and livestock for prolonged periods. In contrast to the national mythology, they were not very well armed and lacked realistic training in frontier warfare. There has been much recent debate over the extent to which colonists actually possessed arms. Historian Michael Bellesiles initiated this debate with a controversial book in 2000, which concluded that few colonists had firearms and that the American "gun culture" was a post Civil War phenomenon. Others have questioned his statistics and believe that gun ownership was wide spread. Anecdotal evidence often reveals the militia and provincials as arriving for duty without arms or poorly armed, but this could mean that they left their weapons at home or, if drawn from the margins of society, were too poor to own them.[64] In any event, civilian firearms were not necessarily muskets or rifles appropriate for combat but might be fowling pieces or other weapons of less value. Certainly the training in volley fire that most militia received was not particularly useful on the frontier.

Indian raids produced swarms of refugees who strained colonial charitable institutions or forced families to cower in crowded stockades and forts while their possessions went up in smoke. Colonial authorities turned to provincial volunteers or draftees for defense, the volunteers sometimes being Indian mercenaries. At the end of this period British regular forces had assumed the primary burden of defending the colonies. For the colonists, war often produced divisions rather than unity. The Confederation of New England, an alliance of Massachusetts, Plymouth, Connecticut, and Rhode Island, collapsed under the weight of King Philip's War. Virginians were not united at the prospect of the Seven Years' War and were unenthusiastic about fighting it. War produced tensions between the frontier and the colonial governments whose political base lay within established communities. It exacerbated religious and ethnic divisions within the colonies. While some colonists capitalized upon the opportunities created by war, the net result was damaged economies and burdensome debt. Yet war did push the frontier forward, and by 1763, Vermont was open to settlement, and the great migration across the Alleghenies had begun. For the colonists, the vast majority of whom earned their living in farming, the wars had been about land. The struggles to control the land had been fought without moderation or humanity, but they were decisive.

NOTES

1. "1868 St. Petersburg Declaration Renouncing the Use, in Time of War, of Explosive Projectiles Under 400 Grammes Weight," in *Documents of the Law of War*, ed. A. Roberts and R. Guelff, 3rd edition (Oxford: Oxford University Press, 2000), 55. The Declaration is more significant for the principle quoted here than the attempt to limit explosive projectiles.

2. Emmerich von Vattel, "Of War," in *The Law of Nations, or, the Principles of the Law of Nature, Applied to the Conduct and Affairs of Nations and Sovereigns*, ed. Joseph Chitty (Philadelphia: T. and J. W. Johnson, 1861), 348.

3. Harold Selesky, "Colonial America," in *The Laws of War: Constraints on Warfare in the Western World*, ed. M. Howard, G. Andreopoulos, and M. R. Shulman (New Haven and London: Yale University Press, 1994), 74.

4. William L. Shea, *The Virginia Militia in the Seventeenth Century* (Baton Rouge: Louisiana University Press, 1983), 15. Shea provides a good account of the Powhatan, sometimes referred to as the Tidewater, wars, as do Ian Steele, *Warpaths: Invasions of North America* (New York: Oxford University Press, 1994), Chapter 3, and J.L. Wright, Jr., *The Only Land They Knew: the Tragic Story of the American Indians in the Old South* (New York: The Free Press, 1981), 60–86. For a reprint of the laws drawn up between 1609 and 1612, see "For the colony in Virginea Britannia lawes divine, morall and martiall, etc.," a Jamestown Document, compiled by W. Strachey and edited by D. H. Flaherty (Charlottesville: The University of Virginia Press, n.d.).

5. For Ireland, see C. Falls, *Elizabeth's Irish Wars* (New York: Barnes and Noble, 1970).

6. Steele, *Warpaths*, 43.

7. I believe that this conclusion may be supported by A. Starkey, *European and Native American Warfare, 1675–1815* (Norman: University of Oklahoma Press, 1998) and the forthcoming *Indian Wars in Canada, Mexico and the United States, 1812–1900* by Bruce Vandervort that I had the opportunity to read in ms.

8. Shea, *Virginia Militia*, 51.

9. Ibid., 134–35. For Bacon's Rebellion, see Steele, *Warpaths*, 55–58.

10. On this point see F.W. Gleach, *Powhhatan's World and Colonial Virginia: A Conflict of Cultures* (Lincoln: University of Nebraska Press, 1997).

11. This approach to war is best described by Patrick Malone, *The Skulking Way of War: Technology and Tactics Among the New England Indians* (Lanham, MD: Madison Books, 1993). For this discussion of Indian attitudes toward war I have drawn on Starkey, *European and Native American Warfare*, 25–31.

12. W. Smith, *An Historical Account of the Expedition Against the Ohio Indians in the Year MDCCLXIV Under the Command of Henry Bouquet . . .* (Philadelphia: T. Jeffries, 1766), 38. This was the view of the experienced frontier commander Colonel Bouquet.

13. Richard White, *The Middle Ground: Indians, Empires, and Republics in the Great Lakes Region, 1650–1815* (Cambridge: Cambridge University Press, 1991), 80.

14. Much of the material in this section is based on Alan Taylor's survey *American Colonies* (New York: Penguin Books, 2001).

15. Taylor, *American Colonies*, 268–69.

16. For this event see Elizabeth Fenn, *Pox Americana: The Great Smallpox Epidemic of 1775–82* (New York: Hill and Wang, 2001).

17. Richard Bourne, *The Red King's Rebellion: Racial Politics in New England 1675–1678* (New York: Atheneum, 1990). Bourne's peaceful portrait of relations may be contrasted with that provided by Francis Jennings, *The Invasion of America, Indians, Colonialism and the Cant of Conquest* (Chapel Hill: University of North Carolina Press, 1975). Jennings sees a pattern of almost unrelieved Puritan aggression against their Indian neighbors.

18. In addition to Bourne, *The Red King's Rebellion*, see Neil Salisbury, "Indians and Colonists in Southern New England after the Pequot War. An Uneasy Balance," in *The Pequots in Southern New England: the Rise and Fall of an Indian Nation*, ed. L.M. Hauptman and J.D. Wherry (Norman: University of Oklahoma Press, 1990), 81–95.

19. Steele, *Warpaths*, 91–93. For an extended discussion of this event see Albert Cave, *The Pequot War* (Amherst: University of Massachusetts Press, 1996).

20. Richard Slotkin, *Regeneration Through Violence: Mythology of the American Frontier, 1600–1860* (Middleton, CT: Wesleyan University Press, 1973), ch. 2.

21. Alden Vaughn, *The New England Frontier: Puritans and Indians, 1620–1675* (Boston: Little, Brown, 1965), 303.

22. Jill Lepore, *The Name of War: King Philip's War and the Nature of American Identity* (New York: Alfred A. Knopf, 1998), 9–11. As Lepore's book makes clear, it would be a mistake to assume that writings during and after King Philip's War accurately reflect Puritan attitudes before the war began.

23. Vaughn, *The New England Frontier*, 303.

24. Daniel Gookin, "Historical Collections of the Indians of New England," *Massachusetts Historical Society Collections*, 1st Ser. I (1792): 154.

25. See Mary Beth Norton, *In the Devil's Snare: The Salem Witchcraft Crisis of 1692* (New York: Alfred A. Knopf, 2002).

26. In addition to the works already cited, the standard account of King Philip's War remains Douglas Leach, *Flintlock and Tomahawk: New England in King Philip's War* (New York: Macmillan, 1958). Also see James Drake, *King Philip's War: Civil War in New England, 1675–1676* (Amherst: University of Massachusetts Press, 1999). Contemporary accounts, which must be used with caution, include William Hubbard, *A Narrative of the Troubles with the Indians of New England. . . .* (London: John Foster, 1677); Increase Mather, *A Brief History of the War with the Indians of New England . . .*

(Boston: John Foster, 1676); and Daniel Gookin, "An Historical Account of the Doings and Sufferings of the Christian Indians of New England in the Years 1675, 1676, 1677," in *Archaeologica Americana: Transactions and Collections of the American Antiquarian Society*, II (1836). Important narratives and documents are to be found in S. G. Drake, *The Old Indian Chronicle* (Boston: Antiquarian Institute, 1836, 1867) and C. H. Lincoln, *Narratives of the Indian Wars, 1675–1699* (New York: Scribner's, 1913).

27. Drake, *King Philip's War*. This argument, which I do not find entirely convincing, is developed throughout Drake's book.

28. Lepore, *The Name of War*, xvii.

29. "A Relacion of the Indian Warre by Mr. Eason of Roade Isld. 1675," in Lincoln, *Narratives of the Indian Wars*, 16–17.

30. James Axtell, *Beyond 1492: Encounters in Colonial America* (New York and Oxford: Oxford University Press, 1992), 239.

31. Bourne, *The Red King's Rebellion*, 36. Bourne concludes that 9,000 people died in the war, one-third of them English.

32. Drake, *King Philip's War*, 4.

33. John Canup, *Out of the Wilderness: The Emergence of an American Identity in Colonial New England* (Middletown, CT: Wesleyan University Press, 1990), 194.

34. I have based my discussion of the refugees on a paper delivered by David Corlett, "Forced to Fly For Our Lives: New England Refugees in King Philip's War," presented at *The Society for Military History 2005 Annual Meeting*, 26 February 2005. I wish to thank Professor Corlett for permission to cite his paper.

35. Petition of James Bat of Hingham (n.d.), Massachusetts Archives, Vol. 67, 240; and Petition of April, 1676, of Lieut. Samuel Niles, his sergeant, corporal and forty men, Massachusetts Archives, Vol. 68, 203.

36. The proposal for the stockade and the response of the towns are in the Massachusetts Archives, Vol. 68, 174, 175b, 176a, 180.

37. "Petition of the Reverend John Eliot, August, 1675," in Nathaniel Bradstreet Shurtleff and David Pulsifer, eds., *Records of the Colony of New Plymouth, in New England*, 12 vols. (Boston: W. White, 1855–61), 10: 451.

38. "The Present State of New-england," in Drake, *The Old Indian Chronicle*, 37.

39. For a discussion of this genre see Slotkin, *Regeneration Through Violence*, ch. 4. Lepore's *The Name of War* provides an important discussion of the literature of King Philip's War. Linda Colley has discussed captivity narratives as part of an imperial experience not limited to North America. See her *Captives* (New York: Pantheon Books, 2002).

40. Wayne Lee, *Crowds and Soldiers in Revolutionary North Carolina: The Culture of Violence in Riot and War* (Gainesville: University of Florida Press, 2001), 127.

41. "Narrative of the Captivity of Mrs. Mary Rowlandson, 1682," in Lincoln, *Narratives of the Indian Wars*, 167.

42. J. Demos, ed., *Remarkable Providences 1600–1760* (New York: George Brazille, 1972), 312.

43. John Williams, *The Redeemed Captive Returning to Zion* (Northampton, MA: Hopkins, Bridgman, and Co., 1853). For a powerful analysis of this episode see John Demos, *The Unredeemed Captive: A Family Story From Early America* (New York: Vintage Books, 1995).

44. Taylor, *American Colonies*, 290.

45. Mather, *A Brief History of the Warr*, 50.

46. Cotton Mather, "Decennium Luctuosum, 1699," in Lincoln, *Narratives of the Indian Wars*, 230.

47. W. Pencak, *War, Politics, and Revolution in Provincial Massachusetts* (Boston: Northeastern University Press, 1981), 17.

48. Norton, *In the Devil's Snare*. Her argument is well summarized in the conclusion, pp. 295–308. See also R. Godbeer, *The Devil's Dominion: Magic and Religion in Early New England* (Cambridge: Cambridge University Press, 1992).

49. Michael Kammen, *Colonial New York: A History* (New York: Charles Scribner's Sons, 1975), 144.

50. Ibid., 152.

51. Ibid., 174.

52. Louisbourg's strategic value is dismissed by N.A.M. Rodger, *The Command of the Ocean: A Naval History of Britain* (New York and London: W.W. Norton, 2005), 247.

53. From Virginia's point of view the Seven Years' War lasted nine years. The name Nine Years War or King William's War had already been taken. The Seven Years' War is also sometimes called the French and Indian War, but one may argue that it was but one of many.

54. For Virginia in the Seven Years' War, see James Titus, *The Old Dominion at War* (Columbia: University of South Carolina Press, 1991). The consequences for the frontier are covered by Matthew Ward, *Breaking the Backcountry: The Seven Years' War in Virginia and Pennsylvania, 1754–1765* (Pittsburgh: University of Pittsburgh Press, 2003). Much of what follows is based upon these two works.

55. Ward, *Breaking the Backcountry*. Ward's claim that the Seven Years' War imposed greater casualty rates than other Indian wars may not stand up to comparison with King Philip's War where a conservative estimate places white deaths at 800 out of 52,000, or more than 1.5 percent. For estimates for King Philip's War see Starkey, *European and Native American Warfare*, 184, n. 59.

56. Jane Merritt, *At the Crossroads: Indians and Empires on a Mid-Atlantic Frontier, 1700–1763* (Chapel Hill: University of North Carolina Press, 2003), 177.

57. Fred Anderson, *A People's Army: Massachusetts Soldiers and Society in the Seven Years' War* (Chapel Hill and London: University of North Carolina Press, 1984), 3–6. Another historian believes that Massachusetts's war mobilization was equal to that of Prussia under Frederick the Great. See William Pencak, *War, Politics, and Revolution in Provincial Massachusetts* (Boston: Northeastern University Press, 1981), xi.

58. Kammen, *Colonial New York*, 327. For the impact of the war upon New York, see pp. 319–36. Anderson finds that only two-fifths of Massachusetts' costs were reimbursed. See Anderson, *A People's Army*, 16.

59. Anderson, *A People's Army*, ch. 2; Harold Selesky, *War and Society in Colonial Connecticut* (New Haven and London: Yale University Press, 1990); Pencak, *War, Politics, and Revolution*, 120–21.

60. Andrew Eliot, "A Sermon Preached October 25th, 1759, Being a Day of Public Thanksgiving Appointed by Authority for the Success of British Arms This Year . . ." (Boston: Daniel and John Kneeland, 1759). See also Pencak, *War, Politics and Revolution*, 121; and Fred Anderson, *Crucible of War: The Seven Years' War and the Fate of Empire in British North Amearica, 1754–1766* (New York: Alfred A. Knopf, 2000), 373–76.

61. Pencak, *War, Politics, and Revolution*, 124.

62. British Library, Bouquet Papers, Additional Manuscripts 21,8150, 350.

63. Merritt, *At the Crossroads,* 294. Her discussion of the Paxton Boys is included in pp. 285–94.

64. Micheal Bellesiles, *Arming America: The Origins of a National Gun Culture* (New York: Alfred A. Knopf, 2000). See also "Forum: Historians and Guns," *The William and Mary Quarterly,* 3rd Ser., LVIX, 1 (2002): 211–41. Participants in this forum attacked the statistics on which Bellesiles based his case. Essentially Bellesiles replied that the statistics were not that important to begin with, but that Americans did not value guns and did not have a gun culture. Bellesiles undervalues the effectiveness of eighteenth-century firearms and does not seem to understand their place in the tactics of the time. See A. Starkey, *War in the Age of the Enlightenment, 1700–1789* (Westport CT: Praeger, 2003), 146. Also, R. H. Churchill in "Gun Ownership in Early America: A Survey of Manuscript Militia Returns," *The William and Mary Quarterly,* 3rd Ser., LX, 3 (2003): 615–42, concludes that "early Americans owned guns. They owned a lot of them" (642).

FURTHER READING

Anderson, Fred. *Crucible of War.* New York: Knopf, 2000. A major survey of the Seven Years' War in America.

———. *A People's Army: Massachusetts Soldiers and Society in the Seven Years' War.* Chapel Hill and London: University of North Carolina Press, 1984. An important social history of Massachusetts in wartime.

Axtell, James. *Beyond 1492: Encounters in Colonial North America.* New York: Oxford University Press, 1985. Important for the cultural interchange between whites and Indians.

Bourne, Richard. *The Red King's Rebellion: Racial Politics in New England, 1675–1678.* New York: Atheneum, 1990. Bourne portrays King Philip's war as a break in the normal pattern of good colonist–Indian relations in New England.

Cave, Alfred. *The Pequot War.* Amherst: University of Massachusetts Press, 1996. The standard account of the 1637 war and the massacre of the Pequot village in Connecticut.

Colley, Linda. *Captives.* New York: Pantheon Books. Colley includes America and North Africa in her discussion of the English experience with captivity.

Demos, John. *The Unredeemed Captive: A Family Story from Early America.* New York: Vintage Books, 1995. An important discussion of the captivity experience of the Reverend John Williams and his family.

Drake, James. *King Philip's War: Civil War in New England, 1675–1676.* Amherst: University of Massachusetts Press, 1999. Drake argues that King Philip's war was unique in that it possessed the qualities of a civil war within an established society.

Ferling, John. *A Wilderness of Miseries: War and Warriors in Early America.* Westport, CT: Greenwood Press, 1980. A standard account of the colonial wars.

Jennings, Francis. *The Ambigious Iroquois Empire.* New York: Norton, 1984. In this and in the two works following, Jennings provides a powerful if somewhat polemical revisionist account of colonial relations with Native Americans. Even if one does not agree with his interpretation it must be considered.

———. *Empire of Fortune: Crowns, Colonies, and Tribes in the Seven Years War.* New York: Norton, 1988.

———. *The Invasion of America: Indians, Colonialism, and the Cant of Conquest.* Chapel Hill: University of North Carolina Press, 1975.

Kammen, Michael. *Colonial New York: A History.* New York: Scribner's, 1975. A valuable survey of colonial New York.

Lee, Wayne. *Crowds and Soldiers in Revolutionary North Carolina: The Culture of Violence in Riot and War.* Gainesville: University of Florida Press, 2001. An insightful analysis of the roots of violence in North Carolina society before and during the American Revolution.

Lepore, Jill. *In the Name of War: King Philip's War and the Nature of American Identity.* New York: Knopf, 1998. An analysis of the way in which late-seventeenth-century New Englanders interpreted and justified King Philip's War.

Merritt, Jane. *At the Crossroads: Indians and Empires on a Mid-Atlantic Frontier.* Chapel Hill: University of North Carolina Press: 2003. Important for understanding the impact of the Seven Years' War on Pennsylvania society.

Norton, Mary Beth. *In the Devil's Snare: The Salem Witchcraft Crisis of 1692.* New York: Knopf, 2002. An important analysis that places the witchcraft crisis within the context of war.

Peckham, Howard. *The Colonial Wars, 1689–1762.* Chicago: University of Chicago Press, 1964. A somewhat dated but still valuable survey.

Pencak, William. *War, Politics and Revolution in Provincial Massachusetts.* Boston: Northeastern University Press, 1981. Places the Massachusetts effort in the Seven Years' War within its political context.

Shea, William. *The Virginia Militia in the Seventeenth Century.* Baton Rouge: Louisiana State University Press, 1983. A valuable account of America's first "citizen soldiers" and how they adapted to conditions in a new world.

Slotkin, Richard. *Regeneration Through Violence: Mythology of the American Frontier, 1600–1860.* Middletown, CT: Wesleyan University Press, 1973.
The first part of an absorbing trilogy on the history of violence in America. Slotkin finds the origins of King Philip's War in Puritanism.

Steele, Ian. *Warpaths: Invasions of North America.* New York: Oxford University Press, 1994. The most up-to-date survey of the colonial wars by a major scholar in the field.

Taylor, Alan. *American Colonies.* New York: Viking Press, 2001. Now perhaps the standard survey of colonial history, drawing on the most recent scholarship and with a broader perspective than previous accounts.

Titus, James. *The Old Dominion at War.* Columbia: University of South Carolina Press, 1991. A valuable analysis of Virginia during the Seven Years' War, a war that Titus finds few Virginians wanted.

Vaughn, Alden. *The New England Frontier: Puritans and Indians, 1620–1675.* Boston: Little, Brown, 1965.
Vaughn provides a positive picture of the Puritans in their relations with their Indian neighbors.

Ward, Matthew. *Breaking the Backcountry: The Seven Years' War in Virginia and Pennsylvania, 1754–1765.* Pittsburgh: University of Pittsburgh Press, 2003. Ward spells out the horrors inflicted upon the frontier during the Seven Years' war. Frontier society collapsed under French-Indian assault.

White, Richard. *The Middle Ground: Indians, Empires, and Republics in the Great Lakes Region, 1650–1815.* Cambridge: Cambridge University Press, 1991. The "middle ground" has become an important concept as a result of this book. White describes the mingling of peoples from different backgrounds and the creation of new societies.

TWO

The American Revolution

Wayne E. Lee

In August of 1777 the British army made a momentous decision, striking out at Philadelphia from its stronghold in New York City, hoping to threaten the Continental Congress, and thus to draw George Washington and his Continental Army into one decisive battle that could end the war. British troops arrived by sea at Head of Elk, Maryland, debarked, and marched overland into Pennsylvania. Initially the British soldiers were surprised and even somewhat spooked by the eerie emptiness of the landscape. Few people turned out to witness the martial spectacle. Many even fled their homes, and the British readily interpreted such abandonment as a sure sign of a rebellious subject, and they promptly appropriated whatever movables they could find. Not all civilians chose flight, however, and as the British army approached Washington's defenses on Brandywine Creek west of Philadelphia, some civilians were overcome with curiosity. Joseph Townsend, all of 21 years old, and eager for a new experience, followed the rumors of the army on the move, and he and some friends, somewhat awestruck, found themselves admitted into British lines. Some British officers asked them about the Americans' whereabouts, and even about Washington's character. As he headed for home, he found himself briefly dragooned into helping tear down a fence to simplify the British advance. Quaker that he was, however, Joseph began to wonder at his own behavior in participating in preparations for battle. He quietly snuck away, but even as he left, the sounds of battle echoed across the rolling Pennsylvania backcountry. Riveted, he found a spot on a hill with some other locals and watched the battle unfold.[1]

Washington's army, despite some moments that seemed to signal hope for the army's future success, could not hold at Brandywine, and they fled north of Philadelphia, leaving the city and countryside around the capital to British occupation. Major Persifor Frazer, an American officer who had participated in the battle, returned to his home in Chester County, Pennsylvania. When he arrived he found two Tories who had taken advantage of his absence by taking up residence in his house. They quickly fled, but Frazer still faced a problem. His allegiances and his military service were of course known to the neighboring countryside, and as the British steadily moved through the area he could be certain that they would eventually target the house of a known rebel officer. Taking the advice of friends, he departed his home, but left his wife, Mary Worrall Frazer, four children, a servant, and three slaves. Mary wisely began secreting the family's valuables in nearby woods and gardens. Within days a British foraging party arrived. The whole family, save Mary and a young slave girl, fled into the woods. Mary bluntly traded insults with one British officer, and troops began to ransack the house even as neighbors gathered to watch. Eventually the commanding officer, Captain De West, entered the house, controlled or removed the most drunken and violent troops, and then searched the house personally. Mary followed him from cupboard to cupboard, and repeatedly protested the propriety of his searches and confiscations. Eventually the British left, and a dismayed Mary realized that she no longer had enough food for her household. Worse yet, possibly on the same day, her husband had been captured, and would spend the next six months in British custody.[2]

These two brief anecdotes from a few short weeks of one campaign encapsulate many of the experiences civilians were faced with in the course of the American War of Independence. Public loyalty to one side brought vulnerability when the other side was ascendant, including the risk of neighbors pointing the way to your home. Women left alone by serving or fleeing husbands faced the whims of soldiery, who themselves were sent from farm to farm to impress supplies. Soldiers in the process of foraging might visit violence upon a family, or show consideration and restraint. Not knowing which of the two to expect, civilians in the path of armies frequently disappeared, hiding themselves and their goods in the surrounding countryside.

With respect to the civilian experience of war, the American Revolution was unique in American history. It was the only occasion in which war was fought between culturally similar peoples within the bounds of American territory in which both sides were intermingled with each other. The Civil War divided the country sectionally along clear boundaries (although admittedly there were zones on the edges where loyalty was less clear), but during the Revolutionary war, people with competing loyalties lived side by side throughout the settled part of the continent. Despite this intermingling of "enemies," eighteenth-century civilians generally expected to be exempt from the activities of armies. The simple needs of armies and the strategic importance of cities, however, inevitably brought armies and civilians face to face. It was this conflict of expectation and reality that framed Mary Frazer's experience—her husband hoped that she would be safe in what turned out to be the dubious sanctuary of their home. Others were less optimistic, and armies could generate waves of refugees. In addition, although the main lines of conflict were between culturally similar

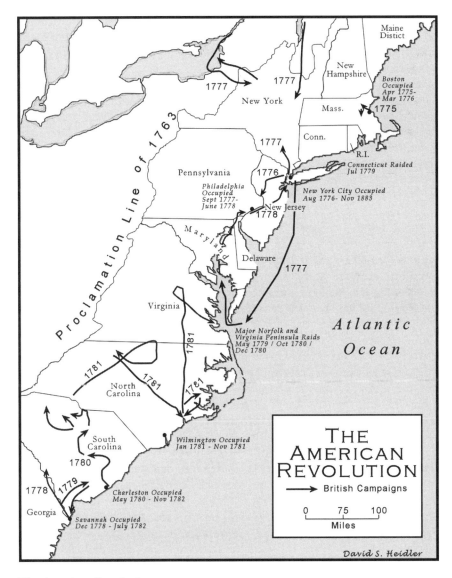

The American Revolution.

European peoples, the war also affected the lives of the Native Americans and black slaves who lived throughout eastern North America. One can only wonder, for example, at the conflicting fears and hopes in the mind of the young slave girl who accompanied Mary Frazer in confronting the British foragers.

Further complicating the expectation and the reality of eighteenth-century warfare was the fact that this was a *revolutionary* war. Ideology and abstract beliefs were at the heart of the conflict for many, if not all, of the participants. The revolutionary and ideological nature of the war led those supporting the cause of independence to argue that "if you're not with us, you're against us." They implemented a system of loyalty enforcement and held an expectation of service to the cause that ran against the grain of the norms of eighteenth-century political warfare. The revolutionaries made the revolutionary war into a "people's war," and in the process created a unique experience for the population living through it. Those people then turned around and plowed that experience back into their conception of the state they were creating. The civilian experience of the American Revolutionary War had a profound impact on the nature of the state that emerged from that war. This essay explores some of those experiences.

CHOOSING SIDES

The Revolution posed many challenges for civilians, but the first problem everyone faced was choosing sides. Historians struggle to explain why the colonists revolted against Britain, and pursuing that question here would divert us from the main purpose of understanding the experience of the war itself. But we cannot ignore the fact that individuals throughout the continent faced pressures to take sides in the struggle. Those pressures framed much of the nature of the wartime experience. An old assumption about the war suggests that one-third of the American population was actively pro-independence, one-third was actively pro-British, and one-third was determined to stay out of it. Those numbers are probably wrong, but they clearly frame the problem. Active supporters tried to pressure the others to shift their posture—to convince the neutral to favor their side and to convince their opponents to act more neutrally.

Some of the pressure could be internal—the pressures of beliefs and hopes. We still debate the extent to which ideology shaped the decision to rebel, but there is little doubt that many Americans had come to believe that the British government was essentially corrupt, and that it sought to impose ever stricter controls over their personal and economic lives. There is also little doubt that many other Americans sincerely believed that the British "constitution"—its evolved system of mixed monarchical and parliamentary government—was the freest and best in the world. These sincere and competing beliefs drove many in their choosing of sides. We can think of these as unofficial pressures on one's choice of allegiances, in which belief rather than force or institutional pressure determined one's side. That such beliefs mattered is most obvious in the way it sometimes split families, with one brother preferring the British and the other the Whigs.[3] The most famous family split was probably that of Benjamin Franklin from his illegitimate, and Loyalist, son William Franklin, but there were many such divisions. Belief, or at least one's posture toward the war, could also be swayed by the success of one side or the other. It is easy to forget the amount of legitimacy that military success could render to a debated cause. That is, after all, what generals in a revolutionary war are hoping to achieve: a military success that will affect the mental posture of the neutral and of the enemy. Nothing makes this more clear than George Washington's successes at Trenton and Princeton in December of 1776 and January 1777. All through the summer and fall of 1776 the British had inflicted defeat after defeat on Washington's army. Literally and symbolically, the rebellion was taking a beating, and willingness to support the cause dwindled. Washington recognized the need for some kind of victory, even a small one, to keep his army together. Most of his soldiers' enlistments were set to expire at the end of December, so Washington gambled. He crossed the Delaware, successfully routed the Hessian garrison in Trenton, and then outmaneuvered British reinforcements in Princeton. There would be other crises, and only in hindsight can we say that these campaigns saved the Revolution, but Trenton and Princeton certainly demonstrate the way in which success could sway belief in a cause.

Committed revolutionaries, however, were not content to rely on rhetoric and ideology to sway the uncertain, nor even to await military success. As they assumed control over the reins of local government, Whigs institutionalized means of determining and fixing the loyalty of the population. British forces would try to do the same in areas they occupied, but for the most part such official pressures on loyalty were instigated by the Rebels. The primary means was the "Test Oath." During the years prior to the Revolution, American protestors had developed more and more thorough methods of pinning down support for their cause—in particular they relied on the public taking of an oath to obey the resolutions of revolutionary committees. In October 1774, in response to Britain's "Coercive" or "Intolerable" Acts passed to punish Boston for the Boston Tea Party, the Continental Congress instituted the "Association" oath, in which all Americans swore to adhere to the terms of a boycott and an embargo on most trade with Britain (some items were exempt). Crucially, Congress recommended that "every county, city, and town" elect a committee to ensure enforcement of the Association, publicize the names of violators, and then "break off all dealings" with them.[4] The creation of the committees projected the power of the revolutionaries down into local government, and quickly those committees became the *only* effective government in many locales. The Association Oath of the protest movement became the model for the wartime Test Oath designed to ferret out Loyalists to the crown.

The Test Oaths were a crucial component of the civilian experience of the war, and they embodied in many ways the unique nature of the war and its impact on the population. Revolution by its very nature allowed little room for neutrality. The Continental Congress acted on that assumption, and in January of 1776 it recommended that the states take "speedy and effectual measures" against Loyalists, including having them "disarmed, and the more dangerous among them, either kept in safe custody, or bound with sufficient sureties to their good behaviour."[5] Some states had already begun requiring loyalty oaths, and the rest would respond to this recommendation at different paces and in differing ways, but in the end they all required oaths of allegiance from all free adult males. Not all locales actively pursued all of the citizens to force them to take the oath—neighbors knew each other's probable loyalties, and often only the suspected or undecided were forced to publicly swear the oath. Refusal could result in a trial, or immediate civil disabilities (being disarmed, barred from office, disenfranchised, prohibited from acquiring or conveying property, inheriting land, or even traveling freely). New York's "Committee and Commission of Detecting and Defeating Conspiracies" supervised 1,000 trials of people refusing the oath between 1776 and 1779. Six hundred men were paroled on bond, others went into exile, a few were confined, and a few relented and took the oath.[6] In Connecticut, some Loyalists who refused the oath were confined in the notorious Simsbury mines, an abandoned copper mine. Others were forced into exile, or at a minimum, labeled by their refusal of the oath, and thus exposed to the ire of rebel supporters.

Consider the experience of Loyalist lawyer Filer Dibblee. Dibblee fled rebel-dominated Stamford, Connecticut in August 1776 for Long Island, soon to be under the control of the British, and notoriously a Loyalist haven. It did not prove a safe haven for Dibblee or his family, however. Within a few months his wife and five children were thrown out of their plundered house "naked into the Streets." Dibblee and his family fled to British-held New York City and slowly built up enough credit to relocate back into Long Island. In 1778 Rebels plundered his new house, and carried him to six months of imprisonment in Connecticut. Eventually exchanged, he returned to Long Island and was "plundered and stripped" there twice more. Finally, with assistance from the British commander, Dibblee moved his family out of the war zone to New Brunswick, joining perhaps as many as 60,000 Loyalists who left the American states for elsewhere by the end of the war. Facing debts he could no longer control, he "grew Melancholy, which soon deprived him of his Reason," and finally in 1784, an agitated Dibblee cut his own throat with a razor.[7]

Dibblee's story is perhaps extreme, and is certainly more tragic than most, but the institutional and forceful pressures on allegiance were pervasive, and those who resisted them suffered. In a more typical case, in December 1776 Elias Long of Northampton County, Pennsylvania rashly described the Continental Congress and the Pennsylvania revolutionaries as "a parcel of damned rascals [who] were selling the peoples liberties."[8] Overheard, he was soon summoned before the County Committee. He was tried and jailed for an indefinite period. From jail Long repented, and he posted a £40 bond for his future good behavior. Subsequently the British occupation of Philadelphia in 1777 badly frightened the Pennsylvania radicals, and they passed an act proclaiming it treason to voluntarily serve the British in any capacity at the penalty of forfeiting all property. The timing is unclear, but Elias Long had become a marked man, and he ended up among the 500 persons eventually named under this act between 1778 and 1781. Elias fled in the spring of 1778, abandoning his wife and children for the next six years. Soon after his departure the state's agents of confiscation arrived to inventory and appraise his property, totaling a relatively modest £145, most or all of which could be claimed by his creditors. Because the estate was so heavily encumbered, the confiscation agents simply distributed the property to creditors on a first-come, first-served basis.[9]

The inventory of Long's estate brings us to perhaps one of the most resented and most legally problematic of the pressure tactics applied by Whig governments: Confiscation. Congress resolved in November 1777 that the states should "confiscate and make sale of all the real and personal estate" of active Loyalists.[10] A number of states interpreted this phrase to include all those who had refused the loyalty oath. North Carolina, for example, had already declared in November 1776 that any person who refused the oath (with a 90-day grace period) would forfeit his estate.[11] The actual confiscation of estates was relatively restrained, and many Loyalists were able to make arrangements with relatives or friends to preserve their property, but the pressure was real. To continue with the example of North Carolina: not all counties followed up on the mandate to impose the oath immediately, and in practice individuals were often given extra chances to take the oath before being punished with banishment or confiscation. In Rowan County, for example, the first oath was not required until August 1777, and only 65 people in the county took the oath in all of that year. In May 1778, the county began a more widespread enforcement of the oath, compiling a list of 577 persons who had refused it. In no way, however, did North Carolina's government confiscate all of those persons' estates. In the whole state perhaps only 110 Loyalists suffered confiscation of their real estate.[12] Nevertheless, the fear remained. Consider the problem: a known Loyalist adult fears being attacked in his home for his adherence to the king, but if he flees he abandons his estate to confiscation. If he flees and leaves his wife behind to hold claim to the estate, she may then become subject to the less than tender mercies of rebels who believed that gender was no guarantee of protection in an environment of revolution.

In some ways this civilian experience of the pressures on allegiance lies at the heart of the military history of the war—this was a people's war. For some the Whigs went too far with their demands for oaths, their threats of confiscation, or the actual mistreatment of suspected Loyalists. Those most outraged responded by taking up arms. Well over 8,000 men served in Loyalist militia units, and Loyalist refugees in New York City supplied as many as 15,000 men to regular British regiments and the navy.[13] Similarly, British missteps drove others into active resistance against the crown. The most famous instance of British use and misuse of oaths occurred in the aftermath of their capture of Charlestown, South Carolina, and their apparent reconquest of that state. On June 1, 1780, British commander General Henry Clinton proclaimed that all the prisoners and active rebels who swore allegiance to British rule would be pardoned, thus preserving their property and status within the realm should Britain win the war. Two days later, in a major about-face, Clinton issued another proclamation, releasing prisoners from parole, but requiring them to take an oath to actively support the British as militia. Many South Carolinians, although prepared to shift from being rebels to being neutral, were not prepared to go the whole distance and fight for the other side. Instead, they again took up arms in the cause of independence.

Although these pressures made neutrality difficult, many nevertheless tried. Some (the majority) tried to abstain from the war simply from a desire to be left alone, but others were members of religious sects committed to a belief in pacifism. Moravians, Mennonites, Quakers, and other sectarians, many of whom lived in distinct, coherent communities in different parts of America, quickly became obvious targets. Most of the colonies had had long experience with pacifist sects, and during earlier wars had passed laws that provided for fees or exemptions from taking oaths or serving in the militia. Within the context of a revolutionary people's war, however, such principled exemptions proved more difficult for some radical Whigs to accept. Rebel recruiters took 14 Quakers from northern Virginia and forcibly marched them to join Washington's army outside Philadelphia in 1777. Eventually Washington learned of their plight and released them to go home, but problems could be more persistent at the local level.[14] In Pennsylvania, for example, Benjamin Franklin convinced the Assembly to pass a resolution urging militiamen to tolerate the sectarian peace churches, and in turn asking those church members to help support the families of absent militiamen. The Northampton County committee, however, ignored the resolution and demanded that the Moravian community supply their quota of riflemen.[15] Part of the problem for the sectarians was their visibility–they tended to refuse service as a community. Less principled individuals who simply avoided service without making public categorical statements might be missed by the rickety state apparatus, but whole communities were hard to ignore and, better yet, easy to target. Statewide in Virginia the Assembly seized £11,221 worth of property as a result of failure to take the Test Oath (all the pacifist churches shared a religious principle against the taking of oaths). Despite the relatively small number of Quakers in the state, £5,191 of that total came from seizures from Quakers.[16] In North Carolina locals quickly assumed that the piedmont Moravian communities were Loyalists and regularly harassed them on that basis.

Sitting on the fence in a revolutionary war proved difficult. The peace churches did so from a principle that at least some Whigs could understand and protect (as did Washington, Franklin, and other local and state leaders on occasion). For the remainder who might hope to stay out of the war it was a riskier proposition, and furthermore, an option that the cash-strapped, manpower-short revolutionary movement could ill afford. Too, the British and their actively Loyalist supporters sought to recapture or at least to stimulate loyalty in the countryside. The neighborhood by neighborhood intermingling of supporters of both sides rendered neutrality perilous. Take for example, the story of Frederick Smith of North Carolina. Late in the war he happened to cross the path of a party of Whig militia who questioned him as to his loyalties. Unsure who was asking, he guessed wrong, and they proceeded to hang him briefly from a tree, cutting him down before he died. Not to be outdone, a Loyalist militia unit that later crossed paths with Smith asked him the same question. Again Smith guessed wrong as to the identity of those asking, and again was half hanged for his trouble.[17] If there was one overarching protection that existed for the hopeful neutrals, it was the sense of some leaders on both sides that not mistreating the population was the only way to gain their loyalty, both as a source of possible recruits and also as willing providers of supplies. This pressure for recruits and supplies framed another major part of the civilian experience of the war.

RECRUITING

As part of their ideology of resistance to Britain, American revolutionary leaders hoped and expected that the fighting would be done by volunteers from the best sort of people. Stable farmers with a vested interest in the state, an interest in order, and an interest in defending their communities were seen as the safest and even as the most efficient kinds of soldiers. The shorthand terminology for this was a preference for a "militia" versus a "standing army." The former would be comprised of virtuous citizens (read "property-holders") while the latter were seen as drawn from the worst sort of folks, easily swayed to the purposes of a corrupt and tyrannical state. In George Mason's words, a "well-regulated Militia, composed of gentlemen freeholders, and other freemen" was the "natural strength, and only safe and stable security of a free government."[18] In the heady days following the opening shots at Lexington and Concord in April 1775, this hope for the efficacy and willingness of the militia appeared well founded. Thousands and thousands of New England militiamen turned out in an upwelling of enthusiasm that historian Charles Royster has called the *rage militaire*.[19] There were so many that the British quickly found themselves besieged in Boston. Their first major attempt to break the siege led to the Battle of Bunker Hill, where the militia seemingly proved its worth, mowing down over a thousand redcoats, and only giving up the hill (actually Breed's Hill) when they ran out of ammunition. Roughly simultaneous with the militia's moral victory at Bunker Hill, the Continental Congress appointed George Washington to command, renamed it the Continental Army, and called for regiments from the other colonies. All of the soldiers who enlisted that summer did so with an expiration date at the end of 1775. The next batch of enlistments (whether new or reenlisting soldiers) were also only for one year, set to expire at the end of 1776. Finally, in the fall of 1776, Congress acknowledged the realities of a long war and set fixed quotas for each state to supply to the Continental Army, with soldiers to enlist for three years or the duration. In all they called for 88 regiments for a total of 63,000 troops.[20]

By the end of 1776, especially prior to Trenton and Princeton, enthusiasm was in short supply. Even after those twin victories, the *rage militaire* was clearly gone forever. The states would never meet Congress's recruiting goals (for a host of reasons not worth recounting here), but they would continue to try, and when recruits for the Continental Army dried up, the states would try shorter term call-ups of the militia, or try to fill their own intermediate-length service "State Troops." Failing their quotas several states quickly resorted to some form of a draft. Massachusetts, for example, drafted half of the militia from four counties for one month's service with the northern army facing General John Burgoyne's invasion of New York in 1777. Finally, in February of 1778, Congress called on 11 of the states to formally institute a draft to pull men from the universal militia into the Continental Army. The states responded, but dreading a standing army, and fearing the unpopularity of a draft, they tended to restrict the draftees' service to 6, 9, or 18 months. All of these demands for troops trickled down to the counties and towns responsible for filling their own quotas, resulting in a nearly constant sense of pressure within local communities to provide more soldiers.

We can begin to assess the impact this constant pressure had on civilians by studying the ways in which the counties and towns tried to deal with it. We cannot get away from the truth that this was a people's war, and much of the problem faced by both sides was who could be persuaded to shed the status of civilian. The system in general is fairly easy to describe. Periodically Congress would assign quotas of troops to the states, who in turn would divide the quota among their towns and counties. The local militia then held a muster of all the available men and asked for volunteers. Although all the recruits would receive some form of enlistment bounty (and often promises of eventual land), depending on the year and the state, volunteers frequently received a higher bounty than those drafted. When, as was nearly inevitable, the number of volunteers did not equal the local quota, the militia officers would begin a draft. Most of the states divided each militia company into "classes," usually four or eight, and each class would be drafted from in rotation. State laws specified that the draft be random from within the class, usually drawing papers from a hat or some other such method, until the quota was filled. The law also allowed those selected through the draft to instead hire a substitute. Over time, particularly as enthusiasm for the war abated, this system, although designed to distribute the burdens of service equally, tended to recruit men from the lower economic strata of society. The draft scooped up men who could not afford a substitute and those men who needed money badly enough to hire themselves out as one. Furthermore, the militia system continued to serve as active military units, not just as a draft pool. So during emergencies, or as a short-term alternative to another draft, militia units (in some states not the whole unit, but one of its "classes") would be called up for two or three months of service. Such service would then be considered, and it prevented those militiamen who served from being drafted at the next quota call.

Such was the system in general. The details from community to community, however, could vary widely. In Maryland, the failure in 1777 to fill their Continental regiments with volunteers led the legislature to institute an "emergency only" draft. They divided the militia into eight classes, which would be drafted to serve for only two months outside the state. But two-month militiamen did not fill the regiments, and so in 1778 the Maryland Assembly determined to institute a kind of targeted draft. They first called for volunteers, then rounded up whatever vagrants could be found and forced them into the army. They then offered the militiamen a chance to provide a substitute at the rate of two militiamen per one substitute; those providing a substitute would then be exempt for as long as that substitute continued to serve. Whatever remained in the local quota was to be made up in drafts from the militia classes in rotation. Even here the system failed to vacuum up the necessary men. In one example from Charles County, Maryland, recruiting supervisor Francis Ware carefully tabulated the results of recruiting for all of 1778. There had been 5 volunteers, 42 substitutes, 59 short-term militiamen provided by the classes, and 39 draftees for long-term service in the Continentals. Of the draftees, however, only 12 successfully joined the army; 19 were "discharged or excused," while eight simply disappeared.[21]

In North Carolina the Assembly used the usual quota system for each county and set a higher bounty for volunteers as opposed to draftees. The law divided the North Carolina militia into four classes, intending to prevent too many men from any one area being called up simultaneously. A quota call supposedly would come from one of the four classes, and that class would not be susceptible to another quota until the other three had had their turn. In practice when there were not enough volunteers, the county militia officers arranged some kind of draft. North Carolina's records indicate a wide variety of methods were employed, as county officers sought to placate the populace as much as possible. In some units names were randomly drawn, while other units, according to the law passed in April 1778, "elected" those who were to be drafted, after the men swore to "vote for those who could best be spared."[22] Social pressure bred changes in practice. In 1779 John Robinson petitioned the North Carolina Assembly, complaining of irregularities in the draft process. He claimed that they had elected those to be drafted (as per the law), but then "the persons Chosen Compleaned, to one of the feild officers, who set aside what we had Done, by Ballot, at a Court Martial held afterward, [then] the Feild officers, presumed to nominateing other persons in their room, But on mature Deliberation, They, the Feild officers, at a subsequent meeting, set aside . . . what they themselves had Done."[23] Others complained that their officers "have pursued the most foul and partial ways and means for fixing those duties [the draft] on the poor and ignorant, or on those against whom they or their friends, and dependants had the most trifling resentment or prejudice."[24]

Quotas for the Continental Army were far from the only pressures on manpower. Invasion scares, Tory risings, Indian raids, requirements to guard prisoners or stores, all generated local call-ups of the militia for short terms.[25] Our records are most complete for the Continental quotas transmitted by Congress, but when one adds in the assorted militia demands, the pressure on communities to part with their able-bodied men over eight long years of war was enormous. Historian Robert Gross calculated that Concord, Massachusetts provided "some 875 men for terms of two months or more–a figure more than two and half times the eligible male population on the eve of war."[26] Jean Lee's work with Charles County, Maryland, looking only at Continental Army call-ups, found that annually the County was expected to provide between 83 and 145 men, to be taken from a pool of roughly 1,500 freemen between 16 and 50. Subtract out the men in their 40s and 50s, as well as those already serving, and one can get a sense of the demand on manpower.

This kind of recruiting pressure naturally bred resistance, particularly in an environment in which support for the war was much less than universal. Many locales experienced violent resistance to the draft, while others, like the Charles County example, found bureaucratic dodges to reduce their response to the quota. Harry Ward has suggested that the worst draft resistance was in Virginia, pointing out that by 1780 only 32 of the state's 72 counties had even attempted to implement the draft. As Virginia was pummeled by successive British invasions in 1780 and 1781, protests against the draft turned into a wave of riots. A Lancaster County mob in December 1780 disarmed their militia officers and seized "papers relative to the draft." A subsequent court-martial condemned numerous offenders, but the county lieutenant found it beyond his power to actually arrest the riot leaders.[27] North Carolina experienced a nearly constant level of active draft resistance, some violent, some creative. Most notably in the latter category were the militiamen in one county who, when asked to elect draftees, simply selected all the top officials of the region, most of whom were legally exempt from the draft, or were not members of the company of those who had "selected" them.[28]

Civilians throughout the colonies were thus constantly experiencing pressure not only to choose sides, but to enlist. Some of them simply resisted that pressure, but a surprisingly large number of civilians would spend some time under arms. As a simple question of numbers, the Revolutionary War more than measures up to America's other "total wars." Roughly 200,000 men served for the Rebels in some capacity, plus an additional 30,000 or so Loyalists supported the British. This breaks out to 9.2 percent of the total population in America, including slaves. The soldiers who served in the American Civil War, combining the Confederate and Union armies and compared to the population in 1860, totaled 9.5 percent of the population. And in America's greatest "total war," World War II, when not only an army, but a navy and an air force had to be filled, the percentage was only 9.1 percent.[29] Despite this relatively high percentage of service, the dominant experience of war for civilians was not *in* the army, but *of* the army.

LOGISTICS, PLUNDER, AND VIOLENCE

A simple but oft-forgotten truth about armies is that their largest impact on the countryside comes not through fighting, but eating. This was especially true prior to the industrial era, when armies represented a concentration of people and animals exceeding that of most cities. Even the relatively small armies operating in North America during the Revolutionary War were huge in comparison to the largest nearby cities. The comparison to cities is apt, because armies, like cities, required food to be brought to them in order to survive. Cities had the advantage of an evolved infrastructure and market system to transport that food. Armies had to invent their own, and it had to come to them wherever they happened to be.

The demand could be extreme. Washington estimated that an army of 15,000 men required 100,000 barrels of flour and 20 million pounds of meat in one year.[30] In contrast to that demand, the Commissary General Joseph Trumbull estimated that Philadelphia, sitting at the center of America's largest flour production industry, could only supply 20,000 barrels of flour.[31] Beyond food, armies required large numbers of horses and carts. One estimate from 1778 suggests that the American army alone needed 10,000 horses, all of which would then need to be fed.[32] None of these estimates account for the simultaneous demand created by the British, who would try to supply themselves from overseas, but would regularly need food and horses from the local countryside.

Setting aside the British system for the moment, to meet this demand the American main army hoped to draw supplies from areas distant from

British soldiers plunder a private residence. (Library of Congress)

their main activities, and unthreatened by the British. Commissary agents traveled the countryside with wagons and small parties of soldiers purchasing flour and beef. They then transported it to supply depots, and from there to the army. An army on the march hoped for supplies coming from those depots, but would also simultaneously send out advance parties to communities in their line of movement, encouraging them to gather together foodstuffs for easy purchase. When desperate, which was often, the army simply sent out parties from its own ranks into the immediately surrounding countryside, and they proceeded from house to house buying food to take back to camp.

Crucially, each of these alternative methods of supply hinged upon money. As will be made clear, American troops were less and less able to pay for the supplies they requisitioned, and even when they had cash, inflation had reduced its value to a point where farmers were less and less willing to part with their produce. Some farmers simply carted their produce to the better paying British. Reluctant farmers were not the only reasons for scarcity within the army, however. Frequently the real problem was a lack of transportation or inefficiencies in the logistical bureaucracy.

At any rate, when this system broke down, and frequently independent militia forces simply had no system at all, the only expedient proved to be the impressment of food and property from the surrounding area.

Both Washington and Congress desperately hoped to avoid impressment, and for much of the early part of the war, the main army was able to do so. But it was clear that it would be necessary, and after 1780 it became much more frequent. Congress and the states therefore required a civilian component to the impressment process: a local magistrate had to provide authorization for taking personal property, with the promise of full payment.[33] Washington struggled to comply with the magistrate requirement, but in the often straitened circumstances of the army, less systematic forcible impressment, or "foraging," became necessary. Conditions in the South were worse, in part because of more dispersed settlement and less developed transportation infrastructure, but also because of deliberate British devastation and the ongoing retaliatory activities of Whig and Tory militias. When General Nathanael Greene took command of the southern army, some estimates suggest that as much as 50 percent of his army's food came through impressment.[34]

When so many soldiers are tasked with getting that much of their food through less than formal means, it becomes very difficult to control their interactions with civilians. There was a fine line between foraging and plundering, and soldiers entering individual homes in order to secure food, officially or unofficially, could easily cross over that line. We have seen how Mary Worrall Frazer experienced British soldiers foraging in her house, and some version of her story could be repeated many times. Although it is impossible to count, there is little reason to doubt that the most common interaction between civilians and armies revolved around this kind of foraging. From a civilian perspective part of the problem with this process was its random quality. One never knew how ill- or well-treated one would be by a party of foragers, nor how often one's house might be subject to the experience. Furthermore, there were whole classes of armed men, popularly referred to as "banditti" who made little pretense at distinguishing between "supply" and "plunder." Thus the unsuspecting civilian might encounter Private Joseph Martin, who on his own personal foraging expedition in 1777, found himself among a flock of "geese, turkeys, ducks, and barn-door fowls," who recalled that he could "have taken as many as I pleased, but I took up one only."[35] Or, the same civilian might confront the extensive, systematic, but still controlled foraging that Mary Frazer had to deal with. Or, worse yet, one might experience the type of plunderer who had little or no connection to an army at all, like the virtually unrestrained whaleboat plunderers who raided from Connecticut across the sound into Long Island. Andrew Miller in Long Island answered the pounding at his door, and immediately was struck with the breech of a musket, which broke the bone over his eye, "tore his eye all to pieses, [and] broke his cheek bone." The raiders plundered his house and left him for dead.[36] Some areas between the armies, perhaps most famously Westchester County, New York, were frequently subjected to both official and unofficial foraging by both sides. Timothy Dwight, serving as a minister in the Continental Army, witnessed the extent of the destruction in 1777 (and it would continue for some years afterward). His description notes the difference between being subject to impressment versus pure plunder, but the result was the same:

These unhappy people were . . . exposed to the depredations of both [armies]. Often they were actually plundered, and always were liable to this calamity. . . . Their houses . . . were in a great measure scenes of desolation. Their furniture was extensively plundered or broken to pieces. The walls, floors, and windows were injured both by violence and decay. . . . Their cattle were gone. Their enclosures were burnt where they were capable of becoming fuel, and in many cases thrown down where they were not.[37]

The random violence of plunderers and foragers did not compare to the destruction and violence that occurred when an army made a deliberate strategic decision to devastate the countryside. For the most part the Continental Army forswore deliberate destruction of a landscape they saw themselves defending. The temptation existed, however, largely as a way of denying resources to the British. General Nathanael Greene strongly encouraged burning New York City (to deny its shelter to British troops who would garrison the city) during the American retreat in 1776, but in the end Congress directed that the city be preserved.[38] Another of Washington's subordinates suggested depopulating the district between the two armies outside Philadelphia in 1777 so as to cut off residents' illicit trading with the British.[39] Washington rejected the suggestion, but he did decide to deprive the British of certain key resources, for example, ordering the Pennypack mills outside Philadelphia to be destroyed and ordering the removal of the millstones from other mills in the region.[40] And General Philip Schuyler did in fact lay waste to the countryside in front of Burgoyne's invading army prior to the battle at Saratoga in 1777.[41]

The British felt fewer restraints when it came to devastation, but they rarely adopted it as a consistent policy. European traditions of war allowed for "fire and sword" strategies when suppressing a rebellion, and British consciences would have been clear. But a number of British officers and senior commanders recognized the "hearts and minds" problem of trying to regain control of the colonies and sought to avoid the devastation option. It could even be argued that part of the British strategic failure in the war was an inability to consistently adopt one or the other strategy. Local commanders sometimes freely chose fire and sword, while others tried to placate and persuade (while also winning battles). William Tryon, the former royal governor of New York, organized a force of Tories on Long Island, and became notorious for his destructive raids across the sound into Connecticut, destroying stores, but also towns. In 1779 he landed at Norwalk with 2,000 Loyalists, joined shortly by the King's American Regiment, and they proceeded to sack and burn the town. The official report to Congress claimed that 80 homes, 87 barns, 17 shops, 4 mills, and 2 churches had been destroyed.[42] Even areas free from the movements of large forces could be subject to this kind of devastation. Jean Lee's study of Charles County, Maryland found that every year until 1783 boat-based raiders landing from Chesapeake Bay destroyed towns, warehouses, and plantations, and this finally ended with the sacking and burning of Benedict in 1783, *after* news of the peace treaty had reached Maryland.[43]

Possibly the worst destruction from deliberate devastation occurred in Virginia in 1781 when General Charles Earl Cornwallis adopted a policy of destruction (a policy he had avoided during the earlier phases of his campaign in the Carolinas). County magistrates in the area compiled lists of those who made claims for damages. St. Bride's Parish in Norfolk County claimed to suffer £39,543 in damage to buildings, livestock, household goods, plantation tools, grain, forage, and even tobacco. Thomas Jefferson, then governor of Virginia, estimated the damage from the six-month campaign to amount to £3 million.[44]

Although the Continental Army may not have engaged in much deliberate destruction, the militias in pursuit of Loyalists often did. One of the problems in this kind of war, where enemies lived side by side, was that partisans of one side or the other felt confident in their knowledge of the loyalties of their neighbors. Often they were right, but that confidence led them to mount raids, or assaults, on the homes of their enemies. North Carolina militiaman James Collins described the procedure that his company used, which combined an interesting mix of restraint and destruction. They would surprise a Tory house, force the doors, extinguish the lights, back the man of the house into a corner, and swing away with swords, "but taking care to strike the wall or some object that was in the way." They would then pull down the house to the roof joists, and spare the Tory himself, provided he left. Collins further claimed that the only property disturbed was the house itself.[45] Other raiders were not necessarily so discriminating. In general, away from the lines of the main armies, where Whigs and Tories faced off against each other, the war generated significantly more violence, and in some regions apparently deteriorated into widespread destruction and vigilantism that caught up in its wake civilians and armed partisans alike.

This level of Whig-Tory violence, as well as the general sense of unease created by being near a large army, generated waves of refugees. If the primary civilian experience of an army was its need to eat, perhaps nearly as many people experienced an army by trying to get out of its way. Refugees in turn created a ripple effect wherever they arrived. The early war American siege of Boston offers a case in point. The prewar population of Boston was roughly 16,000. During the long American siege of the British garrison, most of the Whiggish population fled, sending roughly 10,000–11,000 people into the surrounding countryside. The

Massachusetts Provincial Congress ordered towns in the area to provide for the poorest of those refugees. Concord, for example, was assigned 66 refugees, and eventually supported 82, with many others taking up residence in Concord at their own expense. By the middle of March, 1776, the population of Concord had risen by 25 percent in one year, an increase that was probably responsible for the outbreak of dysentery in the town that year.[46] Reversing the situation, at least politically: when the British garrison finally evacuated Boston, they took with them to Halifax some "102 officials of the Crown, 18 clergymen, 105 rural residents, 213 mechanics and similar tradesmen, as well as some 382 farmers."[47] When the British re-established themselves in New York City, it became a center for Loyalists fleeing the kind of treatment described by James Collins. By 1777, its population had grown by 11,000 (not including the British army);this increased population was packed into a less-habitable city, for New York had seen about one-third of its buildings burn down during the American Revolution in 1776.[48]

Armies moved, struggled, ate, straggled, and burned their way across much of the continent during eight years of war—America's longest war prior to Vietnam. In the process they visited trying times on countless civilians. Many civilians, however, were prepared to acknowledge that war carried with it certain risks. Property (especially food) would be needed by armies, and probably taken, hopefully with payment, and soldiers would die in battle. With that recognition came a certain fatalistic resignation. While on foraging duty for the Continental Army in Pennsylvania, Joseph Martin noticed that the inhabitants seemed resigned to the necessity and never abused him (although he doubted whether his fellow New Englanders would have been equally sanguine).[49] One Captain McDowell of the British army, while with a foraging party in Charlotte in 1780, was challenged by a woman who asked whether it was "soldier-like to plunder a helpless family so, and leave us nothing?" McDowell replied: "But, madam, we must have something to eat, and these rebels won't bring it in." Having tried his honor, the woman then tried his conscience: "And have you no women and children at home?" she asked. Only on discovering that they had the same last name did McDowell call back his men saying they had taken enough from that house, reminding his men that it was "likely ye have some of your family amongst the rebels [as did McDowell]; but it is the fortune of war. Good bye! It is the fortune of war."[50] Such acknowledgement of the "fortune of war" had limits, however, and civilians reserved the right to judge when they felt those limits had been overreached. Residents of the Salisbury district in North Carolina complained not that impressment was done, only that it was often done illegally.[51] It was in this capacity to judge, in the midst of a people's war, that a civilian's power lay. Enough mistreatment and enough violations of expectations of conduct in war, could lead a civilian to support, or even take up arms, for the opposite side. As widespread as it was, the experience of foraging, plundering, and violence was not nearly as universal as the experience of the economic consequences of the war.

ECONOMICS, CURRENCY, PRICES, AND SHORTAGES

To understand the impact of the war on currency, prices, and the availability of goods, one must begin with the nature of the colonial economy. Aside from the relative few who were purely subsistence farmers (and most of them resided deep in the backcountry), the American economy prior to the outbreak of war depended heavily on the export trade. Furthermore, the entire colonial economic system had evolved in a codependent relationship with the British empire. Most colonial products were sold in virtually guaranteed markets in Britain or the British West Indies. Food (beef, grain, and fish) from New England and the mid-Atlantic states flowed to the slave populations of the West Indies. The shipbuilding and carrying trade of New England depended on the activity of British commerce. Even the specialty products of the South—Chesapeake tobacco, North Carolina naval stores, and Carolinian rice—were all at least initially destined for merchant connections in Britain. Intercolonial coasting trade had been growing, and the northern colonies' economies had become quite diverse, but all were still dependent on export over water. There were a growing number of farmers in the interior with little access to overseas markets who produced grain and meat for local urban markets or simply for subsistence, but even that population had become caught up in the latest economic component of the imperial relationship: consumerism. By the 1750s Americans had begun their long relationship with materialism, and all of those goods came from Great Britain.

American production did not balance out American consumption, much to the joy of mercantile theorists in Britain, who believed that colonies should produce wealth for the home country—not for themselves. One result of this imbalance was a serious shortage of "hard" currency, or specie (meaning money actually made from a precious metal), in colonial hands. To keep trade flowing individuals relied on paper debt, essentially IOUs passed from merchant to merchant, and on paper currencies issued by colonial governments on the promise that the paper would be "retired" (or sunk) at a fixed point in the future, by using tax income to repay all the holders of paper currency with hard currency. Colonial paper currency was usually issued in response to a crisis (typically a war) and served to pay soldiers, purchase supplies, and otherwise energize the economy during wartime. It invariably lost value as its holders lost faith that the government would be able to retire it at face value. Despite failing to maintain value, it was frequently the only currency widely available in a colony, and it served crucial economic functions. This basic system was well understood by the colonists, who had had long experience with such currency during the series of eighteenth-century imperial wars and because of the general shortage of specie in the colonies as a whole.

The imbalance of trade—resulting in both American debt and a shortage of currency—as well as the overall management of the imperial economy were major issues in the protest movement that led up to the revolution. Almost inevitably, therefore, one of the tools used by American protestors was a boycott, or nonimportation movement, later combined with a nonexportation movement. Perfectly suited to the environment of political protest, such tactics were less suited to preparing for war. Nonimportation and exportation were never perfectly enforced, but nevertheless had two side effects. Americans began a program of home manufacture to replace banned British-made goods, but Americans also began to experience shortages. Ironically, the war converted a voluntary but leaky program of nonimportation into an involuntary (but still leaky) British naval blockade. In April 1776 Congress officially ended the nonimportation movement and opened their ports to all nations, save Britain. Wartime conditions, especially the demands of the army and the British blockade, however, imposed shortages and restructured the market. Traditional outlets for many American products were closed, but, as Harry Ward describes it, "capital moved from the trade sector to domestic and war-related industries. Despite war adjustments, domestic production thrived in such diverse areas as clothing, flour milling, distilling, tanning, lumbering, and meat processing."[52]

Despite early efforts by the Continental Congress to organize the economy, and despite some successes in the movement of capital into domestic production, the break in the long orientation of the economy toward export to British possessions created serious disruptions. For simplicity's sake we can break down the economic component of the Revolution into three stages, and we will see that a number of different developments roughly coincided chronologically. From the outbreak of hostilities the Continental Congress found itself at the head of a war effort, but because of the separate past histories of the individual colonies and their fear of a too powerful central government, the Congress utterly lacked coercive power, was denied the power to tax, and remained dependent on contributions from the tax-collecting states. Forced to finance a war, however, the Congress relied on past precedent and began issuing bills of credit (essentially paper money). The first issue was for only $6 million, but lacking real revenue, the Congress repeatedly returned to the printing presses as their only source of money. By 1779 they had issued $200 million in paper, had not retired any of the previous issues, and had received virtually no payments from the states. Furthermore, the states continued to raise their own military forces (in addition to Continental regiments, which were nominally financed by the Continental Congress), and therefore each state printed its own money as well.

Nevertheless, during this first economic stage of the war, Continental (and state) currencies, although depreciating, continued to hold some value. In some ways the flood of currency stimulated local farming economies. High prices and heavy military demand brought relative prosperity to farmers in backcountry New England and in the breadbasket of Pennsylvania and Delaware—at least until the British invasion of the latter area in 1777, when the grain trade from Philadelphia shrank to between one-fifth and two-fifths of its prewar size.[53] Furthermore, during this period American merchants established a brisk trade with France and other European powers in the West Indies, although the British blockade limited its expansion. Toward the end of this period the currency began to collapse, and an inflationary spiral began that characterized the next stage. Beef in New England went from $0.04 per pound in 1777 to $1.69 per pound and rising in 1780.[54] In Maryland, a bushel of wheat fetched 4 shillings (abbreviated as "4s"), 8 pence (abbreviated as "8d") in November 1777. In early 1778 it had climbed to 7s 6d, but by spring had risen to 70s. The winter of 1779 found it at 150s, and the spring and summer of 1780 saw wheat soar to a range from 420s to 720s.[55]

The second stage began in 1779 as the Continental currency began to utterly collapse, although the French entry in the war and the subsequent weakening of the blockade actually spurred American foreign trade. Despite the peak in exports, inflation raged out of control. Continental currency, which had traded at 4 to 1 ($4 Continentals for $1 hard currency) in January 1778, surged to 100 to 1 in January 1781, and 167.5 to 1 in April 1781.[56] Facing these conditions, Congress saw no choice but to shift the responsibility for the war effort wholly onto the states. Acknowledging financial impotence, Congress recommended that the states collect taxes in goods, which could then simply be delivered to the troops. Meanwhile Continental soldiers collecting supplies in the countryside could only offer certificates for what they took, essentially receipts, and although not denominated in dollars or pounds, they increased the level of debt assumed by the central government and undermined efforts to restore value to the currency. The "tax in kind" program at the state level also failed as a system, if for no other reason than the lack of transportation facilities to move bulk commodities to where the army needed them.

The states finally began to collect taxes in a consistent way in 1780, and then in 1781 a conservative faction gained control of Congress and helped initiate a new stage of national economic mobilization. The Continental currency was revalued on a realistic basis, most active military operations ended after Yorktown, and the inflationary spiral slowed down. Even ending inflation, however, proved painful. Massachusetts, for example, demanded new taxes payable in specie only. Because specie was virtually inaccessible, prices plunged into a deep depression, and farmers found themselves unable to pay their taxes and faced losing their land. Additionally, 1782 and 1783 proved to be the worst period for American foreign trade as the British navy focused its efforts on catching and destroying American merchant ships.

Overall this inflationary spiral and interruption of trade made civilian life more difficult, but not uniformly, and it is difficult to make a single characterization. The leading authorities on the colonial economy summed it up thus: "The War of Independence enriched some men, made others poor, created some new chances for success, and led to some lasting structural changes in the economy. In particular, the war increased the relative importance of the domestic sector, encouraged industrial development, and promoted internal improvements. Nevertheless . . . the net effect of war was a sharp decline in individual income [primarily because of the loss of exports]."[57] Inflation had been particularly hard on those living on a fixed income, including notably laborers, clerks, clergy, teachers, and soldiers. They found their agreed upon salaries dramatically losing value. Farmers experienced a whole new level of demand for their produce, and those who could expand to take advantage of it could do quite well. The British attracted supplies to their army by paying with specie, and one calculation suggests that they consumed 37 tons of food, 38 tons of hay and oats, and (during the winter) huge supplies of wood *per day*.[58] Even in locally oriented farming communities hardships abounded (manpower shortages around Concord, Massachusetts actually led crop yields per acre to drop), but the struggles of producers for export were even worse. We have already mentioned the specifics of the damage to wheat and flour exporters around Philadelphia. Georgia saw its prewar rice production of 35,000 barrels drop to 2,000 in 1780. South Carolina produced 155,000 barrels of rice prior to the war. In 1782 it was only 23,000, but it rebounded in 1783 to 65,000.[59]

Such massive disruptions to exports meant an overall decline in income, but even with income, there was often little to buy. Shortages of finished goods, and frequently even of food, lasted throughout the war. Domestic production of certain necessities (clothes, shoes, etc.) increased enough to keep most civilians supplied, but some commodities remained scarce. Food shortages were rarely continuous, but could be extreme. Richard Durfee of Rhode Island explained the food scarcity by the constant calls on the militia, depriving families of needed labor. He recalled that "some people were under the necessity of grinding flaxseed and cobs together to make bread, and of making potato bread, and of stewing down sweet apples and grinding cornstalks to obtain the juice to boil down as a substitute for molasses."[60] Other families, like Mary Frazer's, could naturally blame shortages on the depredations and demands of armies. Over one 10-month period, from 1780 to 1781, Concord was called upon to furnish 42,779 pounds of beef for the army—roughly the equivalent of 100 head of mature cattle. Such demands seriously depleted the cattle available to the Concordians themselves.[61] Considered as a continent-wide problem, however, food shortages of any duration tended to be limited to areas of active army operations. The vast majority of the population was essentially agricultural, and, provided their food was not directly impressed or stolen by a passing army, most families found a way to subsist.

Specific shortages or crises, however, brought civilian reaction. A long European tradition supported the "lower sorts" in their right to riot when the basics of life were either unaffordable or unavailable. They took to the streets to set prices and to protest the movement or hoarding of necessities. In the revolutionary context such crowds often acted in concert with revolutionary committees, which had attempted to set ceilings on both prices and wages. Women were particularly active in these riots, as was traditional when the issue involved subsistence. Even after the repeal of the largely unsuccessful attempts to control prices, crowds still took to the streets to act according to their sense of a just economy. Barbara Clark Smith has identified at least 30 occasions in towns and cities in Massachusetts, Connecticut, Rhode Island, New York, Pennsylvania, and Maryland, between 1775 and 1779, where crowds of civilian men and women rioted to lower prices of goods or claim access to food (although it is worth noting that many of these riots involved specialized imported commodities such as salt and sugar, and not bread per se).[62] In one example in late 1777 in Boston, 900 people gathered in an unofficial town meeting, resolved to offer paper money for goods they believed merchants were holding, but swore they would take the goods "in some other way" if necessary. The next day 500 of them converged on the store of Jonathan Amory. Sensing trouble, he appealed to Boston's revolutionary committee, who agreed to appoint intermediaries, who set a compromise price, and then allowed it to be sold. The crowd paraded the hoarded sugar to a nearby storehouse and left it in the care of the three designated intermediaries. They then added the sugar held by other merchants in town, which the agents disbursed at a set price for most of the next year.[63]

DISEASE

Civilians' physical encounters with the armies were often unpleasant, but rarely fatal. Similarly, the economic disruptions and shortages caused by the war, although nearly universal, did not result in famine or widespread death. The greatest threat to life experienced by civilians during the American Revolution was disease. Until the medical advances of the late nineteenth century, sanitation issues and a misunderstanding of contagion made armies notorious carriers of disease. To return to the "army as city" analogy, the close quarters and questionable hygiene of a city (the normal breeding places for disease) applied with even greater force to an army. What was worse, armies moved. In this limited, but still lethal sense, the War of Independence did not differ from any other war of the period—the normal camp-based diseases inflicted their usual misery upon armies. Uniquely, however, the movements of armies and refugees on such a massive geographic scale unleashed a continent-wide pandemic of smallpox. European populations had long experienced smallpox, and its endemic status in the high density areas of Europe usually prevented it from assuming plague-like proportions. Europe's descendants in America, however, not to mention the Native American population, did not live in such close quarters, and the prewar incidence of smallpox had been significantly less.[64] The accidental introduction of the disease in America, probably via infected British soldiers in Boston and in Quebec, and the subsequent mobility of soldiers and refugees sent the disease careening around the continent. The war also witnessed a surge in Americans' willingness to undergo inoculation for small pox. The practice was controversial in America, because it involved purposefully contracting a milder form of the disease to gain immunity against the naturally transmitted variety. Inoculated individuals could still spread the fully virulent form of the disease, however, and their movements (including those of inoculated soldiers) helped spread the disease around North America. Elizabeth Fenn has estimated that the epidemic killed at least 130,000 people from the Atlantic to the Pacific.[65]

WOMEN

In one sense every aspect of this essay has included women, whether or not they have been specifically mentioned. Women's experience of the war deserves separate treatment, however, because although *civilians* like others, they were civilians in a special sense. First, no one in the eighteenth century expected women to act as combatants. In theory they could even avoid the pressure of having to choose sides, being instead "forced" into one side or the other by their husbands' and fathers' choices, and then nominally protected by that decision. As the war dragged on, however, and as the new states wrestled with the revolutionary implications of the war itself, the nominal protection afforded women as civilians eroded. In addition, women faced special problems not associated with civilians more generally. Those left behind by husbands called to war (or by exiled Loyalist husbands) faced new problems of responsibility and vulnerability.

Women left alone, in what we have already established were difficult economic times, struggled to keep the family land or business intact. Some men, with long-term military or political commitments to the Rebel cause might be gone for years at a time, and exiled Loyalist husbands who had left their wives behind created truly long periods of responsibility for their wives. For some women the responsibilities and challenges of war became an opportunity. Historian Joan Gundersen found in a study of spousal correspondence that "more than one woman began the war writing to a husband about 'your' farm, then called it 'ours,' and finally 'my' farm."[66] Other women, continuing from the days of the boycott of British goods, found new economic roles in domestic industry, particularly weaving. Hannah Adams recalled of her years during the Revolution: "I learned to weave bobbin lace, which was suitable, and much more profitable to me than spinning or knitting, which had previously been my employment."[67]

Such opportunities came at a cost. Along with all the normal challenges created by the wartime environment, women faced some special vulnerabilities. Being alone in the house meant facing the uncertain behaviors of soldiers who came calling. Isabella Reid of Lone Cane Creek in South Carolina, recalled that while her husband was away fighting, a group of Tories broke into the house and "stripped . . . [the women] of all their clothing except their undergarments."[68] Not to be outdone, many Loyalist women in their petitions to Parliament claimed that they too, left behind by their husbands, had been "turned naked out of doors" by the Rebels. Neill McGeachy left his wife behind in North Carolina in 1776 while he went to serve with the British army. She successfully maintained their house until 1781 when it "was forcibly taken from her by the enemy who without Compassion or Remorse stripped and turned her out of doors with a Young Child."[69] Sometimes the vulnerability of women extended to rape, although there is some disagreement among historians about the prevalence of rape by British or American troops. It was certainly considered a perquisite of war by soldiers in many European contexts, but hard evidence for rape is relatively scarce in the records of the Revolution. Showing a memorable lack of concern, Lord Lawdon commented in 1776 that with so many British troops in the area "a girl cannot step into the bushes to pluck a rose without the most imminent risk of being ravished, and they are so little accustomed to these vigorous methods, that they don't bear them with the proper resignation, and of consequence we have the most entertaining courts-martial every day."[70] In fact, there is a relative dearth of such court-martial records, and it is possible that Lawdon was joking with his correspondent.[71] There is similarly a dearth of rape proceedings in the court-martial records of the Continental Army.[72] There can be little doubt that women experienced fear on that score, however, and Whig propagandists made much of the possibility of being ravished by British, and especially Hessian troops, and the Congress widely propagated their investigation of rapes reported by several women in New Jersey in 1776.[73]

Loyalist women faced more than physical vulnerability. They were also politically vulnerable. Despite a patriarchal system that assumed the subservience of women to men, and thus should have rendered them beyond the punishment of Rebel governments, Loyalist women, especially those left behind in an effort to preserve family property, found themselves targets for exile and confiscation. The cash-strapped Rebel governments saw the confiscation and sale of Loyalist estates as a ready means of income. A woman who stayed behind, even a woman who might actively have chosen the Rebel cause and deserted her husband, could not stop them. As Joan Gunderson points out, the states "found their excuse in coverture."[74] Under English common law, the husband owned all the property, therefore, the state could seize it regardless of the wife's ostensible loyalty. Complicating the situation for the states, however, common law also provided protections of a wife's property for her own support. In June 1780 Pennsylvania tried to ease the problem by simply banishing the wives and children of men who had joined the British.[75] Elias Long's wife, discussed previously, was not banished, but did have to suffer through all her property being sold out from under her. Other state legislatures experienced significant twinges of conscience on this issue. North Carolina's 1778 confiscation law allowed the wife and children of an absentee Loyalist to inherit as if he had died. In 1779, however, they tightened the act to allow only the traditional widow's one-third to remain in the family. Some members of the house protested this provision, arguing that the act's elimination of an allowance for families amounted to warring "against aged parents or against Women & Children, more especially being as in this Case, our fellow Subjects." In the end, the act allowed wives to retain only the one-third, but an amendment was added to ensure that none of the household furniture or produce could be confiscated under the law.[76]

SLAVES AND INDIANS AS "CIVILIANS"

There were other special categories of civilian caught up in the turmoil of the Revolutionary War, and their experiences of that war differed wildly from those of the white Americans who had begun it. Most of the roughly 500,000 slaves in North America were *civilians* in the strictest sense as noncombatants, although many did succeed in becoming soldiers for both sides as a means to freedom. Different Indian peoples had different responses to the war; most ended up fighting on the British side, a few allied with the Americans, and many tried to remain neutral.

A Patriot woman employs a strategy of accommodation with British officers. (Library of Congress)

Even the combatant tribes, however, had women, children, and the aged who experienced being a civilian in unique ways.

Every colony had at least a small population of slaves who lived in different conditions from region to region, although the vast majority of slaves were concentrated in Virginia and South Carolina. Their dispersion also meant that they experienced the war in different ways. Virtually all of them, however, would experience the pull of the British in some fashion. At the very beginning of the conflict in November 1775, the royal governor of Virginia, John Murray, the Earl of Dunmore, made a radical pronouncement promising freedom for slaves who rallied to his cause and took up arms against the Rebels. Hundreds of Virginia slaves fled to his lines and engaged in active service on his behalf. Dunmore, however, was already in a tenuous position, and would shortly find himself literally driven offshore, confined to launching small raids from ships and from coastal islands, and eventually leaving the area altogether. The slaves who had joined him suffered tragically, many of them dying of smallpox while crowded aboard ship or on Gwynn's Island. Other longer-lived British garrisons also served as magnets for fleeing slaves. First Boston and then New York City attracted such refugees. Many of them went to work for the British, but without much clarity in their legal status, as the British Parliament sought to avoid antagonizing the white population with a general policy of emancipation.

The situation changed dramatically when the British moved their main operations into the slave-heavy South. Part of the rationale for that shift was in fact the large numbers of slaves who might perhaps rise against their masters or be made directly a part of the British war effort. General Henry Clinton, prior to departing on that campaign, issued a proclamation promising to sell any blacks captured in rebel service, but also to protect and grant at least a certain measure of freedom to any slaves who fled into British lines. As the British army campaigned through Georgia, the Carolinas, and Virginia, countless slaves faced a choice. Sylvia Frey has pointed out that the choice was not as simple as we might conceive it in hindsight. Thousands of slaves did choose to flee to the British, either to the garrisons in Savannah and Charlestown, or to follow in the wake of Cornwallis's army. Many others feared the consequences of such a choice, recalling the fate of past escapees or slave rebellions, or unsure of how to traverse the countryside with a family in tow, and so the majority of slaves remained on their plantations.[77] For those who did join the British, the majority would find freedom, although some were returned to Loyalist owners. Those who remained on the plantation experienced a particularly acute version of the uncertainties of war. The shortages and scarcities that afflicted whites were hard on the already ill-provided for slaves. Furthermore, they lived in fear of partisans from one side or the other swooping through a plantation and claiming their bodies as plunder. Infamously, South Carolina militia officer Thomas Sumter proclaimed that militiamen who joined his forces could claim a slave taken from a Loyalist farm as part of his enlistment bounty (officers were to receive more than one according to rank).

The revolutionary era produced highly mixed results for slaves. Some evidence suggests that the fatalities among those who fled to the British were as high as the total suffered by white patriots during the war. Some 80,000–100,000 slaves fled their owners and gained at least momentary liberty. Tens of thousands of those then departed with the British from Savannah, Charlestown, and New York City.[78] In the deep South, where hopes for a postwar economic recovery were pinned to the availability of slave labor, the mass exodus resulted in a resurgence of slave importation—from within North America and from across the Atlantic. Contrarily, during the war in the North, every northern state save New York and New Jersey passed provisions to end slavery. New York and New Jersey followed more slowly after the war. These provisions did not affect the experience of war much, however, because all of them were designed to produce gradual rather than immediate emancipation. The upper South also saw a move toward abolishing slavery, but it faded in the postwar years, although there were several years in which many planters emancipated their slaves on a large scale. The ultimate political settlement of the Revolution chose to fix slavery into the national political system rather than abolish it, but for slaves, the war itself had provided choices on a vast new scale. Some had been able to take advantage, and some not, but the Revolution certainly created a vast new class of free blacks and endowed them with the experience to help in their continued efforts for change.

If the experience of the war was mixed for slaves, it was an unqualified disaster for Native Americans. The frontier from New York, through Ohio, and down into the Carolinas and Georgia contained roughly 70,000 Indians divided up among many different peoples, most of whom were disinclined to follow each other's lead. During the Revolution they never acted as a unified body, and in fact some peoples, especially the Iroquois and the Cherokee, actually divided over the issue of how to respond to the Rebellion, literally generating a kind of civil war among the Iroquois peoples. Most Native Americans looked on the rebellion as a war between brothers, and as such, an inappropriate venue in which to intervene. Fortunately for the British, many peoples were inclined to identify the imperial government as their best hope against land hungry Americans who were already encroaching on their lands west of the Appalachians. Furthermore, the British were much more prepared to continue to provide the trade goods that Indians had come to depend on as a part of their lifestyle (in particular guns, gunpowder, and alcohol). As the British-American war escalated and dragged on, many Indians found it increasingly difficult to remain neutral, particularly in the face of indiscriminate attacks by American militia. Most Indian peoples sided with the British, unknowingly choosing the losing side, and they suffered accordingly. Even most groups who joined the Americans did not emerge from the war any better off or any more secure in their claims to land. The best way to consider the Indian experience of the war is to take a brief look at the choices and consequences of a couple of examples.

The Confederacy of the Six Nations of the Iroquois in upstate New York, consisting of the Mohawk, Oneida, Onondaga, Tuscarora, Cayuga, and Seneca peoples, experienced the war in a particularly bitter form. Long considered the most militarily potent confederacy of Indians, both Whigs and Tories put forth every effort to persuade the Iroquois to join their side. The Iroquois as a group initially tried to cling to neutrality, but the pressures of war gradually overwhelmed that desire, and tragically, the individual tribes split, with the Oneida and the Tuscarora choosing the Americans, and the remainder siding with the British. But such a simple division fails to do justice to the complexities of the split among the nations. In Colin Calloway's study of the Oneida town of Oquaga, for example, he demonstrates how its policies swayed back and forth between the two sides, seeming to outsiders to be inconstant in its alliances, and thus subject to the destructive vengeance of both sides.[79] Furthermore, the Americans were notorious for failing to distinguish between friendly and enemy Indians, and even more notorious for forgetting their allies in the aftermath of war and lumping them all together as targets for dispossession. Indeed, even those groups who lived in coherent communities within the frontier, such as the Stockbridge Indians of Massachusetts or the Catawbas of South Carolina, who had quickly and, in the end, correctly judged the political winds and aligned themselves with the Rebels, found themselves constantly trying to remind the ungrateful new republic of their service.

Simply the fact that the bulk of the Indian population lived in the path of Americans hoping to expand into the western territories meant that Indian proponents of neutrality regularly died at the hands of Americans who either could not or would not distinguish between enemy, friendly, or neutral Indians. When an Indian people felt they could no longer remain neutral, usually because the younger men of the tribe could no longer be restrained from taking revenge for indiscriminate American attacks, their actions in turn exposed their women, children, and old men to a particularly terrifying kind of war. Americans fighting Indians over the previous century and more had come to recognize that the normal battle-centered European mode of fighting did not function versus Indians who desperately wanted to avoid the human costs of that kind of warfare. When confronted by a large white expeditionary force, Indians simply melted into the countryside. Partly from strategic necessity, and partly from a racial dislike of Indians, Americans had resorted to devastating Indian villages and capturing and killing women and children. There were many such incidents during the Revolution, but the willingness to engage in such destruction can be found even in the orders of George Washington. Responding to Iroquois raids in 1778, Washington ordered the Continental Army into the Iroquois country in 1779, specifying: "the immediate objects [of the expedition] are the total destruction and devastation of their settlements and the capture of as many prisoners of every age and sex as possible. It will be essential to ruin their crops now in the ground and prevent their planting more." Washington hoped that these actions would create a "disposition for peace," but he ordered that any such overtures be ignored until "the total ruin of their settlements is effected—It is likely enough their fears if they are unable to oppose us, will compel them to offers of peace." Peace would then be maintained through hostages, which were "the only kind of security to be depended on."[80] In the end, the Continental expedition killed few Indians, and took only a few hostages, but they destroyed 30 to 40 Iroquois, allied towns, burned 160,000 bushels of corn, and girdled thousands of fruit trees.

The willingness to inflict this kind of violence on Indians extended right down through the ranks to the individual soldiers. Consider William Skaggs's casual attitude toward taking a female prisoner, presumably to act as a slave, which he recounted in his application for a pension. In the spring of 1779 he enlisted in the Virginia militia and marched to attack the militant Cherokees living on the Chickamauga River. They marched to the Indian town and "invaded[,] killing many Indians; after they put to flight & destroyed the inhabitants of the place, they put fire to the town and entirely consumed it." Afterward, one of the militia captains proposed searching for those who had escaped. The captain, Skaggs, and about 20 soldiers "left the main army and marched . . . across the Cumberland mountains. Shortly after they had crossed the mountain they discovered an encampment of the Indians, which they immediately attacked invaded and killed three of the Indians and took three prisoners the said William states that in that attack he had the good fortune to take a squaw as a prisoner."[81] Qualitatively speaking, this was a completely different experience of the violence of war than that experienced by whites in the main theaters of conflict.

Such experiences have led historians to suggest that the physical scars of the war had significant social and spiritual implications. Postwar Native societies struggled to reestablish their normal patterns of life. In a telling anecdote related by François Marquis de Barbé-Marbois, the secretary of the French legation to the United States, one can see the internal fragmentation created by divided loyalties within the tribes and the breakdown of social norms of behavior. Visiting an Oneida village in September 1784, Barbé-Marbois saw two young men in their twenties begin to quarrel, and one finally struck the other with his club. The two men were brothers, the father intervened to end the fight, and they shortly made up. Barbé-Marbois commented that "these quarrels are all the more frequent as they stem from the war that is just over. The nations, and even families, are divided. One of the two brothers had served in the British army, and the other had joined the Americans. On several occasions we had heard the latter call his brother a Tory; for in taking part in the quarrel, the Indians adopted the names 'Whigs' and 'Tories.'"[82] This kind of social fragmentation, the increased exposure to disease, and the sense of having been abandoned by the British at the treaty table left Indians "increasingly bereft of a sense of sacred power and customs."[83] In the years to follow, many Indian groups would undergo various kinds of spiritual revivals, but there seems little doubt that the war had led to a new, even if momentary, nadir in most Indians' lives.

CONCLUSION

The American Revolution unleashed powerful ideas, sparked social unrest, brought the United States political independence, undermined the positions of Native Americans east of the Mississippi, and brought freedom for many slaves while merely tantalizing the vast majority. The Revolution also brought the experience of war into the lives of white Americans around the continent. It dramatically rearranged the American economy during eight long years of warfare, and while the economy would recover fairly quickly, the war may have urged or at least speeded the country down the road to industrialization and market capitalism in the process. Where the economic effect of the war was universal, the physical presence of the war was less so. Some locales experienced the physical presence and danger of armies nearly constantly, while others dealt with armies and Whig-Tory partisan fighting for intense but limited periods.

Indian atrocities on the frontier were often blamed on the British. (Library of Congress)

For most the war was a kind of lurking shadow. One never knew when it would come calling. When it did, it might come as a demand to serve, or it might be the sudden arrival of a commissary agent with his wagons and certificates of impressment. It could be a force of militia, or British soldiers come to harass or arrest at the instigation of a neighbor suspicious of one's allegiances. Or, perhaps worst of all, from the sheer uncertainty of it, one might be visited by hungry soldiers—with or without officers in charge. Surely the distant sounds of cannon fire must have brought many hearts into many mouths.

Given this experience of warfare, it seems reasonable to ask about its longer term consequences. One of the major debates among historians about the larger revolutionary experience is the extent to which it changed anything, and if so, how much? Believing that something changed, how much of it can be laid at the door of the war itself, rather than the process of political transformation implied by the Declaration of Independence and the Constitution? Did the lurking shadow of violence and the wrenching experience of inflation make common folk more or less radical in their political ideals? This, after all, was a people's war; loyalties and the ideas that went with them were regularly put to the test.

Historians have argued that a key indicator in testing these questions lies in Americans' attitudes toward virtue. Prior to the war Americans saw republican virtue, or civic responsibility, as perhaps the key explanation for the corruption of Britain (that is, British society no longer cultivated civic responsibility). More importantly, they saw the possession of virtue as crucial to their own probable success. It was in this sense, for example, that Americans predicted the victory of a virtuous militia over a corrupt standing army. They would win not in spite of being militia, but *because* they were militia: the virtuous representatives of the whole people. Civic virtue would also sustain the people's commitment to the cause. They would not flag or fail in the face of misfortune or personal loss, but carry on and sacrifice for the greater good.

Unfortunately, the actual experience of the war led to questioning the virtue of the people. Citizens proved reluctant to surrender their produce for worthless paper money. They proved even more reluctant, if not openly rebellious, at reporting for military duty when asked. Nor did virtue seem to contain the violent propensities of many militiamen, or keep hungry and cold soldiers from taking private property to eat or burn. During the war, some people acknowledged the failure of virtue and increasingly hoped for a more a hierarchical order to enforce virtue. Late in the war Presbyterian minister Samuel McCorkle preached a lengthy diatribe against plundering. While abhorring private vengeance, he wished the state had moved more swiftly and forcefully against the guilty, bringing to bear "one bold martial stroke of exemplary vengeance on the first [plunderer] who dared to offend."[84] For some, the ability to enforce virtue became the best recommendation for the Whig governments—they were simply doing a better job than the British occupation forces. In the Continental Army the failure of virtue led both to a soldiery recruited heavily from the outcasts of society and eventually to a more thorough approach to the centralized control of armed force. In the years after the war a number of state governments experienced new rebellions, most famously Shay's Rebellion in Massachusetts in 1786 and the Whiskey Rebellion in Pennsylvania in 1794, but there were others as well. We can interpret the swift and forceful reply to these rebellions as in part a response to the experience of war. No one wanted a return to that kind of uncertainty. The conservative reaction of the late 1780s is often blamed on the experience of a weak central government during the war. Its inefficacy in raising money and running a war frustrated many and led some leaders (including George Washington and Alexander Hamilton) to demand a more powerful government. It is also possible that the civilian experience of wartime violence had a similar effect on a more popular and more visceral level. Some revolutionary leaders had lost their confidence in the ability of virtue to contain excessive violence, and now instead looked to establish stronger forms of authority. The Constitution of 1787 carefully divided authority over the military, but it also centralized that authority in new ways.

In the end it remains a question worth asking not only for the Revolution, but for any intense civilian experience of war. What is the relationship between the experience of war and political reaction? Does the memory fade and with it the desire to reform? Or is the experience burned into the soul, permanently changing the ideological and political stances of those who experienced it?

NOTES

1. Wayne Bodle, *The Valley Forge Winter: Civilians and Soldiers in War* (University Park: The Pennsylvania State University Press, 2002), 79–820.

2. Persifor Frazer, *General Persifor Frazer: A Memoir* (Philadelphia, 1907), iii, 157–60. The full story of the British search of the Frazer house is quite revealing of the almost random mix of restraint and violence. De West promised that nothing that belonged to the lady of the house would be taken, and on that basis Mary several times prevented De West or individual soldiers from taking certain personal items—although she lamented the loss of two glass cream buckets. The house was being used to store clothes and equipment belonging to an American unit, and when those were found, they were of course completely (and legitimately) confiscated. The British further took salt, liquor, horses, and food. Prior to De West's arrival the soldiers may have been beginning to get out of hand; Mary Frazer recalled that one soldier was preparing to strike her when De West intervened.

3. "Whig" is one term for those who actively favored independence from Britain—similarly, "patriot" or "rebel."

4. Library of Congress, *Journals of the Continental Congress, 1774–1789*, 34 vols. (Washington, D.C.: GPO, 1904–1937), 1: 75–80 (quote p. 79), hereafter abbreviated *JCC*.

5. *JCC*, 4: 20. A table of the various state Test Laws can be found in Claude Halstead Van Tyne, *The Loyalists in the American Revolution* (New York: Peter Smith, 1929), 318–26.

6. Harry M. Ward, *The War for Independence and the Transformation of American Society* (London: University College of London Press, 1999), 38.

7. Wallace Brown, *The Good Americans: The Loyalists in the American Revolution* (New York: Morrow, 1969), 140–41.

8. Francis S. Fox, *Sweet Land of Liberty: The Ordeal of the American Revolution in Northampton County, Pennsylvania* (University Park: Pennsylvania State University Press, 2000), 53.

9. Ibid., 53–56.

10. *JCC*, 9: 971. A table of the various state confiscation laws can be found in Van Tyne, *The Loyalists*, 327–41.

11. Walter Clark, et al., eds., *The State Records of North Carolina*, 25 vols. (Winston and Goldsboro: various publishers, 1895–1907), 23: 985–86, hereafter abbreviated *NCSR*.

12. This number represents sales of real estate in 1786–1787, when most such sales occurred. Robert O. DeMond, *The Loyalists in North Carolina During the Revolution* (Durham: Duke University Press, 1940), 180 and appendix B.

13. Dorothy Denneen Volo and James M. Volo, *Daily Life During the American Revolution* (Westport, CT: Greenwood Press, 2003), 178, 211.

14. Tract Association of Friends, *Biographical Sketches and Anecdotes of Members of the Religious Society of Friends* (Philadelphia: Tract Association of Friends, 1870), 159–60.

15. Fox, *Sweet Land*, 76.

16. Arthur J. Mekeel, *The Relation of the Quakers to the American Revolution* (Washington, D.C.: University Press of America, 1979), 265–66.

17. E. W. Caruthers, *The Old North State* (Originally published as: *Revolutionary Incidents and Sketches of Character chiefly in the "Old North State"*; Philadelphia: Hayes & Zell, 1854–56; reprint, Greensboro, NC: The Guilford County Geneaological Society, 1994), 171–72.

18. Fairfax County Committee of Safety Proceedings, 17 January 1775, in Robert A. Ruland, ed., *The Papers of George Mason, 1725–1792* (Chapel Hill: University of North Carolina Press, 1970), 1: 212.

19. Charles Royster, *A Revolutionary People at War: The Continental Army and American Character, 1775–1783* (New York: W.W. Norton & Co, 1979).

20. *JCC*, 5: 762 and 6: 944–45.

21. Jean B. Lee, *The Price of Nationhood: The American Revolution in Charles County, Maryland* (New York: W. W. Norton & Co., 1994), 165.

22. *NCSR*, 24: 154–55.

23. Petition of John Robinson, 1 November 1779, Gen. Assy. Session Records, Oct.–Nov., 79, Joint Papers, Petitions to General Assembly, North Carolina Department of Archives, Raleigh, NC.

24. Remonstrance and petition from a number of inhabitants of the district of Salisbury, North Carolina, Gen. Assy. Session Records, Apr.–May, 1782, Joint Standing Committees, Propositions & Grievances—report and Papers, North Carolina Department of Archives, Raleigh, NC.

25. As an example, during the *quietest* period of the war in North Carolina, from 1777 to 1779 there were seven separate major calls for men totaling 11,348.

All of these were for expeditionary forces (militia and Continental), and thus did not include numerous local militia musters for routine enforcement or in response to several local Tory risings during this period. These numbers also do not include those who were already serving in North Carolina's Continental regiments in Washington's army to the north. Nowhere near 11,348 men actually responded to those requests, in part because that number was roughly 15 percent of the white male population of North Carolina, but it is indicative of the recruiting pressure on the state. Wayne E. Lee, *Crowds and Soldiers in Revolutionary North Carolina: The Culture of Violence in Riot and War* (Gainesville: University Press of Florida, 2001), 305 n. 34.

26. Robert A. Gross, *The Minutemen and Their World* (New York: Hill and Wang, 1976, 2001), 146.

27. Ward, *War for Independence,* 114–16.

28. Depositions in Inquiry on Drafting of troops in Anson County, Military Collection, Misc. Papers, North Carolina Department of Archives, Raleigh, NC; *NCSR,* 13: 150–51, 158–59.

29. Statistics derived from the U.S. Department of Commerce, *Historical Statistics of the United States: Colonial Times to 1970* (White Plains, NY: Kraus International Publications, 1989); John Resch, *Suffering Soldiers: Revolutionary War Veterans, Moral Sentiment, and Political Culture in the Early Republic* (Amherst: University of Massachusetts Press, 2000), 261 n. 22; John Richard Alden, *The American Revolution* (New York: Harper & Row, 1954), 87–88; Robert A. Doughty et al., *American Military History and the Evolution of Warfare in the Western World* (Lexington, MA: D.C. Heath & Co., 1996), 453–54; Maurice Matloff, ed., *American Military History* (Washington, D.C.: Office of the Chief of Military History, U.S. Army, 1969), 192.

30. Don Higginbotham, *The War of American Independence: Military Attitudes, Policies, and Practice, 1763–1789* (Boston: Northeastern University Press, 1983), 304.

31. Volo, *Daily Life,* 178.

32. Volo, *Daily Life,* 170.

33. In theory, *impressment* was simply a forced sale. The "forced" part was necessary because either the army did not have enough money or the farmer considered the money worthless. Frequently the Continentals resorted to giving certificates or even paying with salt. *Foraging* often denotes soldiers simply taking food without authorization or payment, although they might or might not be under orders to do so.

34. E. Wayne Carp, *To Starve the Army at Pleasure: Continental Army Administration and American Political Culture, 1775–1783* (Chapel Hill: University of North Carolina Press, 1984), 98.

35. James Kirby Martin, ed., *Ordinary Courage: The Revolutionary War Adventures of Joseph Plumb Martin,* 2nd ed. (New York: Brandywine Press, 1999), 60.

36. Harry M. Ward, *Between the Lines: Banditti of the American Revolution* (Westport, CT: Praeger, 2002), 39.

37. Timothy Dwight, *Travels in New England and New York,* ed. Barbara Miller Solomon (Cambridge: Harvard University Press, 1969), 3: 345.

38. Richard K. Showman and Dennis M. Conrad, eds., *The Papers of General Nathanael Greene,* 12 vols. to date (Chapel Hill: University of North Carolina Press, 1976), 1: 295; Philander D. Chase et al., eds., *The Papers of George Washington, Revolutionary War Series,* 14 vols. to date (Charlottesville: University Press of Virginia, 1985–), 6: 200–201, 252, 273; *JCC,* 5: 733.

39. Wayne K. Bodle, *The Valley Forge Winter: Civilians and Soldiers in War* (University Park: Pennsylvania State University Press, 2002), 214–15.

40. Pension Record of William Hutchinson, in John C. Dann, ed., *The Revolution Remembered: Eyewitness Accounts of the War for Independence* (Chicago: University of Chicago Press, 1980), 151; Brooke Hunter, "Wheat, War, and the American Economy during the Age of Revolution," *William & Mary Quarterly* 3d Ser., 62 (2005): 511.

41. Richard M. Ketchum, *Saratoga: Turning Point in the America's Revolutionary War* (New York: Henry Holt & Co., 1997), 330.

42. Volo, *Daily Life*, 221–22.

43. Lee, *Price of Nationhood*, 144.

44. Sylvia R Frey, *Water From the Rock: Black Resistance in a Revolutionary Age* (Princeton, NJ: Princeton University Press, 1991), 210–11.

45. James Collins, *Autobiography of a Revolutionary Soldier* (Clinton, LA: Fleiciana Democrat, 1859; reprint New York: Arno Press, 1979), 66.

46. Gross, *Minutemen*, 134–35.

47. North Callahan, *Royal Raiders: The Tories of the American Revolution* (New York: Bobbs-Merrill, 1963), 76.

48. Volo, *Daily Life*, 212–14.

49. Martin, *Ordinary Courage*, 69.

50. William Henry Foote, *Sketches of North Carolina: Historical and Biographical* (New York: Robert Carter, 1846), 417.

51. Petition of Sundry Inhabitants of Salisbury and Parts Adjacent, General Assembly Session Records, Apr.–May, 1782, Joint Standing Committees, Propositions & Grievances—Report and papers, North Carolina Department of Archives, Raleigh, NC.

52. Ward, *War for Independence*, 151.

53. Hunter, "Wheat, War," 509.

54. Gross, *Minutemen*, 140.

55. Elizabeth Cometti, "Inflation in Revolutionary Maryland," *William & Mary Quarterly* 3d Ser., 8 (1951): 230.

56. Paul A. C. Koistinen, *Beating Plowshares into Swords: The Political Economy of American Warfare, 1606–1865* (Lawrence: University Press of Kansas, 1996), 18.

57. John J. McCusker and Russell Menard, *The Economy of British America, 1607–1789* (Chapel Hill: University of North Carolina Press, 1985), 366.

58. James A. Henretta, "The War for Independence and American Economic Development," in *The Economy of Early America: The Revolutionary Period, 1763–1790*, ed., Ronald Hoffman, John J. McCusker, Russell R. Menard, and Peter J. Albert (Charlottesville: University Press of Virginia, 1988), 74.

59. Frey, *Water From the Rock*, 208–9.

60. Dann, *Revolution Remembered*, 33.

61. Gross, *Minutemen*, 143.

62. Barbara Clark Smith, "Food Rioters and the American Revolution," *William & Mary Quarterly* 3d Ser., 51 (1994): 3–38.

63. Smith, "Food Rioters," 23.

64. Persons who survived smallpox were rendered immune to any future outbreaks.

65. Elizabeth A. Fenn, *Pox Americana: The Great Smallpox Epidemic of 1775–82* (New York: Hill & Wang, 2001), 274.

66. Joan R. Gundersen, *To Be Useful to the World: Women in Revolutionary America, 1740–1790* (New York: Twayne Publishers, 1996), 161–62.

67. Ward, *War for Independence,* 167.

68. George C. Chalou, "Women in the American Revolution: Vignettes or Profiles," in *Clio Was a Woman: Studies in the History of American Women,* ed., Mabel E. Deutrich and Virginia C. Purdy (Washington, D.C.: Howard University Press, 1980), 84.

69. Loyalist claim of Neill McGeachy, AO 12/36/62, Public Records Office, Kew, Great Britain.

70. Armstrong Starkey, *European and Native American Warfare, 1675–1815* (Norman: University of Oklahoma Press, 1998), 28–29.

71. There are British accounts that acknowledge rape by British soldiers, but they are usually in the context of the offenders being caught by their officers and punished. Banastre Tarleton, *A History of the Campaigns of 1780 and 1781, in the Southern Provinces of North America* (Dublin: Colles, Exshaw, et al., 1787), 297–98. Cf. Armstrong Starkey, *War in the Age of the Enlightenment, 1700–1789* (Westport, CT: Praeger, 2003), 96.

72. James Neagles, *Summer Soldiers: A Survey & Index of Revolutionary War Courts-Martial* (Salt Lake City, UT: Ancestry Incorporated, 1986).

73. Carl Berger, *Broadsides and Bayonets,* rev'd ed. (San Rafael: Presidio Press, 1976), 15–16.

74. Gundersen, *To Be Useful,* 161.

75. Holly A. Mayer, *Belonging to the Army: Camp Followers and Community During the American Revolution* (Columbia: University of South Carolina Press, 1996), 11.

76. *NCSR*, 13: 897–98; 991–92; *NCSR*, 24: 211–12, 268.

77. Frey, *Water From the Rock,* 113–14.

78. Frey, *Water From the Rock,* 211.

79. Colin G. Calloway, *The American Revolution in Indian Country: Crisis and Diversity in Native American Communities* (Cambridge: Cambridge University Press, 1995), 108–28.

80. Washington to Sullivan, 31 May 1779, Otis G. Hammond, ed., *Letters and Papers of Major-General John Sullivan, Continental Army,* 3 vols. (Concord, NH: New Hampshire Historical Society, 1930–39), 3: 48–53.

81. Pension Record of William Skaggs W2182, Revolutionary War Pension and Bounty-Land-Warrant Application Files, National Archives, Washington, D.C.

82. "Barbé de Marbois's Journal of his Visit to the Territory of the Six Nations, 23 September 1784," in Stanley J. Idzerda and Robert Rhodes Crout, eds., *Lafayette in the Age of the American Revolution: Selected Letters and Papers, 1776–1790* (Ithaca: Cornell University Press, 1983), 5: 250.

83. Ward, *War for Independence,* 205.

84. "Sermon Against Plundering," Samuel E. McCorkle Papers, Duke University Special Collections, Durham, NC.

FURTHER READING

The simplest truth about the civilian experience of the American Revolutionary War was that it varied a great deal from place to place. This list of reading therefore includes a number of local studies that provide a feel for the nature of the war in those locales. Such studies are the best way to understand wartime life.

Bodle, Wayne K. *The Valley Forge Winter: Civilians and Soldiers in War.* University Park: Pennsylvania State University Press, 2002. Probably the single most useful source that directly asks about the interaction of armies and civilians. In addition to being a military history of the British invasion and occupation of eastern Pennsylvania from 1777 to 1778, the author also imaginatively uses the sources to reconstruct what it might have been like to experience life in the midst of conflict.

Brown, Wallace. *The Good Americans: The Loyalists in the American Revolution.* New York: Morrow, 1969. Probably the best and most accessible of a series of studies that exist on the Loyalists. The author covers their experience in all of the colonies, but also manages to convey the pungency of their individual experiences. This is a good reference for the Loyalist motivations, the legal mechanisms used against them, and for their subsequent postwar choices.

Buel, Joy Day, and Richard Buel. *The Way of Duty: A Woman and Her Family in Revolutionary America.* New York: W. W. Norton & Co., 1984. A striking account of one family's experience of life in Connecticut before, during, and after the war. Furthermore, this account focuses on the choices and challenges faced by a woman whose husband was frequently away fighting.

Calloway, Colin G. *The American Revolution in Indian Country: Crisis and Diversity in Native American Communities.* Cambridge: Cambridge University Press, 1995. This is the standard work surveying the Indian experience of the American Revolution. It is particularly appropriate for the experience of war, because it is essentially a series of local studies, examining in great detail the vagaries of war within individual communities, but the author also achieves breadth by examining Indian communities from many different areas east of the Mississippi.

Conway, Stephen. *The War of American Independence, 1775–1783.* London: Edward Arnold, 1995. A valuable and up-to-date overview of the war, especially useful for the ways in which the author places it within a wider context. He argues strongly for the revolutionary nature of the war itself; he makes an important contribution to understanding the war as a "people's war."

Frantz, John B., and William Pencak. *Beyond Philadelphia: The American Revolution in the Pennsylvania Hinterland.* University Park: Pennsylvania State University Press, 1998. An edited collection of studies of the counties outside Philadelphia during the war. Essentially a series of local studies, the individual chapters provide excellent insights into the workings of county revolutionary committees, the experiences of Loyalists, and the effects of the passages of armies.

Frey, Sylvia R. *Water From the Rock: Black Resistance in a Revolutionary Age.* Princeton, NJ: Princeton University Press, 1991. The best and most up-to-date account of how slaves in North America experienced the war. The author ranges widely beyond just the American Revolution, but it forms the core of the book, and she aptly conveys the complexities of their situation.

Gross, Robert A. *The Minutemen and Their World.* New York: Hill and Wang, 1976, 2001. A classic work on Concord, Massachusetts during the war. The author has carefully researched the social history of virtually all the residents of the town, and although he frames the book around their experience of the opening shots in Concord in April 1775, he also tracks the economic and social implications of the war on the town's population.

Gundersen, Joan R. *To Be Useful to the World: Women in Revolutionary America, 1740–1790.* New York: Twayne Publishers, 1996. An able summary of much of the new work that has been done in early American women's history.

Higginbotham, Don. *The War of American Independence: Military Attitudes, Policies, and Practice, 1763–1789.* Boston: Northeastern University Press, 1983. Probably the standard military history of the war. Useful for civilian experiences in that the author also tracks the interactions between military operations and the wider world, surveying the social, political, economic, and international implications of the war.

Lee, Jean B. *The Price of Nationhood: The American Revolution in Charles County, Maryland.* New York: W. W. Norton & Co., 1994. A massively researched study of one Chesapeake county in Maryland. The author covers virtually every aspect of Maryland society, both in the decision for war and independence, in their experience of the war, and in its ultimate effects on the county.

McCusker, John J., and Russell Menard. *The Economy of British America, 1607–1789.* Chapel Hill: University of North Carolina Press, 1985. This is simply the standard work on the nature of the colonial and revolutionary economy.

Resch, John, and Walter Sargent, eds. *War and Society in the American Revolution.* Chicago: Northern Illinois University Press, 2006. An edited collection of the best new work examining the relationships between military activity, politics, culture, and society. Includes studies of the extent of the recruiting pressures, refugee experiences, Iroquois reactions to their own civil strife, the nature of wartime violence in the backcountry, and more.

Ward, Harry M. *The War for Independence and the Transformation of American Society.* London: University College of London Press, 1999. A short volume that covers a lot of ground. The author marches topic by topic through the Revolutionary era, recounting how Americans experienced the war and what changes that experience wrought on American society. An excellent starting point for further research on a variety of topics.

THREE

America's War of 1812

Richard V. Barbuto

When the U.S. Congress declared war on the British Empire on June 18, 1812, hardly anyone in Congress or in President James Madison's administration expected a long conflict. Great Britain was locked in deadly war with Napoleon and France, her fleets occupied in the blockade of nearly every European port, and her armies overextended defending British dominions and battling the French in Spain. Britain had few troops in Canada. Surely it would be as Henry Clay had boldly proclaimed to Congress back in 1810, "I trust that I shall not be deemed presumptuous when I state that I verily believe that the militia of Kentucky are alone competent to place Montreal and Upper Canada at your feet."[1]

Reality disproved Clay's optimism as the war dragged on for 31 months. Today, Americans familiar with this chapter of history recall the attack on Washington, D.C. and the burning of the White House. They may recall as well Jackson's overwhelming victory over an invading British army at New Orleans. Canadians remember that the stalwart stand taken by militiamen against the American invaders marked the birth of their nation, while Britons are hard-pressed to remember that they fought two wars against the United States. Native Americans find that the War of 1812 is just another in a long series of conflicts, which resulted in diminishing native lands and sovereignty.

However, this war was hard on the common people—American, Canadian, and native alike. Wars disrupt lives and sunder communities, and this war was no different. Those who chose or were chosen to perform military duty left their homes, farms, or trades to travel to distant frontiers where daily life was strange, strenuous, unhealthy, and at times deadly. Those remaining at home experienced financial stresses due to severe economic dislocations. Prices soared, and produce rotted in warehouses. Armies raided across the national borders to destroy valuable mills and to confiscate military stores and food. Villages too close to military operations were sometimes burned in retaliation for a previous raid or other violations of the law of war. Deaths among noncombatants were rare but not unheard of, particularly in those lands contested between native and white. The War of 1812 was also marked by shifting loyalties as many had to choose whether to remain an American citizen, or a British subject, or to swear allegiance to the current military power. Perhaps the least popular of America's early wars, the War of 1812 witnessed shocking partisan politics and growing dissent that could have resulted in destruction of the Union established in 1776.

AMERICA: A YOUNG REPUBLIC

The United States in 1812 was a decidedly different country than it was in 1776. The population of whites and blacks was approximately 6 million, twice that of colonial America. Roughly 1 million lived west of the Appalachian Mountains. Congress admitted five new states to the union: Vermont, Kentucky, Tennessee, Ohio, and Louisiana. Congress also had organized the rest of the lands ceded by Britain or purchased from France into territories administered by appointed governors. As the population of the territories grew, the settlers could expect statehood and expanded representation in the national government.

An overwhelming majority of Americans did not live in cities or towns. Only 15 percent of the population lived in urban areas larger than 500 people. The remainder lived on the family farm or plantation in rural communities or in crude cabins on the frontier. The distinction between frontier and rural community is imprecise but worthy of discussion. The frontier community consisted of itinerant white hunters and trappers living among native villages and widely scattered white settlements. All lived at a subsistence level of economic development, producing just enough food to feed themselves with little left over for trade. The majority of white people lived on a family farm, spending long hours working the soil to feed themselves. As this first generation of white frontier settlers extended the amount of land under cultivation and as their livestock increased, they produced enough food to barter for the implements that they could not produce on the farm. Artisans and traders appeared on the frontier to provide these implements. Thus, production of food in excess to the needs of the settlers led to specialization, which in turn transformed the frontier into rural America.

Seeking land and opportunities, more white families settled on the former frontier or struck out for themselves to push the boundaries of the frontier farther westward. The frontier was moving relentlessly; former frontier settlements, once stockaded to defend against native attack, were growing into villages and towns with touches of civilization.

As the frontiers were secured from conflict with the Native Americans by peace treaty or relocation of natives, plantation owners moved westward to expand their holdings. In the South, slaves cleared the land and planted tobacco and cotton. Plantations existed among family farms, native and white settlements, in a mosaic society with an integrated and growing economy.

Regardless of whether they were on the frontier, in rural America, or between cities, roads were abysmal. Villages grew up along rivers to take advantage of growing water traffic. It was more than 10 times cheaper to move people or cargo by water than by animal-drawn wagon. Major rivers, like the Ohio and Mississippi, were crowded with small rafts, keelboats, and other craft moving settlers westward and produce eastward. State legislatures debated opening public roads and building canals to connect villages with the larger cities. However, these public works projects were hardly begun in 1812. Many roads, bridges, and ferries were private affairs with the proprietors charging for their use. Larger cities and villages had regular coach traffic that moved people along rutted, dusty roads. Rains turned the road beds to rivers of sticky mud, all but stopping wheeled traffic. In the North, ice was welcomed as road traffic resumed on sleds and sleighs. The newly invented steam engine powered a small number of craft moving people and mail between New York and Albany.

The larger cities on the coasts, such as New York, Boston, Philadelphia, Baltimore, Charleston, and New Orleans, continued to thrive. Economic specialization was at its peak, and the use of coin and paper currency had long ago replaced barter. The coastal cities had been centers of commerce since colonial days, but business was growing fast. The wars of the French Revolution, and now the wars of Napoleon, had created widespread opportunities for commerce. Britain's Royal Navy was actively blockading the ports of France and her allies. French commercial vessels were either hemmed in port or captured at sea. American shippers took up the slack, carrying goods between French colonies and ports throughout the world. America was the world's largest commercial shipper after Britain. Shippers borrowed from banks, insured their cargoes from capture or accident, bought trade licenses and paid duties and could still turn considerable profits from even one or two successful voyages. Laborers could usually find work on the wharves, and the life of a sailor, while not without risk, provided a reasonable livelihood for those who could adapt to life at sea.

American cities were also undergoing an economic transformation due to increasing industrialization. Water power, harnessed at mills, turned wheels and moved belts, which in turn made possible the widespread use of machinery. Heavy machinery increasingly replaced muscle power. Factories, which housed hundreds of lesser-skilled laborers, replaced small shops,

The War of 1812.

which accommodated a handful of skilled artisans. American craftsmen in cities were slowly being transformed into laborers and owner/managers, with social repercussions that would be realized in later decades.

As the frontiers and population moved westward and as the economy grew, American politics came to reflect the wide variety of interests. Persons active in government formed parties that generally aligned with these interests. The Federalist Party, the party of second president John Adams, represented the commercial and business interests and was pro-British. The Federalists established the beginnings of a national economy, stabilized the currency, and funded military preparedness with a system of taxation. Under Federalist administration, the country saw a massive expansion of foreign commerce and with it, growing prosperity.

However, the Federalists were perceived as elitist by a society that was increasingly democratic. Thomas Jefferson offered an alternative that was more focused on expanding the liberties of the common man. His followers organized in opposition to the Federalists. Formally titled Democratic-Republicans, Jefferson's adherents were more commonly known as simply Republicans. Distinctly anti-British in sentiment and unhappy with taxation that supported what was perceived as an unnecessarily large naval and military establishment, the Republicans convinced enough Americans to vote Jefferson into office in 1801. Jefferson reduced the army and navy in order to reduce taxes. Political partisanship was at a level that could hardly be comprehended today. Newspaper owners declared for one party or the other and subsequently ran the very real risk of having their presses and type destroyed. In cities, politicians and their hooligans resorted to slander and physical assault of their opponents. When the vote for war came in 1812, it reflected political divisions that had been festering for years.

In 1812, there was no way that the United States could land an army on the British Isles and march on London. However, British territory was close at hand. At that time, "Canada" was just a geographic expression. British North America consisted of four separate provinces, two of which included Canada in their names. Nova Scotia, New Brunswick, Lower Canada and Upper Canada were settled by approximately half a million white inhabitants. Lower Canada, which had the largest population of the four by far, is the present province of Quebec. It was called Lower Canada because it was downriver of the Great Lakes and the St. Lawrence River water system. Upper Canada, modern-day Ontario, was up river of this major water system. Lower Canada was originally "New France," and about 90 percent of the people spoke French as their mother tongue. New Brunswick also had a sizable French-speaking segment, but many of the remainder of white Canadians were of British stock—largely English and Scottish in origin. A surprising number of Americans had emigrated to Upper Canada in the two decades before the war, and their presence lent an unknown quality to the level of loyalty the king could command. Likewise, the Governor General of British North America was never entirely certain of the loyalty of the 300,000 French speaking citizens.

Canada was not as economically well developed as the United States. Harsh weather and limited good soil kept agriculture barely above subsistence levels. Farmers had enough surplus to feed the people in the three major cities of Quebec, Montreal, and Halifax. Americans also sold large quantities of livestock, salt, and grain to Canadian merchants. However, the government in London typically had to send food from Europe to feed the 6,000 or so soldiers and sailors stationed in North America. There was hardly any industry in Canada, and the Canadians depended upon trade from Britain to provide manufactured goods of all kinds.

The War of 1812 was not just a conflict between Britain and the United States. The native populations of America and Canada were deeply involved. In fact, the United States was waging two parallel wars: one against Britain and her native allies in Canada, and one against the Creek Red Sticks in the Mississippi Territory. The Creek War was particularly brutal and damaging to that native nation.

THE ROAD TO WAR

The three major causes of the War of 1812 were the seizure of American commercial vessels and cargoes, the impressment of American sailors, and the smoldering conflict between the United States and the natives living within America's borders. The wars of Napoleon on the continent of Europe were the source of Anglo-American tension on the seas, while the inexorable migration of American settlers westward fanned the flames of conflict with the Native Americans.

With the exception of a short respite between 1801 and 1803, Britain and France were locked in war from 1793 until the Battle of Waterloo in 1815. The British strategy was not to confront France on the continent with its small army but to use its powerful navy to choke French trade. Both nations had colonies in the Caribbean that produced sugar and rum for consumption in Europe. The Royal Navy successfully swept French merchant vessels from the sea. However, the Royal Navy required huge numbers of sailors to man its ships. Few were left for British commercial carriers. Seeing an opportunity, American merchants stepped in and carried French goods between Europe and French colonies. As American agriculture produced increasing surpluses, grain, meat, furs, whiskey, and naval stores were sent to European markets. American exports increased dramatically.

Britain resented that American shippers were profiting from Britain's military success and invoked international law to dampen American trade. Claiming that neutral shippers could not legally carry French cargoes, British war vessels stopped American ships on the high seas and diverted them to British admiralty courts. The courts confiscated the cargoes and oftentimes the vessels as well. The crews were left stranded in port and had to find their own transportation back to the United States. British ships even entered American territorial waters to stop ships and check cargoes. Hundreds of American vessels were seized and crews scattered. Merchants, shippers, and investors were ruined as cargoes disappeared into British warehouses. Shipping insurance rates rose dramatically making the cost of trade prohibitive for many.

While British activity to squelch American trade drove up costs, ruined some merchants, and irritated the nation, it was the impressment of American seaman that inflamed many to call for war against Britain. The Royal Navy was a voracious consumer of sailors. Losses from disease, desertion, and combat had to be made up. British naval captains began stopping vessels on the high seas to take back British crewmen who had deserted. Officers would line up the crews and demand that each sailor speak. Those exhibiting a British accent were immediately sent over in chains to the British ship. It was not unheard of for the captain to hang one of the presumed deserters as a lesson to the others. Often short of crewmen, British captains often drafted American citizens as well. The U.S. Department of State listed more than 6,000 sailors who claimed American citizenship yet were impressed into the Royal Navy. Despite repeated attempts at negotiations, the British were unwilling in principle to give up impressments although promising to curb excesses in practice. Jefferson was not satisfied.

It was in the midst of this trade war that British heavy-handedness at sea almost triggered war. In June 1807, the British warship *Leopard* hailed the American warship *Chesapeake* and demanded that it stop so that a British party could board and search for four deserters. The American captain refused, and the commander of the *Leopard* fired several broadsides into *Chesapeake,* killing 3 and wounding 18. The British removed the four suspected deserters and hanged one of them.

The nation exploded in anger. A newspaper in Norfolk, Virginia, reported that the incident "produced a degree of agitation beyond anything we ever witnessed or can attempt to describe."[2] Norfolk citizens wore black armbands for 10 days in memory of the American dead. The governor of Virginia called out the militia. A town meeting of citizens of Wilmington, North Carolina, proclaimed the attack was "tantamount to a declaration of war, or a flagrant violation of our sovereignty."[3] Even Federalists called for war at the outrage. It was one thing to stop a commercial vessel but an entirely different matter to fire upon a warship. Jefferson, had he wanted war, could have led a united nation. Instead, he waited for diplomacy to resolve the issues. Britain disavowed the attack, but it was not until 1811 that she completed a settlement. The call for war in the United States slowly receded, but anti-British feelings were deep and widespread.

Hoping to avoid any incident that might trigger a war, Jefferson ordered an embargo. American ships were prohibited from carrying cargoes to European countries or their colonies. The embargo was a diplomatic and economic failure. Ships deteriorated in port and American products rotted in warehouses. Exports dropped 80 percent in a single year. The economy entered a depression. Farmers, merchants, and investors were broken, and sailors were out of work. The Federalist Party experienced a resurgence as Americans lost faith in Jefferson. Congress eventually ended the embargo and permitted trade with all nations except Britain and France. These two countries hardly felt the sting of the embargo. Each found substitute markets as other nations provided the shipping service that was once dominated by Americans.

Ascending to the presidency in 1809, James Madison was not about to give up the use of trade as a diplomatic weapon. In May of 1810, the Congress passed Macon's Bill #2. This measure reopened trade with the British and French Empires but promised to reimpose restrictions on either party if the other rescinded its restrictions on American trade and neutral rights. Napoleon accepted the offer but had no intentions of actually respecting American trade. The French freed some American vessels for show but continued to seize others and their cargoes. Nonetheless, Madison chose to accept Napoleon's word in good faith, and in February, 1811, he ordered all trade with Britain and her colonies to cease. Short of a total embargo, this was perhaps the worst of all results for American commerce. Clearly, Jefferson and Madison had overrated the withholding of American trade goods as diplomatic lever.

In 1811, the march toward war left the Atlantic and moved to the Indiana Territory. For several years, the Shawnee leader Tecumseh had led a movement for spiritual renewal and active cooperation among the western tribes. His enticing idea was that a confederation of tribes could successfully stop further white settlement on native lands. It was widely held throughout the western states that the British were actively arming the natives and encouraging them to war against the Americans.

Tecumseh's followers established a center called Prophet's Town in what is present-day Indiana. William Henry Harrison, governor of the Indiana Territory, was determined to stop what he considered to be a conspiracy that would lead to open war. Indian activity had frightened hundreds of settlers to abandon their farms and to seek shelter behind stockade forts. While Tecumseh was visiting southern tribes in an attempt to woo them to join his confederacy, Harrison marched on Prophet's Town. A large force of regulars and militia were camped near Tecumseh's village when natives struck before dawn. Suffering approximately 200 casualties, Harrison's men eventually drove off their attackers and continued on to burn Prophet's Town.

President James Madison, who had succeeded Jefferson in 1809, had had enough. He sent a secret message to Congress on the first of June outlining hostile British actions. The House and Senate voted largely along party lines, which also reflected sectional differences. In the closest vote on a declaration of war in American history, the southern and western regions voted for war while the northeastern states voted against. For the most part, however, the declaration of war was met with enthusiasm. In cities, crowds cheered as the President's war message was read. People burned candles in their windows in the evenings. In rural villages, men fired weapons into the air and militiamen fired the village cannon in celebration. Even Americans overseas were joyous. Samuel F. B. Morse, studying art in England, had been raised in a Federalist household. Nonetheless, he was a nationalist first. "The only way to please John Bull is to give him a good beating and such is the singularity of his character, the more you beat him, the greater his respect for you."[4] "John Bull" was the commonly used personification for Britain. The British referred to Americans collectively as "Cousin Jonathan."

Early in the war, even before American and British soldiers had traded volleys, the war's effects were significant. The economic dislocations caused by interrupted foreign trade had inflicted suffering throughout the United States. Mob violence had caused numerous deaths and injuries. Political partisanship degenerated into ugly exchanges, accusations of treason, and calls for punishment. Settlers on the frontier were gathered in forts for protection. Families were disrupted as men joined together, ready to move on their enemies.

PREPARING FOR WAR

Congress, led by Republican War Hawks, had been preparing for war since January, 1812.[5] The regular army was miniscule: fewer than 6,000 officers and men at the end of 1811. Congress expanded the regular army, authorizing more than 35,000 regular soldiers to fight what was hoped to be a short war. Congress also authorized 50,000 one-year volunteers and 100,000 militia to be called up for six months. Perhaps the most significant effect the war had on American society was the unanticipated absence of young men from farms and shops where their skills and muscle power contributed so much to the well being of the household. The government, however, concentrated on other issues. How would these soldiers be recruited, trained, and equipped? Who would lead them?

The first order of business was to select the officers, because they would conduct the recruiting. Because regiments were recruited on a state basis, the senators and representatives submitted lists of potential officers to the secretary of war. The congressmen, of course, nominated officers in order to pay back political debts or to secure future support. Those nominated were almost entirely from the social and economic elite, lawyers and gentlemen planters predominating. While some had basic military training in the state militias, most did not. They were largely ignorant of their new trade—soldiering.

There were significant legal distinctions between officers and enlisted soldiers. An officer could legally order an enlisted soldier to do just about anything, from personal service to making a suicidal attack. The officer–enlisted relationship represented class distinctions that were evident throughout the country. While not as severe as in Britain or Russia, they were significant nonetheless. Officers did not do manual labor. They could resign their commission at will, unlike the enlisted soldiers who were required to serve out a full enlistment. An enlisted soldier would routinely receive physical punishment for minor infractions while officers would not, except for the most severe crimes—treason or cowardice. Despite these distinctions, American officers by and large guarded the health and safety of the soldiers who had volunteered to fight alongside them.

These new officers saw military service as an opportunity to improve their social standing or to further their political ambitions. The esteemed veterans of the Revolution had risen to high positions; the new officers hoped that a successful war would have a similar effect for them. However, it would be wrong to ascribe only selfish motives for military service. The overwhelming majority of new officers were Republicans, imbued with a high level of patriotism and persuaded that the war was entirely just. Nevertheless, their enthusiasm would not entirely compensate for their lack of military skill.

Militia and volunteer units differed from the regular army in important ways. The country had militia organizations from the earliest days of the colonies to protect the community from Indians, pirates, or foreign armies and navies. Law stated that every white male citizen between the age of 18 and 45 was required to enroll in the militia. The governor appointed the senior officers. However, most communities elected their junior officers. On an infrequent basis, perhaps two days a year, the militias gathered to check the rosters, to drill, and to listen to the politicians running for office. These were social occasions for the entire family, because it was an opportunity to go to town, to meet acquaintances, and to see what was new in the stores. Lydia Bacon, who accompanied her husband, a regular soldier, on the Detroit campaign, had this to say: "The malitia [sic] are very different from regulars, most of them have no idea of order & discipline, they think they can do as they please."[6] The militia had a major drawback in addition to poor training. The constitution gave the president the authority to call out the militia to suppress rebellion and to repel invasion. This was generally understood to mean that the militia could not be required to serve outside the borders of the United States.

There was no formal draft to fill the ranks of soldiers, yet many soldiers ended up in militia units involuntarily. When Congress called for 100,000 militia, it allocated quotas among the states. When the governor received his quota, he suballocated quotas to his various militia brigades. The quotas cascaded downward until militia company commanders received their allocation. For example, a militia company of 80 might have to provide six soldiers for six months. The company commander would first ask for volunteers. In the heightened patriotic mood sweeping much of the country with the declaration of war, volunteers often stepped forward in sufficient numbers to meet the quotas. If not, then the company commander would draft the number necessary to meet the quota. This could be done by drawing from a hat or other lottery method. It was generally understood that everyone would serve one tour of active duty before anyone would be drafted for a second tour of duty. These selected citizen soldiers would then be formed into temporary regiments and sent off to training camps. Their families remained behind to manage the farm or business.

The volunteer organizations represented another aspect of community service. Many communities, particularly in the east, had companies of volunteers. Volunteer companies were private organizations. These men bought their own uniforms and weapons and equipment. They elected their own officers and drilled much more frequently than the common militia. It was an honor to be asked to join a volunteer company, and the members represented the upwardly mobile segment of society. Volunteer companies typically chose to form elite military organizations such as riflemen, artillery batteries, dragoons, and hussars; they preferred to wear the ornate uniforms associated with these types of units.

However, the Congress had a different concept when it authorized 50,000 volunteers. States would be responsible for forming these regiments, and governors would appoint the officers. The recruits would enlist for 12 months only and would provide their own uniforms and equipment. These soldiers would not receive the enlistment bounties or the free land at the completion of military service that regulars could expect. Yet, volunteer regiments proved highly popular. Soldiers served together with friends and acquaintances from their local communities. The officers were known to them. And finally, 12-month enlistments were preferable to the 5-year enlistments then required of the regulars. All the men in many of the volunteer companies joined the new volunteer regiments. Because the volunteers were exactly that, they could, unlike the militia, be ordered to cross international borders. Yet the volunteers suffered from problems similar to those of the militia, which made their value in combat dubious. Hubbard Taylor, a Kentucky politician and friend of James Madison, wrote to the President of the near impossibility of turning volunteers into soldiers. "The difficulty of restraining volunteers within the due bounds of discipline is almost at first commencement impossible."[7] Taylor blamed the ill discipline on the practice of the men being allowed to vote for their sergeants and officers. American democracy worked against military effectiveness.

It might be concluded that the persons who enlisted in the regular army would be those marginal to society and to the economy—the poor, unskilled, and unemployed. However, records do not support this assertion. Those who stepped forward to serve in regular units represented a broad spectrum of males in America. Most were farmers or artisans (shoemakers, carpenters, blacksmiths, tailors, etc.), roughly proportional to those segments of the population. Only 13 percent of enlistees were foreign born, only slightly higher than the 11 percent of the population believed to have been born outside the United States. Most foreign-born soldiers were Irish, but many hailed from Canada, Britain, Germany, and France. Although records did not usually list the race of an enlistee, there is evidence that a few hundred blacks were recruited, mostly from New England and Pennsylvania.

Why did a man enlist in the regular army? Certainly patriotism and a desire for adventure motivated many, but service in a volunteer regiment would satisfy these goals. Recruits in the regular service were offered incentives unavailable in the volunteers or the militia. Enlistment bounties started at $16, a considerable sum in 1812. Also, recruits received 160 acres of land upon completion of five years of service. For a young man wanting to own a farm, military service proved the opportunity he might not otherwise have.

Once a soldier enlisted, he and his company were marched to large camps closer to the border. The first arrivals slept under the stars until tents arrived from Philadelphia where they were made by hundreds of seamstresses hired for the task. The officers organized guard details to keep thieves out of the camps and to prevent desertion. Work details set off to improve camp roads, fetch food and water, and to build latrines away from the tents. The officers drilled the soldiers constantly in marching and in firing their weapons. Drill was repetitive and boring, but new soldiers would need considerable training to meet Britain's superb army.

Training was grueling; hard work and discipline problems could not be avoided. If the stern look or punch from a sergeant was not sufficient to bring a soldier into conformity, more drastic measures were quickly applied. When a commander came across a soldier who refused to cooperate with his training regimen, fell asleep while on guard, challenged his sergeant, or perhaps had stolen from a farmer or another soldier, that soldier could receive a court-martial. A soldier found guilty received punishment commensurate with the crime. Congress had outlawed whipping as punishment prior to the war. Yet commanders could be quite creative in finding appropriate punishments. Typically, punishment took the form of humiliation such as wearing a sign around one's neck or standing on a stump for an hour a day for a week. A soldier who had stolen a duck was forced to wear the dead duck around his neck all day while standing at attention in camp. Deprivation of the whiskey ration or a few months pay was common. As the seriousness of the charge increased, so did the punishment. While whipping was outlawed, paddling was not. Whipping cut the skin; paddling only bruised it. Confinement for a month or two was a frequent punishment when the unit was stationary. Sometimes the court wanted the punishment to be inflicted quickly. A guilty soldier could be sentenced to sit astride a fence or on a rail for hours with heavy weights tied to his feet. While abhorrent to us today, these punishments were consistent with those awarded by civilian courts.

The military courts reserved the most serious punishments for desertion. Most deserters succeeded in escaping the army. Only about 20 percent were captured and returned to camp. Draconian means were taken to discourage soldiers from desertion. Branding the cheek or forehead with a "D" was common, as was cropping one or both ears. This maiming prevented the soldier from enlisting in the future and carried social consequences in civilian life. As one might imagine, execution was also within the legal bounds of a court's prerogative. Executions rose dramatically during the war as desertion increased. Three soldiers were executed in 1812, 32 in 1813, and 146 in 1814.

In Brigadier General Winfield Scott's camp in Buffalo in 1814, several deserters were tried by court-martial and sentenced to be executed by firing squad. Scott assembled his entire brigade. The five unfortunate soldiers were marched to the front of the formation where they stood by their wooden coffins and freshly dug graves. Five firing squads lined up opposite the condemned men. The order was given, and the five execution squads fired in unison. All five deserters fell. Then one of them stirred. Scott walked over to Private William Fairchild and pulled the bound and blind-folded soldier to his feet. Because of his extreme youth, Scott had secretly given Fairchild a reprieve. Scott walked the shaken soldier over to his company commander. The point was made and desertions in Scott's Brigade all but ceased.[8]

Another reality of life in camp was disease. Because Americans over-whelmingly lived in rural areas, many had never caught the childhood diseases taken for granted today. Crowded together in tents, eating out of a common cooking pot, inadequately clothed in the rain and snow, soldiers became ill and died at alarming rates. As was true in all of America's wars until the widespread use of antibiotics in World War II, many more Americans died of disease than from enemy action or accident. Soldiers who were wounded in battle had poor chances for survival. Stomach and chest wounds were almost always fatal. Bullet wounds to the limbs were universally treated by amputation. This was often successful, but the amputee was eventually discharged from service and, with only his severance pay and grant of land, was returned to society. Even with the care from his family, life of an amputee was extremely hard. He could barely earn a living as an artisan or contribute to working a farm. As harsh as life in the army sounds to us today, it was no more difficult than life on America's frontiers.

ON THE FRONTIERS

In 1795, the number of nonnative inhabitants west of the Appalachians was approximately 150,000. By 1812 that number had increased dramatically to more than 1 million. Kentucky, Tennessee, Ohio, and Louisiana were added to the union. Congress divided the remainder of the Old Northwest and Louisiana Purchase into territories under governors with strong powers. White settlers streamed into primeval forests and wide prairies hoping to start new lives.

The land wasn't free, and the settlers were uniformly impecunious. How did they come to own a plot of soil? Those who had military service were rewarded with a piece of federal land upon discharge, but this was only a fraction of settlers. Typically bankers and businessmen from the east coast cities, or even Europe, pooled their assets to form development companies. The company bought property from the government, often sight unseen, and sent managers into their new purchases. The manager surveyed squares of land, typically in 40-acre blocks. The managers would also pick out locations for small villages, often called stations. Typically, these potential settlements were on rivers. Surveyors laid out streets enclosing smaller plots. Meanwhile, the development company in the East enticed settlers to head to the West.

Settlers would meet with managers, choose plots of land, and begin their new lives. As the settlers cleared land, they made their mortgage payments in firewood and lumber. When the farms started producing surplus, the settlers paid in grain, pigs, or cattle. Their first order of business, however, was security, both physical and economic.

Physical security meant avoidance of disputes with natives and defensive measures if coexistence was not possible. Land managers worked with federal Indian agents to meet with tribal leaders to negotiate trade and settle disputes. However, settlers who struck out on their own and squatted on tribal lands took grave risks and frequently were burned out by the natives or forced out by federal soldiers and marshals. As soon as the population was large enough to support a militia, settlers met to elect officers and to establish regular training sessions. Local communities looked to themselves for security first, and to territorial or federal authorities later.

Economic security meant throwing up a crude, small cabin and clearing and cultivating the land as soon as possible. On the farm everyone worked, often long hours and often without breaks, even on Sundays. Settlers burned or chopped trees and dug up boulders and large rocks. The stones were used to build chimneys and sometimes stone fences to pen in farm animals. The mule was essential in breaking up the ground, laden as it was with roots and rocks. Settlers brought seed with them from the East or purchased it from the land managers. For the first year or two, the settler family grew enough to feed itself, but each year more and more land was brought under cultivation until the farm began producing surplus. Grain, corn, fruit, pigs, and chickens in excess to family needs could be used in barter or as payment for debts.

While the settler families worked hard to produce surplus, the land companies advertised in the cities of the East for professionals to journey west and take up residence in the settlements. The first professionals on the frontier were the lawyers. Disputes over land and other property were a major problem. State governments and territorial governors were often slow in establishing courts served by trained judges. The land manager and the settlers very often selected their own judges from among themselves or from the newly arrived lawyers. Justices became de facto governments and filled the gap until state or territorial authorities could establish more formal governance.

Besides lawyers, land managers tried to attract artisans such as blacksmiths and coopers and professionals such as doctors and teachers. These new arrivals populated the stations and served the settlers in their scattered farms. Depending on the perceived threat from the native population, the land manager would surround his station with a timber fortification.

Typically settlers were available between planting season and harvest season and sold their labor to the manager to build the defensive structures. Labor was another way for the settler to pay off the mortgage. As whites flowed into the frontier, they moved into native territories regardless of government injunctions to respect borders established by treaty. Consequently, they increasingly clashed with the native populations.

The native population was becoming increasingly dependent upon trade goods provided by the governments of the United States and Britain. Muskets and rifles largely replaced bows as hunting weapons. Steel knives and tomahawks replaced bows and clubs as implements of war. Machine-woven cloth supplemented or replaced furs and leather as clothing. Wool blankets were prized as were iron pots and pans. White traders eagerly sought pelts in exchange for these manufactured goods. The pelts would be fashioned into hats and other items of outer dress for Europeans as well as Americans. Yet, with this trade of useful commodities also came whiskey, which had a debilitating effect on native society.

The American settlers in the West had two desires—land and security. The natives and the British stood in the way of both. Social organization among the natives was loose in the extreme. While the tribal elders would attempt to forge a consensus for policy, individuals were always free to dissent and act on their own. Into this chasm of two societies, white and native, strode Tecumseh, perhaps the most influential Indian leader of the period. Tecumseh saw no plausible way in which the native population could live at peace with the white settlers, given the huge numbers pouring into frontier lands. It was clear to him that the purity of native life was being defiled by white encroachment, which brought disease and the debilitating effects of alcohol with it.

Tecumseh preached a return to traditional values and the expulsion of whites from native lands. To bring his program to fruition, he forged a wide-ranging confederation of like-minded natives. Tecumseh's confederation was formed not so much by tribes but by individuals drawn to Tecumseh's charisma and his message of unity and reform. Thus, Tecumseh gathered about him hundreds of young warriors—Shawnee, Kickapoo, Potawatomi, Delaware, and others—eager to fight the Americans and throw them back across the Appalachians. Other natives were decidedly neutral, unsure of the wisdom of challenging the numerous Americans who could very well defeat the British and then take vengeance upon their native allies.

In 1812, the native population was not united in opposition to the Americans and neither were the Canadians. The white population of Upper Canada was fractured along economic and social fault lines. The first white inhabitants of the territory that would become Upper Canada were the French-speaking fur traders. They moved easily among the natives, often marrying among them and forming both family and business ties. After the American Revolution, the British evacuated thousands of American Tories, those who had fought against the rebels and were no longer welcome in the new United States. Many moved to the sugar islands of the Caribbean. Others sailed to New Brunswick and Nova Scotia, hoping to rebuild their lives. Eventually Britain opened Upper Canada to settlement, and thousands flooded in, settling along the shores of Lakes Erie and Ontario. These hardy settlers were thoroughly British in manner and loyalty. Canadian settlement mimicked that of the American frontier. Eventually, the earliest Canadian settlers grew prosperous. They farmed large tracts of land and became the social and political elite of the new province. As British subjects, they sought order, which would lead, in turn, to stability and prosperity.

As families on the American frontier gained physical and economic security, they too, like their Canadian counterparts, were increasingly moved to achieve stability and prosperity. As more and more settlers arrived, or passed through to establish their lives farther west, the frontier was slowly transformed into rural America.

RURAL AMERICA

The vast bulk of white and black Americans lived in rural America—in villages smaller than 500 people, on the family farm, or on large plantations. Much of America, mostly east of the Appalachians, was no longer frontier. Patterns of economic and social activity were well developed. West of the mountains, rural America was newer, and communities grew or withered away with economic development and the movement of settlers in search of land and prosperity.

On the farm, most time and effort was still directed at producing food to eat or sell. The farm family dedicated most of the arable land to the production of grain. Cultivation followed an annual cycle of plowing, sowing, weeding and watering, and harvesting. Spring plowing and autumn harvesting were labor intensive allowing families some spare time in summers. At harvest, the farmer retained some of the seed for use in next year's sowing. However, the family transported most of the grain to the mills to be transformed into flour, paying the miller with part of the product. Flour or corn meal excess to the family's needs was packed into barrels, and the farmer could sell this at the village market or to grain merchants. Grain merchants, buying from dozens of local farmers, transported flour to the larger cities to be sold at a profit. In larger villages, transport businesses arose. These shippers moved cargoes, such as barrels of grain or cattle, by boat or wagon, to city markets or to large ports, such as New Orleans. There, dock workers loaded huge cargoes onto ocean-going vessels for movement to the cities on the east coast or Europe.

Back on the rural farm, not all land was dedicated to grain. Families supplemented their diet with home-grown fruit and vegetables and meat from pigs and chickens. Younger children, unable to contribute much to the hard labor required of plowing or harvesting, were adequate to the task of feeding and caring for barnyard animals. They could also weed and water vegetable gardens and pick berries and beans and other small produce. Families kept dairy cows for milk, butter, and cheese. The males in the family hunted a variety of animals for food or to remove predators such as fox and coyote. To this end, many families maintained hunting weapons such as shotguns or fowling pieces. For the most part, these weapons were not particularly useful for military service. All family members could fish in ponds and streams, and this added variety to an otherwise monotonous meal.

Rural families wanted more than just food. The production of surplus food brought in currency or credit, which was exchanged for metal products (pans, nails, tools, blades, etc.), sugar, salt, cloth, and sometimes niceties like ribbons, books, writing paper, and ink. One of the first business activities in the growing village was the general store. The proprietor bought needed products in bulk from traveling vendors or ordered them from manufacturers in the cities. Coins and paper money were still in short supply, and barter was still an accepted mode of commerce. The farmer could exchange bags of grain, eggs, chickens, or baskets of fruit and vegetables directly to the merchant who would sell them at a profit to villagers for currency or for other services.

Economic activities in town continued to be specialized as craftsmen and common laborers focused their talents. Blacksmiths created a variety of metal products, while carpenters built beds, tables, chairs, and chests of all sizes. Coopers assembled barrels to hold meat, whiskey, grain, and other produce on its way to the big cities. Tin smiths and leather workers created a wide variety of items useful in the house or on the farm. While farmers sometimes made their own soap and candles, it was becoming simpler to acquire these through purchase or barter.

One of the biggest differences between frontier and rural society was the density of settlement. On the frontier, settlers could go days or weeks without seeing another person. In rural America, the next farm was typically less than a mile away, and the village was within one or two hour's walk. Farm families typically traveled to town on Saturdays to buy and sell and returned on Sunday for church service.

America was an overwhelmingly Protestant country. Catholic communities existed in larger cities and in territory that was initially settled by France or Spain. Small Jewish communities were present in large cities as well. But in rural America, Protestant faith communities of all denominations prospered. These denominations differentiated themselves by degrees of hierarchy or autonomy and in the level of ritual present in services. Services centered on scripture, and the bible was the first book most families owned. Groups of worshippers pooled their resources to build churches and meeting halls and to hire clergy to minister to the faithful. Some ministers were itinerant, traveling to new settlements and out to the frontier to bring the Christian faith to all.

During this period, most Americans could hardly read or write. Notable exceptions were lawyers and clergy and the upper classes in general. The notion of universal public education was still far off, especially in rural America. Teachers, educated in eastern schools, moved to rural communities to eke out an existence while bringing the rudiments of numeracy and literacy to children. Like any other craftsman or businessman, their pay was often in the form of farm produce. Those families who saw education as a means to self-improvement and prosperity sent their children to school during the periods when their labor could be spared. Because education was not free, families often gave priority of education to males.

While literacy was uncommon, people still yearned for news and entertainment contained in books and newspapers. Unlike the cities where private libraries existed, rural villages had a paucity of books. Teachers and wealthier citizens owned books and often loaned them out to friends. A literate family member read from the bible, a novel, newspaper, or even an almanac by candlelight to the rest of the family on evenings after they had completed their work. Few villages could support newspapers, although these were common in larger cities. Still, literate persons subscribed to newspapers, and these arrived in the mail, often days after publication.

Mixed in among the family farms were plantations. The plantation was a business that produced staple crops such as cotton or tobacco. Cultivation on this scale required far more labor than the family members could supply. Labor came from three general sources, common laborers, sharecroppers, and slaves. Farm laborers offered their service for money or food and shelter. The plantation owner employed them as needed to clear land, plow, sow, and harvest. This meant that the farm laborer was on his own during slow seasons and during the winter. Then he might hire his services in town to other craftsmen or businessmen. The sharecropper was a free citizen, typically white. This farmer and his family did not own their own land but lived on the plantation working a sizeable plot of the owner's land. Most of the sharecropper's produce went to the planter, but he could keep a smaller share for his own use or to sell. In states in which slavery was legal, plantation owners were also slave owners.

European traders brought black Africans to America as slaves as early as 1619. The laws that regulated slavery had been in existence since colonial times and were largely continued by the states after the Revolution. The vast majority of slaves were owned by planters and used as agricultural laborers, although many were taught crafts useful on the plantation such as carpentry or blacksmithing. Planters trained selected slaves in domestic duties such as cooking, cleaning, and serving. Paul Jennings, one of President Madison's house servants, recalled of his master that "Mr. Madison, I think, was one of the best men that ever lived, I never saw him in a passion and never knew him to strike a slave, although he had over one hundred, neither would he allow an overseer to do it."[9] Madison was probably an exception. Slave owners typically inflicted physical punishment to keep slaves working. Social distinctions existed between the house slaves and the field hands, with the house servants achieving higher status. Laws prohibited teaching slaves to read and write. Other laws regulated social behavior in order to maintain rigid boundaries between whites and slaves and free blacks.

While the vast majority of black Americans were slaves, free blacks lived in many urban and rural communities. Many slave owners, upon their deaths, freed some or all of their slaves. For example, in 1810 a full 20 percent of blacks in Maryland were free while only 7 percent were free in neighboring Virginia. Once freed, the former slaves' children were also free. Many southern states prohibited free blacks from living within their boundaries, and free blacks migrated to northern cities or even moved west in search of land and a new life. Local and state laws and customs regulated the economic and social activities of free blacks, which maintained boundaries between the races, even in the North. Communities deprived blacks of voting and property rights and denied access to education. Church communities were often segregated with free blacks creating their own faith communities.

Islands of native communities also existed within rural America. For the most part, the native population away from the frontier had acquiesced to white sovereignty and had extensive lands reserved for their exclusive use. Unlike the western natives, those living near white settlements had become more agrarian. On the Niagara Frontier, for example, the Seneca and Tuscarora kept cattle and hogs and grew corn, vegetables, and wheat. Several settlements had their own sawmills, and cabins were replacing traditional long houses. The Seneca settlement on Buffalo Creek had over a thousand inhabitants, dwarfing the nearby village of Buffalo. The political status of Native Americans was ambiguous. The federal government considered them to be noncitizens but who nevertheless composed sovereign "nations." The federal government reserved the exclusive right to negotiate treaties with the various Indian tribal groups.

Canada had rural areas that were less well developed than those in the United States. One characteristic of Canadian society, however, is germane to the conduct of the war. In the first decade of the nineteenth century, thousands of Americans emigrated from the United States into Upper Canada. Perhaps a majority of white settlers in western Upper Canada had either been born in the United States or were the children of former Americans. They moved to Upper Canada because the land was cheap and taxation low. The British authorities required these immigrants to take an oath of allegiance to the king, but most newcomers treated this as *pro forma* and not as a sincere change in their loyalty. This numerous group of immigrants took what was left over by the former Tories. They brought with them a spirit of independence and democratic notions that were utterly foreign to the loyal subjects who had fled such anarchic conditions in the new United States. British officials and the loyal classes feared that when war came, the former Americans would join the invaders. The fear was not unfounded.

Canadian Loyalists formed a hard core in every militia regiment, but the disaffected, mostly former Americans, avoided duty when possible. This was not just a matter of loyalty, however. Militia duty meant leaving the farm for an unspecified time. Farmers completed their planting by June 1812, but the harvest would mean widespread desertion as militiamen returned to their fields to get the crops in. British military commanders were never sure how many militiamen would be present for duty at any given time.

On the eve of the war, British General Isaac Brock ordered an oath of allegiance be administered to all whites in Upper Canada. Those who refused to take the oath were dispossessed of their lands and given a short time to leave the country. Hundreds fled to New York. Many took the oath reluctantly in order to keep their farms but would assist the American forces entering Canada. The Iroquois nation was a large group of tribes that was encircled by rural communities. The Iroquois were in a precarious position because their scattered reserves straddled the border. While most Iroquois lived on their traditional lands in New York, hundreds had departed after the Revolution. These natives in Canada were disposed to assist the British in defending that land. The New York Iroquois chose to remain neutral, at least in the beginning. Before the war was over, Iroquois fought Iroquois with lasting effects on tribal unity.

LIFE IN THE CITIES

Approximately 15 percent of Americans lived in communities larger than 500 persons. It was in these larger communities that economic activity was most specialized and diversified. Urban dwellers had access to a large range of goods and services. The cities were not only residential areas but also industrial communities in which laborers lived within walking distance of their places of employment. During colonial and revolutionary times, manufacturing operated within the guild system. The master craftsman owned the business and held the range of skills to create consumer goods. Goods produced within guild workshops included clothing, shoes and other leather products, glassware, metal products, furniture, books and newspapers, beer and wine, baked goods, and a myriad of other items.

The master took in apprentices to assist him in production. The master established a long-term understanding, an unwritten contract, with the parents of the young apprentice. The apprentice, usually a young teenager, performed the unskilled labor in the shop. In return, the apprentice typically received room and board but most importantly, the master passed on the secrets of his craft to the apprentice. A wealthy master might bring on several apprentices. As the apprentice attained increasing skill, the master promoted him to journeyman. The journeyman eventually was able to construct a product entirely by himself and received wages for his work. In larger shops, the master might spend his time purchasing materials and selling products, while leaving actual production to the journeymen. Eventually, the journeyman would either purchase or inherit the business from the master. He was now the master craftsman. Apprentices, journeymen, and masters, although occupying different rungs on the social and economic ladder, identified themselves with their specific craft.

With widespread use of water power and with the advent of steam power, the guild system slowly collapsed. Evidence of the breakdown of the guild system was evident before and during the war. Successful masters sought credit from bankers to expand their production facilities. These entrepreneurs located factories along waterways to take advantage of this free source of power. Wheels turned huge arrays of belts, which in turn powered machinery such as looms, lathes, and cutting tools. Cloth, metal hardware, tools, building materials, and a wide variety of finished products poured out of American factories to make life a little easier and a little nicer for much of society.

With the steam engine, factories no longer had to be located near moving water. Former master craftsmen, now businessmen, established factories in cities to be close to the labor force and the customers. During the War of 1812, in cities such as Philadelphia, Boston, and New York, small shops coexisted alongside larger factories and tenements. However, water and steam-powered machinery slowly worked a dynamic that damaged the guild system and created class distinctions between business and labor.

Machines such as looms and lathes did not require a journeyman's level of skill for their operation. By breaking the production process into its component parts, a few skilled laborers and many unskilled or semi-skilled laborers could assemble most goods. As this occurred, factory owners stopped taking in apprentices and passing their skills to journeymen. Instead, the factory owner, or a foreman in his place, hired laborers as needed with no commitment beyond the end of the day. The foreman trained the laborer in a small piece of the process and paid him or her at subsistence levels.

Apprentices and journeymen were almost entirely males, but now females made up an increasingly larger portion of the labor force. Young women worked at looms producing cloth or as seamstresses piecing together clothing. In many sectors of production, factories could produce goods more cheaply than the master working with a few journeymen in a small shop. The smaller businesses could not compete with the factories, except in service and for the production of unique items such as jewelry. This dynamic was just getting started during the early nineteenth century but would pick up speed as the nation approached the Civil War. Politically, however, owners and laborers saw their interests being guarded by the different parties. Owners increasingly aligned themselves with the

Federalists, while journeymen and common laborers increasingly became active Jeffersonian Republicans.

People living in cities had much greater access to education. However, this applied to those who could afford schooling. The children of the middle and upper classes, not needed in the fields or the factories, were free to attend school regularly. Children of the laboring classes were often laborers themselves, but even if they were free to do so, their parents could not afford to educate them. Schools concentrated on a liberal arts education with studies of language (particularly French, Latin, and Greek), geography, and history as well as basic mathematics and economics. The sons and daughters of plantation owners went to boarding schools in the larger cities where they met other students like themselves, made important connections, and acquired a class identity.

Those men with an aptitude for academics (and the money to do so) pursued baccalaureate studies in fields that led to professional employment—law, medicine, theology, and education for example. Women might be sent to finishing schools to acquire skills in music, needlepoint, and art, as well as literature and language. Civil engineering was only taught at the military academy at West Point. Graduates of this institution, founded in 1802, were very prominent in the building of roads, canals, and rail lines after the war. Children of the wealthiest Americans might be sent to Europe for a year or two of higher education. They returned ready to enter a profession, or in the case of young ladies, ready to marry one of their class.

The beginning of industrialization also sharpened gender roles. On the frontier and in rural communities, work was task oriented and responsive to natural cycles. Work was done when it needed to be done whether it was plowing, sowing, harvesting, or preserving. In cities, the men typically left the home to work in shops, offices, factories, warehouses, and docks. Meanwhile, women remained in the home, doing all that was necessary to run the household—cooking, shopping, cleaning, and sewing. To a male returning from daily outside work, the house or apartment was a refuge from degradation and exertion. Work accomplished outside the home was compensated while no remuneration accrued to domestic work, unless the women of the household took in work such as laundry or sewing. With the males out of the house, the females took on the greater portion of the task of childrearing, which included educating the children. In colonial times, the man of the household provided the primary moral compass and religious education but, more and more, this role was transferred to the woman of the house. These differences tended, over time, to sharpen gender roles.

Caught in the house with only young children for company, women sought opportunities outside the home. By and large, it was unmarried women who worked in the textile factories while married women took in piece work. Typically, more women than men joined churches. This provided opportunities for a social life outside the home. Women organized prayer groups, missionary support groups, and various moral reform groups to support causes such as abolition, temperance, or public education. Starting slowly in the first decades of the nineteenth century, these movements gained strength after the war.

Black neighborhoods sprang up in many northern cities as slaves who had been freed chose to leave the hostility in states in which slavery was protected by law. While there was certainly hostility in northern cities, moving to black neighborhoods mitigated its worst effects. Many blacks, men and women, became domestic servants. Black women took in laundry from middle and upper class white households. Black men, who might have spent much of their life as agricultural laborers, now worked in shops and factories and received wages lower than white workers. Many black males signed on as seamen. Once in their new communities, recently freed blacks rejected their classical or diminutive forenames and chose instead English or biblical names. As slaves, blacks used the surname of their master or no surname at all. Overwhelmingly, freed slaves selected common English surnames. Very often, blacks placed the word *African* in the names of their churches and social groups. Even in 1812, black urban communities gave evidence of their own distinct cultures.

WAR STRIKES HOME

American society in 1812 was diverse and dynamic. From the beginnings of industrialization in the cities, through vast areas of rural farming, to subsistence living in the deep forests of America's frontier, black, white, and Native Americans sought increased security and prosperity. The War of 1812 put these efforts on hold for most Americans as contending armies passed through the frontier borders and struggled over coastal cities and towns. The results for many were economic dislocation, family separation, loss of property and homes, and the specter of disease, wounds, and death.

The United States initiated the war and formed a plan for quick victory. The American strategy in the West was to cross the Detroit River and invade Upper Canada, clearing the British from the Great Lakes, diminishing their influence over the native tribes. American leaders expected support from those inhabitants of Upper Canada who had recently emigrated from the United States. General William Hull, who led the American forces at Detroit, issued a proclamation that recognized the assistance that he might receive from this disaffected segment of Canadian society. "I doubt not your courage and firmness; I will not doubt your attachment to Liberty. If you tender your services voluntarily they will be accepted readily." Hull portrayed the invading Americans as liberators, and he urged the civilians to remain neutral, warning them, "If contrary to your own interest & the just expectation of my country, you should take part in the approaching contest, you will be considered and treated as enemies and the horrors, and calamities of war will Stalk before you." Hull explicitly promised the worst punishment for any Canadian civilian who fought with Tecumseh's forces. "No white man found fighting by the Side of an Indian will be taken prisoner. Instant destruction will be his Lot. . . ." It was a common attitude among frontier whites that the worst treason was to join a native force in its attacks upon settlers.[10]

THE NORTHWEST

The war immediately went poorly for the Americans. Despite the staggering odds against the British in numbers and the loyalty of its citizens, they threw back all American attempts at invasion and even moved into American territory. Their native allies were key to these developments. Mackinac Island guarded the strait between Lakes Huron and Michigan. Before the American garrison there was even aware that war had been declared, it was attacked and captured. The British attackers reflected the social variety of the fur trading regions: British regulars, Canadian militia, French-speaking voyageurs, and an array of native warriors—Sioux, Chippewa, Winnebago, Menominee, and Ottawa. The natives coveted scalps as physical totems of victory and bravery. The British commander, unwilling to kill soldiers or civilians after surrender, mollified the natives by providing them with large quantities of captured cattle, firearms, blankets, and whiskey.

The Americans at Fort Dearborn were not so fortunate. Fort Dearborn was a tiny log fortification on land that would later become the metropolis of Chicago. General Hull ordered the soldiers and families at Fort Dearborn to evacuate the fort and seek safety at Fort Wayne. The commander at Fort Dearborn, Captain Nathan Heald, had negotiated safe passage for the 93 soldiers, women, and children with the Potawatomie chief, Black Bird. He gave the natives supplies to buy their good will but refused to give up firearms and whiskey. Heald's column had hardly departed their stockade when the natives fell upon them, killing most and capturing the few survivors. One of those survivors, John Kinzie, wrote afterward of the natives among the women and children. ". . . here was perpetuated one of the most shocking scenes of butchery perhaps ever witnessed . . . the tomahawk & knife performed their work without distinctions of age or condition."[11] Black Bird himself intervened to spare Kinzie and his family.

News of the disaster at Fort Dearborn reached Hull. Hull was not a military man and was not up to the task given him. With his supply lines cut, Hull pulled the Americans back across the Detroit River and into Fort Detroit. Major General Sir Isaac Brock followed Hull and opened up a bombardment upon the American fort. A young mother, Mrs. M. McCarty, remembered, "hour after hour how I passed thus alone, listening to the booming cannon and the startling and shrieking as a ball whizzed by the house, sometimes feeling almost sure that it was a mark for the enemy and thinking perhaps the next shot would terminate my existence."[12]

Tecumseh and Brock tricked Hull into believing that they outnumbered the Americans. Brock informed Hull that he was not certain that he could restrain the natives if the combined British–native force assaulted the fort. Hull was struck with the fear that the soldiers and families in Fort Detroit would be massacred. The unfortunate Hull surrendered his command to the smaller enemy force. Tecumseh kept his followers under tight control. Brock released several hundred Ohio militiamen, and he marched the captured American regulars off to prison in Quebec. The U.S. Army court-martialed and convicted Hull for cowardice. The court sentenced him to death, but the president granted a reprieve, citing Hull's service during the Revolution. With three dramatic victories over the Americans, more natives flocked to Tecumseh or made war on their own. In the words of frontier minister William Gurley, the news of Hull's surrender "fell on our ears like a thunderbolt."[13] Settlers by the hundreds abandoned farms and fields and fled to the relative security of forts scattered throughout the western theater.

President Madison had to overcome the humiliation of losing Detroit, and he sent Major General William Henry Harrison, the victor of Tippecanoe, to do so. Harrison marched on Detroit along three routes. One column, commanded by Brigadier General James Winchester, drew up to a small settlement on the River Raisin, only 35 miles south of Detroit. The British commander at Detroit, Henry Procter, boldly gathered every soldier, militiaman, and native warrior available and struck Winchester's contingent at dawn. Fighting for their lives, the Americans—regulars and volunteers from Kentucky—put up a gallant struggle but eventually surrendered, after receiving Procter's word that he would protect them from the natives. Hundreds of Americans marched off as prisoners, but the wounded, somewhat fewer than one hundred, remained at the battlefield to await wagons to evacuate them.

The following morning, hundreds of native warriors, anxious to collect scalps, fell upon the wounded Americans. They took some as prisoners, but at least 30 were tomahawked and scalped. Bodies were left where they lie, many to be devoured by wild hogs. The Indians were very likely retaliating for their defeat at Tippecanoe and several other American attacks on native villages. This was already a war of atrocity, but the American reaction to the massacre at the River Raisin was electrifying. Hardly a family in Kentucky was not touched by the fighting. The cry of "Remember the River Raisin" would be heard on battlefields throughout the west.

The American and British armies in the West received supplies along lines that stretched back to Philadelphia or Quebec. Both sides desperately needed control over Lake Erie to simplify their supply problems. As the war stretched into 1813, British Commander Robert Heriot Barclay built a small flotilla of brigs, schooners, and gunboats at Amherstburg at the southern mouth of the Detroit River, while Commodore Oliver Hazard Perry did the same at Presque Isle Harbor near Erie, Pennsylvania.

These shipyards were primitive in the extreme, and virtually everything needed to construct a warship, except the lumber, came from eastern cities. The sailors to man the vessels came from many sources as well. The U.S. Navy sent Perry a few hundred sailors who were unemployed in American harbors blockaded by the Royal Navy. Unlike the land forces, free blacks were heavily represented among seamen. Perhaps as many as 10 percent of Perry's sailors were black. However, the numbers of able-bodied seamen were insufficient to sail the newly constructed ships. Where would the rest come from?

Perry sought the help of the army. He asked for volunteers, and nearly 200 soldiers—regulars, Kentucky riflemen, Pennsylvania militia—stepped forward for what would prove to be the adventure of their lives. On September 10th, Perry's small undermanned flotilla of nine vessels met six of the Royal Navy in the shallow waters of western Lake Erie. The fighting was incredibly bloody, but within a few hours, the American flotilla was victorious. Twenty percent of the American sailors, soldiers, and marines were killed or wounded. However, the military significance of this short, violent exchange was dramatic. The British at Detroit were cut off from supplies.

Procter and Tecumseh immediately evacuated their forces from American territory. Without a British force and British weapons and supplies, Tecumseh could not fight the Americans with any prospect of success. General Harrison was quick to pursue. Catching up at Moraviantown on the River Thames, Kentuckians had their revenge for the River Raisin. Mounted riflemen rode down the British infantry, and Kentucky dismounted volunteers attacked the native contingent with unmatched ferocity. When it was all over, Tecumseh was dead, his body hidden by his followers. The war in the Northwest was over, and American settlers slowly left the wooden stockades and returned to their farms. The fighting had shattered native families, with the loss of so many young warriors. Within a few years, the U.S. government ordered native tribes westward.

THE CENTRAL THEATER

Farther east, along the Niagara River between Lakes Erie and Ontario, the war was particularly destructive for both civilians and citizen-soldiers. After the declaration of war, the Americans sent regulars and militia to the Niagara Frontier to prepare for an invasion across the Niagara. Unfortunately, supply for these hastily assembled troops was unsatisfactory. There were few tents or cooking implements, and food delivery was intermittent. Militiamen called away from their farms and villages lived in the open with only the blankets or coats they brought from home. A militia officer wrote home, "We are every few days, deluged in water, such storms of rain and wind I think I never experienced, and cloth of my Tent is mere sieve stuff; every third night I get wet as a Muskrat."[14] The supply system could not replace shoes worn out during training. The newly recruited regular soldiers who joined them were hardly better off. They were clothed in summer uniforms of linen, because wool coats were unavailable until the following year. The men fell victim to sicknesses of all kinds.

In October, 1813, the Americans finally invaded, crossing the Niagara and landing at the small village of Queenston. Because of the lack of boats, only about one-third of the regulars and militia crossed in the first wave. After a few hours of fighting, the Americans consolidated their position on the Canadian shore and sent their wounded back to the New York side of the river. However, when the American militia saw the broken, bloody wounded, they balked. Insisting that the general could not order them to cross into a foreign country, they refused repeated entreaties to get into the boats. American officers tried their best to coax the militia to cross now that victory was at hand but to no avail. Within hours, the British assembled a force of Iroquois, regulars, and militia and counterattacked the American lines. The Americans were completely unnerved by the war whoops of the natives. With their backs to the river and no boats available, the Americans surrendered—nearly a thousand of them. The British released the militia, but they sent the regulars into captivity.

In 1813, there began a train of events that transformed the war from one in which chivalry and the law of war was embraced by both sides to one in which retaliation and revenge threatened to control events. In April, an American force of about 1,500 soldiers crossed Lake Ontario to the city of York, the capital of Upper Canada. Their commander, the famed explorer Zebulon Pike, had warned them that acts of looting or vandalism would be dealt with severely. Once on land, Pike led his men into battle and pushed the British, Canadians, and natives into York. As Pike paused to interrogate a captured sergeant, the British blew up a powder magazine in a fort guarding York. The explosion was immense, and hundreds of Americans were killed or wounded in a rain of stone. Pike was among the casualties and died within hours.

Inflamed by the death caused by the explosion and without Pike to control them, hundreds of Americans began looting the homes of the citizens of York. They also released prisoners from the city jail, many of whom were American sympathizers who had refused to take an oath of loyalty. Through the night, groups of soldiers and disaffected Canadians went beyond looting and set fire to both public and private buildings. Eventually, the soldiers were brought under control, and the Canadians disappeared into the backwoods. But the damage had been done.

The following month, a larger force of Americans assaulted Fort George at the mouth of the Niagara River. Despite determined resistance, the British garrison and Canadian militia were forced to withdraw. With a powerful force of Americans on Canadian soil, many sympathizers came out and offered assistance to their American liberators. About 130 volunteered for military service under the command of Joseph Willcocks, a former member of the assembly of Upper Canada. Calling themselves the Canadian Volunteers, these mounted soldiers gathered information from sympathizers and terrorized loyal Canadians. They captured prominent loyalists and often burned their homes.

In December, 1813, the Americans decided to abandon Fort George and cross the river into New York. Fort George was about one mile from the village of Newark. Virtually every male of military age had departed Newark, and the city was occupied by women, old men, and youngsters. The American commander, a militia general, gave orders to Willcocks to burn down the unoffending village. Willcocks ordered the villagers out of their homes and into the snow. Without giving them time to remove their possessions, Willcocks ordered the homes set afire. Willcocks's men plundered the homes and robbed some of the women of the money they were carrying. The soldiers carried the ill Mrs. William Dickson out of her home on her bed. They then torched her home. Two women of Newark gave birth that horrible evening. The inhabitants of Newark trekked off in the wind and snow, seeking refuge farther inland from their destroyed village.

Sir Gordon Drummond, the British commander, moved immediately to retaliate. Nine days later, on 19 December, Drummond ordered a night attack on Fort Niagara, across the river from the destroyed village of Newark. The British attacked with the bayonet and forced the gate of the ancient fortress. Taken by surprise, many Americans surrendered after a short resistance. However, wounded and ill soldiers in the infirmary put up a stout resistance. After awhile, however, seeing that further resistance was futile, many Americans dropped their weapons and offered their surrender. The British refused their offers and bayoneted dozens of Americans. The war was growing increasingly bitter.

Drummond then sent additional attacks along the length of the Niagara River. The British burned Lewiston, Black Rock, and Buffalo and every dwelling in between them. Drummond was unable to keep his native allies under tight control, and several American civilians were scalped and killed during the week-long British attack. Like the citizens of Newark, hundreds of Americans along the Niagara sought refuge from the blustery winter among the townspeople farther inland from the desolated border.

In May 1814, Colonel John Campbell led a force of 800 regulars and militia from Erie, Pennsylvania, across Lake Erie to the village of Dover, Upper Canada. Campbell's men burned 6 mills, 3 distilleries, 30 houses, and about a dozen barns. They then went about shooting livestock, leaving the carcasses to rot. Amelia Harris, a Canadian, recalled the destruction of her family's farm, "what at early noon had been a prosperous homestead, at noon there remained only smouldering ruin."[15] Campbell announced that the destruction of Dover was specifically in retaliation for the burnings along the Niagara the previous winter. Campbell subsequently stood before a court of inquiry, which censured him for his conduct. Mills and distilleries, although private property, had been considered legitimate targets because of their role in feeding enemy troops. However, Americans were desperately trying to limit damage done to civilians who enjoyed protection by the customs and laws of war as practiced by them and by the British. The British were not mollified by the slap on the wrist administered to Campbell, and Sir George Prevost sent out orders to continue acts of retaliation. Ultimately, Prevost's order would result in the burning of Washington.

When British General Gordon Drummond unleashed his natives on the Niagara Frontier in December of 1813, his actions drew unanticipated effects. Although most of the natives who fought for the British on the Niagara were Iroquois, a party of them destroyed a Tuscarora village near Lewiston. The Tuscarora were also Iroquois. The New York Iroquois had declared their neutrality in the war and had repeatedly tried to persuade their tribesmen in Canada to do the same. When the Canadian Iroquois brought destruction upon the Tuscarora, however, political loyalties changed. The Seneca living in their large settlement near Buffalo decided that it was time to join the war as allies of the Americans.

The Americans welcomed the Iroquois. Nearly 600 males and an unknown number of females formed a military unit under the elder Seneca statesman, Red Jacket. When the Americans under Major General Jacob Brown invaded Upper Canada, the Iroquois joined them. On 5 July 1814, at the Battle of Chippewa, Brown sent the Iroquois to clear the woods around the American camp. Moving quickly into the forest, the Iroquois overran small clusters of western Indians, remnants of Tecumseh's followers. Often the natives chose to fight to the end rather than to surrender. Proceeding deeper into the forest, they came into desperate, sharp fights with local militia and some Canadian Iroquois as well. When the fighting in the forest was over, half of the 300 Canadian militia and natives were dead or wounded. Nearly every household along the Niagara River, native and white, had been punished by the war.

Red Jacket's warriors returned to the forest the next day to recover the bodies. They found three wounded natives. Slitting the throats of two western natives, they recognized one Canadian Iroquois. They gave him a canteen of water and left him to die. They then brought dozens of scalps to an American general and asked for payment. Brigadier General Peter B. Porter of Buffalo refused to pay for scalps. Americans had criticized the British for that practice since the Revolution. However, he did pay for 20 prisoners taken by Red Jacket's men. In disgust, the New York Iroquois burned the scalps and threw them into the Niagara.

The War of 1812 in the Central Theater was hard on civilians, soldiers, and natives alike. Whole villages were burned: Newark, Lewiston, Dover, Black Rock, and Buffalo. People on both sides of the border were forced to declare their allegiance and sometimes pay the price of loyalty. Treason abounded, sometimes in the form of illegal trade with the enemy and sometimes in making war against one's countrymen. The scars of the war extended well into the nineteenth century. Canadians are not unaware that their lands were twice invaded by Americans. They justifiably see their determined defense as the birth of the Canadian nation. Events on the Atlantic coast would have a similar result among Americans.

THE ATLANTIC THEATER

Throughout the war, British naval parties raided isolated coastal villages looking for food, salt, and seamen to impress into involuntary service. Joshua Penny of East Hampton remembered the day when he was forcibly taken. "My wife followed us to the door and shrieked; upon which a sergeant of marines struck her with the breech of a gun, the point of which he thrust at her left breast with such violence that she is unwell from that cause to the present time."[16] The most violent raids, however, occurred farther south.

In April 1813, Rear Admiral Sir George Cockburn conducted an extended raid into Chesapeake Bay. His crews burned or captured dozens of American vessels, destroying the livelihood of hundreds of families. The British landed at village after village, taking flour and cattle and destroying foundries and mills. When the militia at Havre de Grace, Maryland, attempted to confront Cockburn's raiders, the British easily drove them off. Clergyman Jared Sparks recalled soldiers and sailors looting homes. "These outrages, to be sure, were not commanded by the officers, but they were not restrained by them."[17] Cockburn then ordered the village burned. The citizens of Havre de Grace fled. James Wilmer remembered that, "the road was filled with the flying distressed women and children, half dressed, in every direction, not knowing where to go or what to do, having been stripped of their all."[18]

The following June, a British raid on Hampton, Virginia, spun out of control. After defeating a small number of American resisters, foreign-born troops under British command began pillaging, murdering, and raping citizens of Hampton. The mortified British officers eventually quelled the mob and returned to their ships. In July, another British squadron proceeded up the Potomac, its mere presence terrorizing the unoffending citizens.

With the abdication of Napoleon in April, 1814, the British government turned its full attention to punishing America for the burning of York and Newark. The Admiralty selected Sir Alexander Cochrane to lead the punitive campaign. Cochrane hated Americans; his brother had died at Yorktown in the Revolution. His orders to Cockburn reflected his sentiments. "Their sea ports laid in ashes and the country invaded will be some sort of retaliation for their savage conduct in Canada, where they have destroyed our towns. . . ."[19] Most of the British naval captains chose to disregard these draconian measures.

Cochrane hoped to enlist the aid of natives and of slaves in his efforts to punish America. He sent agents to negotiate with the Choctaw and Creeks. However, these tribes refused to act unless they were accompanied by a large British force. While the Royal Navy freed hundreds of slaves in raids on the coast and resettled them in the Caribbean, there was no general slave uprising in the South.

In August of 1814, Cockburn and Brigadier General Robert Ross landed at Benedict, Maryland, with a few thousand soldiers. They scattered a large militia force at Bladensburg and marched on Washington. First Lady Dolly Madison, upon learning of the British advance, was determined to save one national heirloom in the White House, the portrait of Washington. Discovering that the frame was screwed to the wall and without proper tools available, Dolly adapted her tactics. "The process was found too tedious for these perilous moments. I have ordered the frame to be broken and the canvass taken out."[20] Upon their arrival at the White House, the British found the table elegantly set and a dinner still warming in the kitchen. After dining in the president's home, the British commanders ordered their men to set fire to that and other federal buildings. Cockburn ordered one newspaper to be burned as well. The *National Register* had repeatedly criticized Cockburn's ways as barbaric and illegal.

Mordecai Booth, a government clerk, recorded as he watched Washington in flames, "a sight so repugnant to my feelings, so dishonourable, so degrading to the American character and at the same time so awful, [it] almost palsied my faculties."[21] Mary Hunter wrote, "You never saw a drawing room so brilliantly lighted as the whole city was that night. Few thought of going to bed—they spent the night gazing on the fires and lamenting the disgrace of the city."[22]

The burning of Washington set off a panic in some quarters. As far away as Georgia, plantation owner Ebenezer Jackson noted the mounting fear of impending attack. "The women and children are flying to the city of Savannah in all directions—among the women some fears are expressed but the men seem generally determined that if the British come it shall not resemble the affair at Washington."[23] The majority of Americans on the coast grimly prepared for the next British move. The citizens of Baltimore, New York, and other coastal cities—rich and poor, Federalist and Republican, black and white—formed in companies to throw up defensive earthworks. These earthworks were extensive. They provided cover for cannon and soldiers alike if the British attacked the cities. Ebenezer Smith Thomas, a resident of Charleston, South Carolina, wrote after the war that, "the British officers that came to Charlestown [sic] immediately after the peace pronounced it the handsomest and best put together piece of field work they ever saw."[24] Local authorities called out the militia who gathered and drilled. In September, it was Baltimore's turn. However, this time the militia fought well. American snipers killed Ross early in the battle. With the land assault stymied, Cockburn tried to press his attack from the sea.

However, the British could not overcome the defiance of Fort McHenry, and they soon withdrew.

The British had better success in the District of Maine. Small forces landed at the villages of Eastport, Castine, and Machias and demanded that the inhabitants pledge their loyalty to the king. Britain planned on retaining this part of the American coast after the war. To their great credit, one quarter of the population refused to switch allegiance. They abandoned their homes and property and moved south rather than give up their American citizenship.

The atrocities in the West and on the Great Lakes reverberated along the Atlantic coast. The Royal Navy prosecuted a destructive, punitive campaign that destroyed lives and livelihoods. The federal government was humiliated by the loss at Bladensburg and the burning of the capital. However, a far worse fate awaited the Creek nation in the Mississippi Territory.

THE SOUTHERN THEATER

The Spanish in Florida, like the British in the Northwest, had been actively encouraging the natives within U.S. territory to resist the Americans. While the Choctaw openly chose to maintain friendly relations with the United States, the Creek nation was split. Many clans had adapted to an agrarian lifestyle peaceably settled within their traditional boundaries. However, Tecumseh's persuasive oratory resonated with a large faction of Creeks. Known as Red Sticks, this group of warriors was determined to throw back white incursions into Creek lands. Under the military leadership of William Weatherford, the mixed-heritage son of a Scottish father and Creek mother, the Red Sticks would become involved in a brutal civil war within the Creek nation as well as a war against the Americans.

As rumors of impending war spread through both native and white communities, a war party of Red Sticks traveled into Spanish Florida to receive weapons. On the return journey, the party was attacked by militia from the white settlements in the Mississippi Territory, and the war began. Peaceful Creeks and white settlers left their farms and withdrew to the relative security of stockaded forts. In August, Weatherford led an attack on the settlement of Fort Mims. Between 300 and 500 Creeks and whites had sought the safety afforded by Fort Mims, but within a few hours of the Red Stick assault, nearly every inhabitant was slain.

The resulting furor among white settlers and Creeks friendly to the Americans was predictable. Multiple columns of Tennessee volunteers under Andrew Jackson, as well as militia and regulars from Georgia and Mississippi, converged on Creek lands. At Creek villages such as Tallushatchee, Talladega, Auttose, and Econochaca, Red Sticks valiantly fought against large contingents of white militia and American-allied Creeks determined to avenge the victims of Fort Mims. Fighting was brutal in the extreme; surrender was neither offered nor accepted. Eventually, the Red Sticks withdrew to their fortified camp at Horseshoe Bend on the Tallapoosa River.

In March 1814, Jackson brought about 4,000 soldiers and Cherokee, Creek, and Choctaw allies to the Red Stick stronghold. There, about 1,000 Red Stick warriors and several hundred women and children prepared to resist. In an extremely hard fought, desperate battle, nearly 900 Red Stick warriors, and some of their women and children, lost their lives. Fewer than 100 whites and native allies were killed. With Jackson's forces now moving unopposed through Creek lands, William Weatherford eventually surrendered. He boldly strode into the American camp, giving himself up and asking for peace. The Creek War was over. Militiamen and natives returned to their farms and tried to take up where they left off. Jackson dictated a treaty that was vindictive in the extreme, resulting in the Creeks giving up half of their territory. As president, Jackson removed the remaining Creeks, as well as his former Cherokee allies, and sent them westward, opening up the land to white settlement.

SUPPORT AND DISSENT

The declaration of war was greeted very much along party lines. Most Republicans were exhilarated that finally something was being done to restore American sovereignty. The War Hawks in particular saw support for the war as proof of one's patriotism. However, even among the majority Republican Party there were several who opposed the war. John Randolph of Roanoke, leader of the "Old Republicans," represented those who espoused small government and traditional republican ideology, which abhorred war except as necessary to defend the nation. Randolph gave a speech in which he responded to a War Hawk congressman:

Sir, if you go to war it will not be for the protection of, or defense of your maritime rights. Gentlemen from the North have been taken up to some high mountain and shown all the kingdoms of the earth; and Canada seems tempting in their sight. Agrarian cupidity, not maritime right, urges the war. Ever since the report of the Committee on Foreign Relations came into the House we have heard but one word—like the whip-poor-will, but with one eternal monotonous tone—Canada! Canada! Canada![25]

Federalists greeted the news of war with dread. Church bells in New England tolled solemnly. Clergymen preached antiwar sermons. Shopkeepers closed their stores. Newspaper publishers lamented the commencement of the war with predictions of failure and loss of life and treasure. Most Federalists opposed the war to varying degrees. Some suggested neutrality, neither opposing war measures nor supporting them. However, most Federalists went into opposition, and antiwar sentiment was strong throughout the struggle. They called the conflict "Mr. Madison's War." The Federalists in Congress published a pamphlet that laid out the reasons for opposing the war, and sympathetic news-paper publishers reprinted the document, giving it national exposure. Republicans condemned the antiwar movement as treasonous. Politics were partisan to a level that would be unthinkable today. Politicians con-ducted themselves uncivilly at best. As an example, after being insulted at a party, Republican Samuel Dexter said of his slanderer, "If he does not retract those words, I'll wring his nose in spite of his popularity."[26] Such exchanges often led to duels between gentlemen, but most citizens were not gentlemen. Republican mobs were active in many cities, damag-ing the property of outspoken Federalists and on occasion attacking their person. The worst partisan activities took place in Baltimore.

Baltimore was growing rapidly and, in 1812, it was the third largest city in the United States with over 40,000 citizens. The population, native-born Americans and European immigrants alike, was predominately Republi-can in sentiment. The editors of a Federalist newspaper, the *Federal Repub-lican,* were fiercely outspoken in their opposition to the war. Even before the declaration of war, the editors were vilified by Republican politicians who reportedly offered a heavy reward to anyone who would tar and feather them. Not to be intimidated, the *Federal Republican* published an antiwar editorial just two days after the declaration of war. The response from the prowar mob was immediate. Crowds of immigrant and native workers gathered in front of the newspaper office and loudly threatened to burn it down. The mayor of Baltimore himself moved among the crowd, pleading for the people to disperse, but to no avail. However, city officials refused to intervene with any strong measures. Night after night, hun-dreds marched through the streets of Baltimore, threatening violence to any who would oppose the war. Some entered a black neighborhood and tore down two homes on the rumor that their owners were sympathetic to the British. Fortunately, city officials called out the militia when crowds threatened to burn down a black church.

For weeks, mobs gathered outside the newspaper office. Federalist supporters, often the sons of the wealthier Baltimore families, rallied to defend the printing press and its owners. Among the defenders was the famed Revolutionary War hero "Light-Horse Harry" Lee, who was in the city arranging for publication of his memoirs. Because of his stature and experience, Lee took charge of the defenses of the building. Federalists argued that they were defending not only their right to oppose the war but also everyone's right to a free and open press. This subtlety was lost on the emotional crowd.

The mob numbered in the thousands and grew particularly ugly one July evening after a particularly inflammatory editorial appeared in the *Federal Republican.* Throwing stones, the rabble broke every window and dared the defenders to fire upon them. Then there was a shot from inside the newspaper building. The crowd scattered in fear but within moments gathered again, this time with weapons of their own. Attacking through the door, a small number of the mob was met by a hail of bullets, which killed one man and wounded several others. The survivors withdrew.

When militia general John Stricker heard the gunfire and learned that the crowd had been fired upon, he reluctantly called out about 30 light dragoons. However, the cavalry commander, Major William Barney, would not intervene until he had signed orders from the civil government. When two city magistrates gave him authority to do so, Major Barney took the defenders under protective custody and moved them a mile down the streets to the jail. This was a timely intervention because the mob had found a cannon and was wheeling it into position to fire upon the newspaper building when the cavalry appeared. As the two dozen Federalists walked toward the jail, members of the mob threw cobblestones at them, wounding two.

The following evening, a huge throng gathered at the jail. Screaming for blood, the self-styled posse assaulted the building. A frightened jailer unlocked the door and the crowd entered the cells and pulled the Federalists outside. The Federalists were repeatedly beaten and stabbed while women called for their deaths and children skipped about playfully. The beatings continued for hours, and the wounded men were thrown into a heap. Burning wax was poured onto their eyes to see if any were feigning death to escape further punishment. The mob killed one man outright. When Federalist citizens approached city officials and militia officers to quell the violence, their pleas were rejected. General Lee, the father of Robert E. Lee, was pummeled so badly that he never recovered. He died in 1818, leaving his family in near poverty.

Federalists were distraught by the refusal of government officials to protect the person and property of those opposed to the war. Where was free speech? The activities of the mobs threatened all social order. Rosalie Stier Calvert, mistress of a Maryland plantation and a Federalist noted, "The same mob only needs a leader like Burr, for example, to come to Washington, throw our poor president out the window, and take the government—nothing could prevent them from doing it."[27] Fortunately from the Federalist perspective, opposition to the war was not quelled for long. Instead, it was the constant backdrop of President Madison's efforts to prosecute the war.

In New England, where Federalist sentiments were strongest, the state governments themselves thwarted the war effort. With wide public support, the governors of Massachusetts, Rhode Island, and Connecticut refused a federal order to call up miltiamen and turn them over to federal service. These governors stated that the U.S. Constitution authorized federal use of state militia only to suppress insurrection or to defend against foreign invasion. Neither of those situations had occurred. The governors would call out the militia to protect the coastal towns and cities from

British raiders, but this hardly helped the federal government's plans to invade Canada. The militia were called away from their homes for weeks at a time but served with their neighbors and remained in their states.

Many citizens of New England were more responsive to their own economic interests than to any patriotic sentiments. The government in Canada had to feed not only the increasing number of British regulars sent there but also the thousands of militia soldiers called up for duty. The demand for food could not be met by Canadian farmers. New England farmers answered the need by selling cattle and grain. Trading with the enemy was treason, and federal authorities acted to stop the smuggling. However, New England farmers stayed off the roads and drove their cattle through the forests toward Canada. At the border, they would allow Canadian traders to lure the beasts across the international border with bushels of corn. By this measure, the Americans avoided violating the letter of the antismuggling laws if not the spirit. Money would exchange hands later. Officials who arrested smugglers could not get convictions in state courts despite convincing evidence. Smugglers grew bolder and assaulted federal customs agents. Throughout the war, New Englanders resisted an unpopular war.

Certainly the activities of some merchants and farmers who traded with the enemy were treasonous. While American justices tended to look the other way, their Canadian compatriots did not. In Upper Canada, many American sympathizers demonstrated their disloyalty by passing information to American officers or in the case of the Canadian Volunteers, by actually bearing arms against their countrymen. British officials settled the score with these traitors in what has been called the "Bloody Assize" of 1814. Bills of high treason were brought against 19 Canadians who had been apprehended carrying arms against the British. Similar charges were made against 50 others who had not yet been brought into custody. A guilty judgment would allow the court to confiscate their property.

Of the 19, 15 were found guilty and 4 acquitted. Seven received the traditional ritual execution for high treason. They were hung until nearly dead, disemboweled, decapitated, and quartered. The others were jailed while awaiting disposition of the legal process. Of these, one escaped jail, four died in prison, and the rest were eventually pardoned on condition that they depart the province and never return. The War of 1812 forced persons to decide where their loyalties lie and sometimes to suffer for their choice.

The most credible threat to national unity came from the Federalists of New England in 1814. While newspapers openly called for a separate peace with England, many merchants and innkeepers refused to pay taxes that would support the war. Many feared that President Madison might introduce a conscription bill to fill the ranks of the army by draft. Calvin Goddard of Connecticut wrote to his senator warning him of the furor that would greet a draft, for "when you propose to violate directly their personal liberty and compel them to fill up the regular army you touch them in a point tenderer than life itself."[28] Citizens met in town meetings to voice their opposition and to prepare demands to their state assemblies for action. The state assemblies, in turn, selected delegates to meet in Hartford, Connecticut, to discuss what steps were appropriate in this continuing crisis. Newspapers likened the convention to the Continental Congress, whose meetings resulted in the Declaration of Independence. The allusion was not lost on the American people who understood full well that New England might take the most drastic of antiwar measures—secession. Delegates met in secret over a three-week period. Supporters of the war and the national government demonstrated peacefully outside the meeting hall. In the end, the moderate delegates had their way. No call for secession emerged. Instead, the Hartford Convention called for seven constitutional amendments such as a single term for the president and no state could provide two presidents in a row. However, these proposed amendments became moot when word arrived that the negotiators in Ghent had prepared a treaty.

THE WAR GRINDS TO A CONCLUSION

In August 1814, American and British negotiating teams met in Ghent, Belgium. For four months, these diplomats wrestled to find a way to end a war that hardly anyone wanted. While the government in London wanted to punish America, perhaps by taking vital territories, the mediocre showing of its army and navy hardly justified such a settlement. In the end, the negotiators agreed that all boundaries would be restored to those of 1812. No word was mentioned about impressments or the rights of neutral shippers. With the war between France and Britain at an end, these issues became moot. On Christmas Eve, 1814, the negotiators signed the treaty ending the fighting and sent it off to the respective governments for approval.

News of the peace treaty was greeted in the cities of America with the peel of church bells and the salute of cannon. The American people were ecstatic. A Brooklyn woman wrote to a friend: "People rushed into the streets in an ecstasy of delight, cannons thundered, bells rang, bonfires were lighted, houses illuminated and flags were unfurled from steeple and dome, strong men wept and grasped each other by the hand."[29] In Boston, Eliza Susan Quincy described a celebratory ball at the state house with some unlikely guests. "Several British officers in full uniform were actively employed in flirting and dancing not in the most graceful manner—but still seemed favorite partners among the young ladies."[30] Unfortunately, news of the peace did not reach New Orleans in time to stop the largest battle of the war.

Andrew Jackson, coming off of his successful campaign against the Red Sticks, moved to defend New Orleans from a rumored British assault.

The U.S. Capitol was only a shell after the British occupation of Washington in August 1814. (Library of Congress)

New Orleans had been under both French and Spanish control before the Louisiana Purchase turned sovereignty over to the United States. The city had a large population of free blacks who made up nearly two-fifths of the city militia. Because of its position on the Mississippi, New Orleans was a major port. Goods from the interior of the continent were trans-loaded from rafts onto ocean-going vessels and dispatched throughout the world. In the warehouses of New Orleans was more than $15 million of cotton, unable to move because of the blockade. Jackson declared martial law in the city, which effectively put the government in his hands. He rallied the militia, and with the aid of Louisiana, Kentucky, and Tennessee volunteers, he prepared defensive works and waited for the British to appear.

The British army at New Orleans consisted largely of well-trained veteran troops under experienced commanders. At dawn on the 8th of January, 1815, thousands of redcoats marched across a flat plain toward the American lines. The Americans had thrown up a breastwork behind a dry ditch running between a swamp and the Mississippi. Standing shoulder to shoulder were French-speaking black and white citizens of the city, Irish immigrants, western frontiersmen, smugglers, Choctaw Indians, U.S. marines, and army regulars. As the fog burned off, American gunners saw their targets and opened a horrendous torrent of cannon and rifle fire. With stunning bravery, the redcoats drew closer, soldiers closing the holes left by fallen comrades. But bravery was insufficient to save the day in the face of musketry and cannon fire. Hundreds of British, including three of the four generals, were killed or wounded in a matter of minutes. Unable to break the American lines, the remnants of a proud British army sailed away. New Orleans was saved and Andrew Jackson achieved heroic stature among the American public.

The people of New Orleans threw a celebration of the victory that saved their city. The troops returned to the city from the battlefield in triumph. Young students from Madame Floriant's finishing school threw flower petals along the path in front of Jackson. Other young women, dressed in white with silver stars on their foreheads, held flags representing every state and territory of the union. Two of Madame Floriant's students crowned Jackson with laurels. The soldiers and citizens entered St. Louis Cathedral where the choir sang a solemn *Te Deum* in thanksgiving. Throughout America, public excitement over the incomparable American victory at New Orleans nearly surpassed that of the announcement of the peace treaty a few weeks earlier. Otis Ammidon, a Philadelphia merchant, wrote to a friend describing the frenzied celebration. "The joy was fully expressed by the laughing, shaking of hands and with congratulations of the passing multitude . . . Strangers in the street did not hesitate to wish each other joy!"[31]

AMERICA IN 1815

With the end of the war, American and Canadian soldiers and militia returned to their homes, farms, and trades. Natives also returned to homes, or finding their villages destroyed, headed west to establish new communities. Notions of native tribes working in unison died with Tecumseh's Confederacy. Those Canadians who had sought refuge in America stayed there. Return to Canada meant imprisonment or worse. War transforms its participants; life is never the same. For many, war was the adventure of their lives. Veterans everywhere gained a level of stature that served them well in their communities. Respected as heroes, those who sought office were seldom disappointed. The thousands who failed to return home left gaping holes in their families and communities.

The war in Europe ended, and the blockade ended with it. American shippers retook to the seas, carrying commodities of all sorts to hungry European ports. The economy experienced a welcomed resurgence. On the political side, the Federalist Party was so thoroughly discredited for its opposition to the war that it faded from the political scene entirely within just a few years.

Perhaps the most significant outcome of the war in America was a renewal of nationalism. While most persons considered themselves as citizens of their state first, there was a growing notion of unity. All Americans took justifiable pride in the victories at Chippawa, New Orleans, and on the waters of Lake Erie and the Atlantic Ocean. The defense of Fort

McHenry prompted Francis Scott Key to compose a poem that was soon put to music. The *Star Spangled Banner* became so popular that Congress declared it the national anthem. America, it was recounted, had fought and won a second war of independence. Self-confidently, America strode onto the world stage and took its place among sovereign nations.

NOTES

1. Speech by Henry Clay, 10 February 1810, in *Annals of Congress,* 12th Congress, 1st session, 50–51.

2. *Gazette and Publick Ledger,* 24 June 1807, from John C. Emmerson's *The Chesapeake Affair of 1807* (Portsmouth, Virginia: n.p., 1954).

3. National Archives, Records Group 45, M124, Miscellaneous Letters received by the Secretary of the Navy, roll 16.

4. Edward L. Morse, ed., *Samuel F.B. Morse, His Letters and Journals,* 2 Vols. (Boston: Houghton, Mifflin, 1914), Vol. 1, 87.

5. The War Hawks were members pf an aggressive faction in Congress committed to redressing grievances against Britain. Because they regarded diplomacy as fruitless, they would eagerly resort to force to defend American rights and honor.

6. Mary M. Crawford, ed., "Mrs. Lydia Bacon's Journal, 1811–1812," *Indiana Magazine of History* 41 (March 1945): 64.

7. "Letters of Hubbard Taylor to President James Madison," *Register of the Kentucky Historical Society* 36 (July 1938): 229.

8. Captain George Howard to Sarah Howard, June 8, 1814. From the George Howard Papers, Connecticut Historical Society.

9. Paul Jennings, *A Colored Man's Reminiscences of James Madison* (Brooklyn: G. C. Beadle, 1865), 17.

10. Proclamation by Brigadier General William Hull made at Detroit, 13 July 1812.

11. Mentor L. Williams, ed., "John Kinzie's Narrative of the Fort Dearborn Massacre," *Illinois State Historical Society Journal* 48 (Winter 1953): 349.

12. Electra M. Sheldon, *The Early History of Michigan From the First Settlement to 1815* (New York: A. S. Barnes, 1856), 401.

13. William Gurley, *Memoirs of Reverend William Gurley* (Cincinnati: Methodist Book Concern, 1850), 234.

14. Major Lovett to Joseph Alexander, 6 October 1812. Taken from Catherine V. R. Bonney, *A Legacy of Historical Gleanings* (Albany, NY: J. Munsell, 1875), 242.

15. James J. Talman, ed., *Loyalist Narratives from Upper Canada* (Toronto: Champlain Society, 1946), 48.

16. Joshua Penny, *Life and Adventures of Joshua Penny, A Native of South Old, Long Island, Suffolk County, New York, Who Was Impressed into British Service* (Brooklyn: Alden Spooner, 1815), 48.

17. Jared Sparks, "Conflagration of Havre de Grace," *North American Review* 5 (July 1817), 162.

18. James Jones Wilmer, *A Narrative Respecting the Conduct of the British From Their First Landing at Spetsutia Island Till Their Progress to Havre de Grace* (Baltimore: P. Mauro, 1813), 8.

19. Cochrane to Cockburn, 24 April 1814 as quoted in James A. Pack, *The Man Who Burned the White House: Admiral Sir George Cockburn, 1772–1853* (Annapolis: Naval Institute Press, 1987), 166–67.

20. Dorothy T. Madison, ed., "At A Perilous Moment Dolley Madison Writes to Her Sister," *Madison Quarterly* 4 (January 1944): 28.

21. Ray W. Irwin, ed., "The Capture of Washington in 1814 as Described by Mordecai Booth," *Americana* 28 (January 1934): 19.

22. "The Burning of Washington," *New York Historical Society Bulletin* 8 (October 1925): 82.

23. Letter of Georgian plantation owner Ebenezer Jackson found in "Letters of the War of 1812," *Magazine of History* 17 (October–November 1913): 169.

24. Ebenezer Smith Thomas, *Reminiscences of the Last Sixty Years*, 2 vols. (Hartford, CT: Case, Tiffany, Burnham, 1840), Vol. 2, 64.

25. Speech by John Randolph, 16 December 1811, in *Annals of Congress*, 12th Congress, 1st session, 533.

26. Lucius M. Sargent, *Reminiscences of Samuel Dexter* (Boston: H. W. Dutton, 1857), 90.

27. Margaret L. Callcott, *Mistress of Riversdale: The Plantation Letters of Rosalie Stier Calvert, 1795–1821* (Baltimore: Johns Hopkins University Press, 1991), 252.

28. Calvin Goddard to David Daggett found in William E. Buckley, ed., "Letters of Connecticut Federalists," *New England Quarterly* 3 (April 1930): 321.

29. Anonymous letter recorded in Margaret A. Cooper's *Some Old Letters & Bits of History* (New York: Privately printed, 1901), 54.

30. Letter by Eliza Susan Quincy recorded in M.M. Howe, ed., *The Articulate Sisters: Passages from the Journals and Letters of the Daughters of President Josiah Quincy of Harvard University* (Cambridge: Harvard University Press, 1946), 15.

31. Otis Ammidon to Jonathan Russell, 20 February 1815, recorded in "Otis Ammidon to Jonathan Russell," *Massachusetts Historical Society Proceedings* 54 (November 1920): 78.

FURTHER READING

Benn, Carl. *The Iroquois in the War of 1812*. Toronto: University of Toronto Press, 1998. Benn explores the diplomatic, cultural, and military history of the Iroquois in their major participation in the war, a level of activity that has been, up to now, minimized by scholars. The settlements of the Six Nations straddled the border, and individuals fought on both sides and, on occasion, against one another.

Borneman, Walter R. *1812: The War that Forged a Nation*. New York: HarperCollins, 2004. A popular work that focuses on causes and results yet also hits the high points of operations. Eminently readable.

Fredricksen, John C. *War of 1812 Eyewitness Accounts: An Annotated Bibliography.* Westport, CT: Greenwood Press, 1997. Fredricksen has collected more than 800 published primary narratives representing diverse perspectives: military members, politicians, women, Native Americans, merchants, and travelers. This is an essential reference work for graduate students of the period.

Gribbin, William. *The Churches Militant: The War of 1812 and American Religion.* New Haven: Yale University Press, 1973. In this classic work, Gribbin reviews the conflicts within American Christianity and attributes the growing multiplicity of church communities to the interrelationship of Protestantism and emerging American democracy: the preeminent religious and secular "faiths."

Hickey, Donald R. *The War of 1812: A Forgotten Conflict.* Urbana and Chicago: University of Illinois Press, 1989. Hickey's focus is on the political, diplomatic, and economic aspects of the war and as such delves into the effects of the war on the civilian communities.

Mahon, John K. *The War of 1812.* Gainesville: University Presses of Florida, 1972. While somewhat dated, Mahon's treatment of the causes and conduct of the war are comprehensive and well documented. Mahon was one of the first scholars to treat the Creek War as an integral part of the wider conflict.

Morison, Samuel Elliot, Frederick Merk, and Frank Burt Freidel. *Dissent in Three American Wars.* Cambridge: Harvard University Press, 1970. Morison writes the chapter on the War of 1812. He opines, with some justification, that this war was even more unpopular than the Vietnam conflict.

Skeen, C. Edward. *Citizen Soldiers in the War of 1812.* Lexington: The University Press of Kentucky, 1999. Skeen describes the experiences of the militia in camp and in battle. He also explores the murky relationship between state and federal governments in the raising, training, and use of these amateur soldiers.

Wilentz, Sean R. *Chants Democratic: New York City and the Rise of the American Working Class, 1788–1850.* New York: Oxford University Press, 1984. Wilentz investigates the dramatic social changes that accompanied accelerating industrialization during the first half of the nineteenth century. As the workshop gave way to the factory, the artisan system inexorably gave way to class divisions between owners and workers.

FOUR

The American Home Front in the Mexican War

Gregory Hospodor

On April 24, 1846, tension mixed with excitement as the soldiers of General Zachary Taylor's "Army of Occupation" performed their duties at camps located across the Rio Grande from Matamoros. Since their arrival in late March, relations with the Mexicans had steadily deteriorated. Now word spread of a polite note from General Mariano Arista, the red-whiskered future president of Mexico, that announced his intention to initiate military operations against the Americans. Although some officers discounted the significance of the message—it was the fourth such notification they had received since arriving on the Rio Grande—all signs pointed to war. Accordingly, General Taylor ordered a cavalry patrol commanded by Captain Seth Thornton to sweep the area west of the American camps and north of the Rio Grande for Mexican forces. On April 25, Thornton, who compensated for his small physical stature with reckless courage, led his 63-man patrol into an ambush. Seeking shelter from a cloudburst, Thornton's men rode toward a group of buildings at Rancho de Carricitos. Suddenly, 1,600 Mexican soldiers hidden in the surrounding chaparral opened fire. In the ensuing fight, 11 Americans died and most of the others were captured, including Thornton. The next day, General Taylor, who would soon become famous for, among other things, his plain speech and even plainer dress, wrote to his superiors that hostilities had commenced. Indeed they had. Within 14 days, major battles at Palo Alto and Resaca de la Palma turned the landscape near Matamoros red. The Mexican-American War had begun.

In the weeks following Thornton's ambush, news of the fighting raced across the nation and generated an ebullient feeling of belligerence almost everywhere it passed. In early May, an Alabama woman described the feeling in Mobile, stating, "We are in the midst of great excitement. The War Fever is raging with vast fury. . . . I have never seen such efforts to animate the slumbering 'War Dogs.'"[1] Likewise, a citizen of New Orleans observed that every steamship brought crowds of volunteers, which led him to believe that the "popular current of the will of the masses of the mighty valley of the Mississippi will sweep everything along . . . until the national honor is vindicated."[2] Lew Wallace, a 19-year-old law student and the future author of *Ben Hur,* left his studies to march through the streets of Indianapolis while soliciting volunteers to the beat of a hired drummer. In Philadelphia, New York, Baltimore, and countless other communities throughout the country, citizens staged prowar rallies. Herman Melville aptly summed up the tenor of the times: "A military ardor pervades all ranks. . . . Nothing is talked of but the 'Halls of Montezumas'"[3] Many believed that the fighting on the Rio Grande forebode momentous events that would inscribe themselves in gloriously large letters upon the history of the nation.

Today, the Mexican War has been largely forgotten in the United States. There are several reasons for this. The war between Mexico and the United States was short (28 months), small (about 100,000 Americans served out of a population of roughly 21 million), and one-sided (the Americans won every major battle, although each was hard-fought). The American Civil War quickly overshadowed the earlier clash of arms. The victors of that titanic struggle comfortably assessed the Mexican War as caused by southerners intent on gaining new land for slavery. Modern historians remain preoccupied with the Civil War; they tend to regard the Mexican conflict as an anecdote to be disposed of quickly in order to proceed on to more substantial topics. Furthermore, many modern academics consider war an aberration, an irrational exercise of violence, which almost always can be avoided by reasoned diplomacy. Thus, they believe that little time need be spent examining the Mexican War beyond appraising how it could have been avoided, recounting the successes and failures of those who opposed it, and labeling it all a big mistake. The Vietnam War generation in particular saw far too many similarities to that divisive conflict to bear scrutiny comfortably. Today, the outcome, the acquisition of more than 500,000 square miles of Mexican territory, does not rest well upon the conscience of a nation that rejects the idea of territorial imperialism. Consequently, few substantial examinations of the war outside of its military aspects exist. Rarely does an event in American history count a study published in 1919, Justin H. Smith's *The War with Mexico,* as essential reading. The Mexican-American War simply does not fit well with the image that modern Americans like to have of the United States and, thus, is best left to slumber in the blissful peace of historical anonymity.

However, to ignore the Mexican War is a mistake. The war is worthy of investigation if only because contemporary Americans perceived it as a seminal event, one that would greatly influence the future of the Republic. Why Americans believed so says something important about them, the war, and the nation itself. Unfortunately, hindsight, the historian's chief asset as well as primary liability, has often obscured the so-called real Mexican War. It is all too easy to look at the many examples of conflict on the home front and ascribe heightened significance to them because we know what happened in 1861. During the 1840s, however, few Americans realistically considered the possibility that the nation could tear itself apart. For most, the war was a nationalist exercise, the fulfillment of America's "Manifest Destiny" and an affirmation of the military, moral, and political strength of the Republic. Therein rests the ironic twist of the Mexican War—the war sublimated many tensions in American society yet engendered sectional stresses that led to civil war. How Americans experienced and participated in the war also provides a revealing snapshot of mid-19th century society and thought. All wars act as mirrors; participation in them changes the rhythms of everyday life and causes consideration of things beyond normal parochial concerns. War demands the sacrifice of blood and treasure. Consequently, wars, especially those involving countries where public opinion matters, bring political questions into sharp focus—What do we stand for? What are the duties of a citizen? The Mexican War revealed that there was a small but important and growing difference in the United States over just such questions. At the same time, the war tested society in other ways. Most Americans experienced the war vicariously through letters from loved ones and communal events or, more frequently, through newspapers and other printed media, which emphasized a romantic and heroic but largely unrealistic impression of the battlefield. It is to the vicarious war experience that we turn next.

THE VICARIOUS WAR

When war came during the spring of 1846, the United States welcomed it. It is fair to say that the young Republic, itself a child of armed struggle, carried on a tempestuous love affair with war. Nothing dissuaded the nation's affection. Memories of the American Revolution, the War of 1812, innumerable Native American campaigns, and the Texas Revolution remained fresh. But the collective memory was selective; the nation chose to remember only heroic deeds, noble deaths, and victory rather than cowardice, rotting corpses, and defeat. The monumental carnage of the Civil War rested unimagined in the future, and even after 620,000 deaths it, too, engendered a popular romantic mythology, especially in the South. Romantic notions of war as the highest test of individual and national character held sway. There were certainly those who knew the awful reality of war, but veterans mostly remained silent, for they had no willing audience.

At first glance, Americans' warlike disposition appears counterintuitive. After all, the Republic was loath to maintain a large standing army or navy and had steadfastly resisted being drawn into the Napoleonic wars. However, it also elevated military men to the presidency and other less grand public offices, and militia service, which resembled playing at soldier more than anything else, was near universal in many parts of the country. Americans were proud of their military accomplishments, particularly the Revolution. Although the most famous revolutionary heroes passed away long before the Mexican War, popular histories and patriotic celebrations kept the memory of the founding age of the Republic alive and promoted nationalism. Through textbooks, the heroes of the Revolution, especially an idealized image of George Washington, served as moral exemplars for the nation's children and taught them how to read, to write, and to cipher. The emphasis on the heroic heritage of the nation caused citizens to personalize their history, to feel an intimate connection with the heroes of their collective past. This connection was far from passive. The deeds and virtues of the Founding generation reminded citizens that they had a precious legacy to maintain. As a contemporary magazine explained, a true patriot "views the deeds of 'the fathers' as examples for imitation, as well as subjects for exaltation."[4] The heroes of the past called men to pursue battlefield glory in their country's cause and the rest of the population to praise and support them as they did so.

Americans also learned about war and heroes from the books they read. Their knowledge was, then, vicarious or second-hand. It would remain so throughout the Mexican War. Americans were confident, however, that they *knew* what war entailed because they had read their military history. Accounts of Napoleon's campaigns were only the most popular examples of a field that was one of the great cash cows for the booksellers of the 1830s and 1840s. Nonmilitary history, such as Thomas Carlyle's *On Heroes, Hero-Worship, and the Heroic in History,* which took the nation by storm in the early 1840s, reinforced a national obsession with the heroic. From Sir Walter Scott's *Ivanhoe* to James Fenimore Cooper's *Leatherstocking Tales,* heroes lived in the most widely read literature of the age. Contemporary art, poetry, and music only augmented the heroic image of war found in books. None of their reading deterred the public from a belief that war was really about the heroic rather than about the horrific, too.

All this served to create an effervescent bellicosity, or war spirit, and a related expectation that the Mexican War would add a rich harvest of heroes to the national Pantheon. Caught up in the excitement, many accepted that this would be a heroic war and left it at that. Others looked deeper. The stock of living heroes, they knew, was diminishing; some veterans of the founding struggle still lived and were treated like living talismans of republican virtue, but they were so rare that newspapers around the nation thought it worthy to reprint the obituaries of those who passed away. The country obviously needed new heroes, but not just to replace the old. The United States of 1846 was different from that of the revolutionaries in at least a thousand ways, and some harbored suspicions that the immense prosperity and growth of the intervening years caused the nation to stray from the republican faith of the Founding Fathers. A new crop of heroes would allay these fears by proving that American manhood continued to possess the right stuff and that the spirit of 1776 was alive and well, and avarice and self-absorption had not triumphed over concern for the common good. Although it worried some, American growth and prosperity gave many others cause for boundless optimism and led to the development of a "go a-head" spirit, as it was called at the time. Consequently, the coming of the Mexican War appeared to reveal new and pleasant possibilities for the Republic and its citizens.

If Americans were confident that the war would produce heroes, they were also sure that a Mexican surrender would soon occur. In early 1846, a Cincinnati periodical asserted that the "Mexicans will be led by this war to think of their weakness and inferiority."[5] Likewise, a South Carolina newspaper asked, "As for the result of a war with imbecile Mexico, who for a moment would fear it?"[6] The question, of course, was rhetorical, and the arrogant certainty of mastery expressed in it was common. "Manifest Destiny," a sense of romantic nationalism that combined near equal measures of idealism and racism, engendered such a belief. The term, coined by New York newspaperman John L. O'Sullivan in 1845, described the generally held opinion that it was the providential destiny of Anglo-Saxon America to spread its people and republican institutions to the Pacific and perhaps farther. The "area of freedom" would thus be expanded. Others echoed O'Sullivan's notions. In July 1846, Walt Whitman, editor of the Brooklyn *Daily Eagle,* wrote, "[W]hat has miserable, inefficient Mexico . . . to do with the great mission of peopling the new world with a noble race? Be it ours, to achieve that mission!"[7] Americans had no doubt that the Republic represented the pinnacle of human government and that they were God's chosen people. On the other hand, Mexico, which had seen only one president serve out a complete term and experienced a leadership change on average every 15 months between 1821 and 1848, was a republic in name only. The reason was clear, or so many believed; Mexicans were an inferior mongrel mix of Spanish and Indian blood and thus unsuited to republican government. The popular pseudoscience of phrenology, the study of the shape of the skull as an indicator of character and ability, supported this conclusion and also challenged the notion that all humans were created equal. Such a degraded people, Americans claimed, could never stand against an aroused nation descended from superior Anglo-Saxon blood. Although some viewed Manifest Destiny as a kind of republican evangelicalism, many others, confident of their racial superiority, thought that the Mexican people were worthy only of either replacement by Anglo-Saxons, which was similar to the attitude toward Native Americans, or domination, which was similar to the attitude toward African Americans.

Armed with these preconceptions, the United States confronted the reality of prosecuting its first foreign war. Considerably less than one percent of the population would serve in the military or accompany the army into Mexico as civilian support personnel or camp followers. The other roughly 21 million—the "home front"—experienced the nation's first foreign war second-hand. The numbers belie the fact that the vicarious war was felt with more immediacy than any other in the young Republic's history.

Americans possessed a voracious appetite for news from the battlefront and other war-related material. Fortunately, the population was more literate than ever before (some contend more even than today) because words, either hand-written or printed, constituted the only truly effective means of long-range communication for the vast majority of citizens. Those with loved ones or acquaintances in Mexico cherished letters above all else.

The public was eager for news about the fighting in Mexico. (Library of Congress)

These "private" letters circulated among a wider circle of people than is common today. But for most Americans, their hunger for tidings of what was happening in Mexico could only be sated by the printed word.

The nation was well equipped to meet the demand for reports on the war. The printed word was cheap and widely available. Serried ranks of new steam-powered cylinder printing presses and other printing equipment stood ready to unleash sustained volleys of penny newspapers, cheap paperbacks, and traditionally bound books upon a willing public.

Newspapers were ubiquitous in the 1840s. They were also cheap, because more efficient methods of mass production lowered prices for city papers with high circulation, and because the small-town editors of newspapers with low circulation and old equipment simply copied interesting stories from wherever they found them, which saved labor costs. Large papers only passed a portion of their cost savings on to the consumer; many devoted some of the remainder to hiring what amounted to a small legion of war correspondents. The big papers, especially those in New York City, committed even more money to creating an express delivery service for the reports from their embedded staff. Several papers quickly pooled resources to create a 2,000-mile express route composed of a combination of pony express riders, steamships, railroads, and telegraph offices. For newspapers large and small, the Mexican War meant big business.

New printing technology also placed books within the reach of almost anyone. For example, the first biography of Zachary Taylor, C. Frank Powell's *Life of Major General Zachary Taylor,* sold for only 25 cents, which compares well with the approximately 3-cent cost of a daily newspaper and 6-cent cost of a weekly. Later books on war-related topics would cost as little as 12.5 cents. If books were cheap, they were also widely available. Publishers rushed to solicit authors and soon had a wide selection of war books on offer. Nationwide distribution took place through well-developed marketing networks. Almost every town had at least one part-time bookseller, who got most of his books from the agents of large northern publishing houses. These booksellers did not just cater to town dwellers; they carried on a brisk mail-order business with rural farmers as well. The big publishers were often willing to sell their products to booksellers on consignment, which boosted sales. In addition, the practice of mailing free copies to newspaper editors ensured both that the reading public would be aware of the book and, in most cases, that the work received a favorable review.

Soon after the start of the war, the nation's publishing industry commenced bombarding the American public with information, and the public manifested little desire for the shelling to cease. The ready availability of cheap printed material, however, did not mean that Americans on the home front received an accurate picture of what was going on in Mexico. To be fair, some, such as the New Orleans *Picayune*'s war correspondent, George Wilkins Kendall, filed mainly accurate reports, but a commitment to accuracy remained largely a matter of personal preference. Even Kendall, who, among other things, compiled precise casualty lists after battles, was not immune to editing his reports creatively. He invented Zachary Taylor's famous order at the Battle of Buena Vista, "A little more grape, Captain Bragg." Taylor's order certainly contained more earthy words, but Kendall, knowing his audience's tastes, altered Old Rough and Ready's words for popular consumption. Kendall's white lie is understandable and perhaps forgivable, but more egregious examples of intentional misrepresentations abound. For example, C. Frank Powell's aforementioned biography of Zachary Taylor provided its readers with an entirely inaccurate picture of the hero as a debonair young general immaculately clad in a full-dress uniform with telescope and sword—the real Taylor was old, corpulent, not prone to sword-waving, and habitually dressed in a plain blue shirt, dirty white pants, and a straw hat.

Authors also often danced around the horrors of the battlefield. The story of Major Samuel Ringgold, the founder of the army's famous flying artillery batteries and one of the first heroes of the war, is particularly instructive. While directing his unit in advance of the main American line at the Battle of Palo Alto, a Mexican cannonball mangled Ringgold's legs as it passed through both his body and his horse. The *Niles' Register*, a paper with national distribution, reported that Ringgold, who survived his ghastly wounds for 60 hours, conducted himself heroically the whole time: "During the night he gave many incidents of the battle and spoke with much pride of the execution of his shot. . . . He continued to grow worse until one o'clock, when he expired."[8] Although it described Ringgold's wounds in detail, the *Register* focused on what those at home most wanted to hear, that the hero died well. Many engravers made Ringgold's heroic image even more palatable by publishing depictions of the Major manfully trying to stand up after what looks like a riding accident in which he suffered minor injuries. The engravers, of course, knew that a realistic picture would never be hung in the family sitting room. Private letters, too, reflected an aversion to describing the horrors of war in detail. Soldiers occasionally wrote home of the work of the surgeon's saw and of stacked bodies. Most realized, however, that the folks back home could not possibly understand the reality of war and that they probably did not want to know. Thus we find Mississippian Joseph Davis Howell concentrating on the heroic in a letter home after the Battle of Monterrey, "there was no room for a man in our regiment to distinguish himself every man fought well and bravely, . . . like incarnate devils."[9] Publishers, editors, and soldiers participated in what amounted to a conspiracy of heroism during the Mexican War. The effect on the home front was predictable; preconceptions of war as romantically heroic were reinforced.

Printed sources and letters were not the only medium through which the heroic character of the war with Mexico was transmitted. Ritual occasions, such as Fourth of July celebrations and mass events honoring volunteers, victories, and veterans of the Mexican War, also defined what the war meant and were the most common way for those on the home front to participate in the war effort. Early war celebrations centered on those who volunteered to serve. On December 5, 1846, in an oft-repeated scene, a young woman presented a handmade banner to the "Old 96 Boys" from Edgefield, South Carolina, while the Star Spangled Banner played in the background. After the presentation, the company's captain swore that his unit would conquer or perish beneath it. Three days later, Edgefield threw the Old 96ers a lavish farewell dinner where both words of praise and liquor freely flowed. The company then stumbled out of town and off to war escorted by a cavalry honor guard of local militia. At Fourth of July celebrations, revelers made an unmistakable connection between the Revolutionary heritage of the Republic and the Mexican War. Across the nation, citizens offered toasts in honor of the Father of the Republic, the Declaration of Independence, and the soldiers of the Mexican War. Frequently, participants made explicit identifications between the Mexican War and the Revolution. At a celebration in Dallas, North Carolina, R. G. McLean proposed this toast, "Gen. Z. Taylor—Actuated and animated by the same spirit that did our fathers in '76."[10] Although specifying Zachary Taylor, McLean's toast reflects the common belief that the soldiers in Mexico were republican heroes. News of victories also threw many into a frenzy of patriotic ecstasy. The rhythm of nineteenth-century military operations, distinguished by a gradual build up to a battle of usually short duration, was matched at home by a cycle of rising tension and jubilant release.

The Battle of Buena Vista, which began on Washington's Birthday in 1847, exceeded all others in the depth and breadth of the public response. Before the battle, some newspapers noted the progress of Santa Anna's march north with dread. Zachary Taylor's little army, stripped of most of its regulars and facing four to one odds, won the transcendent victory of the Mexican War. Effusive praise poured forth from governing bodies, but paled in comparison to public celebration of the victory. Citizens across the country built bonfires, participated in parades, and held public meetings. In St. Martinville, Louisiana, Catholic parishioners staged a Sunday parade to their church accompanied by martial music. They chanted the *Te Deum* in a sanctuary draped with banners inscribed in gold with the names of Buena Vista and other battles. As the ceremony progressed within, artillery fired salutes outside. In Raleigh, North Carolina, bells rang at sunrise, cannons fired a 100-gun salute, citizens paraded, and the city was illuminated in honor of the victory. To most, the victory confirmed that God was indeed on America's side, that 1 sturdy volunteer could lick 10 Mexicans, and that the spirit of '76 was alive and well.

The soldiers' return also engendered a commemorative impulse. The typical celebration included a parade, music by a local band, speeches, toasts, presentation of tokens of the community's esteem, and a picnic.

Homecoming fetes could be very elaborate affairs. In Memphis, an immense amount of planning went into providing enough hot food for a quarter mile of tables lined up end to end. In New Orleans, Zachary Taylor's arrival occasioned the construction of a 60-foot tall by 40-foot wide triumphal arch in what is now Jackson Square. Its construction was but a prelude to the grand festivities planned to honor the hero's return home, which included, among other things, firework displays, a 50-unit parade, and a religious ceremony at the Saint Louis Cathedral. New Orleans also witnessed perhaps the ultimate example of delirious patriotic civic-mindedness as one citizen offered to ignite his fine home in order to make "a splendid bonfire" in homage to the returning paladin.[11] Not every hero, of course, returned home alive. Most of the dead were buried in Mexico, but a few, officers mainly, were sent home. The reception for the bodies of Colonel Butler and Lt. Colonel Dickinson of South Carolina's Palmetto Regiment in 1848 gives some idea of the spirit of these affairs. As minute guns fired and bells tolled, a military honor guard escorted the lead caskets and led a half-mile long procession through Columbia to the State House. Once there, William C. Preston, president of South Carolina College and former U.S. Senator, delivered a eulogy that extolled the heroic virtues and deeds of the men and, by all accounts, dimmed every eye with tears. Through public events such as these, the home front affirmed, in one way or another, its preconceptions of war.

The *real* Mexican War was tragic and ironic beyond description. Very few, however, tried to communicate even a semblance of the reality of the war to the folks back home. What the home front learned instead was what they already *knew* was true—that American soldiers were heroic republicans cast in the mold of their forefathers, that war was a romantic adventure, and that the nation's Manifest Destiny would be realized. The real war remained inaccessible even after the soldiers returned home. Mexican War veterans did little to alter the prevailing conception of the conflict; veterans knew that those who stayed home could never comprehend *their* war and, indeed, did not really want to understand it. As such, the Mexican War did not lead to public maturity where the general question of warfare was concerned; rather, the vicarious war perpetuated ideas that prepared a generation to march blithely off to the battlefield in 1861. Indeed, so prevalent was the nation's obsession with military heroes and the heroic that a Presbyterian minister worried that Americans' predilection for "this modern apotheosis of individuals" might provoke God's wrath, because it attributed to the flesh that which only Providence could bestow.[12] Others worried that the proliferation of heroes might diminish the meaning of the word. A pessimist lamented in 1848 that "to be a hero is a very common affair—indeed, nothing but the sublimation of simple rowdyism" and consequently "our galaxy of great men is obscured."[13] But most Americans were optimistic about the bumper crop of heroes that the war with Mexico produced. Heroes, it seemed, were just what the nation needed.

Men, Women, and the War

Armed with patriotic fervor and naive notions about the heroic, romantic nature of war, the men and women of the Republic quickly responded to the news of the clash of arms on the Rio Grande. For most, antebellum beliefs about gender differences dictated the public roles that each would play; men would fight the war and women would support them as they did. One might assume, then, that a dichotomy—active males and passive females—existed regarding each sex's response to the Mexican War. Such was not the case. Women played an essential part in the war effort. In their own way, they helped to prosecute the war to victorious conclusion and contributed to the general popularity of the conflict. Of course, American men confronted one decision from which women were excluded, the choice of whether or not to volunteer.

The United States welcomed war with Mexico, but it was woefully unprepared to wage it. The strength of the U.S. Army in 1846 was approximately 5,500 men, which was roughly one-third of the size of Mexico's professional force. To rectify the deficiency in manpower, Congress authorized President James K. Polk to enlist 50,000 volunteers on May 13, 1846. Polk soon summoned 20,000 men from southwestern and western states for immediate service. The balance, from the east coast mainly, was to be organized as reserves. From the start it was clear that volunteers, those who willingly enlisted in either regular or volunteer units, would play a large part in war.

The Republic's men rushed to answer the call to the flag. It is difficult to capture the intensity of the *rage militare* that gripped the country during the early months of the war, but the volunteer mania gives some idea of its scope. In Virginia, one company, organized by a Richmond Whig, volunteered even before the president issued a requisition for troops to Governor William Smith. Baltimore met its quota in 36 hours. In Tennessee, 10 times the number required tried to enlist; in Kentucky, 4 times the number required; in Illinois and North Carolina, at least 3 times the number required. So many companies applied for selection to the First Regiment of Mississippi Volunteers that late arrivals had to be turned away, which caused some disconsolate souls to hang Governor Albert Gallatin Brown in effigy in front of the Governor's Mansion in Jackson. Brown's response is instructive; he desperately, if unsuccessfully, solicited Secretary of War William Marcy for a greater allotment. Other governors resorted to lotteries in an effort to avoid the wrath of angry, disappointed volunteers. Many men did not wait to be called by their respective state governments and either went to New Orleans to enlist individually or formed complete companies that enrolled in volunteer regiments from other states. To be fair, not every community responded with equal fervor, especially those in areas where the call was for service in the reserves. Some made no effort at all. But it should be remembered that even Massachusetts, a hotbed of opposition to the war, met its quota within a month. To many, it seemed that Congress was the only thing limiting the size of the force sent to chastise Mexico. The patriotic frenzy of mid-1846 eventually subsided, but later recruiting efforts always met their quotas, although with more difficulty than before.

All told, 100,454 soldiers served during the Mexican War (26,922 with the regular army and 73,532 with volunteer units). Few ever saw combat in Mexico; some were mustered out almost as soon as they enlisted. The vast majority was native-born. For our purposes, the volunteer phenomenon is significant, because enlistment constituted the most substantial way for men to participate in the Mexican War. The motivations of those who signed up, as well as the perceptions of the volunteers by those who stayed home, also reveal much about antebellum culture, especially those aspects that touched on war.

Accounting for roughly 100,000 men's motives for joining up is problematic at best. But one thing seems clear, the patriotic fervor engendered by the war encouraged enlistment, which was the ultimate expression of love of country. History required the current generation of men to prove itself worthy of its republican forefathers. In a speech to returning volunteers in 1847, Francis Marion Aldridge expounded on this link,

It was by deeds of gallantry that our liberty was won, it must be by deeds of gallantry and self sacrifice that our liberty shall be maintained—Hence he who falls in his Country's cause becomes so identified with that liberty that they seem to the closest inspection to be one and the same—The one must live or die with the other— . . . Wrapped in the silvery garments of fame they [the honored dead] are martialed [*sic*] by Washington.[14]

Volunteer Chatham Roberdeau Wheat agreed. He wrote to a friend that after they had died in battle "and when our comrades on earth should prove triumphant—we would, with Washington & the heroes that have gone before, hang out our banners from the battlements of Heaven."[15] An Alabama woman also perceived that the spirit of the Founding generation was alive in the volunteers: "There is a company now here from Montgomery who are so eager for the fight that they have sent a messenger to Gen. Gaines, to say they will go to war without pay, and are willing to be killed without any compensation whatever! . . . There speaks the noble spirit of our forefathers!!"[16] These Americans were not alone in making the symbolic connection between those who volunteered and the Revolutionary heritage. It seemed natural to associate the volunteers, the contemporary heroes of the age, with the Revolutionary heroes of the Republic. The Revolution dominated the nation's historical consciousness and supplied citizens with the ideological substance of their beliefs as well as their symbols and allusions. In a very real sense, Americans fought and thought during the Mexican War era with their ideological fathers looking over their shoulders.

The contemporary generation also bore the burden of the reputations of their states, localities, and sometimes even their families. Volunteer regiments, for example, marched under the flag of the United States, but bore the name of their state and were composed of companies recruited locally. Tennessee's governor encouraged the men of the Volunteer State, a nickname gained during the War of 1812 and affirmed during the Texas' revolution during the 1830s, to bear "the time-honored standard of Tennessee to the field of battle and glory . . . [and] never permit it to be lowered in the face of the enemy, whilst your regiment has one soldier left to hold it proudly in the breeze."[17] Josiah Pender explained that the men in his regiment "came to do honor to her [North Carolina] and we will sacrifice our lives on that altar."[18] Similarly, West Pointer Ambrose Powell Hill informed his parents: "There is one regiment . . . on which I would stake my life and that is the one from dear old Virginia. I would fight for its honor and reputation as soon as I would for my own."[19] Thomas Marshall was merely following in the footsteps of his father and grandfather, both officers during the Revolution, when he accepted an appointment as brigadier general of volunteers in 1846. One South Carolinian believed that the family name had been diminished because his brother did not go off to Mexico; H. H. Townes lectured his sibling: "I wish you had volunteered. Mother ought to have made you volunteer. I will always regret our family was not represented in the army of Mexico."[20] For many, the intertwined call of duty to nation, state, neighborhood, and family proved too strong to resist.

Although the promise of tangible rewards such as land bounties convinced some to volunteer, even more perceived that in valiantly defending the honor of their country they could win lasting individual fame. The notion that fame was a powerful inducement as well as the reward of the courageous soldier was not new. A correspondent to a Charleston, South Carolina paper in 1789 wrote:

What but the love of enterprise, and of applause, would induce the soldier to exchange the peaceful joys of a domestic life for the rougher scenes, the hardships and dangers of a camp? What but the grateful tribute of his country's thanks, could persuade him to leave security, and jeopardy his life in the field of battle? The thought of sharing the honors of the brave, and of rising to glory, give courage to the hero, and adds strength to the warrior's arm.[21]

The piece could just as easily have been written during the Mexican War. Americans shared a republican conviction that those who fought for their country were worthy of the highest praise, because they manifested the ideal of civic virtue, using one's talents for the benefit of all rather than oneself alone. Put another way, just as it was the duty of males to defend the Republic, it was also the duty of those who stayed behind to exalt the sacrifice made in their behalf. Richard Henry Stanton clearly understood this when he exclaimed in a speech at Maysville, Kentucky: "He who devotes himself to danger and to death in the defense of national rights and national honor, is a hero of the noblest order."[22] Similarly, John Campbell wrote to his nephew in Mexico: "Some are prepared as you will find on your return to your native land to bind your victorious brows with the wreaths of military glory and to shout your praises in every section of our great & powerful country."[23] This connection goes a long way toward explaining why little public dissent outside of partisan politics surfaced during the war; simply stated, to criticize the war was to also criticize the heroes who fought it.

Certainly, romanticism also played a role where the idea of fame was concerned. Occasionally, for example, one hears echoes of the poem by Thomas Osbert Mordaunt, which appeared as a chapter header in Sir Walter Scott's popular *The Tale of Old Mortality:*

> SOUND, sound the clarion, fill the fife!
> Throughout the sensual world proclaim,
> One crowded hour of glorious life
> Is worth an age without a name.[24]

It is a mistake, however, to dismiss talk of fame or reputation as so much romantic fluff. Volunteers were passionately self-interested men, but, like many of their Revolutionary forefathers, the quest for fame on the battlefield enabled them to reconcile their individual ambitions with the public good. They knew that a military reputation carried weight back home, especially in the political arena. It was no accident that the Republic's two most prominent military heroes, George Washington and Andrew Jackson, were also presidents; a military reputation, all knew, had its uses. Few volunteers, of course, aspired to the presidency. More common were the sentiments expressed by volunteer Thomas Sumrall's uncle, who encouraged him to "win a laurel that may perhaps smooth your path through life . . . from the good wishes and respect of all good people."[25] We should remember, too, that, although the connection between self-sacrifice and fame was plainly understood, the judgment of the worthiness of a public figure was ultimately a subjective decision; fame is fickle as more than one returning soldier-turned-politician found out.

Victorian notions of gender differences stressed that women were inherently more moral than men. As such, women served individually as paragons of moral and republican virtue and collectively as the moral conscience of American society. But women in the 1840s were expected to exercise their influence upon society in a private manner. They did not possess the right to vote, nor were they encouraged to take leadership roles in public. Women, especially those from the upper and middle classes, were sheltered from the outside world, because it was believed to be corrupt. At the same time, they were expected to exercise their felicitous influence upon society. Some women, like Elizabeth Cady Stanton and Susan B. Anthony, challenged this confinement of women's so-called place to the home and church by founding, leading, and participating in organizations that aimed both to reform American society and to change women's position in it. Public feminist activism was, however, the exception rather than the rule, and the Mexican War did little to change this. Most women accepted that their proper sphere of influence was within the home where they served the family as the primary agent of moral instruction.

Although American women's sphere of influence was more confined than it is today, they played a key role in how the Mexican War and those who fought in it were perceived. As the moral conscience of society, women provided essential justification for men to participate in the hostilities. "Respectable" women were more than just an audience who cheered on their men as they marched off to and returned from the war; they did not just sanction violence, but often actively encouraged it. The influence of women extended beyond their role as society's moral conscience; their public support of the war also tended to reinforce traditional gender roles—the masculine warrior–protector and the feminine, patriotic and self-sacrificing republican woman. In a Fourth of July speech given before the Mississippi legislature in 1846, a male orator expressed the prevailing conception of the role of women in relation to the Mexican War:

Ladies: if it be true that you govern the world, that you possess a ruling influence upon men, then you are omnipotent, then a great duty devolves upon you, then you are the Guardian Angels of our Republican liberties. Prove yourselves worthy of the unbounded confidence this unlimited power reposes in you. Smile upon prudent valour, frown upon dastard fear. Let the coward and the traitor to his country find no solace in your company, and he will soon be brought to rights . . . Show yourselves to be worthy of our mothers, of our Revolutionist heroines, of our patriotic dames.[26]

Had women publicly opposed the war or withheld their blessing, the story of the Mexican War would have been drastically different.

Women demonstrated their support for the Mexican War in many ways. Most often, they organized community functions to support the volunteers. To one observer at a farewell celebration for a volunteer unit, it seemed that the mere presence of the women of the community could "inspire them [the volunteers] to scale the strongest rampart in Christendom."[27] One of the most common ways of demonstrating support was to present some token of approbation to the volunteers before they left or as they returned from Mexico. Often these public symbols of approval took the form of flags that the men would carry into battle. Such presentations were accompanied by brief orations that affirmed the dominant interpretation of the Mexican War as a worthy and just endeavor. After delivering a banner from the ladies of Jackson to the Mississippi State Fencibles, a volunteer company, Fanny Mayrant explained that:

An insult has been offered to the American Union . . . Mexico, and through Mexico, all the world must be taught that the American Flag is not to be assailed with impunity—they must be made to know that the soil of Freedom is sacred, and that the hostile tread of an invading foe will meet with a chastisement commensurate with the dignity of a nation that acknowledges no superior. Volunteers, you have gallantly tendered your aid to inflict upon Mexico, the punishment her treachery so richly deserves. You have resolved to go forth, to battle in the cause of your country, and to peril your lives in the vindication of her honor and the promotion of her glory. In doing so, you sever for a while, the ties of affection that bind you to your homes—you leave behind you, those whose hands cannot participate in your patriotic struggle, but whose hearts will ever be with you, and whose prayers for your success, will daily and fervently ascend to the God of battles.[28]

Kate McCarthy, representing the women of Columbus, Mississippi, presented the Lowndes Guards, the local militia unit, with a banner inscribed with the belligerent motto, "Victory or Death." In Nashville, the Female Academy presented the returning volunteers of the First Tennessee Regiment with a banner that read: "Weeping in solitude for the fallen brave is better than the presence of men too timid to strike for their country."[29] These women left little doubt of what was expected of the soldiers who served in Mexico.

Mayrant, McCarthy, and students of the Female Academy were not alone in presenting an image of militant, one could say Spartan, womanhood. As one newspaper related, "Let us read no longer the classic pages of Grecian history; the conduct of American women has given a more than Spartan glory to her character."[30] Louisa Quitman, the daughter of Major General John Quitman, chafed at her forced inactivity; she wrote to her father in Mexico that "I very often quarrel with Fate, for having placed me among the weaker portion of human kind and frequently threaten to run off, join the army and offer myself as your aide."[31] When asked at a banquet if she was worried about her husband's safety in Mexico, Eliza Quitman, Louisa's mother, responded, "I would rather be the widow of a man who had fallen fighting in the battles of his country, than the *wife of a living coward.*"[32] After hearing of the rout of the Third Indiana Regiment at Buena Vista, Captain Thomas Ware Gibson's wife stated that she would rather see her husband "face the enemy head on and be killed" than run away like a coward.[33] The powerful cultural resonance of traditional gender roles inspired the militant rhetoric of women, which in turn helped limit public dissent.

In private, however, many women were less fervent in their support for the war. The patriotic and bellicose public stance of women masked deeper worries about the war's potential to damage the welfare of their families and male friends. While husbands, sons, fathers, sweethearts, and friends might prove their honorable manhood in Mexico, they could also lose their lives. American women found themselves in a dilemma as they confronted the issue of the Mexican War—they were supposed to protect their families and society while dutifully supporting the men who volunteered to protect them. Women were correct to worry about the fate of the men who left for Mexico, for the conflict proved deadlier than any in American history—110 out of every 1,000 who served died, per year of the conflict; for the Civil War and World War Two, which cost far more in terms of total loss of life, the numbers are 85 and 30.

Although not all women felt obliged to keep their concerns about the war private, the vast majority did. Margaret Fuller, the antebellum feminist and author, publicly proclaimed that the Mexican War was unjust and delayed her return to the United States from Europe as a result. But Fuller was exceptional. Most women expressed their concerns within a sphere circumscribed by friends, relations, diaries, letters, and private conversations. For example, a young South Carolina woman represented the feelings of many when she confided to a correspondent: "Ah how my heart sickens when I reflect on that war and the feeling is always kept first in my mind as we have the portrait of five of our brave boys that have fallen there."[34] Another young woman, Lucy Ruggles, wrote that she feared so much for her brother's safety that "I dread to look in a newspaper [for news from Mexico] yet I grasp them with utmost eagerness." Later, after a male friend said "that he was afraid that my brother would not have another opportunity to distinguish himself [in battle]," Ruggles replied, "I hope he will not."[35] Feelings such as these might have surfaced in public had the war lasted longer than it did and had American arms suffered serious setbacks.

The decision of married men to join the volunteers often caused conflict between domestic partners. Undoubtedly, many women were successful in influencing their husbands not to volunteer. For example, Howell Cobb, a booster of the Mexican War from the start, wrote to his wife, Mary Ann, "I prefer to do the fighting myself and leave them [his children] a peaceful legacy."[36] She disparaged his plans to resign his seat in Congress and join the army. Cobb did not volunteer because of his wife's wishes and because male friends and relations convinced him that he could better serve the war effort if he stayed in Congress. The tension between Cobb and his wife ended with his decision not to enlist. Tension and conflict, of course, were more likely to persist if a husband decided to ignore his wife's protests. Diarist Franklin Smith reported that volunteer Captain Gholson's

wife never for a moment repined or complained at any thing since their marriage until he took this step [volunteering]—and . . . during their lives he never crossed or opposed her wishes in any thing of any moment until he came on this expedition— And when he left her weeping and prognosticating evil it almost broke his heart.

Unlike Cobb, Gholson felt honor bound to join the volunteers. Smith then solemnly added that, "This story is in the main applicable to hundreds now in Mexico."[37] Likewise, Varina Howell Davis told her husband, Jefferson

Davis, that she was unhappy with his decision to join Mississippi's volunteers. Davis encouraged her not to lament his service publicly and wrote, "my love for you placed my happiness in your keeping, our vows have placed my hono[r] and respectability in the same hands."[38] The implication here is that for Varina to act publicly in any role other than that of a supportive and patriotic wife could injure her husband's reputation or honor. Alabama volunteer Sydenham Moore agreed; he advised his brooding wife that all who "witness this gloom and despondency, . . . [will] naturally say, what a cruel being her husband must have been to have left his wife prey to such feelings."[39] Davis and Moore heeded their husband's advice and played the role Victorian society prescribed for them, although they never surrendered their reservations.

Mothers, too, often wished that their sons would not go off to Mexico, but they did the best they could to live with it. Mothers' responses were as varied as the individuals themselves and ranged from resignation to affirmation. Volunteer Joseph McNeir's brother wrote, "Your course has been a matter of great grief to Mother—but she has struggled hard, and has to some degree become reconciled to it."[40] Fletcher Archer's mother wished he had not left for Mexico and worried that he might fall from the path of righteousness so far from home. Her only solace was the belief that God watched over those who worshipped Him. Thus, she wrote to Fletcher, "let not your heart forget to cherish, and beat in unison with the spirit of God, who will certainly guide you in the way of all Truth."[41] Franklin Smith reported that the mother of one volunteer "had done all she could to persuade him not to come but when she found she could not she resigned herself to it and the last word[s] she said to him were to stand firm and fight like a man!"[42] This woman clearly understood the demands that the close association of courage, reputation, and manhood placed upon her son. She also discerned that the masculine ideals that impelled her son to embark on a dangerous adventure threatened the well-being of the household she was obliged to protect.

Many women recognized that the masculine desire to be considered fearless could cause the men in their lives to act recklessly and intoned against it. Eliza Quitman may have publicly wished to be married to a dead hero over a live coward, but privately she advised her husband not to expose himself unnecessarily. "Do not be too valiant," she wrote, "I shall think none the worse of you for obeying my commands. Return to us the first opportunity you have of releasing yourself honorably." Later a despondent Eliza would ask, "[W]here is the glory for which you are fighting?"[43] Apparently, Molly Walker shared Eliza Quitman's concerns for her soldier husband felt obliged to advise her: "Don't be too alarmed for my safety. We go with too large a force to expect a hard fight." Molly must have suspected that her husband might still act with reckless bravery because he added, "I am sorry that we go with such a large force for it will spoil all the sport."[44] North Carolinian James Slade's wife wrote to him from New Orleans: "you have been very imprudent since you have been in Mexico venturing your life in battle . . . this will render me miserable and unhappy until you return."[45] Martha Barbour also agonized over the fate of her husband, Philip, a regular officer. Unlike Mrs. Slade, Martha's worst fears were realized as her husband was killed on September 17, 1846, at the battle of Monterrey. Although most women during the war were never put in Barbour's tragic situation, all who had dear ones in Mexico shared anxiety over their fate.

Some American women played a more active role in the war effort than those described here. Women followed the U.S. Army during its campaigns in Mexico as wives, cooks, mistresses, prostitutes, nurses, laundresses, entertainers, and merchants of various stripe. Their numbers are impossible to assess with any accuracy, but certainly there were hundreds. For example, army regulations permitted, rather than mandated, four laundresses per company. Tradition held that these women were usually the wives of soldiers, who often cared for their children in addition to performing their prescribed duties. Other than that they were ubiquitous; we do not know much about the female camp followers, because none left accounts of their experiences. Some women attempted to follow a loved one into the service and were usually discovered during the first formal inspections. One at least, Eliza Allen Billings from Maine, claimed that she joined the army disguised as a man, served with General Scott during his march to Mexico City, and even suffered a wound in combat. She wrote a book, *The Female Volunteer,* about her experiences. Although there is reason to doubt the veracity of Billings' tale, there is no doubt that the most famous American woman to come out of the war was Sarah Borginnis (sources refer to her by several last names), an Irish laundress.[46] Borginnis, who was best known as "The Great Western" because she was, by all accounts, over six feet tall and had a personality to match her imposing physical stature, became a legend. When the Mexicans bombarded Fort Brown opposite Matamoros for seven days in April 1846, she disdained shelter, set up her tent in the center of the fort, nursed the wounded, and began dispensing food, water, and coffee to the garrison. Afterward, the soldiers celebrated her exploits, and Borginnis resumed her normal duties while proudly wearing a bonnet pierced by a Mexican bullet. The horde of newspapermen that descended on Fort Brown quickly picked up her story and ran with it. The Great Western followed the army into northern Mexico, and, on the battlefield of Buena Vista, moved among the soldiers shouting encouragement, distributing cartridges, and aiding the wounded. In 1866, she died at Fort Yuma and was buried with full military honors.

The women who actively participated in the Mexican War challenged traditional gender roles as dramatically and directly as their more famous sisters who gathered at the Seneca Falls Convention in 1848. But these women represented the wave of the future, and their numbers were small. At war's end, the tension between the private domestic concerns of women and the public demands of Victorian manhood remained unresolved. Indeed, traditional gender norms were affirmed rather than challenged in any significant way. The friction between Victorian male and female culture would reappear during the great war that lay in the nation's future, a war that touched almost every family and was neither short nor uniformly victorious for either side.

If one only considered the home front's vicarious experience and the response of men and women, the conclusion that few divisions over the issue of the Mexican War could easily be reached. Such, however, was not the case. As befitted a nation that prized free speech, a multitude of citizens expressed differences over topics ranging from the causes and management of the war to the question of whether warfare was morally justifiable. The heroic, romantic image of the war certainly affected the terms of the debate, but did not squelch it altogether. Thus, we now turn to politics and nonpolitical dissent in our effort to understand the home front during the Mexican War.

POLITICS AND DISSENT

In 1846, Richard Gholson, a volunteer officer in Mexico, told a friend that he joined up because he was Democrat. Gholson explained that as a Democrat and an early supporter of the annexation of Texas, he had publicly pledged "to offer up his humble fortunes in defense of her [the country's] rights" if war came.[47] Although today it might appear that Gholson was merely a political extremist, he was far from alone in placing party politics center stage when considering a response to the Mexican War. Most white men—the franchise (right to vote) had been greatly extended during the so-called Age of Jackson and voter turnout tallied the highest levels in American history—largely defined who they were through their political affiliation. In short, party politics mattered more during this period than they do today. Political rallies, barbeques, and marches were often better attended than church services; the vast majority of newspapers were politically affiliated; election day was a kind of secular holy day. Despite the fact that the vote had not yet been extended to many segments of society, most notably women or blacks, the centrality of politics, broadly defined, in American life cannot be denied, for this was also an era of reform. Advocates of various moral and religious causes, including many women, organized and worked diligently in attempts to see that their reform agendas became national or local policy. The Mexican War did not escape their attention. It seems natural, then, that political activity and discourse played a large role in how Americans experienced and reacted to the Mexican War.

Let us turn first to the political parties. There were two major national parties in 1846, the Democrats, the party founded by Andrew Jackson and his supporters, and the Whigs, established later to oppose the supposed depredations of the man they called King Andrew the First. In the early 1840s, both parties were closely matched in electoral strength and rigorously national in their organization—they generally avoided anything that might cause their members to think that they were first northerners, westerners, or southerners rather than Democrats or Whigs. However, both parties showed signs that sectional concerns could no longer be sidestepped by focusing on economic questions. The annexation of Texas in 1845 and the related issue of the expansion of slavery rocked the parties and boded ill for their future and the future of the nation. In 1846, the parties were only in disarray rather than in obvious stages of outright decay. This, then, was the stage upon which the partisan battle over the Mexican War would be fought.

Because most newspapers focused on the ongoing negotiations with Great Britain over Oregon in the spring of 1846, news of the opening of hostilities on the Rio Grande rolled like a sudden and unexpected thunderstorm across the nation. The Democratic president, James Knox Polk of Tennessee, was among the first in Washington to hear the news when Adjutant General Roger Jones arrived at the White House at six in the evening of Saturday, May 9. The report of Thornton's ambush galvanized Polk to action. Although small in stature, the president possessed big plans, which involved territory belonging to the Republic of Mexico. Frustrated in his earlier attempts to gain Upper California, especially the glittering prize of San Francisco Bay, and to settle other disputes with Mexico by negotiation, the president had already determined that force was necessary to achieve his goals; he wrote in his diary on April 25 that the time had arrived to "take redress for the injuries done us into our own hands."[48] He had only been restrained from ordering the military into action by congressional Democratic leaders and members of his cabinet who counseled patience. Wait, they said, let Mexico fire the first shot. Now word of Thornton's ambush removed the last barrier on the road to war. By 7:30 P.M., the cabinet had hastily assembled and soon unanimously agreed that a message asking for a formal declaration of war be sent to Congress on Monday.

The message articulated the president's interpretation of the causes of war in the strongest possible terms. Despite every amicable attempt to settle the differences between the two countries, Mexico, Polk argued, had chosen war. With the attack on Thornton's patrol, "the cup of forbearance had been exhausted." Indeed, he chided those who had heretofore advised a policy of diplomacy and restraint; "Had we acted with vigor in repelling the insults and redressing the injuries inflicted by Mexico . . . , we should doubtless have escaped all the difficulties in which we are now involved." Put another way, an aggressive preemptive policy would have avoided the current situation where Mexico had struck first, "invaded our territory, and shed American blood on the American soil." The president concluded: "Now war exists, and, not withstanding all our efforts to avoid

it, exists by the act of Mexico herself, we are called upon by every consideration of duty and patriotism, to vindicate, with decision, the honor, the
rights, and the interests of our country."[49] This necessary, yet unsought
war, Polk implied, would be fought with a sword in one hand and an olive
branch in the other. Significantly, he mentioned neither California nor any
other territorial ambition.

Reprints of the president's war message quickly appeared in almost
every newspaper. The message struck the first blow in what was soon to
become a bitter partisan battle over the Mexican War. It also established the
basic political position that the Democratic party would defend throughout the Mexican War and served as the touchstone for any debate on the
war. As such, the message played a crucial role in defining the direction
that the political argument over the question of the war would take. Any
opponent of the war had to come to terms with the president's logic. Democratic supporters of Polk's policy both within Congress and back at home
consistently reiterated the main points of the message of May 11. It was
a drumbeat they would keep up for the entire war, which they claimed
was a just and honorable conflict. Indeed, one Democratic newspaper editor went beyond mere vindication when he affirmed, "there never was a
more righteous war than this."[50] Democratic partisans argued that those
who opposed this "righteous" war were unpatriotic at best and traitors at
worst.

The key to Polk's war message and the various defenses of it by his
supporters was a theory of just warfare that linked the honor, interests,
and rights of the nation together. The question of the justice of the war
revolved around notions of whether or not warfare, specifically this war,
constituted justifiable behavior for the Republic. As the model republic,
Americans believed that their nation should be held to a higher standard
of morality than any other country. The United States was different from
the imperial powers of Europe, they thought; she was a republican city on
a hill, an example for the world, and should act accordingly. A war waged
primarily for territorial aggrandizement was obviously not in keeping
with this idealized belief in the mission of the Republic. Americans considered the political party in power as caretakers of the nation's precious
republican heritage as well as its rights and interests. Thus, the majority
party, in this case the Democrats, who controlled the Presidency and both
houses of Congress in 1846, would be held accountable for the actions of
the Republic. For Democrats then, it was absolutely essential that the justice of the war with Mexico be established beyond dispute. The continued
electoral success of the party, not to mention the reputation of the Republic, demanded it.

The practical appeal of the Democratic interpretation of the Mexican
War rested firmly upon its accordance with the sensibilities of individual male social relations. Concerns over defending the honor, rights,
and interests of the nation were not mere romantic fancies. The war

message artfully cast Mexico in the role of the proverbial schoolyard bully, who acted with concern only for his own selfish interests and willfully trammeled over those of others. Consequently, it took little imagination to appreciate the logic of the argument. For example, the editor of a Mississippi Democratic newspaper succinctly related that the same principles that governed individual conduct applied to international relations as well.

It is a principle which is well established among mankind–clearly demonstrated in all their transactions–that, *submission whether as regards individuals or nations provokes insult and aggression.* Study the history of nations . . . and the truth of the same principle is evident. It is true that peace, a *dishonorable* peace, has been frequently the result of submission. Yet it was but temporary, though purchased at so great a sacrifice. New encroachments would soon follow–concessions more unreasonable than the first would be demanded, and at last the party that had submitted to a sacrifice of their rights on the altar of ambition, and for the 'sake of peace,' were compelled to resort to arms enervated, and shorn of their strength. The cloud of war slumbered in the distance only to gather contents still more destructive, and to scatter them over the earth with redoubled fury.

  Look to individuals in their private transactions . . . to discern the same well established principle. If a man is not tenacious of his rights, and with the fear of 'difficulties' ever before his eyes, quietly submits to unjust encroachments in one instance, it is afterwards expected and even demanded that he should continue to pursue this policy. The final result is the occurrence of the very event which he so much dreaded. On the contrary the man, who 'knows his rights and knowing, dare maintain' is permitted to enjoy them unmolested, and is free from those misfortunes which a craven, cowardly, temporizing course of conduct begets.[51]

Few other Democrats felt compelled to make clear the precise equation described here. They simply made the argument that the nation was threatened and trusted their readers or listeners to make the obvious connection. One might disagree that the offenses committed by Mexico warranted a resort to arms, as most Whigs and a few Democrats did, but a common set of cultural values supported the mainstream Democratic explanation of the reasons for war, which made it difficult to deny. Its power, then, rested upon what at first glance seemed like common sense.

Americans, the Democrats often pointed out, need only look into the recent past for an example of a just war fought, at least in part, for reasons similar to those now provided. The nationalist War Hawk faction in Congress, whose most prominent members were Henry Clay and John C. Calhoun, used arguments equivalent to those of President Polk and his supporters to justify America's declaration of war against Britain in 1812. For example, Calhoun listed the impressment of American seamen and the violation of American trade among the wrongs perpetrated by Great Britain. "These rights," he asserted in 1811, "are essentially attacked, and war is the only means of redress." The United States was "bound in honor

and interest to resist."[52] Calhoun maintained that war was the only alternative left to the nation because:

Wrongs submitted to produce contrary effects in the oppressor and the oppressed.
The first wrong, by universal law of our nature, is most easily resisted. . . . Let that
be submitted to; let the consequent debasement and loss of national honor be felt,
and nothing but the grinding hand of oppression can force resistance. . . . In submission then there is no remedy; our honor lost; our commerce under the control
of the oppressor.[53]

In 1848, an Arkansas Democrat spoke for many others when he noted
the connection between the earlier war and the one with Mexico: "In
1812 we went to war with Great Britain, one of the mighty powers of the
earth. . . . Compare the causes in the two cases. It seems to me that the list
of aggressions is longer on the side of Mexico."[54]

Whatever their inspiration, Democrats in the House and Senate demonstrated overwhelming support for the president's interpretation of
the road to war. In the House of Representatives during early May 1846,
Kentucky Democrat Linn Boyd succeeded in attaching an amendment
that paraphrased the war message to a bill providing 50,000 volunteers
and $10 million for the war. Thus, the vote on the amended appropriation
bill served either as a benchmark of support for Polk's war message or as
a measure of the unwillingness to oppose the war message if it also meant
not supplying the troops. The bill passed the House 174 to 14 with every
Democrat and many Whigs voting "yea." The story was largely the same
in the Senate where the bill passed with an overwhelming majority.

The words of Democratic congressmen mirrored their votes. An excerpt
from a speech by Senator William Allen of Ohio gives some idea of the fire
and brimstone being preached by Democrats.

If we meet this act of aggression promptly, vigorously, energetically, . . . we shall
furnish a lesson to the world which will be profitably remembered hereafter. . . .
We have but one safe course before us. . . . Let us enter the Mexican territory, and
conquer a peace at the point of the bayonet. . . . [I]f delayed, there will be other
parties than Mexico who will soon mingle themselves in this affair; and the consequences may be felt throughout the civilized world.[55]

Likewise, Representative Hugh Haralson of Georgia declared that "the
blood of our people shed upon the Rio Grande . . . cries aloud upon us for
prompt, speedy, definite action."[56] The words of Polk and his supporters
in Congress would not just echo throughout the nation during the coming
months; they were repeated and amplified by hundreds of dutiful editors
and thousands of the party faithful.

Democrats desired a free hand to wage their president's war. Hence,
they painted their Whig opponents as both disloyal and dishonorable.
Put another way, Democrats endeavored to shame their opponents into

supporting or at least acquiescing in President Polk's war policy. In his December 8, 1846, annual message, Polk himself argued that the Whigs' vigorous criticism provided "aid and comfort" to the Mexicans.[57] In his diary, the President also characterized the Whigs as "Federalists," a reference both to the 1813 accusation that Connecticut Federalists had displayed blue lights to a British blockading squadron to thwart Steven Decatur's attempt to slip out of New London and to the "treasonous" Hartford Convention of 1814.[58] The President was not alone in making this connection as Democrats mercilessly beat the theme like a proverbial rented mule. Polk wrote the sheet music, and Democratic political organs across the country played the tune as they variously styled Whigs as, to name but a few, "traitors," "Blue Light Federalists," "Tories," "Prophets of Evil," "Mexican Whigs," "Massachusetts Federalists," "Federal Whigs," and, finally the ever popular if simple, "Federalists," in articles that graced their pages.[59] Alabamian E. A. O'Neal wrote to a friend in Washington of the hoped for result of all this Whig bashing: "You have traitors in Congress, as well as we have among us. But the masses . . . will put their *mark* on them."[60] Electoral dominance rather than principled belief in the propaganda they were pushing was the primary Democratic motive.

Although President Polk was largely able to wage the war in the manner he desired, Democrats proved unable to ride the tidal wave of patriotic sentiment to political ascendancy. The midterm elections of 1846 proved a disaster. Overall, the Democrats lost 30 seats and the majority status in the House of Representatives, but they gained a few seats in the Senate. Even after accounting for the traditionally Democratic seats in the House lost due to reapportionment, party managers faced the inevitable conclusion that accusations of disloyalty, cowardice, or partisan feeling had failed to stick. Simply stated, few Whigs paid the hoped for price at the only place it really mattered, the ballot box. The reasons for this are complex and can only be hinted at here. Americans expected a quick war and by election day no end was in sight. Certainly, there was growing recognition of and solicitude over the territorial objectives of the President, but just as important were concerns over traditional partisan issues unrelated to the war, especially the enactment of an independent treasury and the Walker Tariff. We must also recognize that midterm electoral success for a sitting President's party is more the exception than the rule in American politics, because no President, or political party for that matter, can ever cure all the ills that afflict the electorate. Finally, the Democratic propaganda machine successfully placed limits on Whig dissent. The moniker of traitor just did not seem to apply to the Whig party, which voted for money to support the troops in the field and supplied both volunteers for the army and its two leading generals, Zachary Taylor and Winfield Scott. It is to political dissent that we now turn.

Not all Democrats adhered to the administration's line on the Mexican War. The national party was not a monolithic entity that marched in lockstep behind its president. Indeed, division and turmoil rived it during the mid-1840s. In the North, the loss of their faction's dominant position in the Democratic party angered the supporters of Martin Van Buren. The Van Burenites' inability to achieve 54° 40' as the boundary line in the Oregon dispute, their lack of control over the party machinery during Texas's annexation, and Polk's replacement of the Van Buren-leaning Washington *Globe* with the Washington *Union* as the party's official organ manifested just how far they had fallen. The so-called Wilmot Proviso, proposed by a former administration supporter who had gradually gravitated into the camp of the Van Buren dissidents, was partly the fruit of this schism.

Shortly after 7 P.M., August 8, 1846, David Wilmot, a first-term Democratic Representative from Pennsylvania, stood up and introduced his famous amendment, which excluded slavery and involuntary servitude from any territory gained as a result of the war. The sectional divisions that both Whigs and Democrats had tried so hard to submerge came suddenly to the fore, and party lines snapped as the amended military appropriations bill passed the House by an 87 to 64 margin. Significantly, all but four northern Democrats voted for it. In the Senate, the bill died with the adjournment of Congress at noon on August 10. Like Wilmot himself, few of the men who voted for the proviso-laden bill were abolitionists or supported the even more radical notion of racial equality. Many claimed to support both the war and expansion, especially northern and western Democrats. However, the proviso did solve the dilemma of reconciling a national desire for territorial expansion with endemic racism and fear of slavery's extension. The simple expedient provided was the potential for a new national domain on the west coast for whites only. The Wilmot Proviso seemed tailor-made for those Democrats who wished to advertise their support for free labor and territorial growth. Of course, it also served to bring the long-avoided issue of the South's peculiar institution to center stage, which was where abolitionists thought it belonged all along. If any who made their way home from steamy Washington that August thought that they had seen the last of the thorny issue, they were sadly mistaken. Pandora's Box had been opened, and come December, the controversy over the extension of slavery was reborn with fiery political rhetoric that resembled the jeremiads of old. The controversy would only find final resolution in the cataclysm of civil war. But again, it should be emphasized that support for Wilmot's proviso was not, for most Democrats, a stance against the war. Indeed, the most contentious question was how much territory should be added to the country—a vocal faction looked beyond just California and New Mexico to all of Mexico. Although it did make financing the war more difficult and irritated Mr. Polk to the extreme, Democratic divisions on the Wilmot Proviso issue little affected their belief that the war was just.

The South, too, had its Democratic dissidents. John C. Calhoun and his small coterie of conservative Democratic disciples frequently bucked national party control. Consequently, Calhoun surprised no one when he proved less than enthusiastic about the war with Mexico. He often traveled the dissenting path alone; some who initially supported his critique of the Mexican War, Congressmen Isaac Holmes, Robert Barnwell Rhett, and William Lowndes Yancey to name a few, abandoned his leadership on the issue and supported the administration's position. Calhoun, however, was never totally alone in his views, although occasionally it must have seemed that way. There were always a few papers in his home state that could be counted on to back him. Still, the story of the Calhounites' attitudes toward the Mexican War is basically the story of one man, John C. Calhoun.

Although the young Calhoun's stance regarding the War of 1812 suggests that he understood the logic of the President's argument, the old Calhoun and his compatriots thought that the war with Mexico was a needless one fraught with danger both for the South and for the Republic. Like others who would disapprove of the war after the fact, they discovered that criticizing an existing war was an entirely different and more difficult proposition than preventing a hypothetical one. Yet they also agreed that national honor demanded that the war, once commenced, be materially sustained and waged to a victorious conclusion. South Carolina Senator Andrew Butler perhaps best summed up the dilemma facing the Calhounites when he admitted, "we are certainly in a difficult position. . . . if we quit the war, it will apparently be with dishonor. If we go on it must end in mischief. The truth is, we are like a shepherd who has got the wolf by the ears! It is hazardous to let go—it is worse to hold on."[61] Thus trapped, Calhoun proposed that American troops withdraw within the present-day borders of the United States and erect a defensive line. He did so for two reasons. First, the explosive sectional controversy unleashed by the Wilmot Proviso led him to believe that an immediate end to the war was essential; and, second, he worried about the growing sentiment to annex all of Mexico, a country inhabited by a race that he considered unsuited to republican government. All the while Calhoun's position evidenced a certain amount of ambivalence; he and his followers continued to vote their support for bills to finance the war. In many ways, Calhoun's course resembled that of the Whig party. Indeed, outside of a small circle of loyal Democratic adherents, Calhoun found support for his position from an unexpected quarter, the Whigs.

Like Calhoun, the Whig party found itself in the unenviable position of having to come up with a stance that did not surrender the war issue to the Democrats, while at the same time not appearing to be disloyal. The powerful cultural symbolism contained in the Democratic interpretation of the war, as well as the memory of what had happened to the Federalist party in the wake of the Hartford Convention, hampered these efforts. Whigs also discovered themselves in other perplexing quandaries. The war, they quickly realized, was more than a defensive one, it was being waged for territory as well, and as a party they were generally committed to intensive development of the nation within existing boundaries before expanding. This stance frayed the bonds of party loyalty, especially during the Texas annexation debate, where sectional interest trumped traditional fears of expansion among southern Whigs. It would reappear during the Mexican War when the Wilmot Proviso gave the territorial debate sectional aspect. Nor was this the only fracture line apparent in the party. The northern tier of states felt most strongly the reformist impulse that grew out of the religious revivalism of the Second Great Awakening. Whig politicians from this same tier of northern states served as the political expression of reform. Thus, we find abolitionist and varying degrees of antislavery sentiment bubbling to the surface during the debates over the Mexican War with obvious ramifications for party unity. This was a political problem that was essentially unique to the Whigs. In general, then, there were Whigs who dissented from the war primarily because the Democrats were for it and those who dissented primarily for reasons of principle. In either case, Democrats had fired the first shot, and Whigs were playing catch up.

Those who placed party loyalty first (henceforth referred to as "loyal Whigs") were easily the most common political animals in the Whig party, especially in the lower portion of the North and West and throughout the South. They rarely argued that the war was morally wrong. Loyal Whigs attacked on a different front by asserting that the Mexican conflict was inconsistent with republican principles and needlessly caused by the Administration's ham-handed management of the border dispute with Mexico. Many loyal Whigs heeded the call to arms, which certainly suggests that they were not of a pacifist bent. For example, Illinois Whig Edward Baker resigned his House seat in December 1846 to join the volunteers in Mexico. Once hostilities were joined in earnest, loyal Whigs contended that the war was being waged for the political benefit of the Democratic party and was bungled in its execution. They responded to Democratic attempts to brand them as disloyal Federalists by painting the Democrats as recalcitrant, inefficient to the point of stupidity, and self-serving. However, there were lines in this partisan battle for the hearts and minds of the American voter that they would not cross. Indeed, loyal Whigs basked in the reflected glory of Whig generals and volunteers, especially local heroes when available, even as they critiqued what they labeled as "Mr. Polk's War." Despite their lack of enthusiasm, loyal Whigs in Congress also consistently voted for war measures, although some, such as Thomas Corwin of Ohio, would refuse to do this as the war dragged on. As a final testament to their divided mind on the Mexican War, the loyal Whigs gleefully supported the presidential candidacy of war hero Zachary Taylor in 1848. Gunpowder, they knew, had its uses.

The experience of Alexander Stephens, a leading critic of "Mr. Polk's War" in the House of Representatives, perhaps best illustrates the problems faced by loyal Whigs. On a sweltering June day in 1846, Alexander Stephens stood and addressed the House of Representatives. His purpose, he said, was to present his views on the Mexican War. The Georgia Whig and future vice president of the Confederacy stated at the outset of his speech that he was not "as some gentlemen seem to be, the advocate of war in the abstract—war for war's sake." Nor was he a "non-resistance man" who believed that all wars are wrong. War was, argued Stephens, "the last resort of nations to settle matters of dispute or disagreement between them, [and] should always be avoided, when it can be done without a sacrifice of national rights or honor." He then went on to explain why the Mexican War did not rise to his definition of a necessary conflict. Stephens asserted, "the whole affair is properly chargeable to the imprudence, indiscretion, and mismanagement of our own Executive; that the war has been literally provoked when there was no necessity for it, and could have been easily avoided without any detriment to our rights, interests, or honor as a nation." He insisted that the immediate cause of hostilities was the advance of Zachary Taylor's army from Corpus Christi on the Nueces River to Matamoros on the Rio Grande. Both Texas and Mexico claimed sovereignty over the land between the rivers. Thus, Taylor's march through it was a move "calculated to provoke, to irritate, and to bring on a conflict, if it was not so designed." Mexico, he pointed out, had made no aggressive moves against Texas before the establishment of an American fort opposite Matamoros. Furthermore, "the President had no right, no power, legally, to order the military occupation of the disputed territory . . . without the authority of Congress."[62]

The Representative from Georgia then shifted gears to inquire as to the aims of the war. Stephens demanded "to know if this was to be a war for conquest." "If so," he added, "I protest against that part of it." Stephens, however, was no enemy to the extension of the borders of the Republic. Indeed, he had voted for the annexation of Texas and looked forward to the fulfillment of what he called "our ultimate destiny, . . . the day when the whole continent will be ours." But he also believed that expansion should only be achieved through voluntary accessions of territory. To him, a war of conquest represented "a downward progress. It is a progress of party—of excitement—of lust of power—a spirit of war—aggression—violence and licentiousness. It is a progress which, if indulged in, would soon sweep over all law, all order, and the Constitution itself." Americans should, Stephens argued, "take a lesson from . . . history, and grow wise by the calamities of others, without paying ourselves the melancholy price of wisdom." Only by maintaining a high order of moral and political integrity could the Republic stand the test of time; "this . . . is not to be done by wars, whether foreign or domestic." "Fields of blood and carnage," Stephens testified, "may make men brave and heroic, but seldom tend to make nations either good, virtuous, or great."[63]

Despite his reservations about the causes of the war, Stephens claimed that the "cause or origin of the flames, whether by accident or negligence, or the hand of the enemy, would have no influence with me on the course

I should pursue in effecting their speediest extinguishment, and using all available and proper means for that purpose. All hands to the rescue would be my motto."[64] Indeed, he had already voted for a bill providing supplies and troops for the war, despite strong reservations about a preamble added by the supporters of the President.

For his efforts, Stephens faced charges of disloyalty and cowardice both in Washington and at home. Verbal resistance to his principal tormentors, Democrats William Lowndes Yancey of Alabama and Herschel Johnson of Georgia, could not answer charges such as these. Stephens felt honor-bound to challenge both men to duels to clear his name. Neither affair ended with shots being exchanged, and Stephens continued his outspoken criticism. Significantly, Stephens' constituents returned him to Congress in the following election. Some loyal Whigs who took similar positions were not so lucky. Abraham Lincoln, a first-term loyal Whig Representative from Illinois, was one of these. His so-called Spot Resolution, which questioned Polk's claim that Thornton's patrol had been ambushed on American soil, is only the most well known of his criticisms of the Mexican War. Like Stephens, he was attacked for his views, but unlike Stephens he challenged no one to a duel, and he lost his seat in the House.

On the reverse of the Whig coin rested the small group of radical Whigs led in Congress by men such as Joshua Giddings of Ohio. These "ultra" Whigs, as they were often called, gave political voice to northern areas where antislavery and antiwar sentiment was common, if not ubiquitous. Their number was small, about two dozen votes in the House on any given issue, but the noise they made was hard to ignore. Most were not abolitionists, but all shared a belief that the Mexican War was a manifestation of an ongoing "Slave Power conspiracy," an attempt to expand both slave territory and slaveholders' power in America, and they expressed their moral outrage in no uncertain terms. For ultra Whigs, financially supporting the war effort was equivalent to surrender and thus unthinkable. Predictably, they were unrepentant about their opposition to the war. Ultra Whig Daniel King of Massachusetts proudly wore the barbs of his political opponents like a crown of thorns; "If an earnest desire to save my country from ruin and disgrace be treason," he exclaimed in the House in 1847, "then I am a traitor: if the fear to do wrong makes a man a coward, then I am a coward."[65] Their stridency, moral certainty, and single-minded commitment to the cause little influenced the direction that the war took from a policy standpoint, but it would be a mistake to say that they had no impact. Southern Whigs found themselves accused by Democrats of being guilty by association with the radical members of their party, which served to push many toward a more clearly sectional position on many issues. In the North, the ultra sermons awakened a growing number of voters to the threat posed by the so-called Slave Power conspiracy. In 1848, many of the ultra Whigs broke with their party and threw their support behind Martin Van Buren, who ran for president on a free soil platform.

Like the ultra Whigs, there were others who opposed the Mexican War on moral grounds. These nonpolitical dissenters were never typical in their unconditional dissent and most often hailed from New England, especially Boston, or other places along the northern borders of the United States. Unlike the ultra Whigs, however, they chose not to express their critiques of the war exclusively through the mechanism of party politics. Moral, nonpolitical dissenters were a diverse lot encompassing people as famous today as Ralph Waldo Emerson and as forgotten as Boston's Baptist minister Dr. Daniel Sharp. Although a belief in the perfectibility of man was common to most, they possessed no centralizing organizational tendency. It simply never seems to have occurred to those who opposed the war on religious, pacifist, antislavery, or other philosophic grounds that they might make common cause with each other in anything other than an informal sense.

Any attempt to survey comprehensively the opinions of nonpolitical dissenters in a few words must meet with failure. This said, one can trace a general outline of the various movements and point to commonalities of thought. Christian religious dissenters were probably the most numerous of the flock, because every denomination contained at least some who believed that adherence to the teachings of the Prince of Peace left no place for war. Of course, it is impossible to measure exactly how many opposed the war on religious grounds. Nor is it possible to trace all the ways in which religious devotion might lead one to oppose it. What can be said is that the only denominations that consistently expressed their opposition were the Unitarian, the Congregationalist, and the Religious Society of Friends. The Roman Catholic, Methodist, Southern Baptist, and Old School Presbyterian leadership countenanced the war. Other Christian sects either were of two minds or made no official comment. Abolitionists opposed the war because they believed slaveholding interests initiated it to expand the South's peculiar institution. They attacked on many fronts, but the most obvious and successful examples of their critique were the satirical publications by James Russell Lowell and Seba Smith of Maine. Pacifist organizations, such as the American Peace Society and the more radical Non-Resistance Society, opposed the war for a combination of reasons, which appear never to have mixed in exactly the same way in individual members. Among their favorites were, the war: conflicted with Christian principles, created a warlike spirit that threatened the Republic and its prosperity, and prevented the creation of a utopian world without war. Public meetings, conferences, publications, and occasionally civil disobedience characterized the pacifist organizations' efforts to get the word out. By far the most famous today but least influential at the time were literary figures such as Henry David Thoreau, Ralph Waldo Emerson, and Herman Melville. Thoreau published *Civil Disobedience* after the war was over in 1848, and Emerson and Melville refrained from public comment. Although they wrote about their feelings with more eloquence and often deeper thought than others, literary dissenters, like the other dissenters mentioned here, saw the Mexican War primarily as evidence of, rather than the cause of, the nation's fall from grace. Although these dissenters might disagree over the reason for declension—the existence of slavery and ignoring God's truth among other things—they did agree that something was terribly wrong with the Republic.

It is easy to overestimate the importance of dissent. In fact, most Americans supported the war although for many this support became more qualified over time, especially once the casualty lists began to come in and President Polk's territorial agenda, determination to send troops deep into Mexico's heartland, and partisan direction of the war effort became obvious. American opinions about the justice of the war and proper policy regarding it mirrored political discourse. Put another way, the mainstream Democratic and loyal Whig political arguments, which never proposed ending the war on any other terms than Mexico's submission, reflected the will of the American people to wage the war to a victorious conclusion. Political discourse, then, encompassed the narrow confines of most public opinion on the war. Simply stated, the war was popular; the American masses evidenced few qualms about the war, its causes, or the territorial acquisitions that resulted from it. Perhaps this was hubris on their part. Hindsight certainly suggests as much. But no matter what the future held, the arrival from Mexico of Nicolas Trist's peace treaty in mid-February 1848 rendered discussions about the justice of the Mexican War and war policy moot. Almost everyone greeted its arrival in the Senate with approbation although each often had very different reasons for doing so. There was something for everyone in the treaty, although seldom all that anyone wanted: moral reformers liked that it promised an end to the war; expansionists liked that it expanded the national domain; anti-expansionists were relieved that it did not include all the territory of Mexico; Democrats saw it as a successful conclusion of "their" war; Whigs were happy that they had successfully countered the Democratic attempt to brand them as traitors and had emerged at first glance stronger politically than before; and, finally, all were relieved that the nation's youth would soon be safely home on American soil. The Senate ratified the Treaty of Guadalupe Hidalgo in early March by a nonpartisan vote of 38–14. Twelve Whigs and 26 Democrats voted "yea," while 7 of each party voted "nay." Calhoun supporter and South Carolina representative H. H. Townes expressed a near universal sentiment: "We are delighted that the Senate has ratified the treaty.... Almost any treaty which will enable us to end the war would be a good one for the country."[66]

CONCLUSION

News of the treaty's ratification by the Mexican Congress arrived at the White House on July 4, 1848. That same day, after considerable festivities, a crowd estimated at around 15,000 gathered on the north bank of the Potomac to dedicate the cornerstone of the Washington Monument. Robert C. Winthrop of Massachusetts, leader of the Whig party and Speaker of the House of Representatives, delivered a two-hour oration, which echoed the idealistic sentiments of Manifest Destiny and encapsulated the ambivalent legacy of the war with Mexico. With the conflict victoriously concluded and almost all of Europe ablaze with revolutionary ardor, Winthrop asserted that the Republic had lived up to the legacy bequeathed by George Washington and the Founders. Liberty was spreading at an unprecedented rate due to the actions of its handmaiden, the United States. There was, then, cause for celebration and optimism. But, Winthrop claimed, the Republic's inheritance required more. He called upon his listeners to remember and to rededicate themselves to the two main tenets of Washington's policy—"first, the most complete, cordial, and indissoluble Union of the States; and, second, the most entire separation and disentanglement of our own country from all other countries." Winthrop realized that one result of the war was the unleashing of "many marked and mourned centrifugal tendencies," which threatened to destroy Washington's creation if left unchecked.[67] For Winthrop, which path the nation would follow—optimistic or pessimistic—remained shrouded in the mists of the future. We, of course, know that work on the Washington Monument ceased in 1856 and was only resumed in 1876, which roughly paralleled the course of political history.

Most Mexican War-era Americans barely paused to ponder what they had wrought. The experience warranted little reflection, because not much happened (or at least was reported) that challenged citizens' preconceptions. Thus, the war appeared to jibe with the Republic's illustrious military heritage and engendered confidence rather than questions. Besides, Americans were much too busy for a period of deep self-assessment. The nation was on the move, and the "go a-head" spirit reigned supreme. The population grew by 36 percent between 1840 and 1850; urban areas, places with more than 2,500 people according to the census, increased by 80 percent during the same period. In 1849 alone, some 800 ships bearing 40,000 gold seekers landed in San Francisco; 450 vessels sat rotting in the harbor, abandoned by their crews. New locomotives clicked along new tracks, their progress tracked over new telegraph lines that traced alongside. On July 21, 1848, Congress passed an act that provided a half-pay benefit to disabled veterans, widows, and orphans of the Mexican War and quickly moved on to more pressing business. Able-bodied veterans were themselves too busy to campaign for pensions, which came in 1887, or to form a national organization, which came in 1874 (149 officers did, however, form the exclusive Aztec Club in Mexico City in 1847). By 1849, the nation's publishing industry began to focus on other topics. Citizens elected Zachary Taylor and other war heroes to office in 1848, but possession of a war record quickly lost its influence as politics returned to normal.

In the immediate aftermath of the Mexican War, the future beckoned, and Americans moved to meet it.

NOTES

1. Anonymous woman from Mobile, Alabama, to Rebecca Gibson Small-wood, 16 May 1846, Wright-Harris Papers, Duke University, Special Collections Department, William R. Perkins Library.

2. D. Hayden to Robert John Walker, 14 May 1846, Robert John Walker Papers, Library of Congress.

3. Herman Melville to Gansevoort Melville, 29 May 1846, *The Letters of Herman Melville,* ed. Merrell R. Davis and William H. Gilman (New Haven, CT: Yale University Press, 1960), 29.

4. "To Whom Does Washington's Glory Belong?" *Southern Literary Messenger,* IX, no. 10 (October 1843): 588.

5. *Casket,* 10 June 1846, quoted in Reginald Horsman, *Race and Manifest Destiny: The Origins of American Racial Anglo-Saxonism* (Cambridge: Harvard University Press, 1981), 236.

6. Abbeville *Banner,* 13 February 1846, quoted in Ernest M. Lander, Jr., *Reluctant Imperialists: Calhoun, The South Carolinians, and the Mexican War* (Baton Rouge: Louisiana State University Press, 1980), 3.

7. Walt Whitman, "Our Territory on the Pacific," *The Brooklyn Daily Eagle and Kings County Democrat,* 7 July 1846, 2.

8. "Death of Major Ringgold," *Niles' National Register,* Vol. 70, 30 May 1846.

9. Joseph Davis Howell to Mother, 9 September 1846, Folder 2, William Burr Howell and Family Papers, Mississippi Department of Archives and History, Jackson, Mississippi.

10. *Charlotte Journal,* 7 July 1848.

11. *New Orleans Commercial Bulletin,* 3 December 1847.

12. A. B. Van Zandt, *God's Voice to the Nation. A Sermon occasioned by the death of Zachary Taylor, President of the United States. By Rev. A. B. Van Zandt, Pastor of the Tabb Street Presbyterian Church, Petersburg, VA* (Petersburg, VA: J. A. Gray, 1850), 14.

13. J.B.D., "On the Causes of the Remarkable Increase of Great Men in this Country, . . . ," *Southern Literary Messenger,* XIV no. 4 (April, 1848): 213.

14. Manuscript address to the returning volunteers of Carroll County [1847], Francis Marion Aldridge Papers, Folder 15, Mississippi Department of Archives and History, Jackson, Mississippi.

15. C. H. Wheat to George Maney, 15 May 1846, John Kimberly Papers, South-ern Historical Collection, University of North Carolina at Chapel Hill Library.

16. Anonymous woman from Mobile, Alabama, to Rebecca Gibson Small-wood, May 16, 1846.

17. *Messages of the Governors of Tennessee, 1845–1857,* Vol. 4, comp. Robert H. White (Nashville: Tennessee Historical Commission, 1957), 126.

18. Quoted in *Chronicles of the Gringos: The U.S. Army in the Mexican War, 1846–1848,* ed. George Winston Smith and Charles Judah (Albuquerque: University of New Mexico Press, 1968), 431.

19. A. P. Hill to Parents, 12 March 1847, U.S. Army—Virginia—First Regiment—Corse's (Montgomery Dent) Company, Virginia Historical Society.

20. H. H. Townes to Brother, 14 December 1846, Townes Family Papers, University of South Carolina, South Caroliniana Library.

21. Anonymous, "Ambition," *City Gazette and Daily Advertiser* [Charleston], 6 June 1789, reprinted in *American Political Writing during the Founding Era, 1760–1805,* Vol. 2, ed. Charles S. Hyneman and Donald S. Lutz (Indianapolis: Liberty Fund, 1983), 713.

22. Richard Henry Stanton, *Speech of Richard H. Stanton, Esq., In Defense of the Mexican War: Delivered at the War Meeting, Maysville, Saturday, December 18, 1847* (Maysville: Kentucky Flag Office, 1848), 1.

23. John Campbell to Col. Wm. B. Campbell, 4 August 1846, Campbell Family Papers, Duke University, Special Collections Department, William R. Perkins Library.

24. Walter Scott first published *The Tale of Old Mortality* in 1816. The poem, slightly misquoted, appears as the heading of chapter 34 and was well known by the American antebellum reading public. See, Walter Scott, *The Tale of Old Mortality,* ed. Douglas S. Mack (New York: Penguin Classics, 1999).

25. T. L. Sumrall to Thomas S. Sumrall, 19 May 1846, reprinted in the Jackson *Mississippian,* 27 May 1846.

26. Manuscript address given before the state legislature of Mississippi by Eugene A. Kennedy in 1846 to commemorate the 70th anniversary of American Independence, Miscellaneous Manuscript Collection, Mississippi Department of Archives and History, Jackson, Mississippi, 25–26.

27. Typescript copy of an undated article [c. 1846] describing the farewell celebration for the Raymond Fencibles, Miscellaneous Manuscripts Collection, Mississippi Department of Archives and History, Jackson, Mississippi.

28. *Vicksburg Tri-Weekly Whig,* 25 June 1846.

29. John Blount Robertson, *Reminiscences of a Campaign in Mexico by a Member of "The Bloody First." Preceded by a short Sketch of the History and Condition of Mexico from her own Revolution down to the War with the United States* (Nashville: John York, 1849), 65.

30. Originally printed in the Paulding *True Democrat,* reprinted in the *Mississippi Free Trader and Natchez Gazette,* 20 June 1846.

31. Louisa Quitman to John A. Quitman, 2 May 1847, Quitman Papers, Southern Historical Collection, University of North Carolina at Chapel Hill Library.

32. Quoted in Robert A. Brent, "Mississippi and the Mexican War," *Journal of Mississippi History* 31 (1969): 202.

33. Quoted in Peggy Mullarkey Cashion, "Women and the Mexican War, 1846–1848" (M. A. thesis, University of Texas at Arlington, 1990), 91.

34. Anna C. Maybin to William S. Johnson, 7 April 1848, William S. Johnson Papers, University of South Carolina, South Caroliniana Library.

35. Both quotations are in Peggy Mullarkey Cashion, "Women and the Mexican War, 1846–1848" (M. A. thesis, University of Texas at Arlington, 1990), 59, 93.

36. Quoted in John Eddins Simpson, *Howell Cobb: The Politics of Ambition* (Chicago: Adams, 1973), 48.

37. Both quotations are in *The Mexican War Journal of Captain Franklin Smith,* ed. Joseph E. Chance (Jackson: University of Mississippi Press, 1991), 67.

38. Jefferson Davis to Varina Howell Davis, 29 July 1846, *The Papers of Jefferson Davis,* Vol. 3, ed. James T. McIntosh (Baton Rouge: Louisiana State University Press, 1981), 13–14.

39. Sydenham Moore to Amanda Moore, 10 November 1846, Sydenham Moore Papers, Alabama Department of Archives and History, Montgomery, Alabama.

40. Thomas S. McNeir to Joseph K. McNeir, 20 June 1846, McNeir Family Papers, University of Virginia Library.

41. P. Archer [mother] to Fletcher Harris Archer, 8 July 1847, Fletcher Harris Archer Papers, Duke University, Special Collections Department, William R. Perkins Library.

42. *The Mexican War Journal of Captain Franklin Smith,* ed. Joseph E. Chance (Jackson: University of Mississippi Press, 1991), 171.

43. Both quotations are from Eliza Quitman to John A. Quitman, 12 July 1846 and 2 September 1847, Quitman Papers, Southern Historical Collection, University of North Carolina at Chapel Hill Library.

44. Both quotations are from W.T.H. Walker to Molly [Wife] [typescript, pg. 68], 19 February 1847, W.T.H. Walker Papers, Duke University, Special Collections Department, William R. Perkins Library.

45. "Cataline" to James Slade, 11 November 1847, William Slade Papers, Duke University, Special Collections Department, William R. Perkins Library.

46. *The United States and Mexico at War: Nineteenth Century Expansion and Conflict,* ed. Donald S. Frazier (New York: Macmillan Reference, 1988), 51.

47. *The Mexican War Journal of Captain Franklin Smith,* ed. Joseph E. Chance (Jackson: University of Mississippi Press, 1991), 67.

48. *The Diary of James K. Polk During his Presidency, 1845 to 1849,* Vol. 1, ed. Milo Milton Quaife (Chicago: A. C. McClure, 1910), 354.

49. All quotations in this paragraph are from *Congressional Globe,* 29th Congress, 1st Session, 1846, 783.

50. *Mississippi Free Trader and Natchez Gazette,* 7 May 1846.

51. *Yazoo* [City] *Democrat* [Mississippi], 6 May 1846.

52. Both quotations are found in "Speech on the Report of the Foreign Relations Committee," 12 December 1811, *The Papers of John C. Calhoun: Vol. 1, 1801–1817,* ed. Robert L. Meriweather (Columbia: University of South Carolina Press, 1959), 77, 80.

53. "Speech on the Loan Bill," 25 February 1814, *The Papers of John C. Calhoun: Vol. 1,* 228.

54. *Arkansas State Democrat* [Little Rock], 21 January 1848.

55. *Congressional Globe,* 29th Congress, 1st Session, 1846, 800–801.

56. Ibid., 793.

57. James D. Richardson, ed., *A Compilation of the Messages and Papers of the Presidents, 1789–1902,* Vol. 4 (Washington, D.C.: Government Printing Office, 1903), 473.

58. *The Diary of James K. Polk During his Presidency, 1845 to 1849,* Vol. 2, ed. Milo Milton Quaife (Chicago: A. C. McClure, 1910), 348, 368–69.

59. For a few examples, see *Wilmington Journal* [North Carolina], 29 May, 10 July, 6 November 1846, 5 February, 9 July, 13 August, 15 October 1847, 18 February 1848; *Mississippi Free Trader and Natchez Gazette,* 29 May, 30 May, 18 June 1846; *Yazoo* [City] *Democrat,* 6 May 1846, 9 February 1847; [Carrollton] *Mississippi Democrat,* 30 December 1846, 18 August 1847.

60. E. A. O'Neal to George Smith Houston, 25 May 1846, George Smith Houston Papers, Duke University, Special Collections Department, William R. Perkins Library.

61. *Congressional Globe,* 29th Congress, 2nd Session, 18 February 1847, 450.

62. All quotations in this paragraph are from *Appendix to the Congressional Globe,* 29th Congress, 1st Session, 946, 948.

63. Ibid., 949, 950.

64. Ibid., 949.

65. Quoted in John H. Schroeder, *Mr. Polk's War: American Dissent and Opposition, 1846–1848* (Madison: University of Wisconsin Press, 1973), 78–79.

66. H. H. Townes to Armistead Burt, 14 March 1848, Armistead Burt Papers, Duke University, Special Collections Department, William R. Perkins Library.

67. Both quotations are from *Oration pronounced by the Honorable Robert C. Winthrop, Speaker of the House of Representatives, on the Fourth of July, 1848, on the occasion of the laying of the cornerstone of the National Monument to the memory of Washington. . . .* (Washington: J. & G. S. Gideon, 1848), 32, 34.

FURTHER READING

The social history of the Mexican War remains to be written. By and large, one must refer to unpublished material—primary sources, master's and doctoral manuscripts—and journal articles to get a broad view of how Americans experienced the war. The list of books below is by no means encompassing but is intended to provide a basic introduction to the historical literature and source material pertaining to the war.

Bauer, K. Jack. *The Mexican War, 1846–1848.* New York: Macmillan, 1974. The best scholarly single-volume account of the war.

DeVoto, Bernard. *The Year of Decision: 1846.* Boston: Houghton Mifflin, 1942. A narrative of one year, 1846, but there is no better place to turn if one desires a feel for the times. DeVoto is the finest writer on this list.

Eisenhower, John S. D. *So Far From God: The U.S. War With Mexico, 1846–1848.* New York: Random House, 1989. A well-written, popular account of the war.

Foos, Paul W. *A Short Offhand Killing Affair: Soldiers and Social Conflict during the Mexican-American War.* Chapel Hill: University of North Carolina Press, 2002. Worth reading as it is one of the few books that addresses the social history of the Mexican War. Foos focuses on the role that class and race played, but he occasionally draws sweeping conclusions his research does not conclusively support.

Frazier, Donald, ed. *The United States and Mexico at War: Nineteenth-Century Expansionism and Conflict.* New York: Macmillan Reference, 1998. The best single-volume reference book on the war. The place to start if you have questions.

Johannsen, Robert W. *To the Halls of the Montezumas: The Mexican War in the American Imagination.* New York: Oxford University Press, 1985. A magisterial account of how Americans experienced and thought about the war. Excellent coverage of published sources from sheet music to biographies. If it was published during the Mexican War and dealt with the conflict, Johannsen has probably read it and written about it.

Lander, Ernest M., Jr. *Reluctant Imperialists: Calhoun, The South Carolinians, and the Mexican War.* Baton Rouge: Louisiana State University Press, 1980. The best of the few published studies of a state's Mexican War experience.

Morrison, Chaplain W. *Democratic Politics and Sectionalism: The Wilmot Proviso Controversy.* Chapel Hill: University of North Carolina Press, 1967. A detailed account of the Democratic politics surrounding the Wilmot Proviso.

Schroeder, John H. *Mr. Polk's War: American Opposition and Dissent, 1846–1848.* Madison: University of Wisconsin Press, 1973. In addition to being well-researched, this is the only book-length study of opposition to the war.

Smith, Justin H. *The War with Mexico.* 2 vols. New York: Macmillan, 1919. Won the Pulitzer Prize for History in 1920. A copiously researched, general history of the war. Necessary reading for any serious student. Watch out for Smith's jingoism and bias though.

Tutorow, Norman E. *The Mexican-American War: An Annotated Bibliography.* Westport, CT: Greenwood Press, 1981. Somewhat dated, but remains one of the best single-volume references for source material, both published and primary, on the Mexican War.

Winders, Richard Bruce. *Mr. Polk's War: The American Military Experience in the Mexican War.* College Station: University of Texas A&M Press, 1997. The best book on the U.S. Army in the Mexican War. Especially good at illuminating the role that politics played in the American military effort.

FIVE

A Very Sad Life: Civilians in the Confederacy

James Marten

"The war was continually rising in front of me," wrote Robert Martin, who, as a boy in the Shenandoah Valley during the Civil War, grew tired of the conflict barring "me from something I wanted, whether food, clothes, or playthings." Although he did, of course, want the South to win, he "grew progressively tired of the continual night alarms," of "surly and threatening strangers" bursting into the house whenever they pleased, of "the ever shorter rations of food that I could hardly eat."[1]

Historians of the American Civil War have studied the southern home front in far more detail than the northern home front, at least partly because contemporaries such as Robert Martin left detailed and often moving memories of their home-front experiences. Economic and political issues, women's experiences, the role of dissent and disaffection, guerilla warfare, and many other topics related to the short-lived Confederate republic have filled bookshelves over the last century. Borrowing from the work of many of these scholars, this essay will focus on the many ways that the war "rose up" in the lives of southerners, from the economic and material effects of the war to the deterioration of the institution of slavery, from the growing disaffection in many parts of the Confederacy to the harsh but hopeful lives of African Americans who escaped slavery's grasp, and from the occupation of southern farms and towns by Union troops to the horror of coming under fire in the battles that raged across the South.

THE ARCHETYPAL CONFEDERATE: EDMUND RUFFIN

Like Robert Martin, Edmund Ruffin was a Virginian whose wartime experiences and attitudes provide a microcosm of the southern home front. A pioneering scientific farmer—he published an agricultural journal for a number of years—he was also a self-styled "missionary of disunion."[2] Proud of his outsider status and used to being ignored, Ruffin nevertheless worked hard to convince his fellow southerners that northern attitudes about slavery and the rise of the Republican Party justified seceding from the Union. Few listened as Ruffin thundered about secession through the 1850s. But that changed when John Brown mounted his "invasion" of Harpers Ferry, Virginia, in October 1859. Ruffin's dire warnings about northern extremism and aggressiveness suddenly began to make sense to more and more southerners.

As the crisis escalated to secession and then to war, Ruffin appeared everywhere: at John Brown's execution, at the Florida secession convention, firing the first gun at Fort Sumter, and marching with a company of South Carolina volunteers to the First Battle of Bull Run. It was at about this time that Ruffin posed for one of the most famous photographs of a civilian from the Civil War era: seated in a chair, musket in hand, white hair flowing over his shoulders, clear, hard eyes gazing at the camera.

Despite his age—he was born in 1794—Ruffin's experiences during the war matched those of many southerners. He pitched in whenever he could. Officials of several states consulted him regarding the disposition of guns and ammunition, and he toured Richmond's Tredegar Iron Works to determine its capacity for supplying the Confederacy with ordnance and inspected a fortification on the James River. Also, knowing that Confederate civilians might be forced to defend themselves from invading enemies, he tutored a pair of women in marksmanship.

Like many ardent southerners, Ruffin's loyalty to the Confederacy sometimes came out in expressions of hatred for northerners. Toward the beginning of 1862 he remarked that, although the North had superiority in resources:

[The Confederacy's] superiority to our enemy is in the much higher moral & intellectual grade of the Southern people, & of the superior principles by which they are actuated, & the holy cause which supports their patriotism & courage. The southern people are defending their just & dearest rights, their property, their families, their very existence, against the fierce & violent assault of enemies who are impelled mainly by the greedy desire to rob us of all that we possess. . . . Their impulses . . . are but those which actuate banditti & pirates in their pursuit of plunder by means of murder.[3]

Ruffin loved to indulge in the worst rumors of Yankee atrocities: according to his diary, the garrison at Washington, D.C., regularly plundered shops, raped women, and murdered southern sympathizers; letters found on numerous battlefields indicated that northerners would be allowed to claim southern land and southerners' possessions if they won the war.

Ruffin and his family were directly affected by the war. Because his plantation, Marlbourne, and his son's plantation, Beechwood, lay near Richmond, they were both in the path of the Union troops during the Peninsula Campaign in the spring and summer of 1862, which culminated in the Seven Days' Battles. Yankees overran Beechwood on their way to the battle of Malvern Hill; foragers and scouts frequently roamed over the neighborhood around Marlbourne. The northerners did considerable damage to the property. Although the buildings remained standing, furniture was smashed, floors were strewn with litter and garbage, and walls were stained with tobacco juice. All of the household supplies, food stores, and livestock were gone, as were most of Ruffin's extensive library and personal papers. Soldiers had also scratched names and graffiti into the walls. Many were insults directed toward Ruffin. Ruffin defiantly wrote that "I take the scurrilous abuse thrown upon myself very complacently—as being the only compliment or eulogism that a low-bred Yankee can bestow on me." He recorded some examples in his diary: "We pity but do not hate the rebels"; "This house belonged to a Ruffinly son of a bitch"; "Old Ruffin don't you wish you had left the Southern Confederacy to go to Hell, (where it will go,) & had stayed at home?"; and "You did fire the first gun on Sumter, you traitor son of a bitch."[4]

In addition, slaves began to leave Beechwood, too, just after Ruffin and the rest of the family had evacuated it. Slaves continued to leave after the white folks returned on June 17. By that time, it was not just men who were leaving, but women and children, too—three entire families, 21 people, left the night after Ruffin came home. Ruffin believed the slaves had been tricked by cynical Yankees: "it appears they have been promised enormous wages, plenty to eat, & no work to do" by the Yankees.[5] Ruffin's son lost nearly 100 slaves while federal troops were in the vicinity.

Although Ruffin maintained his defiant stance toward the North, the war continued to take its toll. A son and a grandson were killed in battle (another grandson was a prisoner of war), his slaves continued to run away, his wealth was scattered. He became increasingly depressed and doubtful that the revolution he had helped to create would succeed. Yet, even in the dark winter of 1865, Ruffin could still write of the "single object for which [I] would now wish any extension of my life—which is, that I may witness the success & triumph of my country in the conclusion of the war, which is now waged against us, in the most atrocious manner, by the vilest & most malignant people & government in Christendom." But he knew that was unlikely, as "every passing month seems to leave the attainment" of such a result "less hopeful."[6]

Ruffin's ardent southern nationalism, his sacrifices of property and family, and his dwindling confidence in the ultimate success of the Confederacy reflect—even as they exaggerated it—the story of the Confederate home front.

THE CONFEDERATE ECONOMY

One of the first challenges facing the new Confederate nation was creating the institutions of nationhood—including a Treasury Department and other elements of a financial system. Economic problems would plague the southern war effort and the home front throughout the conflict. Confederate financial policy, hastily made after secession but before the real fighting began, guaranteed that, unless its armies won a quick victory over the Union, the Confederacy would suffer from economic instability and inflation. Early on, loans from some of the newly seceded states helped the country pay its bills. However, because the country had very little specie—gold—in its treasury, according to the historian Emory Thomas, "gifts, loans, and the printing press became the chief sources of support for the Confederate government."[7] The government placed a lot of confidence in a plan by which investors would buy bonds from the government and collect a guaranteed return some years in the future (the guaranteed interest ranged between 5 and 8 percent; the bonds were to be redeemed in 20 or 30 years). In essence, investors were loaning money to the Confederate government, betting that it would win its battle for independence and survive long enough to pay its creditors. The Confederacy also instituted various taxes, but due to an inadequate bureaucracy, a deteriorating transportation network, and citizens' resistance, the government collected only a fraction of the money its citizens owed.

But bond sales never matched the Confederacy's economic needs, and the government increasingly relied on the printing of paper money to pay its bills. Less than a year after the war began, three-fourths of the government's income came from issuing paper money. Having so much currency in circulation inevitably led to inflation. In 1863, for instance, the value of a Confederate dollar plummeted, from a value of $.33 in gold in January to only a nickel ($.05) in December.

Another economic difficulty facing the Confederacy was a serious shortage of food—or, more accurately in some areas, inadequate means of transporting the food that existed to hungry southerners. The conversion of southern agriculture from cash crops like cotton and tobacco to foodstuffs was slow and painful for most planters. Federal troops occupied or threatened livestock and grain-producing regions in central Virginia and middle Tennessee. Absent farmers and planters slowed down production, and the already limited network of southern railroads, few of which were more than local or, perhaps, regional lines, wore down as new rails and equipment became too expensive or too difficult to get, and as Yankee troops destroyed or took over more and more of the region's railroads.

The shortages were most severe in southern cities, where civilians rioted in protest of food shortages and government mismanagement of the supply system. The most famous disturbance occurred in Richmond in April 1863, when a group of women—wives of factory workers struggling to keep up with inflation in the Confederate capital—gathered to present a petition to Virginia Governor John Letcher. Eventually several hundred women—joined by a few men and a number of youth—confronted the governor. He could give them no answers, and when he returned to his mansion, the crowd turned into a mob, and a peaceful protest became the Richmond "Bread Riot." Stores and markets on 10 city blocks were broken into and looted; the rioters took not just food, but also jewelry, clothes, and anything else they wanted. The violence did not stop until President Davis appeared before the crowd and ordered a company of soldiers to fire on them if they did not disperse in five minutes. The protestors went home, but other riots broke out in Atlanta, Macon, Columbus, and Augusta, Georgia; in Mobile, Alabama; and in Salisbury and High Point, North Carolina.

If it is somewhat surprising—at least superficially—that an agricultural economy had difficulty feeding its people, it is probably less surprising that it was unable to create an industrial base. It is a commonplace that the Confederacy lagged far behind the Union in its manufacturing capacity when the war began. In 1860, the latter had produced 97 percent of the country's firearms, 94 percent of its cloth, 93 percent of its pig iron, and over 90 percent of its boots and shoes. And most of the South's factories were located in the upper South, including Kentucky, Maryland, and Delaware—states that did not join the Confederacy. Despite this early handicap, however, the Confederacy actually was able to supply its armies with arms and ammunition throughout the war. The effort to convert the economy to a military footing affected everyone. Agents and army officers scoured the country, confiscating homemade liquor stills and church and plantation bells for metal to be melted down and formed into weapons. Soldiers and, after the firing stopped, boys roamed battlefields looking for lead and damaged weapons to salvage.

With help from free and enslaved African Americans, young boys and old men, and young women and girls, the CSA became a major manufacturer of war materiel. By 1863, for instance, 10,000 people were working in war industries in Selma, Alabama, alone. The biggest iron production facility in the Confederacy, the Tredegar Iron Works in Richmond, employed 700 people in 1861 but had increased to 2,500 by 1863. Much smaller establishments sprang up in cities and towns throughout the Confederacy. These ranged from two or three men putting together pistols in backyard sheds to a gunpowder factory in Augusta, Georgia, the largest at that time in North America. Shipyards produced 50 ships for the Confederate Navy, including 22 ironclads. However, despite the Confederacy's success in producing arms and ammunition, it was never able to come close to matching the North in producing other manufactured products—and it just barely kept its armies and civilians fed.

Shortages of basic necessities, coffee, sugar, butter, and household items that had been imported from Europe before the war, forced Confederate civilians to be creative. Southerners substituted sawdust for soap, salt for tooth powder, pigs' tails and ears for Christmas tree ornaments, leaves for mattress stuffing, and okra seeds and chicory nuts for coffee beans. They published recipe books that offered ways to make apple pie without apples and lemonade without lemons and recommended home remedies based on locally grown plants. Women made blankets from old carpets, shoes from worn out saddles and furniture, and battle flags from wedding dresses.

One product for which there was no substitute was salt. Modern Americans barely think about salt, but for people living without refrigeration, it was a basic need; there was no other way to preserve meat, which in the Confederacy meant that if no salt was available, thousands of hogs could not be turned into pork and bacon. Its scarcity was reflected in the skyrocketing prices asked for it; the price for salt rose from $2 a bag before the war to up to $60 as early as 1862. Southern governments anxiously developed new sources of salt, which promptly became targets for Union military operations in Florida and in Saltville, Virginia.

As in any war, an accurate count of the cost in civilian lives is nearly impossible. Newspapers in the Confederacy struggled simply to remain in print, and battlefield news dominated the headlines. But the conditions brought on by the war obviously affected the nutrition of southerners, whose diets came to lack much in the way of vegetables and fruits. The war also limited the amount of medical care they received when they fell ill, as many physicians had become surgeons in the military. The respected Civil War historian James M. McPherson has suggested that as many as 50,000 noncombatants—white and black alike—may have died from the effects of malnutrition, exposure, and disease.

The severity of the suffering, the outbreak of riots like the one in Richmond, and the complaints from Confederate citizens to their local, state, and federal officials encouraged local and county governments to create programs that provided food and allowances for the families of soldiers and to open city controlled markets to prevent speculators from charging predatory prices. Some towns and cities purchased basics like flour, salt, and meat in bulk and sold them to individuals at cost, while others set up markets where the neediest families could pick up free food. Skilled craftsmen and farmers were exempted from military service in order to keep the civilian economy going. These programs apparently had the desired effect, as no other major disturbances were reported after the flurry of "bread riots" in 1863. But Confederate resources continued to shrink with the continued demands by the army for white soldiers and black laborers, as more farm land was occupied by Union troops, and as the blockade and transportation problems limited the government's ability to import and transport necessities. As a result, the hardships brought on by the war continued to chip away at Confederate civilians' loyalty and determination.

The war brought hard times to almost all southerners, but at least one, the newspaper humorist named Charles Henry Smith, who wrote under the name Bill Arp, declared in one column—an open letter to Abraham Lincoln—that the South would never give up. "Mr. Linkhorn, sur, our peepul git more stubborn every day," he wrote in the colorful style of many nineteenth-century columnists. "They go mighty nigh naked, and say they are savin their Sunday klothes to wear after we have whipped you. They just glory in livin on half rashuns and stewin salt out of their smoke house dirt. They say they had rather fight you than feed you, and swear by the ghost of [John C.] Calhoun they will eat roots and drink branch water the balance of the time before they will kernowly to your abolition dyenasty."[8] Home-front southerners would, for the most part, live up to Arp's proud declaration, made halfway through the war. But as the challenges facing them mounted, it became increasingly difficult to sustain hope in the Confederate cause.

MOBILIZING FOR WAR ON THE CONFEDERATE HOME FRONT

Historians have frequently debated the extent to which the Civil War was a so-called total war—a conflict in which all of a country's resources are mobilized on behalf of the war effort and during which all of those resources become targets of the enemy. There is no question that some elements of the Civil War did become "total," especially when viewed from the Confederate side. Most of the destruction of property took place in the South, of course. Between 750,000 and 850,000 men served in the army—at least 75 percent of the military age population (which by the end of the war included men ranging in age from 17 to 50).

But the mobilization of the civilian population for war also suggests that, at least on the Confederate side, the Civil War was a total war. Because such a large percentage of the adult white males were drawn into military service, the lives of the people they left behind changed dramatically. Farm and plantation wives and sons took over the day-to-day operations when husbands and fathers left for the army. They managed slaves, marketed crops, and dealt with all the complexities of administering an agricultural operation. Perhaps a quarter of a million Confederate soldiers died in battle or of disease; and many left behind families who now looked to mothers as heads of household.

Women and girls converted all of the skills they learned as wives, daughters, and mothers to a war footing, knitting and sewing for the soldiers and acting as nurses when armies fought or marched close by. Throughout the war they raised money for hospitals and other soldiers' causes by holding church bazaars, organizing raffles, and staging concerts and tableaux. Sunday School classes created soldiers' aid organizations that collected supplies and money to be sent to camps. And throughout the Confederacy, children of all ages spent idle time "picking lint" from rags and old clothes to be packed around wounds on the battlefield. Most contemporaries and a number of historians have also highlighted the importance of women's patriotism in encouraging wavering young men to join the army. At least during the first year or two of the war, women were famous for disdaining healthy men who remained at home, or those who joined "home guard" or militia companies that were unlikely to see service. As one southern woman declared in a letter to a friend, she would hate "a man who would flinch, even from martyrdom for his Country."[9]

In addition to their fundraising and domestic activities, women also took on jobs that broke a number of social barriers. The informal nature of female nursing during the early part of the war turned into a much more official role for a number of women when the Confederate Congress authorized the hiring of civilian matrons and female nurses in military hospitals. One woman, Sally Louisa Tompkins, actually received a captain's commission in the army so her clean, efficiently run hospital could be an official military installation. Confederate Treasury Department and other government bureaus employed women as clerks; many spent hours every day copying by hand the Secretary of the Treasury's signature onto the millions of dollars of currency rolling off Confederate printing presses.

The absence of most able-bodied men during the war left many southern women to fend for themselves. (Library of Congress)

Other young women and girls were forced to take on manual labor. Hundreds made uniforms and other war material at private and government-owned plants in Georgia. Over 300 women and girls between the ages of 12 and 20 also worked at the Confederate Laboratory on Brown's Island in Richmond, where late in the winter of 1863 an explosion killed 36 and injured 30 more. As the grim casualty list at Richmond shows, virtually all southerners mobilized for war.

CIVILIANS UNDER FIRE

The most extreme civilian experience came when the battlefront and the home front intersected. Civil War armies normally fought their battles away from population centers, but civilians inevitably came under fire on many occasions. The widow Judith Henry at First Manassas and Jenny Wade at Gettysburg are only the most famous examples of civilian battle deaths—the phrase often used in modern wars is "collateral damage"—but countless other southerners came under fire at one point or another during the war.

The danger was greatest, of course, when a city was under siege. And the most famous—and, perhaps, the worst siege endured by southern civilians—occurred at Vicksburg, Mississippi, in the summer of 1863. The constant combat, the stench of rotting horse and human flesh broiling in the Mississippi heat, and the nightly shelling of the city created nearly unbearable conditions. Soldiers and civilians alike suffered from dysentery and malaria. Noncombatants often huddled in caves burrowed into the city's many hillsides. Supplies dwindled steadily until, by the end of June, Confederate soldiers subsisted on rationed water and tiny amounts of rice and peas, and the women and children of the city survived on about the same. But the shelling was the worst trial. Mrs. W. W. Lord described the "horrible shells roaring and bursting all around" her family and neighbors, "the concussion making our heads feel like they would burst." However, she proudly reported, her "children bear themselves like little heroes. Every night, when the bombardment began and it was time to run for their cave shelter, "they spring up . . . like soldiers, slip on their shoes without a word and run up the hill."[10]

Another woman who survived the siege described the cave shelters in which her family and many other found refuge. Mary Ann Loughborough's "cave," hollowed out of the hill behind her house, had three rooms—a six feet deep entrance, fitted with a cloth "door," branching into a "T" with a bedroom on one side and a dressing room on the other. Although she had to crouch in the front room and bedroom, enough earth had been scooped out in the other room for her to stand upright. In this little space she "went regularly to work, keeping house under ground," fixing meals of corn bread and bacon, and slowly growing accustomed to her "shell-expectant life."[11]

Although it is surprising that so few civilians were hurt or killed given the many tons of Union shells fired into the city, there was, nevertheless a cost. Letters from a woman living in Vicksburg detail the cost to the civilians of Vicksburg, including the news that at least three women had been decapitated by Union shells, that a little boy had died in a cave, and that the young son of an Irish couple living near her home was killed during the shelling. A neighbor had "heard screams down [in the kitchen] one morning and ran down there. A piece of shell had passed through the bed where the child was laying cutting it in two and its legs were sticking out of the wall where the shell had driven them and still kicking." The horrifying scene had "killed" the sick mother, "and the Father rushed all about town screaming and going on terribly."[12] "How very sad this life in Vicksburg," wrote Mary Ann Loughborough, with words that any southern civilian who experienced the sharp end of war could share.[13]

That sadness—along with fear and a sense of helplessness—came to other parts of the Confederacy whenever Union and Confederate forces met in battle. According to one resident of Harpers Ferry, Virginia, which changed hands several times during the war, "the great objects in life were to procure something to eat and to keep yourself out of light by day and your lamps . . . hidden by night" so as not to draw the fire of Union pickets.[14]

One of the most famous diaries of the Civil War offered a child's-eye view of the siege of Atlanta. Ten-year-old Carrie Berry recorded near misses when shells and grapeshot crashed into her family's back yard or through the roof—once destroying a bed on which someone had been sleeping a short time before. Kept inside by her rightfully worried parents, Carrie complained, "I get so tired of being housed up all the time. The shells get worse and worse every day."[15] Carrie spent much of her time knitting, cooking, ironing, sewing, and caring for her newborn sister. She also sorted through burned houses looking for usable nails and commented on the comings and goings of Confederate troops and, after the Battle of Atlanta, Union troops. And for many months, her diary never mentioned a single instance in which she played or went to school. For this little girl, and for countless other boys and girls around the South, childhood had simply ceased to exist.

A HARD WAR: THE OCCUPIED SOUTH

Union forces occupied huge swaths of the Confederacy between 1861 and 1865. The United States never gave up control of northern and extreme southeastern Virginia, and by the spring of 1862 had taken over northern Arkansas, coastal North Carolina, and, more importantly, New Orleans and southern Louisiana. The surrender of Vicksburg a year later opened the entire Mississippi Valley to occupation. Even south Texas was briefly occupied by Union forces in late 1863 and early 1864. As a result, a common home-front experience in the Confederacy was dealing with occupation—and with the occupiers.

The U.S. government's policy toward Confederate civilians evolved over the course of the war. Early on, armies were ordered not to disturb southerners any more than was necessary: personal property was to be protected, supplies taken from southern farms were to be paid for, slaves were not to be encouraged to run away (some were even returned to their owners after they ran into Union lines), and women were to be shown the utmost respect. This so-called soft war was meant to win southerners' hearts and minds and to encourage their loyalty to the United States. However, it became apparent by the second year of the war that this policy was not working, and the government and military began to change course. A series of Confiscation Acts passed by Congress punished suspected rebels by seizing their property; these laws, in effect, gave escaped slaves the protection of the U.S. Army. An 1863 General Order also gave commanders the authority to destroy private property that could be used by Confederate forces. Moreover, armies were given permission to "live off the land"—to forage at will throughout the Confederate countryside. These so-called hard war policies led inevitably to the strategy pursued by Gen. William T. Sherman, whose "March to the Sea" from Atlanta to Savannah in late 1864 was meant, as he told Gen. Ulysses S. Grant, to "make Georgia howl"—but also to deprive the Confederacy of vital supplies and transportation facilities.

The demographics of most places occupied by federal forces had changed dramatically from the beginning of the war. Of course, the Confederate army had already evacuated a location before the blue coats arrived, and high-ranking civil officials and local politicians were arrested—or worse— if they were captured by Union troops. Most of the healthy men between the ages of 18 and 50 were in the army by the end of the war, leaving boys, old men, and invalids. Wealthy residents were the most likely civilians to leave, taking with them as much moveable property as they could carry and many of their slaves. As a result, most of the civil and social leaders of southern communities were gone by the time northern forces took over.

The challenges of living in an occupied region were many. Northern soldiers confiscated personal property, livestock, and food for their own use. Although property rights were far more likely to be respected by soldiers serving garrison duty than by soldiers who were just passing through—it was safer to live in occupied Memphis, for instance, than to live along the path of Sherman's March—southerners could rarely feel totally secure in their possessions. Economic distress, worry over absent family members, and countless other sources of stress and disappointment wearied people living in occupied territory. And the uncertainty of who was in charge—their own civil authorities or the U.S. military—weighed heavily on southern civilians, who often had to swear oaths to the United States to move about the country, conduct business, or execute legal documents.

And there was always the threat of personal danger. Although soldiers actually harmed relatively few noncombatants, that was small consolation to southern women and children, and the possibility of violence was a painful worry for most southerners in occupied areas. More common than actual attacks on people were assaults on personal property. Yankees would storm into houses, go through personal possessions, destroy photographs and other personal belongings, and force women and children out of bed in the middle of the night. Their often rude and aggressive behavior inspired anger, fear, and resentment. "It makes my blood boil," one woman wrote, "when I remember that our private rooms, our chambers, our very inner sanctums, are thrown open to a ruthless soldiery."[16]

Perhaps inevitably, rumors were spread around the South of alleged atrocities—and some were true. A newspaper reported that Union troops had murdered a little boy because he was named for a noted Confederate general; a Florida Confederate claimed that three Yankees had raped a 10-year-old girl; and a Louisiana woman reported that soldiers had abused a girl so badly that she went insane. Perhaps 600 Union soldiers were court-martialed for raping black and white civilians, mainly in the South, and the army executed at least 22 men for sex crimes against civilians.

New Orleans became the most talked about occupied city in the Confederacy. As a major port and the South's largest city, the loss of New Orleans was a serious blow to the Confederacy. Captured in April 1862, New Orleans and the southern parishes of Louisiana became a laboratory for the creation of "loyal" governments in the occupied South. By 1864, a party of moderate prewar Unionists had formed and been elected to the major posts in the new government. Although "provisional" governments were established in a few other parts of the occupied South—on a tiny sliver of coastal North Carolina, in extreme south Texas, and in Arkansas, for instance—the wartime government of Louisiana was the most successful experiment in wartime reconstruction.

But New Orleans became famous as an occupied city because of the man who served as its first Union commander: Gen. Benjamin Butler. Butler earned the nickname "Beast" when he ordered the execution of a man who tore down a Union flag. He further angered southerners by instituting a plan to arm African Americans (mostly free blacks who had formed their own militias earlier in the war). His men attempted to enforce the loyalty of the citizenry; soldiers even searched schools for evidence of Confederate sympathizers. Tension arose in the city—as it did in all occupied parts of the Confederacy—between residents still committed to the southern cause; residents who had no love for Yankees, but saw no reason to resist them; and those who rejoiced with the Union occupation and eagerly cooperated with developing a loyal government. Even among the latter, however, a debate raged over whether or not to abolish slavery and to extend voting rights to black men (neither was actually accomplished).

Butler's most infamous action as commander of New Orleans, how-ever, was his famous "woman's order," issued after a woman emptied her chamber pot onto the head of a Union officer. Butler ordered that any woman who continued to insult Union troops would "be regarded and held liable to be treated as a woman of the town plying her avocation"—as a prostitute![17] Combined with his other policies, this order made Butler one of the most hated men in the South, and some southerners reportedly placed his portrait on the bottoms of their chamber pots.

On the other hand, occupying forces and residents of occupied regions tended to fall into relatively peaceful relationships. This was particularly true when Union troops remained in the same place for extended peri-ods of time; troops marching quickly through a region rarely perceived the people they encountered as anything other than possible sources of food or as abstract, generic enemies. In an occupation situation, however, individual families often grew fond of the young men stationed near their houses and farms, who often took a special interest in the children they met. A few teenaged girls in occupied towns retained their fierce Confed-erate loyalty and recorded in their diaries the names of classmates who flirted or even talked to attentive Yankee soldiers.

A HARD LOT: REFUGEES

The hard hand of war drove many southerners to flee from the Yankees as they occupied larger portions of the South. It is impossible to deter-mine how many families became refugees—voluntarily or involuntarily, as in the case of Atlantans in the fall of 1864, when Gen. William Sherman ordered all residents to leave the city. Many left their homes for brief peri-ods of time, or simply moved in with relatives in another county or state. But it is safe to say that tens of thousands of Confederate civilians were displaced during the war. Although southerners from all classes became refugees, they tended to be planters and their families—men who feared being arrested because they were local political leaders—and families with property, including slaves, that they feared would be taken by invad-ing Yankees. They crowded into supposedly safe places anywhere from Richmond to East Texas, looking for work and provisions.

One of the most famous accounts of a refugee family is the journal of a young woman named Kate Stone, whose father-less family packed up and moved from Brokenburn, their plantation near Vicksburg, and spent the sec-ond half of the war as refugees near Tyler, Texas. The Stones, who in peace-time lived very comfortably with dozens of slaves, endured weeks of travel, sleeping on hard ground or bug-infested beds, eating indigestible food, and, for the first time in their lives, experienced a shocking lack of respect shown them by African Americans they encountered along the way.

The Stones provide one version of the southern refugee experience. Once they finished their difficult passage through Louisiana to Texas, they returned to their normal roles and pastimes. The younger children—Kate had two little brothers and a sister, along with older brothers in the Confederate Army—attended a local school, while the women managed their makeshift home and went visiting other families in the refugee community. Kate occupied herself with reading, sewing, gossiping, visiting, and receiving visits from young army officers. Indeed, Kate admitted once that the last year in Texas was the most pleasant of her young life.

Local residents often viewed refugees with suspicion—especially rich refugees whose war seemed less demanding to less fortunate southerners. And Kate shared the contempt that wealthy refugees often expressed about their new neighbors. "The more we see of the people," she wrote shortly after the Stones settled in, "the less we like them, and every refugee we have seen feels the same way." She chalked the Texans' attitude up to "envy, just pure envy. The refugees are a nicer and more refined people than most of those they meet, and they see and resent the difference."[18] At a Texas barbecue, a refugee friend complained about their less than perfect surroundings and asked, "why should we dine with plebians?" After making an appearance and seeing "the animals feed," in the memorable words of Kate's mother, the Stones returned home.[19] Sometimes the tension between locals and refugees exploded into violence; Kate's teenaged brothers got into frequent scrapes with Texas youngsters and were even challenged to duels.

The Stones were hardly representative refugees. Most had far fewer resources at their disposal than the Stones. The diary of a much less fortunate woman, Cornelia Peake McDonald, shows another family headed by a woman, that was forced to move from one small Virginia town to another for most of the conflict. After losing their soldier-husband and father early in the war, she and her children were often sick. Her youngest child died, and the survivors endured extraordinary poverty. Encountering unfriendly Yankees at every step and sometimes unable to find food—some days all she consumed was coffee and bread—Cornelia barely made ends meet by teaching drawing and French. Her sons also brought in a little money cutting firewood for the Confederate government, and friends could be counted on for small loans. Like most refugees, Cornelia was affected by the rampant inflation in the Confederacy. One time she discovered that $100 in Confederate money bought only poor bacon, three candles, and a pound of nearly rancid butter. Unable to afford new clothes, Cornelia clothed her children in hand-me-downs from friends, or created new pieces out of old cloth. When her 17-year-old son, Harry, finally convinced her to allow him to join the army (he enlisted in the Army of Northern Virginia just in time to surrender with it at Appomattox), Cornelia made his uniform out of the course material used to make clothes for slaves before the war.

A number of slaves became refugees, too. The Stones had taken their best slaves with them to Texas, where they were hired out to local planters

The prospect of freedom but also an uncertain future awaited slaves as the Confederacy's fortunes ebbed. (Library of Congress)

and farmers. Texas was often seen as the safest spot to protect slave property, and hopeful and desperate planters transported tens of thousands of their most valuable slaves to the Lone Star State to preserve them from Union troops invading Louisiana and Mississippi; some came from as far away as Virginia or South Carolina. A Mississippi slave remembered having to walk along the side of the road on the way to Texas, because so many wagons were going the same way; "it look like everybody in the world was going to Texas."[20] The forced emigration often separated families, as children and old people were left behind and only healthy young men—the slaves worth the most on the open market and most able to work hard—were taken along. Slaves who became ill, even women about to deliver babies, were literally left at the sides of roads.

The refugee experience can be summarized by the comments made to a newspaper reporter by a poor woman he encountered on the road in Tennessee: "It's a hard lot, gentlemen, to have to leave your house in this way and look for another among strangers."[21]

THIS SAD WAR: MORALE

Although historians frequently argue that southerners retained a remarkable constancy to their fledgling country despite these and other hardships, the Confederacy was plagued by frequent, and sometimes crippling, amounts of disaffection and even disloyalty. Some of this stemmed from the poverty, danger, and dislocation that accompanied the war in some regions; some southerners simply could not spare the energy required to maintain their support for the Confederacy.

But philosophical differences among Confederates also played an important part in the dissent that contributed to the erosion of home-front morale. Several events had unified southerners in April and May of 1861: the attack on Fort Sumter, President Lincoln's call for troops to put down the rebellion and imposition of a naval blockade on the rebellious states, and the secession of the upper South states of Virginia, North Carolina, Tennessee, and Arkansas. However, the unity inspired by the immediate crisis only temporarily concealed prewar divisions among southerners. During the election of 1860 and the "secession winter" of 1860–1861, secessionists had urged action, cooperationists had argued for caution, and Unionists had argued that southern interests were best served in the Union, not in an independent country. But even these three categories of southerners were divided into subgroupings; some Unionists, for instance, were unconditional in their support for the United States, while the loyalty of others was conditional—they would support the Union only as long as the government refrained from interfering with slavery.

Once the war began, support for the Confederacy surged, and most Unionists chose their region over their country. But significant dissent emerged fairly quickly. Every state had a few die-hard Unionists who remained loyal to the Union despite its war against the South; some of them were convicted by state courts of various forms of disloyalty and executed or jailed, a number of them fled the Confederacy, and thousands joined Union army regiments formed entirely of southerners who remained loyal to the United States. In Texas, for instance, the First and Second Texas Cavalry were composed largely of German–Americans and Mexicans, respectively.

Another category of dissent stemmed from the ways in which the war challenged the assumptions on which the Confederacy was based. Although the larger issue for which Confederates fought was, of course, the notion of states rights—a doctrine Americans had struggled with since the Constitution was adopted—they also sought to preserve a way of life and a social philosophy. Even white southerners who did not own slaves (perhaps three-fourths of the population) steadfastly defended the moral justice and economic value of the institution. Slavery and the racism at its roots were the bases for the South's social, political, and economic systems, and although most public defenses of secession and war cited the need to defend southern rights under their interpretation of the Constitution, southerners knew they were also fighting to defend slavery and the plantation-based, cash crop economy it supported.

As a result, when the dire circumstances in which the Confederacy frequently found itself required drastic measures that threatened southern

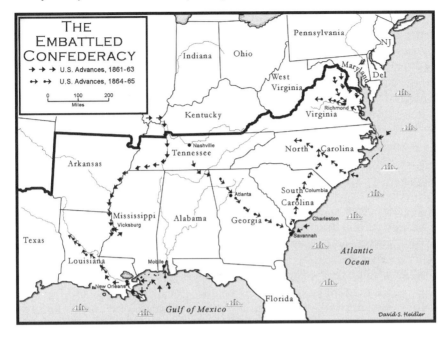

The Embattled Confederacy.

assumptions, southerners responded negatively. The states' rights foundation of the Confederacy crumbled as the government was forced to institute military conscription (the first national draft in American history), which eventually included all white males between the ages of 17 and 50; to raise taxes to pay for the cost of the war (including wide-ranging license fees on most businesses and a graduated income tax—the first in American history—as well as the hated "tax-in-kind," which required farmers and planters to contribute 10% of their crops and livestock to the war effort); and to institute martial law in some regions of the Confederacy in order to enforce conscription and to collect taxes. The Confederate Congress passed bills that required planters to grow less cotton and more food, allowed the government to impress slaves to work on Confederate fortifications, and regulated the kinds of cargoes that blockade-running ships could carry into Confederate ports (they were to devote a certain percentage of their cargo space to necessities rather than the luxuries that earned them much higher profits). They also exempted from military conscription men who owned or supervised at least 20 slaves. By the end of the war, the Congress had even passed a measure authorizing the army to recruit and to arm slaves to fight in the Confederate army, although none of the black recruits saw action.

Opposition to these policies grew throughout the course of the war. Vice President Alexander Stephens was one of the most vocal critics of

President Jefferson Davis's administration, but he was joined by a host of other critics, ranging from Sen. Louis T. Wigfall of Texas to Gov. Zebulon Vance of North Carolina. The historian Frank L. Owsley went so far as to say that the Confederacy, plagued by opposition to its policies by states' rights demagogues, "died of state rights." Members of the opposition did not form a national political party, but in the 1864 state and Congressional elections, so-called Peace Parties ran against government candidates, doing especially well in North Carolina.

Political differences led to very public examples of dissent. But the loyalty of many other residents of the Confederacy waned in the face of the deprivations and violence of the war. This brand of disaffection was particularly severe in areas of the South where slavery was less prominent than in regions dominated by large plantations. It often took the form of support for deserters and draft evaders. When deserters from the Confederate army went into the bush, sometimes encouraged by their wives and mothers to leave a hopeless cause, they were often protected by networks of friends and kinfolk who often foiled the attempts of the military to track them down. They were often joined by men seeking to evade the draft. The most famous example of an entire region's turning away from the Confederacy occurred in Jones County, Mississippi, where many residents claimed to have seceded from the Confederacy to form the Free State of Jones, although the extent of their dissent has been clouded by legend. Sometimes, however, communities struck back at dissenters. In the fall of 1862, for instance, in what was probably the largest case of community vigilance against dissenters, pro-Confederate militiamen rounded up 150 non–slave-holding Unionists and hanged nearly 40 of them after informal trials.

Dissent in the Confederacy took many forms, and although historians have tried to generalize about its origins—in some areas, it seems that non–slave owners were more likely to resist the Confederacy than slave owners, although that was not the case throughout the region—local conditions and attitudes muddied the waters. In some parts of the South, especially in Appalachia and in the border state of Missouri (although Missouri never officially seceded from the Union, many state residents sympathized with the South and formed a Confederate government-in-exile, which was recognized with a star on the Confederate flag), the conflict was very personal and often not directly related to the war. Guerilla conflicts in those areas pitted southerners against southerners. Men like William C. Quantrill styled themselves Confederate officers, but were basically outlaws preying on families on both sides. His most spectacular "battle" came when he and his men rode into Lawrence, Kansas, in August 1863; they burned the town to the ground and killed 150 civilians.

Part of the drain on southern morale came from the "culture of death" that surfaced in the Confederacy. Especially in the cities and towns, residents grew accustomed to the constant funerals, which devolved from elaborate affairs with military honor guards to small, nearly unnoticed affairs simply because of the overwhelming number of soldiers coming home in coffins. At least 260,000 Confederate soldiers died in combat or in battle—about a third of all the men who served in the Confederate army!—and one of the most striking images from first-hand accounts of the home front are the crowds that would gather outside telegraph offices, where the latest casualty reports were posted. Teenaged boys would read the names to the crowds in some places; in others, women and children crowded around bulletin boards hoping not to find the name of a son, brother, or neighbor. Death was a constant companion to home-front southerners, which was acknowledged in a number of the schoolbooks produced by Confederate publishers for southern schools. With names like the *Dixie Primer* and the *Confederate Speller and Reader,* the texts often promoted the southern cause; arithmetic books offered boastful problems like "If one Confederate can kill seven Yankees, how many Yankees can seven Confederates kill?" But several books portrayed a darker side of war. Mrs. M. B. Moore's *Dixie Speller* included the following heartbreaking but grimly patriotic passage by a fictional boy: "This sad war is a bad thing. My papa went, and died in the army. My big brother went too, and got shot. A bomb shell took off his head. My aunt had three sons, and all have died in the army." Not surprisingly, the boy hoped "we will have peace by the time [I] am old enough to go to war."[22]

Southerners' evangelical religion also played a role in the ups and downs of their morale. Like their northern counterparts, Confederates believed that God was on their side. President Davis declared a number of fast days and thanksgiving days; southern ministers were famously devoted to the Rebel cause. But the Christian confidence projected by southerners onto the war effort also meant that, when things went badly—when their armies were defeated and when family members were killed in futile battles—their faith inspired doubt. They wondered if God was, indeed, on the side of the Confederacy. If not, what had they done to bring His vengeance on their shoulders? If God's will would determine the outcome of the war and of all earthly events, as most southerners believed, then their possible defeat called into question many of their basic assumptions.

Despite the desperate circumstances in which many southerners found themselves, and despite the political and philosophical differences that divided Confederates, southern morale did not simply spiral steadily downward throughout the war. Not surprisingly, military successes and failures profoundly affected morale; in spite of increasing shortages and hardships, for instance, the victories at Second Manassas and Fredericksburg in 1862, and at Chancellorsville in 1863, and even the bloody stalemate in the Wilderness of northern Virginia in the summer of 1864, sparked surges in Confederate confidence. Indeed, shortly after the vicious fighting in the Wilderness had cost the Army of Northern Virginia more than 11,000 men killed or wounded, the ardent Confederate nationalist J.D.B. DeBow could still write, "We must succeed in this conflict or all is lost. Reconstruction is but a dream of fools, traitors, or weak-minded men at the South and deluded ones at the North."[23]

SLAVE LIFE IN THE CONFEDERACY

There were, in effect, two sets of parallel experiences by southern civilians, determined by race and by the ultimate effect that the war would have on them. White and black southerners shared a number of experiences, especially in terms of the material conditions they endured. But the ways in which the races viewed the war, not surprisingly, differed drastically.

Every facet of slaves' lives was affected by the Civil War. As shortages forced white southerners to tighten their belts, black southerners had to tighten theirs even more. Slaves found old routines upset and provisions scarce. While the white folks had to give up tea and coffee, slaves ate mostly corn bread, corn mush, and potatoes, with occasional helpings of stringy meat. In many parts of the South they were forced to scrounge in fields and forests for wild greens and game. Although some slaves apparently died of starvation, some, including the future black leader Booker T. Washington, recalled that their already basic and meager diet changed little.

One of the most important effects of the war on slavery and slaves came when masters and overseers went off to war. They were replaced with less experienced sons and wives, or with men unaccustomed to managing slaves. This often translated into poor relationships between the enslaved and the enslavers, as the new overseers often reduced rations, resorted to harsh punishments, and demanded more work than prewar masters and overseers. One slave recalled that his wartime overseer had made the slaves so miserable that he no doubt went "to hell when he died, but I don't se how de debbil could stand him."[24]

Although the number of slaves living in southern cities had been in decline during the 1850s, the war reversed this trend. Thousands of slaves came to towns and cities with their refugee owners, were hired out by plantation owners to work in the manufacturing establishments that sprang up everywhere, or came with their masters when the latter entered the military and then stayed on to work in army camps and hospitals. In the cities slaves were anonymous and more free; although they shared their wages with their owners, they were normally allowed to live on their own and to spend at least some of the money they earned. Moreover, the anonymity of the city made it easier to escape when Union troops came nearby.

Even worse conditions faced those slaves and free blacks forced to build Confederate fortifications (the latter could be fined $100 or jailed if they refused). Thousands dug trenches, built forts, and installed gun emplacements for the Rebels. When the Union army invaded southeastern Virginia in the spring of 1862, for instance, more than 1,300 slaves were put to work on the defenses around the Confederate capital. The owners of slaves working for the army commonly complained of the harsh conditions their human property had to endure, and Confederate newspapers reported poor and scanty rations, disease, punishing work schedules, and abusive discipline. Fed only three-quarters of an ounce of meat and a few ounces of unleavened bread and water three times a day, the slaves were expected to put in long hours of heavy, sometimes dangerous labor. Many planters complained about the feeble condition in which their slaves returned home, while others castigated the government for failing to reimburse owners whose slaves had died.

With hundreds of thousands of white men in the Confederate army, the 3 million slaves living in the Confederate states made up over 40 percent of the home-front population. Obviously, if they had chosen to, they could have undermined the entire Confederate war effort. "If every mother's son of a black had thrown 'way his hoe and took up a gun to fight for his own freedom along with the Yankees," one declared, "the war'd been over before it began." Nevertheless, "we couldn't help stick to our masters. We couldn't no more shoot'em than we could fly."[25] Martin Jackson's father offered grim reasoning for remaining faithful: "He kept pointing out that the War wasn't going to last forever, but that our forever was going to be spent living among the Southerners after they got licked."[26]

Despite the harsh conditions under which they lived, few revolted openly, however, and many remained hard working and faithful to their masters throughout the war. "The negroes, as a general thing," reported one newspaper soon after Appomattox, "have acted very well towards their owners and the white residents of the South, during the disturbed condition of the country for the last four years." A few joined "the invaders, "but only because of their "ignorance and the superior control of the white man."[27]

Although the Confederacy did not accept African Americans into the army until the last few months of the war (and they did not see action), a number of slaves actually accompanied their masters to war to tend horses, nurse the sick and wounded, or act as personal servants. A few were wounded or killed; some even took up arms against the Yankees. Younger slaves mourned the deaths of masters and masters' sons. Some slaves provided dramatic evidence of their loyalty. When federals captured his master, William Byrd walked all the way from Virginia to Texas and waited until after the war to be freed. Henry Smith marched with the Texas Brigade through the siege of Petersburg, where his master's son was killed. Henry buried him and carried his belongings back to the plantation in Texas, where he continued working after the war. After the conflict, white southerners used stories of such determined faithfulness to prove that African Americans had not minded being slaves.

But not all slaves were so cooperative, and many tested the boundaries of the institution. "I could not begin to write you," a Texas woman complained to her husband late in 1863, "how our negroes do all the little things." They had become surly and reluctant to do their work and sometimes actually resisted the overseer—an apparently ineffective wartime replacement for her absent husband—when he tried to punish them. Like other slaves in the neighborhood, they ran away for days at a time. The situation had gotten so bad, the woman reported, that "a great many" of her neighbors "are actually afraid to whip the negroes." One slave, threatened with a beating by an elderly man living nearby, "cursed the old man all to pieces, and walked off in the woods."[28] Other slave owners and a few southern newspapers made similar comments, although, in keeping with southern tradition, trouble with the slaves was rarely mentioned in public.

FROM SLAVERY TO FREEDOM: CONTRABAND

But the most dramatic form of resistance on the part of slaves during the Civil War came when they simply ran away. Even before the serious fighting started, slaves had begun to flee to Union lines. Among the first slaves to escape appeared in the spring of 1861 at Fortress Monroe, an old Federal installation near Norfolk, on the southeastern tip of Virginia. They had been working on nearby Confederate fortifications, and took advantage of the proximity of Union lines to flee. The problem was that no one in the federal government had yet decided about the status of fugitive slaves; should they be sent back to their owners, should they be cared for by the army, should they be considered free people? The fort's commander, Gen. Benjamin Butler—the same man who would earn infamy in New Orleans later in the war—declared them "contraband of war" and promptly "confiscated" them under international rules of war. Although Congress later passed a series of acts further refining federal policy toward slaves, the basic approach—and the term by which they were known, contrabands—were set during that first summer of war. Butler also established the contours of those escaped slaves' lives. The former slaves received food and shelter, but were also immediately put to work. Although at first the status of the escaped slaves was unclear, it soon became apparent that they would not be returned to their masters, and as U.S. government policy evolved during the next two years, those African Americans who managed to get into Union lines were, for all intents and purposes, declared free men and women. By July 1861, at least 900 slaves had gained their freedom at Fortress Monroe.

Over the next four years, tens of thousands of African Americans changed their status from slaves to contrabands by fleeing to Union army posts and occupied territory. Most escaped to northern and southeastern Virginia, the Sea Islands off South Carolina, parts of Tennessee, and other places taken over by Union forces; at least 50,000 crowded into enclaves along the Mississippi River, from Cairo, Illinois, all the way south to Vicksburg and Arkansas.

Some of the camps grew into functioning villages, with schools, churches, and shops. Freedman's Village, built along the Potomac River on the site of Robert E. Lee's property in Arlington, Virginia (and now occupied by Arlington National Cemetery), was created to relieve the severe crowding among 10,000 or so black refugees living in the District of Columbia. The government built white-washed duplexes for the refugees in the village, employed them in workshops and on government farms, and provided a school, chapel, and hospital.

Another model contraband camp grew near Corinth, Mississippi, where slaves from northern Mississippi and Alabama and southern Tennessee began arriving in the spring of 1862. The contrabands built themselves log cabins along the streets laid out and numbered by the army. The little town was even divided up into wards. Like Freedmen's Village, the camp at Corinth soon had a school, hospital, stores, an administrative office, and a church. Within a few months, some of the African American men had been organized into a kind of militia, relieving white troops of the necessity of guarding the camp. A number of American Missionary Association workers came to Corinth to teach and to preach, and by the summer of 1863 there were nearly 400 pupils attending the school. The Union Christian Church of Corinth, as the missionaries called their little chapel, regularly attracted hundreds of worshippers to services that sometimes featured the preaching of four black ministers recently escaped from slavery. More than 300 children attended Sunday School classes. Families were also encouraged to grow their own food in individual gardens; a little cotton field and a large field of vegetables for the hospital were also maintained. The Corinth camp, by the summer of 1863, had become a fully functioning little town.

However, most contrabands did not experience such well-organized and improving conditions. In some places, freed slaves had to live in old packing crates, tobacco barns, sod huts, and, if they were lucky, abandoned houses. Single rooms sometimes housed six families. The supplies that were supposed to be distributed to the contrabands were sometimes sold on the black market by army officers, and the medical care in the camps (usually provided by army surgeons) was unreliable. Many camps offered material deprivations rivaling if not exceeding those of the plantations from which they had escaped. A northern woman working at a hospital for freedmen in the middle of a muddy field near Washington began her description by writing, "If I were to describe this hospital it would not be believed." In this place "are gathered all the colored people who have been made free by the progress of our Army." The overburdened hospital cared for "all cripples, diseased, aged, wounded, infirm, from whatsoever cause." Their patients included black army teamsters beaten nearly to death by white soldiers and desperate mothers carrying dying children into camp. Up to 50 sick, injured, or simply exhausted men, women, and children arrived each day. At least one baby was born daily, but nurses "have no baby clothes except as we wrap them up in an old piece of muslin." "This hospital consists of all the lame, halt, and blind escaped from slavery."[29]

Conditions in some makeshift camps were even worse. An agent for the Cincinnati Contraband Relief Commission revealed the horror of some contrabands' lives when he described a temporary shelter near Davis Bend, Mississippi. In an open cattle shed lived 35 "poor wretched helpless negros [sic]." The band consisted of a nearly blind man, 5 women, and 29 children all under the age of 12.

One of the Women had the small pox, her face a perfect mass of Scabs, her children were left uncared for except for what they accidentally rec[eive]d. Another woman was nursing a little boy about 7 whose earthly life was fast ebbing away, she could pay but little attention to the rest of her family. Another was scarcely able to crawl about. They had no bedding. Two old quilts and a soldiers old worn out blanket comprised the whole for 35 human beings. I enquired how they slept, they collect together to keep one another warm and then throw the quilts over them. There is no wood for them nearer than half a mile which these poor children have to toat [sic] . . . hence they have a poor supply, and the same with Water . . . the only vessel they had to carry it in was a heavy 2 gallon stone jug, a load for a child when empty. . . . They were filthy and will all probably have the small pox and a number of them likely [will] die.[30]

Not surprisingly, the death rates in the teeming camps soared, especially among the children. Out of the 4,000 black refugees living in Helena, Arkansas, in 1863–1864, about 1,100 died. In Memphis, 1,200 out of the 4,000 contrabands died in only three months, while the camp at Natchez suffered a nearly 50 percent mortality rate in 1863. To make matters worse, Confederate guerrillas frequently attacked defenseless contraband settlements, sometimes kidnapping and selling men, women, and children—each of whom brought as much as $100 on the slave market.

These men, women, and children rarely received food and shelter free of charge. Contraband of all ages had to work in return for the security, rations, and housing the army provided. By the age of 10 or 12, as they had as slaves, freedchildren took their places in the fields alongside older African Americans.

But many of these newly freed-children—not to mention adult contrabands—also had access to schools. After living their entire lives in a society that actually made it illegal for them to learn to read and write, the contraband eagerly crowded into schools of all sizes and in all conditions almost as soon as they reached Federal lines. A contraband opened one of the first schools for black students in Norfolk in the fall of 1861; two years later there were 21 teachers in 11 schools with 3,000 day and night students of all ages. Scores of individuals, missionary associations, and even the army, sponsored or staffed schools throughout the occupied South; over 1,400 men and women were teaching in 975 schools in the year after the war ended. Schools ranged in size from a few girls being taught by a single teacher (sometimes the young daughters of Union army officers) to the 1,422 in public schools run by the military in New Orleans and more than 14,000 in schools operated in rural parishes in southern Louisiana.

A number of the teachers in contraband schools were African Americans—some recently escaped slaves themselves! In fact, the American Missionary Association's first school in Norfolk opened under the leadership of Mary Smith Peake, the free daughter of a white man and a mulatto woman. The school would later become Hampton Institute, alma mater of Booker T. Washington and other notable black leaders. Some teachers, such as "Uncle" Cyrus White, who taught school in Beaufort for several months in 1863; William D. Harris, a plasterer; and his assistant, Amos Wilson, who taught in Grosport, North Carolina, were former slaves. But most black teachers came from the North in the employ of the American Missionary Association. Edmonia Highgate of Syracuse, New York, had lectured and raised money for the AMA before the war and had taught in the Binghamton public schools; she became a teacher and principal in Norfolk during the war. Her colleague, Sara G. Stanley, came from Cleveland via Oberlin College. A teacher at the AMA school at Camp Barker in Washington, Stanley was a former slave, but she had been an educator and writer in Brooklyn for 20 years before joining the AMA. Northern publications produced flash cards and textbooks for contraband schools; the American Tract Society even published a monthly magazine, *The Freedman,* to be distributed to black soldiers and to be used in contraband schools.

NOTHING TO REGRET BUT FAILURE

The Confederate States of America ceased to exist with the surrender of its armies, which began with Gen. Robert E. Lee's surrender of the Army of Northern Virginia at Appomattox on April 9, 1865, and ended when Gen. Edmund Kirby Smith gave up the Rebel forces west of the Mississippi River. Members of the Confederate government had fled Richmond on April 2; Union troops finally captured Jefferson Davis five weeks later in Georgia. The Civil War was over.

Most southerners grimly picked up the pieces of their lives. But not a silver-haired old Virginian in failing health. Edmund Ruffin spent the two months after Lee's surrender planning the end of his personal war. Weary of mind and body, he wrote that with "nothing left for my support & no means for aiding others . . . I can do no good in any way. I am now merely a cumberer of the earth, & a useless consumer of its fruits, earned by exertions of others." Although he did follow the news from around the country closely, he finalized his last will and testament and wrote letters to close family members. He continued to scribble into his diary vitriolic attacks on northerners. In his last entry, he declared:

[M]y unmitigated hatred to Yankee rule—to all political, social & business connection with Yankees—& to the Yankee race. Would that I could impress these

The war left many southern cities in ruins, as this photograph of part of Richmond, Virginia, shows. (Library of Congress)

sentiments, in their full force, on every living southerner, & bequeath them to every one yet to be born! May such sentiments be held universally in the outraged & down-trodden South, though in silence & stillness, until the now far-distant day shall arrive for just retribution for Yankee usurpation, oppression, & atrocious outrages.[31]

Then he sat down in a chair, placed the muzzle of his musket in his mouth, and pushed the trigger with a forked hickory stick. Edmund Ruffin died with the revolution he had helped to start.

Ruffin would not be witness to the next two or three decades of daunting economic, political, and racial challenges and antagonisms. The South as he knew it would never be restored, yet by the 1890s white southerners had regained control of their state governments and had virtually restored the racial caste system that had been the economic, social, and political bedrock of the antebellum South. And by the late nineteenth century, the "Lost Cause"— a nostalgic, defiant, and conservative movement that memorialized a mythic "old South" and paid tribute to the valor and sacrifices of Confederate soldiers—would provide common ground for southerners seeking to remember a dignified and heroic past. A significant part of the Lost Cause, promoted by the women of organizations like the United Daughters of the Confederacy, recognized the sacrifices and contributions to the Confederate war effort of southern civilians. Southerners' pride in the exploits of Confederate armies and the toughness of Confederate civilians was perfectly asserted in a southern newspaper in May 1865: "Men must not suppose that because the Southern Confederacy is dead, its memory will become odious either to this generation or to the generations that are to follow. . . . The southern people have nothing to be ashamed of or to regret except failure."[32]

NOTES

1. Robert Hugh Martin, *A Boy of Old Shenandoah*, ed. by Carolyn Martin Rutherford (Parsons, WV: McClain, 1977), 45–46.

2. Quoted in Betty L. Mitchell, *Edmund Ruffin: A Biography* (Bloomington: Indiana University Press, 1981), 2.

3. William Kauffman Scarborough, ed., *Diary of Edmund Ruffin*, 3 vols. (Baton Rouge: Louisiana State University Press, 1972), vol. 1, 278–79.

4. Scarborough, *Diary of Edmund Ruffin*, vol. 2, 419–20.

5. Ibid., 346.

6. Scarborough, *Diary of Edmund Ruffin*, vol. 3, 705.

7. Emory M. Thomas, *The Confederate Nation: 1861–1865* (New York: Harper & Row, 1979), 73.

8. Charles Henry Smith, *Bill Arp's Peace Papers* (New York: G. W. Carleton, 1873; New York: Gregg Press, 1969), 33.

9. Quoted in Anne Sarah Rubin, *A Shattered Nation: The Rise and Fall of the Confederacy, 1861–1868* (Chapel Hill: University of North Carolina Press, 2005), 72.

10. Mrs. W. W. Lord Journal, typescript, Library of Congress.

11. Mary Ann Loughborough, *My Cave Life in Vicksburg* (New York: D. Appleton and Co., 1864), 60–62.

12. Lavinia Shannon to Emmie Crutcher, 13 July 1863, Crutcher-Shannon Family Papers, Center for American History, University of Texas at Austin.

13. Loughborough, *My Cave Life in Vicksburg*, 81.

14. Annie P. Marmion, *Under Fire: An Experience in the Civil War*, ed. By William Vincent Marmion, Jr. (N. p. 1959), 7.

15. Carrie M. Berry Diary, 23 August 1864, typescript, Atlanta History Center.

16. Quoted in Stephen V. Ash, *When the Yankees Came: Conflict and Chaos in the Occupied South, 1861–1865* (Chapel Hill: University of North Carolina Press, 1995), 201.

17. Quoted in James M. McPherson, *Battle Cry of Freedom: The Civil War Era* (New York: Oxford University Press, 1988), 551–52.

18. John Q. Anderson, ed., *Brokenburn: The Journal of Kate Stone, 1861–1868* (Baton Rouge: Louisiana State University Press, 1955), 238.

19. Ibid., 292.

20. George P. Rawick, ed., *The American Slave: A Composite Autobiography* (Westport, CT: Greenwood Press, 1972), vol. 7, 221.

21. James M. Merrill, ed., "'Nothing to Eat but Raw Bacon': Letters from a War Correspondent, 1862," *Tennessee Historical Quarterly* 17 (June 1958): 152–53.

22. Mrs. M. B. Moore, *The Dixie Speller* (Raleigh: Branson and Farrar, 1864), 23.

23. Quoted in Rubin, *A Shattered Nation*, 24.

24. Rawick, *American Slave*, vol. 4, pt. 1, 15.

25. Ibid., pt. 2, 134.

26. Rawick, *American Slave*, vol. 5, pt. 4, 14.

27. Marshall (Texas) *Texas Republican*, 2 June 1865.

28. Lizzie Neblett to Will Neblett, 13 August 1863, Lizzie Neblett Papers, Center for American History, University of Texas at Austin.

29. Henrietta Stratton Jaquette, ed., *South After Gettysburg: Letters of Cornelia Hancock, 1863–1868* (New York: Thomas Y. Crowell, 1937), 33–35.

30. Quoted in Henry Rowntree, "Freedmen at Davis Bend, April 1864," ed. James T. Currie, *Journal of Mississippi History* 46 (May 1984): 122.

31. Scarborough, *Diary of Edmund Ruffin*, vol. 3, 940–41, 949–50.

32. Marshall (Texas) *Republican*, 26 May 1865.

FURTHER READING

Ash, Stephen V. *When the Yankees Came: Conflict and Chaos in the Occupied South, 1861–1865* (Chapel Hill: University of North Carolina Press, 1995). In this excellent book on a relatively unexplored topic, Ash describes not only military policy, but also relationships between occupiers and the occupied and the economic consequences of occupation by Union soldiers.

Blair, William. *Virginia's Private War: Feeding Body and Soul in the Confederacy, 1861–1865* (New York: Oxford University Press, 1998). Blair suggests that the needs and hardships brought on by war led Virginians to demand, and Virginia officials to provide, government-sponsored welfare programs.

Bynum, Victoria E. *The Free State of Jones: Mississippi's Longest Civil War* (Chapel Hill: University of North Carolina Press, 2001). Bynum puts the legendary events that supposedly led to the "secession" of a part of Mississippi from the Confederacy in their historical and mythological contexts.

Clinton, Catherine, ed. *Southern Families at War: Loyalty and Conflict in the Civil War South* (New York: Oxford University Press, 2000). This anthology of original essays explores a number of ways in which the war unleashed tensions affecting gender relations, black families, courtship and marriage, religious belief, family economies, and other issues vital to the southern home front.

Faust, Drew Gilpin. *Mothers of Invention: Women of the Slaveholding South in the American Civil War* (Chapel Hill: University of North Carolina Press, 1996). Faust suggests that the hardships and responsibilities forced on southern women during the war moved them outside their traditional roles and into more public and more demanding positions as military nurses, plantation managers, and government employees, to name just a few; many welcomed their new authority and responsibilities.

Gallagher, Gary W. *The Confederate War* (Cambridge: Harvard University Press, 1997). Contradicting historians who have suggested that the South collapsed partly because of dwindling morale and disaffection, Gallagher argues that southerners actually maintained surprising devotion to the Confederate cause despite their extraordinary sacrifices.

Grimsley, Mark. *The Hard Hand of War: Union Military Policy Toward Southern Civilians, 1861–1865* (Cambridge: Cambridge University Press, 1995). Grimsley provides the best account of the reasons the U.S. military's treatment of southerners evolved from a "soft" approach, designed to restore Confederates' loyalty to the Union, to a "hard" approach designed to punish Confederates for their disloyalty.

Marten, James. *The Children's Civil War* (Chapel Hill: University of North Carolina Press, 1998). Every facet of northern and southern children's lives were touched by the war; this book examines how the war affected children's literature and schooling, forced them to take on the economic roles of absent fathers and brothers, and encouraged them to immerse themselves in the home-front war efforts of the Union and Confederacy.

Massey, Mary Elizabeth. *Refugee Life in the Confederacy* (Baton Rouge: Louisiana State University Press, 1964). In the only book-length study of southern refugees, Massey focuses on their daily struggles, relationships between refugees and other Confederates, and on the economics of refugee life.

Mohr, Clarence. *On the Threshold of Freedom: Masters and Slaves in Civil War Georgia* (Athens: University of Georgia Press, 1986). One of a number of books published in the last 20 years about the collapse of slavery in the Civil War South, this book examines the changing dynamics of master–slave relationships and the ways in which slaves tested the boundaries of freedom as the war closed in on the Confederacy.

Rable, George C. *Civil Wars: Women and the Crisis of Southern Nationalism* (Urbana: University of Illinois Press, 1989). Rable describes the effects of the war on southern women, but also details the ways in which they were politicized—often reluctantly—by the war, which forced them to insert themselves into the political system by writing letters to government officials and urging their husbands and sons to consider their responsibilities to their families over their devotion to the Confederacy.

Rubin, Anne Sarah. *A Shattered Nation: The Rise and Fall of the Confederacy, 1861–1868* (Chapel Hill: University of North Carolina Press, 2005). Rubin takes a fresh look at the ideology of southern nationalism as it promoted the Confederate cause and was reshaped by defeat and reconstruction.

Sutherland, Daniel E., ed. *Guerrillas, Unionists, and Violence on the Confederate Home Front* (Fayetteville: University of Arkansas Press, 1999). An anthology of essays on the political and paramilitary confrontations between Unionists and Confederates in isolated regions of the Confederacy, particular on the frontier and in mountainous areas where slavery was not a vital part of the economy.

Thomas, Emory M. *The Confederate Nation: 1861–1865* (New York: Harper & Row, 1979). Part of the New American Series, this is the classic survey of the political, military, and economic history of the Confederacy.

SIX

The Northern Home Front During the Civil War

Paul A. Cimbala

By the spring of 1865, residents of the free northern states had discovered that America's Civil War had insinuated itself into the most ordinary of their activities. As early as August 1861, Ralph Waldo Emerson warned that such would be the case. The war, he wrote, will "engulf us all," and "no preoccupation can exclude, & no hermitage hide us."[1] Almost a year later, Nathaniel Hawthorne concurred with Emerson's view. In an *Atlantic Monthly* article published in July 1862, he explained, "There is no remoteness of life and thought, no hermetically sealed seclusion, except, possibly, that of the grave, into which the disturbing influences of this war do not penetrate."[2] Northern writers and philosophers had the luxury to engage in hyperbole, but in this case they spoke the truth.

Too often, the devastation in the Confederate states and the revolutionary consequences of emancipation obscured the reality of the war's impact on the civilian population of the North. To be sure, much of the ordinary matters of northern life progressed as they had done before the war. However, if northern children continued to attend school and learn the lessons that had been common fare in antebellum America, they also added to their daily concerns the welfare of brothers, fathers, and uncles who were in the army. If families continued well-worn economic routines, they did so in a market place influenced by new government policies and the pressures of a wartime economy. If women continued to practice the domestic arts, they frequently redirected their talents to furthering the war effort. If some town and city residents chose to shut their eyes to gruesome battlefield reports from the South, they could not long ignore the consequences of a diminished male population, the maimed veterans, and the funerals that became common fixtures on their streets, or the spontaneous celebrations that followed Union victories. If African Americans in the free states still experienced discrimination, they expected a better future in the implied promises they discerned in the Emancipation Proclamation. And while northerners had always been close to death before the war, they came to learn how to grieve in different ways, especially when as a nation they mourned for their assassinated president.

All of these intrusions add substance to the July 1861 assessment of Vermont businessman William Y. Riply, who explained to his son that despite ideas politicians in Washington might have about the conflict, "This war is a war of the *people*."[3] Politicians planned to defeat the rebels, and soldiers suffered in the campaigns to bring those plans to fruition, but civilians also sacrificed much for victory. In the process, they opened their lives to the extraordinary circumstances created by secession and war.

NORTHERNERS CONFRONT SECESSION

The election of Republican candidate Abraham Lincoln in November 1860 led northerners to wonder if southerners would now act on their threats to break up the union. That Lincoln had not won any of their electoral votes, northerners might have assumed, was a good indication of the unhappiness of the residents of the slave states in the election's aftermath. Still, just how far those southerners would go was not immediately clear. Assessing the outcome of the recent election, Philadelphian Sydney Fisher wrote in his journal that "the overwhelming voice of the northern people" backed the newly elected president. Would southerners, he rhetorically asked, "dare forcibly oppose their pigmy strength to this formidably array of power and opinion?"[4]

The sectional tension apparent in 1860 had increased since the Compromise of 1850, but such tension had waxed and waned from the inception of the Union. It was the rise of the Republican party in the mid-1850s, however, that changed the way both southerners and northerners approached politics. The party, formed in reaction to the Kansas–Nebraska Act of 1854, appealed to northerners who accepted the necessity of keeping slavery out of the new western territories. It united individuals committed to providing white men with the opportunity to become independent farmers unhindered by competition from a slave oligarchy.[5] The new party also provided white southerners with a political focus for their fear and hatred, for they considered it a threat to slavery, which was the foundation of their way of life.

After Lincoln's election, Republican protestations that they would not tamper with slavery where it already existed could not abate southern anxiety. The first wave of secession began with the exit of South Carolina from the Union on December 20, 1860, quickly followed by the other deep South states. A lull after Texas seceded in early February 1861 allowed northerners to continue to disagree about the proper response, but the firing on Fort Sumter at Charleston, South Carolina, united loyal citizens to support Lincoln's subsequent call for troops. The secession of Virginia, North Carolina, Arkansas, and Tennessee, which quickly followed, however, bolstered northern resolve.

Northerners expected a quick fight to put an end to the southern folly, but a few wary citizens were skeptical of such an outcome. Friends told Theodore Upson, an Indiana farm boy, "that it would all be over soon; that those fellows down South are big bluffers and would rather talk than fight." Upson, however, questioned their optimism. He had witnessed the spunk of his southern relations and concluded, "I am not so sure about that."[6]

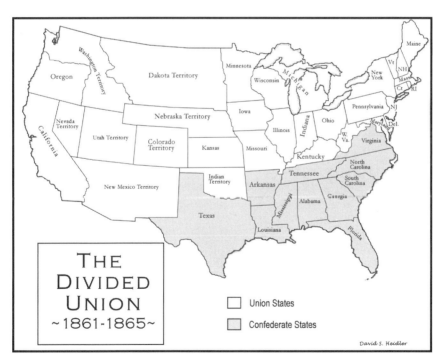

The Divided Union.

NORTHERN REACTION TO THE FIRING ON FORT SUMTER

Northerners reacted to the events in Charleston harbor with shock and anger. Upson and his father, who had family in the South, were husking corn on their Indiana farm when a friend informed him of the firing on Fort Sumter. The elder Upson "got white and couldn't say a word." He stopped work for the day and returned to the family house, and spent some time alone pondering events before he finally discussed them with his wife. By that point, the elder Upson appeared to have aged a decade.[7] That sort of somber reaction, however, soon gave way to more belligerent responses across the North. Alfred Bellard, an 18-year-old English-born resident of Hudson City, New Jersey, recalled that "my military spirit along with the rest of the people in the Northern States rose to boiling pitch."[8]

The troubling but thrilling times that came with war disrupted the rhythms of everyday life throughout the North. For many, Lincoln's call to arms immediately changed everything. Ulysses S. Grant remembered, "Business ceased entirely" in his town of Galena, Illinois.[9] At the University of Vermont, students found it hard to concentrate on their studies "or do anything but get excited."[10] People gathered in town halls and town squares and at school houses and opera houses to hear patriotic speeches, condemnations of southern traitors, and plans of action. They assembled near telegraph and newspaper offices to track national news. Flags flew from public and private buildings, including churches, and along city streets and rural byways, while communities large and small steeled themselves for the coming fight.

Ministers added to the patriotic mood by reminding their congregations of the divinely ordained destiny of the nation that the slaveholders would now spoil. Newspapers exhorted men not only to fight secessionists, but also to revive the spirit of the North, stop disruptive party squabbling, purge Washington of corruption, and restore honor lost in the scramble for material gain. Patriotic sacrifices would foster an appreciation for the rights protected by the Constitution. Fighting secession would revive public virtue and absolve the North of its sinful cooperation with southerners in maintaining slavery.

Patriotism united the people where political interests, business concerns, and caution had divided them only a day earlier. Even individuals who had been sympathetic toward the southern states now saw secessionists as members of a slave power conspiracy to undermine American freedom. The mendacious slaveholding oligarchy had long contemplated secession, they concluded, as they came to understand present events in light of the past sectional controversies.[11]

War making at this time was very much in the hands of state governments and local patriots, thus it was fortunate that outraged northerners were committed to bringing a swift end to the so-called Confederacy. Wealthy individuals and businessmen pledged funds to outfit volunteers or to help the families of men who went off to war. Town meetings called to raise money for the war effort often concluded with men volunteering for military companies that state governments gathered up into regiments. In 1861, the assumption that the war would be short prompted men to rush to arms as individuals, as members of antebellum independent volunteer companies, or as established state militias. Connecticut citizens enthusiastically filled the state's first regiment of 90-day volunteers in 3 days. In 3 weeks, they had volunteered in numbers sufficient to make up almost 6 regiments and also filled 2 3-year regiments almost immediately after Lincoln called for them.[12]

African American northerners were just as eager as their white neighbors to enter the fray. They met in their communities to proclaim their devotion to the nation and formed voluntary military companies or offered extent organizations to fight for the Union and more. Black northerners tactfully avoided mentioning emancipation, but theirs was indeed an antislavery war—if the nation would allow them to fight. In 1861, only a few abolitionists would contemplate such a radical notion. When white men took up arms, they did so expecting to fight a short, white man's war with the sole purpose of restoring the nation's antebellum constitutional status quo.[13] Confronted with that reality, most northern blacks tempered their support for the conflict until the emancipation became a declared goal. In the meantime, black northerners, veterans of the antebellum abolitionist movement, turned their attention to helping the contrabands who were beginning to make their way into Union lines.[14]

THE INITIAL RESPONSE OF WOMEN TO THE OUTBREAK OF WAR

At the outset of the war, some women were reluctant to see their men join the army, because they well understood the economic and emotional consequences of such action. These wives and sweethearts urged caution and counseled patience, but they were in the minority and could not drown out the drumbeats that rallied communities to war. Indeed, most women supported the war and contributed to its conduct in numerous ways. Clothing the first round of volunteers was but one way that they contributed to the initial rush to arms. They also nursed sick recruits and fed healthy soldiers at rendezvous camps. Women rose to such challenges not only because they had the valuable skills of homemakers, but also because they, like their men folk, had developed organizations ranging from sewing circles to temperance groups that allowed them to rally for quick collective action.[15] It was these groups of women who frequently sewed and then presented the regimental flags that became symbols of home and honor to their soldiers.

Northern women came to grips with their own ambivalent feelings as they bade farewell to their husbands, sons, brothers, and fathers. They were proud, but they readily grasped the seriousness of the situation perhaps better than the soldier boys they were sending off to war. When one Maine regiment left the state capital of Augusta in early June, its recruits briskly trotted off to the train cars to the sounds of "sobbing mothers, wives, and dear ones."[16] At Jersey City, New Jersey, women at the station "were crying and wringing their hands, while the boys who were off for a soldier, were laughing and cracking jokes and doing their best to make everyone else feel as happy as themselves."[17] These women, however, knew that they had to adjust to the extraordinary circumstances. After sending off her husband in the spring of 1861, Iowan Emiline Ritner wrote that she "felt as if I had been to a funeral;" nevertheless, "I must train myself, and get used to it."[18] Women wept as they said their goodbyes, but they were willing to make sacrifices for their nation.

THE COMMUNITIES THAT WENT TO WAR

The national government was a distant entity to these men and women who went to war in 1861. Washington rarely intruded into the people's lives before Fort Sumter, neither overburdening them with taxation nor providing assistance for them in their personal times of trouble. The average citizen came into contact with the federal government through the postal service and in some areas might know of it from nearby light houses, courts, customs houses, armories, or naval establishments.[19] Before the war, politicians funded these enterprises as well as a meager frontier army in ways that only indirectly touched people's pocket books. The federal government mostly relied on land sales and import duties for revenue; indeed, in 1861, tariffs made up over 90 percent of the government's income. For over half a century before secession, the federal government had not tapped into an internal revenue source, except through a few excise taxes.[20]

States were equally adept at limiting unpopular taxation. New Jersey, for example, avoided levying direct taxes altogether by relying on money paid to the state by railroad and canal companies.[21] Towns such as Springfield, Massachusetts, offered limited services, and therefore could rely on local government's traditional tax on property, which property owners did their best to keep low.[22] If special needs arose, municipalities could borrow money. Jacksonville, Illinois, relied on private subscriptions or county and town bonds to pay for transportation improvements.[23]

Between 1861 and 1865, this relationship changed. Northerners saw the federal government asserting increased control over many aspects of their lives. Not only did the government establish a military draft, it also raised taxes, sold bonds, and printed paper money. It impinged on judicial due process by occasionally suspending the writ of habeas corpus, and it altered the status of a legally sanctioned institution by enforcing emancipation. By the end of the war, some northerners came to expect more from the national government, if only in limited ways for a limited time, as they coped with wounded veterans, war widows, and ex-slaves. Even so, the war's legacy did not include a more powerful or intrusive federal government.

Northerners remained closely tied to their localities and states despite the war's centralizing forces.[24] If anything, the war reinforced those connections. Military companies recruited among neighbors carried an enduring local identity to war, and regiments took their states' names into battle. These practices helped to nurture feelings of loyalty and affection in the folks back home, even among those who did not have loved ones at risk, because communities closely followed the progress of their local boys.

Northerners, even those who had moved about before the war, found in their communities the institutions that brought stability and a sense of belonging to their lives. Just as important, if not more so, were those institutions within the communities that shaped a commonly held set of values shared by a majority of northerners. Northerners cherished their schools, churches, political parties, town meetings, civic celebrations, voluntary organizations, and other associations not only because they helped to anchor them in a community, but also because they recognized them as the *free* institutions that provided the foundation for their liberties. As young people matured and participated in these institutions, they learned

UNCLE SAM. "Go ahead, Boys; I'll take care of the Wives and Babies. GOD bless you!

Northern soldiers bound for the front are assured that the country will take care of their families. (Library of Congress)

the importance of individualism, self-control, personal sacrifice, discipline, hard work, democracy, moral righteousness, and the manifest destiny of their nation. They might not have thought much about the mechanics of the national government with its various bureaus and departments, but they intuitively knew that their free institutions—the very essence of their nation—could flourish only within an environment of law and order provided by the Constitution. Both their spiritual happiness and material success depended on the survival of what they considered to be the best government in the world, a government now threatened by the selfish actions of a regressive oligarchy of duplicitous, traitorous slaveholders.[25]

In 1861, northern communities were still primarily rural and agricultural, but the region as a whole was evolving into a more modern and dynamic one than that of the South. The North was becoming an urban, industrial region, where even the large midwestern farms featured efficient, modern agricultural methods. The greater use of technology on the farm and in the factory, as well as the development of a railroad transportation network and a capitalist financial system, all contributed to these changes.[26] White men and women of European heritage formed the bulk of the northern population at the outset of the war. The large numbers of Irish, German, and other immigrants who came to the country in the years before the war gravitated to the northern economy, because it did not require them to compete with slavery. Milwaukee, Wisconsin, for example, benefited greatly from the large German population whose numbers at the outbreak of the war not only dominated the laboring classes there, but also occupied numerous positions among the professional and merchant classes.[27] Textile factories in the mid-Atlantic states provided work for Irish and English immigrants, but even New England mills, noted for their early use of female employees, began to turn to such workers before the war.[28] Soldiers from the textile town of Rockville, Connecticut, marched off to war saying their farewells "in almost every language spoken in Europe."[29]

Many immigrants, especially Catholics, shied away from the Republican party with its Protestant reformer connections. However, they joined Republican Protestants in embracing the belief that hard work could make for better lives, a core concept of free-labor ideology that flourished in the intellectual and economic environment of the free states. And they did work hard, whether it was in a factory or on a farm. Farm laborers, for example, found their days consumed from sun up to sun down with breaking sod, digging wells, planting, and harvesting during the growing cycle, while they spent the rest of the year engaged in other kinds of hard labor, such as logging.[30] Factory workers averaged 11 hours a day on their feet, regulated by the requirements of their machines rather than their own rhythms.[31] Indeed, the hard outdoor toil of the farm hand and the disciplined if boring labor of the factory worker might very well have made them better suited to the rough and regimented life of soldiering than their southern counterparts assumed.

Only 226,000 free blacks lived among these white northerners (more than 95% of the black population of the United States still lived in the slave states).[32] In 1860, major northern cities had only a small number of black residents. The largest urban black population in 1860 was the approximately 22,000 blacks who lived in Philadelphia, yet this represented only 3.9 percent of that city's population. Cincinnati, Ohio, was home to the second largest black community with some 3,700, but that was only 2.3 percent of the total population. Boston's population of over 2,200 blacks made up a mere 1.3 percent of its population, while New York City's population of almost 12,500 African Americans was just 1.5 percent of the total.[33]

Many relatively prosperous northern blacks were prominent because of their involvement in reform movements and were notable for their middle-class status. By the time of the war, a small black professional class existed in Boston, but some laborers, such as porters, also enjoyed a privileged place in the black community because of their steady employment.[34] Blacks in New York City were sufficiently religious, prosperous, and proud to sustain substantial African American churches, but smaller northeastern cities such as Newark and Jersey City, New Jersey, while home to middle-class blacks, could boast only few property holders among them. Most blacks in New York City who owned property were of modest means, and while landowning black farmers in New Jersey enjoyed a degree of prosperity, farther west in Ohio, rural blacks were most likely to work the soil as laborers or tenants on someone else's land.[35] In fact, most northern African Americans lived the hard lives of laborers primarily concerned with providing the basics for themselves and their families.

Regardless of their economic situations, northern blacks endured racial discrimination and segregation because of custom and law, and their freedom was something less than the liberty claimed by their white neighbors. In 1860, for example, some northern states prohibited blacks from offering testimony in court cases involving whites, and all of the northern states, except Massachusetts, barred blacks from jury service.[36] Indeed, such discrimination frequently kept working blacks from improving their station. In antebellum New York City, the ever increasing number of Irish immigrants led to the replacement of black domestic servants with Irish women, while Irish men dominated the carting trade to the exclusion of blacks until a small number of African Americans began entering the occupation in the mid-1850s.[37]

FILLING THE LABOR GAPS LEFT BY THE RECRUITS

Countless farms, factories, and businesses would miss the labor of the soldiers who left for the war. The economy of the New England states, for example, had to deal with the absence of 363,000 men, which constituted more than 10 percent of the region's total population.[38] Likewise, the midwestern states of Ohio, Indiana, Illinois, Michigan, and Wisconsin had to continue to keep farms productive while sending to war about 680,000 men who served for more than a short-term enlistment; on average, every other farm family in those states made due without a worker.[39] Nevertheless, agriculture grew to keep up with the requirements of the war as farmers perceived their profitable labor as an extension of their patriotism. Northern farmers also continued to make use of technology to ease the labor short fall. In 1864, northern farmers purchased a record 80,000 reapers and mowers, bringing the total of these machines employed on farms in that year to 250,000.

Increased mechanization helped to make up for lost workers as farmers expanded cultivated acreage. But machines did not do it all. A new supply of German, Swede, and Norwegian immigrants entered the agricultural labor pool, probably attracted to the northern states by the Homestead Act of May 1862. Young boys and girls assumed new tasks, and women not only managed farms but also did the hard chores previously performed by men.[40]

Soldiers' relief organizer Mary A. Livermore's recollections of her travels during the summer of 1863 through the farm communities of Wisconsin and eastern Iowa provided testimony for the way that midwestern farms rose to the challenge posed by the wartime economy. From her rail car she witnessed "what seemed a continuous wheat-field" and, over the course of six hours, she counted hundreds of "two-horse reapers" harvesting the bounty "in a wholesale fashion that would have astonished Eastern farmers." Furthermore, she observed women performing every type of task required by the harvest. "Women were in the field everywhere," she noted, "driving the reapers, binding and shocking, and loading grain." One of the women told Livermore that with all the men off in the army and with her husband unable to hire farm hands even though he could pay them, she and her daughters had to come to his assistance. As one of the farmer's daughters explained, "Harvesting isn't any harder, if it's as hard as cooking, washing, and ironing, over a red-hot stove in July and August—only we do both now." The consensus among the women was that the country needed the grain, and the army needed to eat, so it was only right that they should take on "men's work."[41] And mechanization on northern farms made a significant difference for them when they went into the fields. As one magazine writer noted in 1863, women could easily replace recruits, because machines made the work so much easier to do.[42]

Industry also had to cope with a reduced workforce, even as the war created the additional burdens of supplying Union armies. Similar to farming, technology filled the gaps, along with children, women, and immigrant workers. By 1865, necessity caused manufacturers to hire so many women and children that their numbers among the North's mill and factory employees increased by 40 percent. By the end of the war, women filled one-third of these industrial positions, up from a quarter

Women shouldered a wide range of responsibilities during the war, including sewing clothes for soldiers, doing their laundry, and helping the wounded keep in touch with home. (Library of Congress)

of the positions they had held in 1860.[43] The growing presence of young women newcomers in factories in Northampton, Massachusetts, was especially noticeable to one New England soldier who whimsically weighed the better matrimonial prospects for single veterans returning to the community.[44]

WARTIME PROSPERITY

By the end of 1862, the northern economy had recovered from the setbacks it had suffered in the aftermath of secession. R. G. Dunn and Company reported 510 business failures for 1864, a significant decrease from 1861's total of 5,935.[45] Compared to earlier periods the economy grew at modest levels during the war, but its discernable dynamism certainly made an impression on northern observers. Traveling across the Pennsylvania countryside during the fall of 1862, Sidney Fisher observed neat, well-cultivated farms and the operation of his late uncle's furnaces and mills near Harrisburg. "I was more impressed than ever with the wealth, resources, and beauty of Pennsylvania," he recorded. "Tokens of redundant prosperity & rapid improvement are visible everywhere . . . The war indeed has revealed to us & to the world the immense power & unbounded resources of the nation."[46]

An obvious indication of the war's impact on entrepreneurialism occurred in communities that directly benefited from the presence of the military. The camps and barracks situated by or in northern communities supplied ready markets for farmers and merchants. During the spring of 1861, farmers near Yonkers, a community north of New York City, sold produce to the men of the 40th New York Volunteer Infantry.[47] The merchants of Keokuk at the southeastern tip of Iowa especially profited from the military presence during the summer of 1861, because rebel control of the lower Mississippi River disrupted the town's normal trade.[48] In 1863, lumberyards on the Mississippi River in Davenport, Iowa, and Rock Island, Illinois, shared a contract for wood for prisoners-of-war barracks.[49] Kansas farmers and freight haulers prospered by providing supplies for the soldiers stationed at the forts in the state.[50] Indeed, businessmen, farmers, and tradesmen who could secure government contracts to provide supplies or services for rendezvous camps and prisoners-of-war camps did quite well for themselves. The war transformed quiet places like Elmira, New York, into bustling profit centers, if only for the duration.[51]

Wartime industrial production was an important weapon in the North's arsenal, but one of its byproducts, the creation of what in October 1863 the *New York Herald* called "the new Northern shoddy aristocracy," worried some patriots and moralists.[52] Such a class of conspicuously consuming entrepreneurs irritated those northerners who believed that the capitalists' self-absorbed desire to increase their wealth could damage not only their character, but that of the nation. Sidney Fisher expressed his disgust with an acquaintance who worried more about his investments than the future of the Union.[53] The Reverend James Remley feared that God would destroy such a selfish nation; in November 1862 he complained to his son Lycurgus about the "Thousands of private citizens" who were "even now speculating in the public misery and trying to make money out of the blood and dying groans of innocent people."[54]

Indeed, the mal-distribution of war wealth began to reveal cracks in the region's free-labor ideology. Mill workers, clerks, and farm laborers went to war confident that their free-labor system protected their independence. They believed that they would never be slaves to any man, even if circumstance compelled them to work for wages. Young men considered working for someone else as a stage on the way to becoming entrepreneurs themselves. Yet capitalists and the land owners were profiting from the war while families of workers struggled. As northern industrial workers and farm laborers were denied their fair share of the benefits of wartime prosperity, the rift between capital and labor became apparent. Working people had to contend with an inflation rate of 80 percent. That rate was certainly modest when compared to the Confederacy's 9,000 percent, but still caused considerable hardship. Wages failed to keep pace with inflation until the end of the war, which significantly diminished workers' purchasing power. And the ranks of the poor continued to increase with widows, orphans, impoverished soldiers' families, and struggling veterans adding to their numbers.[55]

WOMEN ADJUST TO WAR

The Union army relied upon volunteers from across the socioeconomic spectrum, but most soldiers were from the middle or working classes, primarily because those were the largest segments of society. By necessity, then, women and children of middling families shouldered most of the burdens of supporting the Union as well as themselves. The pay sent home by soldiers was critical for their support, although state governments and some municipalities helped by disbursing funds to the most hard-pressed families of absent soldiers. In addition, as the war continued, enlistment bounties increased, which eased the financial strain for families of new recruits.

Nevertheless, inflation, new taxes, problems encountered while trying to gain access to soldiers' relief funds, and the irregularity of soldiers' pay all placed strains on household budgets. Voluntary pledges by community leaders to care for soldiers' families were especially vulnerable as the war dragged on longer than first anticipated. Initially, community leaders in Dubuque, Iowa, for example, rallied to the needs of the families of men who went off to war, but their efforts soon foundered as the war went on longer than they had expected and longer than their resources lasted. The city's Volunteer Fund Board pledged assistance to two companies of 90-day volunteers in April 1861. A third company volunteered for three years' service, and its members received a pledge from the board to assist their families. In January 1862, the board was helping 116 families, but had disbursed all of its funds and could do no more.[56]

In such circumstances, even minor setbacks could become major crises. Thus the war took a psychological as well as an economic toll on women coping not only with money matters but also with obstreperous in-laws, pregnancies, willful children, illness, aging parents, family deaths, loneliness, and anxiety over the safety of sons and husbands. Her husband's absence and the burdens of motherhood placed a considerable strain on Rachel Cormany, who suffered from depression throughout the war. During the fall of 1863, she felt herself gloomy and at her wits' end as she dealt with her demanding little daughter, Cora. "Last night & today Cora cried so much that my patience quite gave way—Indeed I wished I had never been born," she complained to her diary in October. "I felt as if I were the most forsaken creature on earth. Indeed I cannot tell how miserable I felt. . . . I often feel my unfitness to be a mother."[57] Aggravating her depression was the intense longing she felt for her absent husband that was only briefly alleviated by his occasional visits home. In March 1864, she noted how one furlough raised her spirits and provided some need physical satisfaction. "O! I was so glad to see him, to be kissed & caressed & to love kiss & caress him," she wrote. After his departure, her melancholy returned.[58]

If visits were rare, letters provided another way of maintaining a level of intimacy with loved ones. Correspondence between the home front and the camp strengthened the family ties and were cherished as artifacts that sustained relationships. Mary Vermilion reread her husband's letters when she felt depressed or lonely, certainly a practice of other wives who carefully preserved their soldiers' letters.[59]

Some relationships, however, unraveled under the rigors of war. Some men roguishly preyed on women left defenseless by the absences of their husbands; some women yearned for physical companionship and succumbed to temptation. Distressing rumors about unfaithful wives found their way to the front, where anxious husbands could only brood about constancy undermined by human frailty. Some stories were maliciously false. Some were based on nothing more than supposedly "scandalous" but actually innocent behavior, such as wives traveling alone. The war also brought the sexual behavior of married and unmarried women, especially those nursing wounded soldiers, under greater public scrutiny.

Allegations of misbehavior could be true, of course, and marital infidelities doubtless contributed to the increased divorce rate during the war. The times, however, placed other strains on relationships as well. Serious quarrels could erupt, for example, over political differences.[60] One Iowa woman sued for divorce "on the grounds that her husband was a secesh" who had beaten her for holding firm to her Unionist beliefs.[61]

Extended families often helped soldiers' wives cope with their problems, but they did not always provide comfort and support. Distance could prevent timely assistance. Indifference could limit the help offered. And political differences also strained familial relations. Elizabeth Ann Butler, for example, found her brothers' "blind adherence" to the Democratic Party objectionable; she also had to bear her uncle's insults about women involved in soldiers' relief work.[62] Democrat in-laws could be particularly trying, as Iowan Mary Vermilion learned when she lived with her husband's Indiana family in a region rife with opponents to the Lincoln administration.[63]

Faced with such irritations, women occasionally vented their frustrations in their letters to the front. In their correspondence, they argued with their husbands and complained about their tribulations. They lectured their men folk about the dangers of a life in the field absent the steadying influence of Christian women and societal norms, fearful that drink, disease, army vulgarity, and violent combat would spoil them for civilian life.[64] Mattie Blanchard was very disturbed when she learned that her husband had taken up card playing, and she made it clear to him that he needed to give it up. "[C]ards can do you no good," she warned; "you are a father now and dont bring disgrace upon your childs head."[65]

Yet, the stoic midwestern farm women Mary Livermore encountered were typical of most northern women who did their usual work and even more with little or no complaint. Mary Austin Wallace of Calhoun County, Michigan, supervised a substantial family farm as well as the construction of the house that her husband had begun before he left for the war in August 1862, all the while caring for her toddler son and infant daughter.[66] Mary Bradbury of Illinois, a mother of several children, received frequent instructions on how to conduct her husband's business affairs; she accepted the challenge and ended up increasing the family's wealth.[67]

Along with these large responsibilities, women took on numerous smaller but essential daily tasks. In November 1862, Emiline Ritner butchered and salted a pig. "We just had to do it," she told her husband. "There was not a man on the hill that we could get."[68] The following year she reported that she planted her own garden in corn and potatoes because, while she was able to hire someone to plow the ground, she could not find anyone to plant it.[69] There was patriotism even in completing these mundane tasks. As Mary Vermilion explained, "A sacred cause makes even the humblest labor dignified and holy," she once wrote to her husband.[70]

Ritner and Vermilion typified countless other northern women who kept their homes running smoothly under difficult conditions. Those fortunate enough to have assets often managed them with a skill that inspired admiration. The less fortunate struggled to keep their families fed and sheltered while fending off angry creditors and demanding landlords. The most desperate turned to crime and sometimes landed in prison, but most took on extra work and, if in their own homes, took in borders. Women found additional opportunities to earn money on farms, in factories, and in school houses as the war consumed more and more men. And just as the war's demands provided new markets for merchants, it presented new prospects for women. They also found work in expanding government offices and engaged in producing uniforms for the ever growing Union army.[71]

At first, the government worked directly with seamstresses to secure the needed uniforms, but a system of subcontracting soon replaced that relationship, with interesting consequences. Businessmen who placed the fabric with the seamstresses took the lion's share of the profits. As a result, women who took on this work might earn as little as $1.50 a week, a meager sum even for that time. Their plight attracted the attention of middle-class reformers, and Philadelphia seamstresses campaigned for higher wages, with some of them considering unionization. Consequently, a sewing women's movement developed in Philadelphia during the summer of 1863 and spread throughout the northeastern states. Increased militancy led to strikes in New York and Brooklyn, while heightening women's interest in collective action.

These women and their reformer allies were trying to establish a new, if still ambiguous, economic reality on the home front. Women might have been dependent on men in their own minds as well as in the eyes of the law, but they still needed living wages. At the same time, women began to expect the government to recognize their needs, because they had sacrificed the company, the income, and in some cases the health and lives of their men. Less fortunate women began to make it clear that they wanted their husbands to return home as soon as possible. If their men had already given their lives for the cause, bereft and impoverished widows expected the federal government to provide them with pensions. In 1862, Congress accepted some responsibility for the dead soldiers' widows, children, or other dependent relatives by making them the beneficiaries of a new pension law that would provide a starting point for future pension legislation down through the end of the century. The benefits could be significant for long-lived war widows and, after 1890, even widows of honorably discharged Union soldiers who had married their husbands after the war had ended.[72]

CHILDREN ADJUST TO WAR

Children experienced the hardships of being without fathers, the agony of loved ones' deaths, and the joy of reunited families. Indeed, everything that touched adults touched children, too, and the war shaped many aspects of their lives. Children explored the new reality by playing war games and creating activities that mimicked the adult world around them, such as raising money for soldiers' relief. Youngsters lived in an environment of songs, books, magazines, and activities that were militaristic in their essence. Children read magazines that described the war in terms they could grasp and created heroes, such as the drummer boy, to inspire emulation. School-aged youngsters learned lessons heavily laced with patriotism. In divided communities they clashed in schoolyards over politics. The war also forced them to set aside normal peacetime activities and shoulder new responsibilities such as extra chores on the farm, tending to younger siblings while mothers worked, or toiling in factories to help support their families. Children might not have fully understood the war, but they certainly knew it had become a central force in their lives.[73]

Following adult examples, children wrote letters to maintain vital connections between home and camp. They routinely received lengthy epistles from their soldier fathers that explained why they were away, described camp life, offered consolation for failures and gave praise for successes, and served up counsel about life in general.[74] Young Jane Bradbury of Illinois sent a letter to her father in which she "made the letters of the alphabet," a feat that earned her the praise of the soldier Bradbury, who lovingly responded by passing on advice to his eldest child about right living.[75] John H. Westervelt, a New Yorker serving in an engineering regiment, sent 68 cleverly illustrated letters to his son Frazee, all leavened with paternal wisdom.[76] And Silas Browning of Massachusetts advised his daughter to "grow good as fast as you grow tall."[77]

The war inevitably made some children orphans. Philanthropists often addressed their needs, increasing their generosity in step with growing wartime prosperity. Several northern states established or assisted existing asylums for war orphans as did religious groups and fraternal organizations, and the federal government eventually established a modest pension for soldiers' orphans. Organizations such as Charles Loring Brace's New York Children's Aid Society received praise for solving two wartime problems at once by placing eastern orphans in western farm homes in need of labor.[78]

PARENTS' CONTINUED CONCERN FOR SOLDIER SONS

Soldier fathers did not abdicate their parental duties when they left home, but neither did mothers and fathers who sent sons off to fight. Parental advice also flowed from the home front to camp, trying to keep up the morale of soldier sons while urging them to live clean lives, trust in God, and do their duty. Considering the makeup of the Union army, this type of correspondence was probably at least as common, if not more so, because northern families sent off their sons and brothers in greater numbers than their husbands and fathers.

Families were especially eager to learn about the details of their soldier boys' new lives. Born of affection, this desire reflected their concerns for absent husbands, sons, and brothers and worries about their physical and spiritual well being. Families also felt that the information their soldiers provided would help them to continue to share in their lives. Thus, Indianan Ovid Butler and his wife asked their son Scot to write frequently. In October 1863, after the Battle of Chickamauga, the elder Butler wrote to Scot requesting information not about the larger matters and issues of the campaign, but about what the boy saw and did, because he and the rest of the family wished to "be with . . . [him] and go with . . . [him] through these conflicts."[79] For Scot Butler's mother, her son's letters alleviated her "despondency and sad forbodings [sic]." "There are times that I grow more anxious about you than at other times," she wrote to him in July 1863. "I think from some unaccountable depression of spirits that I feel, that All [sic] is not well with my absent boy, when here come a letter . . . and the cloud is lifted from my spirits for the time."[80]

The connection between parents and their sons away at war could alter old and established relationships. As the war dragged on, boys became men with opinions and experiences shaped by camp life and battle. In fact, sons often began to influence the views of parents who were forced to accept the rapid maturation of their boys. For example, War Democrat Andrew Evans of Brown County in southern Ohio had always expected his son Sam to help with the family smithy and farm. Once Sam left for the army, the son was no longer under the constant supervision of the father who gradually came to realize the significance of the son's new life experiences. In 1863, when Sam took a position as an officer in a black regiment, his father was not pleased. However, Sam remained true to his new commitment despite risking paternal disapproval. In the end, Andrew moved closer to Sam's views. The elder Evans supported the 13th amendment and became an advocate of black suffrage, at least in part because of his increased respect for his son.[81]

LEARNING ABOUT WAR

The lack of reliable information about what soldiers were experiencing at the front often frustrated northerners, whether they were parents or not. Philadelphian Sydney George Fisher sought out men who had fought in battles or witnessed their aftermath for their testimony about their experiences.[82] Many of Fisher's fellow northerners, just as hungry for details about battle, also talked to soldiers, something that was easy to do early in the war when three-month volunteers returned to their communities after their short term of service. After the Battle of Bull Run in July 1861, easterners had dramatic evidence of the war's toll when their 90-day men came home. In New Haven, Connecticut, people greeted the returning First Connecticut Volunteer Infantry, veterans of that first great battle of the war. In the spring they had sent their men off to war all pressed and polished, and now those men returned ragged and worn, a sight that made the state's governor weep.[83] There would be other opportunities to satisfy civilian curiosity later in the war when civilians witnessed the condition of returning regiments. In February 1864, the people at St. Paul who came out to receive the First Minnesota learned something about war when they registered the price their men had paid over the past three years. They had sent off a regiment of 1,200 men and now welcomed home 325 soldiers.[84]

Throughout the war, home folk received battlefield relics from their husbands, sons, or friends as well as letters with vivid descriptions of battles that probably increased everyone's anxiety. Civilians gathered at telegraph offices when they learned that armies were clashing, and they read battle reports in weekly and Sunday newspapers as well as special editions printed to keep pace with breaking stories. Erroneous information often confused people, and the stylized, unrealistic engravings in magazines such as *Harper's Weekly* misled them. A few northerners saw the more realistic if sometimes posed consequences of battle captured in photographs; more had the opportunity to do so when entrepreneurs turned them into stereoscopic images and reproductions for sale to the general public.[85] Photographs of dead soldiers, however, could have a shocking effect even as they enthralled viewers. They reminded northerners of the unnatural, violent deaths of their men and the unsentimental handling of the remains of their heroes.[86]

MILITARY CAMPS, SOLDIERS, AND CIVILIANS

Few civilians could ever fully understand the war, because they were isolated from combat. Northerners living near the Canadian border, on the Great Lakes, and along the southern border worried about Confederate raids, but they rarely saw even a Confederate uniform (except for those on prisoners-of-war), let alone a battle. The summer of 1863 was a dramatic exception, but the war even then did not directly touch most northerners. Instead, the home front witnessed war in other ways.

At the outset of the war, rendezvous camps where soldiers gathered and prepared to head to the front edified nearby communities about the new, burgeoning volunteer army. Permanent camps and barracks provided long-term social connections between civilians and soldiers, but such installations could also reveal the darker side of army life. Throughout the war, farmers coped with soldiers who stole chickens and fruit or cut down their trees for fuel; city dwellers grimly abided men in blue who became public nuisances or worse.

Blue uniforms might call to mind their heroes at the front for mothers and sweethearts, but soldiers' bad behavior confirmed their worst fears about the army's negative influence on their men. Civilians were especially concerned, because they assumed that good men made good soldiers and bad men made bad soldiers, with the latter being incapable of seeing the battle through to victory. The notion that ill-mannered professional warriors could still fight well and win wars remained alien to most Yankees.[87] Civilians became troubled when faced with the fact that not all soldiers were virtuous, even if the war they fought was.

Bored and apprehensive soldiers frequently turned to liquor, which could make them rowdy and lascivious, spoiling for fights and looking for prostitutes. Some communities saw problems caused by soldiers worsen as unsavory characters enlisted for bounties or for fees paid to draftees' substitutes. These types often deserted and blithely committed crimes while on the run. Places like Sandusky, Ohio, a railroad depot town, were plagued by such men, and some counties in the Midwest were racked by roving gangs of deserters.[88] In December 1864, the editor of the *Indianapolis Daily Journal* was sufficiently exasperated with these people to publicize an execution at a nearby camp as a warning to potential deserters and bounty jumpers of the fate that awaited them.[89]

WOUNDED SOLDIERS EDUCATE THE HOME FRONT

Northerners were doubtless most worried about the physical safety of sons, brothers, and fathers. Their concerns were amplified when they saw wounded soldiers returning from battle. Riverboats and trains brought the wounded to military hospitals throughout the North, filling them after a major fight. The District of Columbia, because of its proximity to the eastern battlefields, was home to an extraordinary concentration of hospitals tending to tens of thousands of men; the poet Walt Whitman once suggested to readers of the *New York Times* that a printed list of the capital's hospitals would compare in length to the directories of churches found in major northern cities.[90] Hospitals far from battlefield also sheltered thousands of soldiers. In the spring of 1862, the people of Keokuk, Iowa, saw the Estes House hotel turn into a hospital for more than 2,000 men.[91] Wounded soldiers filled New York City's civilian hospitals, forcing the town fathers to establish a network of municipal facilities; the city eventually became the site of government-built military hospitals.[92] In the greater Philadelphia region, there were several hospitals that provided beds for 157,000 wounded men during the war.[93]

Citizens near these hospitals could see first hand what a lead rifle ball could do to a human body and what it was like for an amputee to recover from the shock of his operation. Some civilians visited hospitals for no other reason than to satisfy their morbid curiosity or, according to Whitman, as others went "to a show of animals."[94] Most hospital visitors, however, were Good Samaritans and family members, and home folk expected to go to their hurt loved ones if circumstances allowed. In May 1863, for example, Rachel Cormany was busy making a traveling dress in case her husband was wounded and needed her.[95] Indeed, some northerners did travel great distances to search for wounded relatives.

As the war progressed, convalescing soldiers and disabled veterans dotted the landscape of town and countryside breaking down the geographic isolation of the home folk from battle. In January 1865, Mary Burwell of Oxford, Michigan, witnessed the psychological devastation of a local soldier who returned home "crazy as he can be."[96] Earlier in June 1863, Iowan Mary Vermillion had a convalescing soldier of her own to nurse when her brother Will came home on leave in an exhausted state. In March 1865, Will returned home again in a weakened condition from a Confederate prisoner of war camp. "People come to see him everyday almost," Mary noted, "and keep him talking about it all the time." The visitors "all want to hear the same story," and Will was always "willing to tell it."[97]

Such sights were not unusual by the end of the war. Almost 22,000 northern men survived amputations to become veterans with empty sleeves or pinned-up pant legs.[98] As a Harrisburg, Pennsylvania, editor pointed out, wounded veterans were a part of the northern landscape by the end of the war. "Every day we notice them in our streets," he wrote; "the spectacle is common to all the cities and towns of the Northern States—a number of disabled soldiers; some minus an arm; some lacking a leg; and many so battered and wrecked in other ways as to require the support of crutches and other artificial means of locomotion."[99]

DEALING WITH DEATH

Funerals were the most jarring reminder of the war, both for communities and for families fortunate enough to retrieve remains from a hospital or battlefield. Americans were familiar with death before the war, but violent deaths in battle or slow deaths from sickness in camps far from home were strange and troubling for them to contemplate. Before the war, death occurred within established rituals; it was a process more than an event that offered comfort to the dying and their family members who stood vigil. People rarely died among strangers, and most families could prepare for the event, grieve the loss, and come to some degree of closure. During the war, however, men commonly died on distant fields, away from their loved ones, leaving families searching for some meaning in the experience that shattered their world and beleaguered them with grief.[100]

Families preferred to recover the bodies of their fallen loved ones and bury them at home. Bringing home dead soldiers, however, was almost always difficult. Finding the body in an unmarked mass grave was hard, and transporting a decomposing corpse in the summer heat was daunting. Metal coffins, airtight coffins, coffins with compartments able to hold ice, and recently invented but infrequently used body bags helped. There were also new, expensive embalming techniques, although most families could not afford them.[101] In fact, everything about transporting a body was costly, as a grieving father informed a local newspaper. To bring his son's remains home from Washington, D.C., to Winsted, Connecticut, he incurred for embalming, a metal coffin, and freight as well as miscellaneous expenses totaling $125 (almost $2,000 in today's money). Furthermore, he noted, "It is hardly possible to effect such a return without the personal attendance of some friend, and every step is attended by some incidental expense."[102] Unable to meet these expenses, thousands of families lived with the knowledge that they would never be able to bury their dead soldiers.[103]

The last trip home concluded with the customary rituals of burial that frequently became public ceremonies. The dead thus became grim reminders of the war's perils. Rachel Cormany, whose husband was in the army, watched a soldier's burial across the street from her home in Chambersburg, Pennsylvania. "The first I ever saw buried," she noted. "I could not help shedding a tear for the brave soldier, perhaps thinking that such may be the fate of my poor Samuel makes me so sad."[104]

Families could find some comfort by gathering as many details as possible about their loved one's passing. The last words of their loved ones could impart an enduring memory of the deceased, and knowing that the death was good or noble, that of a true Christian, or a consequence of heroism could be consoling.[105] Families were sometimes fortunate to receive this information in condolence letters written by the deceased's comrades in arms.

Religion helped relatives cope, and fatalism allowed some family members to accept what they could not change. Moreover, religion helped northerners find deep meaning in these sacrifices. Abraham Lincoln and other politicians found religious language a natural way to hallow war deaths, in part because evangelical Christianity was so integral to northern society. Northern ministers reminded their congregations that these sacrifices were part of God's plan.[106] For many churchmen, God's will guided the nation to emancipation, which would lead to its salvation while furthering its grand purpose as a beacon of liberty to the world. Dead northern soldiers thus became martyrs for this holy cause, one certain of success because, as Methodist bishop Matthew Simpson made clear in his famous patriotic speeches, the United States was essential for the fulfillment of God's plan on earth.[107]

AMUSEMENT AND WAR

Civilians broke their daily routines with amusements that were much different from those before the war. Social activities included church services, concerts, and visits with friends. Civilians enjoyed the outdoors, visited the seashore, picnicked, ice skated, and participated in sporting events. The intellectually curious attended lectures and frequented libraries.[108] Men, women, and young people continued their prewar habit of reviewing the events of the day in their journals. Some diarists such as Sidney George Fisher, Maria Lydig Daly, and George Templeton Strong left behind more than just brief records of their lives; they composed substantial historical accounts of the northern home front that included their own intelligent reflections on war, politics, and other matters.[109] Letter writing, however, became the most common literary effort of the many individuals who had family members in the military.[110]

Elites continued to spend money on yachting events, horse races, expensive dinners, and other exclusive affairs. Wealthier families visited Newport, Rhode Island, and other fashionable resorts. By the end of 1862, the revived economy made it easier for them to frequent more formal entertainments, such as the opera and the theater, which were readily available in the North's larger cities. But the rich had no monopoly on recreation. The middle and lower classes had minstrel shows, circuses, agricultural fairs, band concerts, and sporting activities. And all sorts of northerners, black and white, either as spectators or participants, devoted free time to the increasingly popular game of baseball.[111]

American boys and men had long played some form of baseball, and soldiers found it to be a welcomed bit of recreation during tedious stays in camp. Black and white northerners, however, watched the game approach a degree of maturity and uniformity on the home front that would launch it on its way to becoming America's pastime. Northern spectators enjoyed town rivalries and attended games played by touring teams. Newspapers recognized baseball's growing significance by covering games. Baseball certainly diverted many a northerner from his or her daily cares, but the sport was not immune to the intrusions of war. Fans attended games that raised money for soldiers' relief funds, and they frequently noticed a team's changing roster as players left the diamond to become soldiers.[112]

Patriotic rituals, such as Washington's Birthday celebrations and the Fourth of July, brought together entire communities to watch parades and hear speeches in honor of the Union that their soldiers were fighting to preserve.[113] Unplanned victory celebrations broke up daily routines and united northerners as communities marked the success of their troops. Mary Livermore recollected the excitement that followed news arriving in cities in the Old Northwest after Grant's victory at Fort Donelson on February 16, 1862. People left their jobs, spilled into the streets, decked the avenues in flags, rang bells, played music, and attended prayer meetings. Spontaneous street parties illuminated with bonfires extended into the night, not ending "until physical exhaustion compelled an end to them."[114]

Livermore also noted that Fort Donelson celebrations involved raising money for wounded soldiers, soon a common occurrence throughout the North that allowed people to socialize while doing good works. Women in particular organized ice cream socials, lectures, and dances to raise relief funds.[115] Civilians attended fairs in towns throughout the North sponsored by soldiers' relief organizations, but the larger cities such as Chicago, Boston, Philadelphia, and New York witnessed extravagant events that brought in enormous crowds of people.

In quieter moments, northerners continued to read, but even here the war reshaped old habits. In New England, for example, newspapers supplanted more frivolous forms of print.[116] Farther west, Mary Vermilion refused to subscribe to "ladies magazines while the war lasts."[117] Vermilion still "read a good deal" while she was away from home staying with a group of women and often read aloud, but even her leisurely reading served a political purpose. She selected literature with the goal of converting other members of the reading circle to her antislavery views.[118]

Not everyone gave up reading fiction, but fiction also catered to the desire of many readers to know more about the war. The war now provided material for writers that attracted an audience already interested in the subject. In 1863, Louisa May Alcott's *Hospital Sketches* brought a fictionalized version of her experiences as a nurse to the attention of the public, while Henry Morford's *The Day's of Shoddy* described the early months of the war in the North and the impact of the first Battle of Bull Run.[119] Some publishers produced sensational war stories in books and periodicals, also introducing story lines that included matters of race and the role of women in the war.[120] Book publishers prospered as their businesses grew during the war, but they helped contribute to the development of northern nationalism even when they printed books that were not overtly designed to be propaganda.[121]

Courtship continued, but its pace was often altered by the war. Private Walter Dunn and Emma Randolph, both of New Jersey, maintained a steady correspondence during the war and married when peace came.[122] Captain John Emory Bryant, a school teacher before the war, and Emma Spaulding, his former student, also conducted a correspondence until Bryant completed his term of service in June 1864.[123] The prolonged courtship rituals in these letters allowed for the couples to grow into their intimate relationships, moving over months and years from conversations between friends to planning for the future between fiancées. On the other hand, the war could accelerate the expected progression of relationships. Some couples consummated their relationships out of wedlock; many couples quickly married before a soldier left for the front. Other couples married when soldiers came home on leave and sometimes under dramatic circumstances. Nettie Butler and her soldier sweetheart married while he was on leave after his escape from Libby Prison.[124] A sadder nuptial involved a young woman who rushed to the side of her wounded fiancée, married him, and then nursed him until his death.[125]

The war also broke down traditional restraints that had previously guided courtship rituals. Single women boldly initiated correspondence with soldiers when they inserted letters in boxes of supplies that they mailed to men at the front or in hospitals. One forward 19-year-old woman "of medium height, of slight build, with blue eyes, fair complexion, light hair, and a good deal of it" asked that the soldier receiving the socks she had knitted "Write and tell me all about yourself."[126] Some young women answered ads placed in newspapers by soldiers who wished to begin corresponding with women other than family members. Eligible women, therefore, provided soldiers with opportunities to stay in touch with the fairer sex and not lose contact with the more civilized patterns of the home front that society provided by the company of women. Corresponding with loved ones was a patriotic act, according to Mary Vermilion, in that it sustained soldiers "by loving, cheering words." Doing the same for strangers and casual acquaintances surely accomplished the same end. Single letter-writing women thus did their patriotic duty and, in turn, were able to enjoy the excitement of developing new friendships. Sometimes the correspondence led to lasting relationships that resulted in marriage.[127]

USING TIME TO AID THE WAR EFFORT

Many northerners, concerned about their contributions to the war effort, accepted that they, too, helped the cause by writing, working, farming, and manufacturing for the Union. Midwesterner Ovid Butler, after recently expanding his landholdings, explained to his soldier son, that with so many men gone to fill the ranks of the military, "he who makes earnest efforts to increase those productions of the earth, which are essential to feed and clothe these Armies and the population is a public benefactor."[128] Community leaders, such as those in Dubuque, Iowa, did what they could by raising funds to assist soldiers' families, but one reason why these efforts might not have endured was that they considered the practical aspects of relief to be women's work.[129] Men remained happy to organize and lead such efforts, but northern women shouldered the grinding work of raising material and money. Such was the arrangement that propelled into being the nation's dominant relief organization, the U.S. Sanitary Commission.

In April 1861, some 50 to 60 New York City women met to establish the Women's Central Association of Relief for the Sick and Wounded of the Army. This attempt to organize local women's groups was soon absorbed by the male-dominated U.S. Sanitary Commission.[130] In June 1861, a group of upper-class men received the federal government's approval to facilitate soldiers' relief, which led to the formation of the commission whose purpose was, as Mary Livermore recalled, "to do what the Government could not."[131] Prominent men such as H. W. Bellows, who became the organization's president; George Templeton Strong; and Frederick Law Olmsted, worked to harness the enthusiasm of the local women's organizations. Avoiding the Christian sentimentality of the women's organization, they envisioned a more a more centralized, scientific, masculine—and thus a more efficient and rational—approach to relief. Using paid agents to promote its agenda, the Sanitary Commission assisted soldiers through a wide range of relief activities, including the recruiting of doctors and nurses for their hospitals. The commission centralized much of the nation's relief efforts, but it continued to rely on the work of local aid groups and its branches located in 10 northern cities. By the end of the war, the Sanitary Commission provided the war effort with relief material valued at approximately $15 million.[132]

The Sanitary Commission's most prominent rival was the Christian Commission, founded in November 1861 by members of the U.S. Young Men's Christian Association. That organization raised approximately $6 million for the relief of soldiers and sailors, but unlike the Sanitary Commission, the Christian Commission paid particular attention to the spiritual needs of soldiers and sailors. It distributed Bibles and religious tracts and sponsored thousands of sermons and prayer meetings.[133] The Christian Commission, like the Sanitary Commission, relied on a network of dedicated women for fundraising at the local level. [134]

Thus the most common way in which women showed their commitment to the Union war effort was by raising money for soldiers' relief. From the beginning of the war, they formed hundreds of local organizations to raise money for soldiers and send boxes of necessary items to the front and hospitals. The Dubuque Ladies Aid Society tended to the needs of soldiers and eventually their families, while women in Bridgeport, Connecticut, went door to door to secure donations for soldiers' relief. [135] The organizer of the Marshalltown, Iowa, Sanitary Commission, Majorie Ann Rogers, visited scattered farm houses to solicit aid.[136] Women living on small farms in Wisconsin, some distance from a railroad line, donated all sorts of goods to the war effort but decided to do even more. "While the need lasted, they could not be satisfied to remain inactive," recalled Mary Livermore, "and so cast about to see what could be done by new and untried methods." Their solution was to ask their farming neighbors for donations of wheat, sell what they collected, and then use the profits for soldiers' relief. Their efforts were impressive. "Sometimes on foot, sometimes with a team, amid the snows and mud of early spring, they canvassed the country for twenty and thirty miles around, everywhere eloquently pleading the needs of the blue-coated boys in the hospitals," Livermore wrote. In the end, they gathered and sold 500 bushels of wheat for soldiers' relief, forwarding the proceeds to the Sanitary Commission.[137]

Such heroic service continued throughout the war. The Sanitary Commission estimated that there were over 10,000 local societies organized during the war that provided as much as $50 million in donations to various state and private entities.[138] But it was difficult work. Local organizations' efforts lagged after 1863 as women and communities tired or directed their attention to veterans in need of charity and assistance. Women in Newport, New York, curtailed their contributions to the Sanitary Commission, because they felt the needy families of their home town soldiers should take priority, while women in Chatham, Pennsylvania, devoted themselves to caring for sick veterans who had returned home.[139] Also, women worried that male-dominated national organizations had a potentially serious flaw in that they lacked the personal knowledge of their soldiers' needs as well as the civilizing feminine touch that was critical for maintaining the soldiers' connection with home. Women also feared that large, impersonal organizations might misuse or misdirect their material contributions, and surgeons might help themselves to the things that they had worked so hard to deliver to the front. Women's groups' came to resent the controlling hand of national organizations, creating a tension between their patriotic commitment to national loyalty and their deep ties to their local communities. This desire for autonomy often found expression in how local groups ordered their priorities, giving preference first and foremost to tending the needs of soldiers from their communities; it also prompted them to organize local fund raising events and fairs that they could control.[140]

Fairs combined the familiar elements of male-run early nineteenth-century agricultural and mechanics' fairs and the female-dominated fundraising fairs that appeared during the 1820s, but on a more spectacular level.[141] Proliferating across the North, local fairs raised funds by selling goods produced by community members or donated by businesses and manufacturers. The larger urban sanitary fairs became the big charitable and entertainment events of the day. Chicago, for example, was home to the first major fair, running from October 27 through November 7, 1863. The event opened with a fantastic parade, cannon salvos, and throngs of attendees, many given leave by their employers to miss work. Volunteers sold donated items from across the North, including all sorts of manufactured goods, pianos, cattle, perfumes, and President Lincoln's signed Emancipation Proclamation, which ultimately secured a bid of $3,000 (more than $40,000 in today's money). Entertainment included musical performances and a lecture by the celebrated young patriotic orator Anna Dickinson. People laughed when Mary Livermore promised that the fair would bring in $25,000.[142] Livermore, in fact, underestimated the enterprise; after the organizers extended the fair's run it had accumulated over $78,000 for soldiers' aid. Other big city fairs exceeded Chicago's success. The organizers of Boston's December 1863 fair could raise admission fees because so many people wished to attend and took in $146,000. New York's Metropolitan Fair, which opened in April 1864, raised an estimated $2 million, and Philadelphia's Great Central Fair, which opened in June 1864, raised well over $1 million.[143]

Women dominated the organization and the execution of these events. In the process, their activities sharpened their social and political skills as well as an awareness of the limitations that society placed on them. Mary Livermore learned that she and an associate needed their husbands' signatures to have a building constructed for the Chicago sanitary fair, even though they would be using their own resources to pay in advance for the work. It was required by law, as all their property legally belonged to their husbands. "We learned much of the laws made by men for women, in that conversation with an illiterate builder," she later recalled. "I registered a vow that when the war was over I would take up a new work—the work of making law and justice synonymous for women."[144] Young women active during the war matched Livermore's determination to do something about such paternalism. Developing and coordinating an extensive network of female-dominated organizations was testimony to their competence and fueled their rising expectations.[145]

African American women initially had no soldiers for whom they could raise relief funds. Nevertheless, black women joined black men to do what they could to assist contraband, those slaves who sought shelter and freedom behind the Union lines. Black communities organized relief efforts for these former slaves gathering in crowded camps.[146] The antebellum alliance of black and white abolitionists developed practical solutions to pressing problems encountered by wartime runaway slaves. In 1862, for example, the Philadelphia black community and the Pennsylvania Abolitionist Society established an employment office for contrabands initially directed by the prominent black abolitionist William Still.[147]

When finally given the opportunity, wives and daughters of African American soldiers took on the same tasks that white women had shouldered from the outset of the war. Antislavery advocate, newspaper editor, and former teacher Mary Ann Shadd Cary most famously went beyond such traditional roles in the women's war effort. Although a resident of Canada who became a British subject in 1862, she returned to the United States in 1863 and worked for contraband relief with the Colored Ladies' Freedmen's Aid Society of Chicago. In 1864, she began recruiting African American men for the U.S. Colored Troop regiments sponsored by Massachusetts, Connecticut, and Indiana.[148]

Some black and white women shared Cary's hunger for more demanding tasks than fund raising. Abolitionist women such as Cary spoke out against slavery, and now they publicly rallied audiences for the Union. Anna Dickenson, a young Philadelphia abolitionist and stalwart lecturer for the Union cause, earned a reputation as a northern Joan of Arc. Other women who shared Dickenson's patriotic sentiments but not her talent became involved in the nation's political discourse in ways that did not attract as much attention.[149] Mary Vermilion, for example, coped with the travails of daily life, but also entered the world of wartime politics by attending Union meetings, which sometimes were all-day affairs, and reading newspapers. She did not hesitate to express her political opinions in letters to her husband.[150] Some women confronted the war head on by hiding their sex and joining the army. Attracted by bounties, moved by a desire to be near loved ones, or propelled by patriotism, they pursued a more unusual course of action than those women who left home to serve the Union cause as teachers and nurses, activities that also came with sacrifices and physical risks.[151]

Women found helping ex-slaves both rewarding and patriotic while maintaining a vestige of feminine respectability. Female teachers and missionaries followed Union armies into the slave states and stayed on after the war. Women traveled to places like Port Royal, South Carolina, and Roanoke Island, North Carolina, as volunteers or employees of organizations such as the American Missionary Association and the New England Freedmen's Aid Society. They witnessed the ugly legacy of slavery and taught freed slaves how to be good Yankees, all the while enduring the paternalism of male supervisors. Teachers courageously stood up to insults, ostracism, intimidation, and violence meted out by white southerners who feared the disruptive social and economic consequences their Yankee ideas would have on their former slaves.[152] Black women who taught ex-slaves in the newly conquered areas of the Confederacy took extraordinary risks, but as one black woman from Newport, Rhode Island, explained in her application for a teaching position, "Who can feel for us if we do not feel for ourselves?" A black woman from Cleveland, Ohio, also explained that she was determined to do something to help bring the ex-slaves "into the family of man." "No thought of suffering, and privation, nor even death, should deter men from making every effort possible," she continued, "for the moral and intellectual elevation of these ignorant and degraded people."[153]

Working in hospitals provided another way for northern women to be more actively engaged in the war effort. Such service allowed them to answer the question that Sarah Emma Edmonds pondered at the outset of the war: "What part am *I* to act in this great drama?"[154] By pursuing the traditional feminine role of caregiver in nontraditional settings, nurses allowed the war into their lives in ways that most home-front patriots could not.

Northern nurses witnessed a kind intense suffering that they never would have seen in ordinary times, while taxing their own physical abilities to the utmost.[155] Louisa May Alcott arrived in the District of Columbia and almost immediately came to know the unhappy consequences of battle and camp. After a night's rest, she commenced her "new life by seeing a poor man die at dawn, and sitting all day between a boy with pneumonia and a man shot through the lungs."[156] Some women committed themselves to the difficult task, adjusted to the unusual circumstances, and became hardened to their surroundings. Quaker Cornelia Hancock of New Jersey, who served in field hospitals close to the front, admitted as much when she noted that "The suffering we get used to."[157] The experience certainly had a lasting impact on her. "I feel assured," she wrote, "I shall never feel horrified at anything that may happen to me hereafter."[158]

Closer to home, women relief workers tended to wounded soldiers and veterans. Sanitary Commission workers supervised transitional homes and "Soldiers' Rests" for the returning men; they also explored other ways of helping the veteran, such as providing clothes and transportation or information about more extensive relief.[159]

PAYING FOR THE WAR: TAXES, BONDS, GREENBACKS

At the outset of the war, states and municipalities rallied to the flag, raised troops, and put off worrying about how they would pay their bills. Still recovering from earlier financial problems caused by the Panic of 1857, as well as the economic downturn prompted by secession, some states lacked immediate resources to cover the new wartime expenses. Voluntary contributions at the local level paid for outfitting many of the first companies of men, and some governors even used their own funds and credit. But the war's staggering costs required a more formal sharing of the burden. In the past, Congress had reimbursed states for comparable expenditures, and states now expected Congress to do the same. In July 1861, the federal government promised to cover the costs involved in mustering state regiments. The law, however, was confusing and relied on an exacting federal bureaucracy. Some disputed state claims would remain unresolved for years after the war.[160]

The war required money from Americans who were not used to heavy taxation at the local, state, and national level. As the conflict dragged on, unexpected and unusual expenses strained purses. For instance, the army's insatiable need for men prompted state, county, city, and town governments to lure recruits with ever larger bounties. By August 1864, Brookfield, Vermont, had paid $6,400 for bounties and expected to pay an additional $14,000 to meet its enlistment quota.[161]

The Lincoln administration resorted to both traditional and innovative funding methods to meet the war's ever growing costs. In the process the central government more frequently intruded into the lives of average northerners. Excise taxes and loans were established ways of raising revenue, while a new income tax and printing a paper national currency were more controversial.[162] In August 1861, Congress passed America's first income tax at a standard 3 percent on annual incomes over $800. It also levied a direct tax on the states based on real estate values that the states could assume and collect as they saw fit. In July 1862, the President signed a bill that broke new ground by authorizing a progressive income tax with a limit set at a high of 5 percent on income over $10,000, while retaining the 3 percent rate on incomes ranging from $600–$10,000. The law also included a slew of other taxes, including excise taxes, stamp taxes, inheritance taxes, and license taxes. These taxes increased the war's financial burden on northerners, especially when businesses increased their prices to cover their own taxes. Income taxes introduced northerners to a new government agency (the Internal Revenue Bureau), the federal tax form, deductions, and the concept of automatic withholding.[163] It also prompted wealthy northerners, as some astonished citizens of Dubuque, Iowa, learned when they perused the published tax rolls, to resort to creative accounting and avoid paying taxes at all.[164]

Early in the war, Secretary of the Treasury Salmon P. Chase expected to finance the war by borrowing money. In February 1862, the federal government increased its reliance on borrowing by authorizing Chase to sell more interest-bearing bonds. However, it was Philadelphia financier Jay Cooke who developed a sophisticated campaign that leavened patriotism with the promise of financial gain to market the two bond issues that he had received the exclusive right to sell. His company used newspaper ads and other printed materials as well as a network of agents to spread the word from cities to isolated farm communities, reaching beyond the banking community to average Americans. Big investors bought up the greater share of these bonds, but sales offices stayed open into the evening to tend to the needs of working people and the middle class. Importantly, the publicity associated with the campaign alerted even those ordinary people who did not buy bonds that the federal government was offering the investment to them and that the government could have a new role in their economic lives. The result was a financial success for Cooke, but the venture also convinced northerners that the federal government could be a source of financial security for themselves.[165]

The new paper currency further connected ordinary people to the national government. Previously Americans satisfied most currency needs by relying on notes issued by state regulated private banks. Sound banks also regulated themselves and won the confidence of their customers.[166] However, this arrangement made it easy to circulate counterfeit and bad bank notes. All of that changed when the Legal Tender Act became law on February 25, 1862. Even Americans who were worried about inflation caused by paper money had to admit that "greenbacks" (the nickname given to federal notes because of the green ink used to print them) were convenient and reliable. They could satisfy all transactions except the payment of import tariffs. A national bank act passed on February 25, 1863, taxed state bank notes at a rate of 10 percent, effectively putting them out of circulation and making greenbacks the dominant circulating currency. Yet paper money had its limits. The federal government continued to pay interest on its debt in specie, a promise designed to encourage the purchase of its bonds.[167]

Early in the war, state and local officials relied on private donations to fund bounties, but as the war continued, borrowing and taxation increased the public burden. Vermont steadily increased its state-wide property tax to cover its expenses.[168] Connecticut, on the other hand, hesitated to tax its citizens. In May 1861, Connecticut spent almost $2 million to put five regiments into the field, which the legislature covered by selling bonds. Resistance to any increase in taxation as well as the conflicting economic interests of businessmen, farmers, and small landowners meant that the state also borrowed money to cover the federal government's initial levy. The legislature's reluctance to tax residents meant a continued reliance on bonds to pay the state's war costs until mounting debt convinced Connecticut's politicians to increase taxes on business and property.[169] Local communities also had to wrestle with increased expenses, especially after they began to pay bounties. Illinois, for example, gave counties and cities the authority to add new property taxes to their usual assessments, which they were to use for extraordinary wartime expenses.[170] Late in the war, Michigan gave county officials the power to borrow money to pay for bounties; Milwaukee, Wisconsin, resorted to additional real estate taxes to cover the cost of inducing men to volunteer.[171]

Northerners reacted to these changes in ways that ran from resentment and cranky complaints to acceptance, usually justified by patriotism. George Templeton Strong believed that paper money as legal tender would be "disastrous" for creditors such as himself, destroying "at least half of what property I possess."[172] One Ohioan from Youngstown, complaining of the inflationary aspect of circulating greenbacks, wrote in 1864 that the paper money was "one great cheat—one grand swindle" and unconstitutional as well.[173] Nevertheless, many northerners thought that greenbacks were justified by the crisis. "They are as good as gold," Mary Vermilion wrote to her husband in June 1863. "While I was traveling

I often heard people refuse to take anything but 'greenbacks'. I would have declined anything else if it had been offered me." But not only did the use of this new money help Vermilion to define her loyalty, it allowed her to judge the loyalty of others. "It is a bad sign to see any one afraid of 'greenbacks'," she observed. "That was one of the signs by which I could always tell the traitors in Indiana."[174]

Though many northerners complained about taxes, virtually everyone was resigned to paying them. In May 1863, one Vermont farmer groused after an encounter with the federal income tax collector, "I would like to know how much mony [sic] they have got to have if all are taxed as I am." But at least he saw a self-interested purpose in his payment. "I am willing to give one half my income if they will let me stay home," he confessed to his brother.[175] Others embraced patriotism as a soothing salve. A Boston businessman explained to his son in March 1862, that "Taxes are & will be enormous for years to come." Nevertheless, "We must not flinch from meeting our duty in this trying conflict."[176] New Yorker Strong groused about the prospects of taxes as well as paper money destroying his net worth, but came to a similar conclusion: "Never mind. I shall not complain if the nation is saved."[177]

Northern economic policy proved effective. Although northerners suffered real hardships of inflation, they never bore the terrible economic burdens and scarcities endured by their Confederate enemies. And while federal, state, and local governments accumulated significant debt, they paid what was necessary to save the Union.[178]

PESSIMISM, CONSCRIPTION, AND DISSENT

Some northerners objected to the war in general both for selfish or principled reasons. Government economic policies confirmed the fears of some conservatives who worried that the war would lead to an unconstitutional growth of federal power and a corresponding abridgement of their liberties. Local political allegiance and an overarching desire to protect local economies even caused some Republican governors to exercise some caution in responding to the demands of the national government.[179] But most of all, northerners with high expectations in 1861 soon found their enthusiasm waning as the war dragged on.

Democratic editors in Connecticut viewed the Confederate success at Bull Run in July 1861 as positive proof of the seceding states' ability to stand as a separate nation; continuing such a fruitless war, they argued, would result only in wasted fortunes, ruined lives, and ultimately a rebel victory.[180] Some New Jersey editors concurred.[181] Even staunchly patriotic northerners who had been all in favor of saving the Union reconsidered their support of the war after Lincoln added emancipation to the nation's war aims. In November 1862, a Connecticut woman wrote to her husband in the army, "the more I see and hear the less confidence I have in our ever haveing [*sic*] peace restored to us again." Her pessimism led her to conclude that "these United States will be a divided land when the fighting ceases if that ever is."[182] Republicans continued to control Congress after the 1862 elections, but the results were an ominous portent for the party. New York and New Jersey gave Democrats victories in the states' gubernatorial races and sent new Democratic congressmen to Washington. Even Lincoln's home state of Illinois elected more Democrats than Republicans to Congress and gave control of the statehouse to Democrats. The Republican Party lost a relatively small but noticeable amount of voter support as northerners began to question the course of the war.[183]

The bloody defeat at Fredericksburg on December 13, 1862, all but thoroughly disheartened northerners. Some families simply wanted their men to come home. That Christmas, Henrietta Parker, a mother from Vergennes, Vermont, was disgusted with how the politicians were conducting the war and urged her son Charles, a captain in the Seventh Vermont Infantry, to resign his commission. "Managed as things now are, the enemy have and will have the advantage," she complained. "I am sick sick Heart sick, of this War, and I want my Son out of it." She told Charles, "I cannot sacrifice you to this Unholy War, They accomplish nothing but the slaughtering of thousands, and to all appearances it is all they will accomplish."[184]

Such sentiments hampered the government's ability to raise additional volunteers. During 1862, northerners responded to recruiting rallies with much less enthusiasm, a problem that continued into the next year. To meet its unrelenting need for men, the government finally considered recruiting blacks. During late 1862 and early 1863, the army began enlisting southern contrabands and free northern blacks. Yet racial prejudice prompted many to wonder if such an effort would do more harm than good. In July 1863 Philadelphian Sidney Fisher was distressed that abolitionists were using black enlistments to further the cause of equality. He recorded in his journal, "All this is as absurd as it is dangerous."[185]

Ironically, by late 1862, the wartime economy provided black men with greater opportunities, making them less enthusiastic about enlisting. Also, many white northerners shared Fisher's attitude, raising legitimate fear among African Americans that they would not be treated as well as white soldiers or that the country would not recognize their basic civil rights. Nevertheless, blacks joined the army, and about 80 percent of the approximately 180,000 men who served in the U.S. Colored Troops were former slaves from the Confederate or Union border states.[186] These black troops made a difference, as did the army's efforts to retain white veteran soldiers. But manpower shortages ultimately forced the government to resort to conscription.

States and municipalities worked hard to avert the necessity of involuntary service. Incentives, patriotic harangues, and shame coaxed northerners into the army in 1862, saving most states from a militia draft. However, the Enrollment Act of March 1863 inaugurated a national draft.

The conscription law was neither as oppressive nor burdensome as it might have been, allowing ample opportunities for individuals to avoid conscription. Men could initially purchase exemptions or hire substitutes at fees that were not beyond the means of gainfully employed draftees. Men eligible for conscription banded together in draft insurance clubs, pooling their resources to pay the costs if anyone was called up. Communities also subsidized fees and substituted payments.[187] Substitute brokers secured replacements for draftees, often with dishonest or at least questionable practices. Brokers in New Jersey preyed on European immigrants who had little understanding of the war and its perils.[188] Before too long, legal draft evasion was sufficiently common to elicit little comment except from soldiers at the front.

For the first two federal drafts, when the commutation was still available, northern men used it liberally; 85,000 of the 133,000 men required to serve in the Army paid the fee.[189] Potential draftees also eagerly sought out substitutes. The quest for substitutes, with ever intensifying competition among northern communities and, thus, ever increasing cost for able-bodied men, continued through the last year of the war. Of the almost 232,000 men selected in the lotteries, more men furnished substitutes than actually went into the army.[190]

Most northerners supported the draft, despite its intrusiveness. Some of them considered conscription a patriotic duty while others thought it to be a good way to spread the burden of service beyond the ranks of the poorer members of society. Some Republicans believed that conscription was the only way to maintain political power, because so many of their constituents volunteered while less enthusiastic Democratic voters stayed at home.[191]

Many northerners, however, found conscription obnoxious and opposed it. It's possible that as many as 50,000 men illegally dodged conscription before the 1863 federal draft, and 161,244 men illegally avoided the subsequent federal drafts.[192] Pacifists understandably quarreled with the notion of forced military service and used moral suasion to try to stop the violence, but they also encouraged conscripts who wished to avoid service.[193] Many Democrats believed that conscription was an extraordinary and unconstitutional act that circumvented states' rights and abridged personal liberty. Democratic politicians remained in loyal opposition, and their party accepted the draft as law, but private citizens with such sentiments often resisted the draft, with violence if necessary.[194]

Direct opposition to the draft took various forms. In August 1862, in Dubuque, Iowa, some Irish dissenters simply fled.[195] During 1862, in Pennsylvania mining areas dominated by Democrats and Irish immigrants, men refused to cooperate with officials and sometimes threatened them.[196] Resistance in these mining communities continued throughout the war.[197]

During the summer of 1863, draft enrollment officers risked life and limb almost anywhere they appeared. In Chicago, snarling dogs and angry

wives greeted their efforts.[198] Hundreds of troops accompanied by artillery put down a protest in Holmes County, Ohio, while in Indiana, draft
resistors killed two enrollment officers.[199] Most famously, New York City
protestors ran riot from July 13 through July 16. A mob, primarily from
the Irish working class, destroyed property, razed a black orphanage, and
committed mayhem and murder. The mob killed at least 105 and perhaps 150 individuals, including soldiers shot or brutally beaten as they
attempted to quell the disorder. Property damage amounted to millions
of dollars.[200]

Opposition to the draft was frequently more than simply a rejection of
forced military service. Working men who tended to vote Democratic—
especially German and Irish Catholic immigrants, in northeastern cities,
Vermont quarries, Pennsylvania mines, and the old Northwest states—
believed that conscription was just one more unfair burden placed on their
shoulders by the Lincoln administration. They conflated the draft with
such government policies as emancipation, their own economic difficulties, and labor problems. They resented the war that they believed favored
the wealthy, the war profiteers, and blacks. New York City rioters, for
example, worried that black men would displace them in the work force if
they were drafted. The Pennsylvania miners staged labor protests for the
same reasons that they had before the war.[201] Iowa draft opponents had
already been protesting taxes and objecting to the war before there was a
draft.[202] Residents of Holmes County, Ohio, believed they were defending
their local liberty from the encroachments of the Lincoln administration's
expanding, intrusive central government.[203]

Significantly, resistance to the draft in these and other places reflected
the values of entire communities that learned the ways of legal draft avoidance from the first threat of conscription.[204] But families and neighbors in
these communities also supported extra legal or illegal resistance.[205] From
late 1864 into the fall of 1865, military forces arrested 2,810 deserters and
3,743 draft evaders in the eastern Pennsylvania mountains alone, numbers
that indicated significant community support for the dissenters.[206] Federal authorities prosecuted citizens who aided resistors and deserters—in
New Jersey, there were 37 convictions for such crimes—but in some communities, sympathetic jurists thwarted the government. [207] In July 1863, a
county judge signed a writ of habeas corpus, freeing two Iowa resistors,
who then filed kidnapping charges against the assistant provost marshal
general and the men who had aided him in arresting them.[208]

Draft resistance was part of the larger national problem of dealing with
dissent in a democracy in crisis. Strident Republicans branded all opposition as treasonous, while Democrats argued that legitimate political dissent was a cherished constitutional right. Some war opponents joined
the Knights of the Golden Circle, the Order of American Knights, and
the Sons of Liberty, secret societies opposed to the war. Republicans saw
dark conspiracies such as secret organizations of "Copperheads," antiwar

men supposedly as treacherous and vile as the deadly snake. Mainstream Democrats struggled to escape the shadow of such charges by claiming that they protected the people's liberty against overbearing Republican power. Democrats also pointed to the Republican secret society known as the Union League, an organization that had its roots in the Wide Awakes, enthusiastic supporters of Lincoln's first presidential campaign. The Union League required "unwavering loyalty and support of the government in all its efforts to suppress the rebellion" and its members "denounced with great bitterness" those northerners who opposed the administration's policies.[209]

Intolerance of reasoned opposition to a war led to mobs attacking Democratic editors, destroying printing presses, and disrupting legitimate Democratic political rallies.[210] Unable to distinguish dissent from disloyalty, Lincoln suspended the writ of habeas corpus at various times during the war, allowing the government to imprison individuals without formally charging them. Some newspapers were shut down. Troublesome Democratic newspaper editors were arrested, as were numerous other war critics. The most famous of these antiwar dissidents was Ohio politician Clement Vallandigham. Vallandigham was charged with treason, tried and convicted by a military commission, and exiled to the Confederacy, even though he urged voters to work within the political system. Far from quieting dissent with its attack on Vallandigham, the Lincoln administration made the Democratic politician into a martyr to "this wild storm of fanaticism," as one Iowa editorialist called Republican policy. Democratic politicians organized rallies in defense of Vallandigham and questioned whether the Republican Party's true purpose in conducting the war was to undermine the liberties of the northern people.[211]

Heated partisanship upset families, disrupted neighborhoods, and even seeped into the sacred quarters of church organizations. Unionists in places opposed to the draft happily turned in dodgers and deserters as well as the neighbors who aided. Tense situations could become violent. Late in the first summer of the war, loyalists and Confederate sympathizers clashed in three different communities in Fairfield County, Connecticut.[212] In March 1863, Mattie Blanchard of Foster, Connecticut, complained about the gloating antiwar men in the community who gathered at the local store and "have a glorious time over the news if it is in favor of the south." These neighbors of hers, she suggested, "ought to be shot" when a time comes for them "to be punished for treason."[213] Albert Hancock, irritated by the antiwar Democrats in his wife's family, declared that "it would do him more good to kill one of his brother in laws, than to shoot Jeff Davis himself."[214] Emiline Ritner of Mt. Pleasant, Iowa, thought that those neighbors who did not support the troops were traitors. "I feel more and more bitter toward them every day." Furthermore, she explained that "When I know a person is a 'copperhead' I *can't* feel that they are *my* friends."[215]

Unionist-dominated religious groups in the Midwest, where antiwar feelings were common, disciplined their apparently disloyal clergy—some had complained about pro-Republican preachers—and put pressure on their Democratic communicants to support the war effort. In 1862, the Illinois Methodist Annual Conference meeting in Springfield forced the retirement of the Reverend William Blundell. The 1863 meeting challenged his status in the church for not joining organizations that supported the Lincoln administration, for neglecting to pray for Lincoln and the Union armies, and for the "gross immorality for failing to observe a day of National Thanksgiving as proclaimed by the President." Other preachers came under fire for various types of allegedly disloyal activities, which generally involved supporting Democrats and opposing Republicans.[216]

Republicans reflexively painted opposition to the Union cause with the blackest brush possible, but events occasionally appeared to justify their anxieties. Some midwesterners discussed establishing a confederacy of their own. Confederate agents made contact with sympathetic midwesterners and financially assisted the Sons of Liberty in Illinois. Sons of Liberty in Indiana had hidden a cache of arms, which was discovered when they were arrested. And a scheme to free Confederate prisoners from Camp Douglas in Chicago was no less alarming because it was badly planned. That conspiracy led to the arrests of 150 people in early November 1864, most of whom were not guilty of treasonous activity. The Chicago conspiracy arrests did not materially improve the city's security, but they did provide an electoral boost to Lincoln and his party in the presidential election on November 8.[217]

Dramatic conspiracies and secret agents aside, antiwar Democrats generally expressed their opposition to Lincoln and his policies in legitimate political activities. Throughout the war, Democratic strength waxed and waned in correlation with battlefield defeats and victories. The draft and emancipation gave them particularly good issues for the 1864 campaign, as did the general accusation that the Lincoln administration was doing serious harm to the constitution. In 1864, Democrats were optimistic because of the country's war weariness and Lincoln's apparent vulnerability. Thus they engaged in the customary political activities as they challenged Lincoln and pressed for the victory of General George B. McClellan.[218]

The 1864 election gave dissenting northerners what would become their last chance during the war to challenge a federal government that appeared to have grown well beyond its constitutional limits.[219] In Philadelphia, Democrats regularly paraded in the streets, much to the annoyance of Lincoln supporters who occasionally attacked the marchers. Indeed, on October 29 Republicans engaged marching Democrats in a knock-down street fight.[220]

For both Democrats and Republicans, however, the public ritual of electioneering provided them once again with opportunities to celebrate their democratic faith even in the middle of a bloody war. They listened to their politicians, priests, and ministers make their points; read political tracts and broadsides; marched in their party's parades; shot off guns and fireworks; and did their best to convince a majority of voters that they and their leaders were the true heirs of the Founding Fathers. The electoral process brought excitement into the streets of northern cities, towns, and villages, but it was political entertainment that culminated in a real, solemn purpose when they voted on election day.[221] Unfortunately for the Democrats, the fortunes of war smiled on Union forces in time for the 1864 election. Northerners gave Lincoln a resounding victory and the assurance that his party would control Congress. As one diarist noted, "*Vox Populi, vox Dei.* So it must be for the best."[222]

VICTORY CELEBRATIONS AND MOURNING

For most northerners, the presidential election following on the heels of their army's victories signaled the beginning of the end of the war. In early 1865, New Jerseyans eagerly grasped at rumors of the surrender of the Confederacy; when disappointed, they still expected the war to end almost any day.[223] Bostonians followed Sherman's advance through the Carolinas, observed Lincoln's second inauguration as a festive day, and followed Grant's efforts to dislodge Lee from his defensive positions in northern Virginia, expecting imminent victory.[224] Chicagoans were losing patience with the rebels and were hoping to make them pay for all of their suffering.[225]

During the spring of 1865, northerners experienced a whirlwind of contradictory emotions, ranging through anxiety, joy, and sorrow as the war moved toward its end. New Yorkers, according to George Templeton Strong, nervously awaited news of Robert E. Lee's surrender of the Army of Northern Virginia after the April 3 fall of Richmond. As late as April 9, Strong was "a little anxious" that there was no word from the Virginia front. When it finally arrive, he concluded, Lee's Army "can bother and perplex none but historians henceforth forward." As far as he and other northerners were concerned, the war was over. The rebel government had disintegrated and "Napoleon could hardly save Joe Johnston's army," the other major Confederate force east of the Mississippi River.[226]

New Yorkers began their end-of-war celebrations when Richmond fell, as did people all across the North. "Isn't it Glorious?" wrote Caroline Woolsey, "New York has stood on its head, and the bulls and bears of Wall street for once left off their wrangling, and sang Old Hundred."[227] Upstate in the village of Homer, jubilant citizens celebrated with bonfires, cannons, and clanging church bells.[228] Boston and surrounding communities rang church bells, listened to speeches, and watched parades.[229] In Jacksonville, Illinois, a spontaneous day-long affair engulfed the town and exhausted the population's energies; the town was too worn out to celebrate Lee's April 9 surrender.[230] Chicagoans remained cautious after the fall of Richmond; memories of defeat coming after assurances of victory made them anxious. But when word came of Lee's surrender, they enjoyed a two-day long city-wide celebration. On the second day, courts, banks, schools, and businesses closed while "At every street corner one caught the sound of martial music."[231] Citizens of Homer, New York, listened to speeches while residents of nearby Courtland held a torch-lit parade.[232] Philadelphia celebrated for a week, while one Boston editorialist described the festivities there as being comparable to a multitude of simultaneous July 4th celebrations.[233]

In New York City, residents listened to the constant firing of guns, although rain stymied greater efforts to commemorate the event. Localized celebrations, however, occupied the city's inhabitants for several days. On April 11, for example, Trinity Cathedral hosted an overflowing crowd for a *Te Deum.* It was an eclectic service that ranged from hymns to an organ recessional that included the "Hallelujah Chorus" and "The Star Spangled Banner." People also began to debate the fate of the rebel president, Jefferson Davis, some expressing a desire to hang him "on a sour apple tree," others arguing for mercy, a debate that individuals pursued across the river in New Jersey and elsewhere.[234] But, as Mary Livermore recalled, "From the height of this exultation the nation was swiftly precipitated to the very depths of despair" when Abraham Lincoln fell to an assassin's bullet.[235]

Confederate sympathizer and popular actor John Wilkes Booth shot President Lincoln on April 14, as the president watched a play at Ford's Theater in Washington, D.C. The president died the next day, and northerners' celebrations turned into mourning ceremonies. Northerners were already used to mourning—the war had consumed over 360,000 of their boys—but Lincoln's death was extraordinary, its impact wide-ranging in part because Lincoln's reputation had risen to new heights after his 1864 reelection. New Yorker George Templeton Strong wrote only a few days before Lincoln's death that the president's "name will be of high account fifty years hence, and for many generations thereafter."[236] Editorialists now eulogized Lincoln, praising him as being second only to George Washington among America's presidents.[237]

The news of the assassination made people "dumb with grief," but united in their anger and sorrow.[238] Individuals who had advised mercy for the defeated South now called for "vindictive justice."[239] New Jerseyan Emma Randolph assumed all Democrats were somehow accomplices in the assassination. "I fell a stronger hatred than ever for the poor Copperheads," she explained; "now they have stooped so low as to murder our loved and honored . . . President."[240]

Some bitter individuals directed their anger against the closest proxies of the moribund Confederacy, all of whom they presumed were connected at least by association to the dastardly act. Some directed their vengeance against individuals who did not show proper respect for the slain president. They attacked paroled Confederate soldiers and southern sympathizers in New York and Washington, D.C., destroyed Copperhead newspaper presses in San Francisco, and besieged Junius Brutus Booth, the assassin's brother, in Cincinnati. New Yorkers fired Irish housekeepers who had expressed satisfaction with Lincoln's death. In the nation's capital, authorities jailed secessionist women who disrupted the mourning routine. The people of Germantown, Pennsylvania, threatened Edward Ingersoll, who shortly after the assassination made an inflammatory pro-southern speech in New York; he was placed in jail for his own protection and soon fled town. In New York City, Unionists tarred a house on Fifth Avenue for "having not been put in mourning;" it took days to remove the mess. Clevelanders mobbed a southern Ohio man who referred to the dead president in unflattering terms. They also chased from the city a prominent local architect, J. J. Husband, for the same sin, and then chiseled away his name from the cornerstone of the county courthouse that he had designed.[241] Northerners would have their satisfaction in learning that soldiers killed Booth as he was attempting to make his escape through Virginia, and that later in the summer the government hanged four of his accomplices and sent four more conspirators to prison.[242]

George Templeton Strong likened the assassination's impact to that of the firing of Fort Sumter in the way that it "invigorated national sentiment."[243] And Lincoln's death touched even individuals who had previously disagreed with some of his policies and produced a surge of national unity.[244] "I felt for some time a mere dull & stupefied sense of calamity," wrote the Philadelphia diarist Sidney Fisher, a strong Unionist who had criticized emancipation and remained skeptical of calls for black rights. "I felt as tho [sic] I had lost a personal friend, for indeed I have & so has every honest man in the country."[245] Even Clement Vallandigham, the famous Copperhead, and other Democrats joined their former Republican antagonists in recognizing the greatness of the martyred president.[246] Thus Strong concluded that "*Death* has suddenly opened the eyes of the people . . . to the fact that a hero has been holding high place among them for four years."[247]

On April 19, the day of Lincoln's funeral in Washington, shops and schools closed across the North. Black-clothed figures crowded into churches decorated with portraits of Lincoln to attend memorial services, walking past lowered flags and buildings draped in black crepe, listening to tolling bells.[248] Northerners paid their respects to Lincoln at the White House, the Capitol, and several cities along the funeral train's route as it brought the president's body to Springfield, Illinois, its final resting place. As many as one million northerners passed Lincoln's open casket before the president was interred on May 4. Northerners unable to attend formal viewings lit bonfires and gathered to pray along the funeral train's route. Farmers doffed hats as the cars passed by their fields. But even as they mourned and demanded justice for the heinous act, northerners attempted to make sense of Lincoln's martyrdom. Many could not fail to acknowledge the proximity of Lincoln's death to Good Friday and Easter: he died to atone for the resurrected nation's sins.[249]

READJUSTMENT

Throughout the North, demobilization manifested itself in several ways. Shortly after the end of the war, a New York City recruiting depot near City Hall once again became park land, and during the summer, the federal government began to liquidate property, including horses that ended up pulling city streetcars.[250] Upstate at Elmira, officials released Confederate prisoners, dismantled entire buildings, and sold surplus material to the locals in what amounted to a giant yard sale.[251] Voluntary associations also ended their war work. In July 1865, the Woman's Central Relief Association dismantled, soldiers' homes closed, and in 1868 the U.S. Sanitary Commission shut down.[252]

Nothing more obviously emphasized the end of the war than the return of soldiers to civilian life. In Washington on May 23 and 24, over 150,000 soldiers paraded through Washington, D.C., to celebrate victory and begin their journeys home. Civilians who witnessed the two-day parade, however, also learned that demobilization had its risks. Men from Sherman's western regiments fought with men from the eastern Potomac army; men from both armies raucously celebrated their survival.[253] Indeed, throughout the spring and into the summer, soldiers returning from the war behaved in ways that seemed to confirm civilians' fear about the effects of camp life and battle. Veterans confined to northern rendezvous camps awaiting paperwork and final orders became impatient and rioted. Undisciplined troops destroyed property and upset the peace of towns along rail lines.[254]

Despite these incidents, many more northerners probably agreed with Samuel Cormany, who believed that he and his fellow soldiers "will be better citizens" because of their wartime experiences.[255] Consequently, northerners joyously welcomed home their heroes. Cities feted them, governors and mayors made speeches, communities staged parades, and families engaged in their own personal celebrations that "were next to heavenly," even while confidence men, pickpockets, "agents and bad women played their arts on unwary" soldiers lingering in camps or walking city streets.[256]

There were, however, indications that some soldiers would never again experience life as they had known in antebellum America, circumstances that had an impact on society and their families. Festering wounds, unhealed amputations, and chronic gastrointestinal problems plagued veterans, affected their families' futures, and led to an expansion of state and federal expenditures as politicians addressed their needs through pensions, soldiers' homes, and hospitals. Some soldiers believed they could

never return to their antebellum lives. Others suffered from the psychological effects of their experiences. New Jersey soldier Walter Dunn, for
example, informed his puzzled fiancée, Emma Randolph, that he could
not return to his parent's household. "I know it would seem verry [*sic*]
diferent [*sic*] the verry quiet life you would have there, to the scenes and
changes of the last four years," she surmised.[257] But Emma witnessed signs
at home that war changed men, even if she did not understand them. In
June 1865, she saw some of Walter's old comrades, and while they looked
well, one of them was "verry dejected and low spirited—not natural at
all." A friend suggested that "he seems like some one laboring under some
heavy grief." And the local minister told her that the boy would not discuss his distress, but appeared to be broken hearted.[258]

Just as states had raised troops, they also orchestrated aspects of the
demobilization effort. New Jersey's governor, Marcus Ward, visited his
state's soldiers in Virginia on several occasions to help speed their demobilization.[259] Connecticut provided transportation for its soldiers, assisted
them with their records, and helped them secure back pay, bounties,
and pensions. The state also expanded New Haven Hospital for invalid
soldiers so that they could convalesce near their home.[260] All told, over
800,000 men from Connecticut and across the Union left the U.S. Army
before the middle of November 1865, a significant addition to the civilian workforce.[261] In some areas, such rapid demobilization placed a strain
on the once booming wartime economy. The Army no longer needed the
quantities of supplies that had kept factories busy, and as a consequence
Connecticut's industries cut payrolls, its ports suffered from a decline in
trade, and the state's residents coped with inflation.[262]

Economic troubles, however, varied throughout the North, and veterans
grabbed what opportunities were available. Taylor Peirce's wife promised
him that "There is all sorts of work to do here and plenty of money to
pay for it with so I feel confident thee will find something to do if thee is
only well enough to work when thee gets home." In fact, her brother had
already found the veteran a job in an insurance company, but he ended up
making his livelihood as an engineer.[263] Government and private citizens
also did what they could for the veterans. New York City, for example,
established job registries that connected veterans and employers, and in
1866 and 1867, William Oland Bourne sponsored left-handed writing con-
tests for amputee veterans in order to prove their competence at clerical
work.[264]

New opportunities absorbed ambitious veterans even as the economy
shifted away from war production. Springfield, Massachusetts, experienced a decline in the labor force at its armory, but investment and innovation kept people working.[265] Postwar Connecticut gained new positions
in the insurance industry, while Chicago veterans, eager to improve their
situations, enrolled in commercial institutes and found employment in
new insurance companies.[266] In northern Ohio and elsewhere, prominent

officers found opportunities in business and politics.[267] And before the end of the decade, one-time Connecticut factory hand Benjamin Hurst, with the help of his wife, established himself as a proprietor of a dry goods store in Rockville.[268]

Some young soldiers, hardly adults when the war began, started new lives from scratch, purchasing land, marrying, and attempting to find domestic tranquility. Older farmers returned to their properties and tried to reconstruct normal lives for themselves and their families, while others sold land, restlessly moved about looking for better prospects, and reestablished themselves in new communities. Samuel and Rachel Cormany returned to their Missouri farm, planted, and engaged in church-related activities, but within a few years moved to Kansas. There would be other changes as the Cormanys experienced the vicissitudes of life, including moves that brought them to Pennsylvania, where they spent their last years.[269]

Women and African Americans, who had fully participated in the war effort, expected to enjoy better lives because of the northern victory, but their postwar goals remained well off in the future. Yankee women remained active and moved from wartime philanthropy into groups advocating women's rights. As Mary Livermore had indicated, their wartime experience had taught them the restrictions of male patriarchy. Georgeanna Woolsey Bacon noted that women who had learned to value their own efforts and abilities during the war "were not willing to fold their useful hands when the war was over, and let the old order of things reestablish itself."[270] She and her sisters Abby and Jane remained active in eleemosynary work and especially in the developing nursing profession.[271] Other women continued their work in helping freedpeople adjust, and many young, white middle-class women as well as northern black women ventured south to teach freedpeople, taking advantage of a unique experience created by the end of slavery.[272] Even so, northern women activists came to resent the fact that their male wartime associates slighted their causes while concentrating on advancing black rights.[273] In 1870, the Fifteenth Amendment guaranteed African American men the right to vote; the nation's women, who had long argued that they had as equal a claim to the ballot as uneducated former slaves, did not enjoy that privilege throughout the nation until 1920, when the Nineteenth Amendment became part of the Constitution.

As indicated by some of the successes of Reconstruction, white abolitionists did not abandon working for greater rights for blacks when the war ended.[274] Their northern black allies, however, better understood the complexities and vagaries of freedom. Not only did they expect a better world for their brethren in the South, but also for themselves that placed them on par with their white neighbors. In the end, black reformers and their allies could claim only partial victory. Frederick Douglass, for example, took comfort in postwar legislation and new constitutional guarantees advancing the cause of the nation's black citizens. Douglass, however, was well aware of the limits of law when confronted with entrenched racism.[275] For example, prejudice limited the access to educational opportunities and consequently to economic advancement for segregated black Bostonians after the war.[276] By the beginning of the 1870s, a black worker in New York City was overwhelmingly more likely to be a longshoreman or a waiter rather than a professional.[277] And by the turn of the century, industrialists preferred European immigrant workers to African Americans, relegating them to the bottom end of the labor market.[278] Also, before the end of the century, northerners exhibited a collected amnesia when it came to black wartime heroism. The aging black veterans who brought up the rear of holiday parades provided telling symbols of the segregation that continued to mark northern society.[279] Instead of changing the attitudes of their former Confederate enemies, northerners came to share their negative racial attitudes.

Northerners seemed to have spent their vindictiveness in the cathartic mourning of their president and the punishment of the assassination conspirators. Their joy in peace soon overpowered their hatred of their former enemies. Jefferson Davis went to prison. Henry Wirz—commander at the infamous Andersonville, Georgia, prisoners-of-war depot—suffered death. Other Confederates were at worst inconvenienced and humiliated by the temporary loss of their political privileges. There was, however, no clamor for a wider range of punishment of former enemies, including the confiscation of rebel property.[280] They relatively quickly admitted that postwar efforts to remake the South in the North's image failed. By the 1870s, the victors were willing to give up Reconstruction as a bad job, blaming its chaos and violence on the inability of the ex-slaves to adjust to freedom. If war had changed these northerners, so too did the peace that followed.

CONCLUSION

Over a short four-year period, as Emerson and Hawthorne had promised, America's Civil War had reached into all corners of northern life. Even if northerners were quick to accept sectional reconciliation, they could not escape the fact that wartime demands had reshaped their families, altered their economic fortunes, and perhaps tested many of them in extraordinary, unexpected ways. Their efforts won a victory that guaranteed the rule of law and preserved what they perceived to be the best possible system of government, while also expanding the Constitution's meaning of liberty. Republican politicians for some time to come waved the "bloody shirt" to remind voters of the wartime perfidy of the Democratic party, old soldiers marched in Memorial Day and Fourth of July parades, and veterans continued to lobby for expanded pension benefits. But there remained more in the collective memory than using the war for cynical self-interest, nostalgia, or brotherly gatherings. The realization of the fruits of victory might have been imperfect, but reconciliation did not mean an abandonment of the ideals that drove the North to resist secession. Recognition of the renewed bond of nationhood could never diminish the meaning of the North's sacrifices. In 1911 Joshua Lawrence Chamberlain informed a correspondent as much. While referring to the experiences of veterans, his words could apply to all who had participated in the northern war effort. "We were fighting for our Country, with all that this involves," he wrote, "not only for the defence of its institutions, but for the realization of its vital principles and declared ideals."[281] As long as people like Chamberlain reminded their fellow northerners that their cause had been and continued to be superior to the cause of their former enemy, the northern experience would have meaning.

NOTES

1. Louis P. Masur, ed., *The Real War Will Never Get in the Books: Selections from Writers during the Civil War* (New York: Oxford University Press, 1993), 124.

2. Ibid., 167.

3. Jeffrey D. Marshall, ed., *A War of the People: Vermont Civil War Letters* (Hanover, NH: University Press of New England, 1999), 40.

4. Nicholas B. Wainwright, ed., *A Philadelphia Perspective: The Diary of Sidney George Fisher Covering the Years 1834–1871* (Philadelphia: Historical Society of Pennsylvania, 1967), 368.

5. Eric Foner, *Free Soil, Free Labor, Free Men: The Ideology of the Republican party before the Civil War* (New York: Oxford University Press, 1970).

6. Henry Steele Commager, ed., *The Civil War Archive: The History of the Civil War in Documents* (Indianapolis: Bobbs-Merrill Company, Inc., 1950; revised ed., New York: Tess Press, 2000), 72.

7. Ibid.

8. David Herbert Donald, ed., *Gone for a Soldier: The Civil War Memoirs of Private Alfred Bellard* (Boston: Little, Brown and Company, 1975), 3.

9. Ulysses S. Grant, *Personal Memoirs of U.S. Grant*, ed. by Mary Drake McFeely and William S. McFeely (New York: Literary Classics of the United States, Inc., 1990), 152.

10. Marshall, ed., *A War of the People*, 24.

11. James H. Moorhead, *American Apocalypse: Yankee Protestants and the Civil War* (New Haven, CT: Yale University Press, 1978), 36–37. For more on the slave power idea, see Leonard L. Richards, *The Slave Power: The Free North and Southern Domination, 1780–1860* (Baton Rouge: Louisiana State University Press, 2000).

12. John Niven, *Connecticut for the Union: The Role of the State in the Civil War* (New Haven, CT: Yale University Press, 1965), 48.

13. James M. McPherson, *The Struggle for Equality: Abolitionists and the Negro in the Civil War and Reconstruction* (Princeton, NJ: Princeton University Press, 1964), 192–220.

14. C. Peter Ripley, et al., eds., *The Black Abolitionist Papers*, Vol. 5: *The United States, 1859–1865* (Chapel Hill: University of North Carolina Press, 1992), 117, 140–42.

15. Jeanie Attie, *Patriotic Toil: Northern Women and the American Civil War* (Ithaca: Cornell University Press, 1998), 33.

16. Oliver Otis Howard, *Autobiography of Oliver Otis Howard,* 2 vols. (New York: The Baker and Taylor Company, 1908), 1: 121–32.

17. Donald, ed., *Gone for a Soldier,* 4.

18. Charles F. Larimer, ed., *Love and Valor: Intimate Civil War Letters between Captain Jacob and Emiline Ritner* (Western Springs, IL: Sigourney Press, 2000), 18.

19. Richard Franklin Bensel, *Yankee Leviathan: The Origins of Central State Authority in America, 1859–1877* (Cambridge: Cambridge University Press, 1990), 101–5.

20. Leonard P. Curry, *Blueprint for Modern America: Nonmilitary Legislation of the First Civil War Congress* (Nashville: Vanderbilt University Press, 1968), 180; Bray Hammond, *Sovereignty and an Empty Purse: Banks and Politics in the Civil War* (Princeton: Princeton University Press, 1970), 48.

21. William J. Jackson, *New Jerseyans in the Civil War: For Union and Liberty* (New Brunswick: Rutgers University Press, 2000), 20, 40; William Gillette, *Jersey Blue: Civil War Politics in New Jersey, 1854–1865* (New Brunswick: Rutgers University Press, 1995), 11.

22. Michael H. Frisch, *Town Into City: Springfield, Massachusetts, and the Meaning of Community, 1840–1880* (Cambridge, MA: Harvard University Press, 1972), 43–45.

23. Don Harrison Doyle, *The Social Order of a Frontier Community: Jacksonville, Illinois, 1825–70* (Urbana: University of Illinois Press, 1978), 81.

24. Historian Phillip Shaw Paludan in his study, *A People's Contest: The Union and the Civil War,* 2nd ed. (Lawrence: University Press of Kansas, 1996), 10–11, stresses the significance of the local connections of northerners.

25. Carl F. Kaestle, *Pillars of the Republic: Common Schools and American Society, 1780–1860* (New York: Hill and Wang, 1983), 75–99; Earl J. Hess, *Liberty, Virtue, and Progress: Northerners and Their War for the Union,* 2nd ed. (New York: Fordham University Press, 1997), passim. Don Harrison Doyle provides an excellent example of the nature of community building and the role of these institutions in a new town in his study *The Social Order of a Frontier Community.*

26. James M. McPherson, *Ordeal by Fire: The Civil War and Reconstruction,* 3rd ed. (Boston: McGraw Hill, 2001), 28.

27. Kathleen Neils Conzen, *Immigrant Milwaukee, 1836–1860: Accommodation and Community in a Frontier City* (Cambridge, MA: Harvard University Press, 1976), 63–125.

28. Thomas Dublin, *Women at Work: The Transformation of Work and Community in Lowell, Massachusetts, 1826–1860* (New York: Columbia University Press, 1979), 145–47.

29. Robert L. Bee, ed., *The Boys from Rockville: Civil War Narratives of Sgt. Benjamin Hirst, Company D, 14th Connecticut Volunteers* (Knoxville: University of Tennessee Press, 1998), 12.

30. Paul W. Gates, *The Farmer's Age: Agriculture, 1815–1860* (New York: Holt, Rinehart and Winston, 1960), 274; David E. Schob, *Hired Hands and Plowboys: Farm Labor in the Midwest, 1815–60* (Urbana: University of Illinois Press, 1975).

31. Edward Chase Kirkland, *Industry Comes of Age: Business, Labor and Public Policy, 1860–1897* (Chicago: Quadrangle Paperbacks, 1967), 342; Bee, ed., *Boys from Rockville,* xvii–xxviii.

32. See McPherson, *Ordeal by Fire*, 5–42, for a comparison of the free and slave states on the eve of the war.

33. James Oliver Horton and Lois E. Horton, *Black Bostonians: Family Life and Community Struggle in the Antebellum North* (New York: Holmes & Meier Publishers, Inc., 1979), 2.

34. Ibid., 10–12.

35. Graham Russell Hodges, *Root and Branch: African Americans in New York and East Jersey, 1613–1863* (Chapel Hill: University of North Carolina Press, 1999), 187–270; David Gerber, *Black Ohio and the Color Line, 1860–1915* (Urbana: University of Illinois Press, 1976), 5.

36. Leon F. Litwack, *North of Slavery: The Negro in the Free States, 1790–1860* (Chicago: University of Chicago Press, 1961), 64–112.

37. Hodges, *Root and Branch,* 232–33.

38. Nina Silber and Mary Beth Sievens, ed., *Yankee Correspondence: Civil War Letters between New England Soldiers and the Home Front* (Charlottesville: University of Virginia Press, 1996), 8.

39. Paul W. Gates, *Agriculture and the Civil War* (New York: Alfred A. Knopf, 1965), 229.

40. Gates, *Agriculture and the Civil War,* 228–29, 234–35, 241–42; Phillip Shaw Paludan, *"A People's Contest": The Union and the Civil War, 1861–1865,* 2nd ed. (Lawrence: University of Kansas Press, 1996), 134–35; James Marten, *Children for the Union: The War Spirit on the Northern Home Front* (Chicago: Ivan R. Dee, 2004), 64.

41. Mary A. Livermore, *My Story of the War: A Woman's Narrative* (Hartford, CT: A.D. Worthington and Company, 1887; Williamstown, MA: Corner House Publishers, 1978), 145–49.

42. George Winston Smith and Charles Judah, *Life in the North during the Civil War: A Source History* (Albuquerque: University of New Mexico Press, 1966), 167.

43. McPherson, *Ordeal by Fire,* 406.

44. Silber and Sievens, eds., *Yankee Correspondence,* 123.

45. Smith and Judah, *Life in the North,* 211; Paludan, *"A People's Contest,"* 127–50; J. Matthew Gallman, *The North Fights the Civil War: The Home Front* (Chicago: Ivan R. Dee, 1994).

46. Wainwright, ed., *A Philadelphia Perspective,* 442.

47. Robert Knox Sneden, *Eye of the Storm: A Civil War Odyssey,* ed. by Charles F. Bryan, Jr., and Nelson D. Lankford (New York: The Free Press, 2000), xiii–xiv.

48. Michael A. Ross, *Justice of Shattered Dreams: Samuel Freeman Miller and the Supreme Court during the Civil War Era* (Baton Rouge: Louisiana State University Press, 2003), 63.

49. Benton McAdams, *Rebels at Rock Island: The Story of a Civil War Prison* (DeKalb: Northern Illinois University Press, 2000), 22.

50. Albert Castel, *Civil War Kansas: Reaping the Whirlwind,* new ed. (Lawrence: University Press of Kansas, 1997), 84.

51. Michael P. Gray, *The Business of Captivity: Elmira and its Civil War Prison* (Kent, OH: Kent State University Press, 2001).

52. George B. Kirsch, *Baseball in Blue and Gray: The National Pastime during the Civil War* (Princeton: Princeton University Press, 2003), 49.

53. Wainwright, ed., *A Philadelphia Perspective,* 401–2.

54. Julie Holcomb, ed., *Southern Sons, Northern Soldiers: The Civil War Letters of the Remley Brothers, 22nd Iowa Infantry* (DeKalb: Northern Illinois Press, 2004), 14.

55. Robert H. Bremner, *The Public Good: Philanthropy and Welfare in the Civil War Era* (New York: Alfred A. Knopf, Inc., 1980), 78–79.

56. Russell Johnson, *Warriors into Workers: The Civil War and the Formation of Urban-Industrial Society in a Northern City* (New York: Fordham University Press, 2003), 245–47.

57. James C. Mohr, ed., *The Cormany Diaries: A Northern Family in the Civil War* (Pittsburgh: University of Pittsburgh Press, 1982), 380.

58. Ibid., 253, 408.

59. Donald C. Elder III, ed. *Love Amid the Turmoil: The Civil War Letters of William and Mary Vermilion* (Iowa City: University of Iowa Press, 2003), 260.

60. Nina Silber, *Daughters of the Union: Northern Women Fight the Civil War* (Cambridge, MA: Harvard University Press, 2005), 110–15.

61. Larimer, ed., *Love and Valor,* 136.

62. Barbara Butler Davis, ed., *Affectionately Yours: The Civil War Home-Front Letters of the Ovid Butler Family* (Indianapolis: Indiana Historical Society Press, 2004), 56–57.

63. Elder, ed., *Love Amid the Turmoil,* 47.

64. Patricia L. Richard, *Busy Hands: Busy Hands: Images of the Family in the Northern Civil War Effort* (New York: Fordham University Press, 2003), 40–78; Marilyn Mayer Culpepper, ed., *Trials and Triumphs: The Women of the American Civil War* (East Lansing: Michigan State University Press, 1991), 106.

65. Silber and Sievens, eds., *Yankee Correspondence,* 115.

66. Culpepper, ed., *Trials and Triumphs,* 268.

67. Jennifer Cain Bohrnstedt, ed., *While Father is Away: The Civil War Letters of William H. Bradbury* (Lexington: University Press of Kentucky, 2003), 3.

68. Larimer, ed., *Love and Valor,* 68–69.

69. Ibid., 164.

70. Elder, ed. *Love Amid the Turmoil,* 85.

71. Silber, *Daughters of the Union,* 41–86.

72. Rachel Filene Seidman, "A Monstrous Doctrine? Northern Women on Dependency during the Civil War," in *An Uncommon Time: The Civil War and the Northern Home Front,* ed. Paul A. Cimbala and Randall M. Miller (New York: Fordham University Press, 2002), 170–88; Megan J. McClintock, "The Impact of the Civil War on Nineteenth-Century Marriages," in *Union Soldiers and the Northern Home Front: Wartime Experiences, Postwar Adjustments,* ed. Paul A. Cimbala and Randall M. Miller (New York: Fordham University Press, 2002), 395–416; Theda Skocpol, *Protecting Soldiers and Mothers: The Political Origins of Social Policy in the United States* (Cambridge: Belknap Press of Harvard University Press, 1992), 107; Amy E. Holmes, " 'Such is the Price We Pay': American Widows and the Civil War Pension System," in *Toward a Social History of the American Civil War: Exploratory Essays,* ed. by Maris A. Vinovski (Cambridge: Cambridge University Press, 1990), 171–95.

73. James Marten, *The Children's Civil War* (Chapel Hill: University of North Carolina Press, 1998); Marten, *Children for the Union.*

74. Marten, *Children for the Union,* 66–76.

75. Bohrnstedt, ed., *While Father is Away,* 128.

76. Anita Palladino, ed., *Diary of a Yankee Engineer: The Civil War Story of John H. Westervelt, Engineer, 1st New York Volunteer Engineer Corps* (New York: Fordham University Press, 1997).

77. Silas W. Browning to Minnie Browning, 4 March [1863?], Silas W. Browning Papers, *A People at War: Civil War Manuscripts from the Holdings of the Library of Congress*, 60 reels (Alexandria, VA: Chadwyck-Healey, 1989–1990), reel 6.

78. Robert H. Bremner, *The Public Good: Philanthropy and Welfare in the Civil War Era* (New York: Alfred A. Knopf, Inc. 1980), 85–90; Marten, *Children for the Union*, 103–7, 164–69.

79. Davis, ed, *Affectionately Yours*, 29, 43.

80. Ibid., 33.

81. Joseph T. Glatthaar, "Duty, Country, Race, and Party: The Evans Family of Ohio," in *The War Was You and Me: Civilians in the American Civil War*, ed. by Joan E. Cashin (Princeton, NJ: Princeton University Press, 2002), 332–57.

82. Wainwright, ed., *A Philadelphia Perspective*, 397, 398, 400, 441.

83. Niven, *Connecticut for the Union*, 63–64.

84. Richard Moe, *The Last Full Measure: The Life and Death of the First Minnesota Volunteers* (New York: Henry Holt and Company, Inc, 1993; New York: Avon Books, 1993), 302.

85. *New York Times*, 21 October 1862; Earl J. Hess, "A Terrible Fascination: The Portrayal of Combat in the Civil War Media," in *An Uncommon Time: The Civil War and the Northern Home Front*, ed. Paul A. Cimbala and Randall M. Miller (New York: Fordham University Press, 2002), 1–26; Earl J. Hess, " 'Tell Me What the Sensations Are': The Northern Home Front Learns about Combat," in *Union Soldiers and the Northern Home Front: Wartime Experiences, Postwar Adjustments*, ed. Paul A. Cimbala and Randall M. Miller (New York: Fordham University Press, 2002), 119–42; Marten, *Civil War America*, 99–111; John R. Neff, *Honoring the Civil War Dead: Commemoration and the Problem of Reconciliation* (Lawrence: University Press of Kansas, 2005), 40; Gunther Barth, *City People: The Rise of Modern City Culture in Nineteenth-Century America* (New York: Oxford University Press, 1980), 79; and Jim Weeks, *Gettysburg: Memory, Market, and an America Shrine* (Princeton, NJ: Princeton University Press, 2003), 13.

86. Franny Nudelman, *John Brown's Body: Slavery, Violence, and the Culture of War* (Chapel Hill: University of North Carolina Press, 2004), 103–31.

87. Gerald F. Linderman, *Embattled Courage: The Experience of Combat in the American Civil War* (New York: The Free Press, 1987), 84.

88. Capt. G. Nagle to Capt. J. W. De Forrest, 17 October 1865, Letters Received, Veteran Reserve Corps Records, Provost Marshal General's Department, Record Group 110, National Archives, Washington, D.C.; *Indianapolis Daily Journal*, 29 December 1864.

89. *Indianapolis Daily Journal*, 24 December 1864.

90. Masur, ed., *The Real War Will Never Get in the Books*, 258–59.

91. Michael A. Ross, *Justice of Shattered Dreams: Samuel Freeman Miller and the Supreme Court during the Civil War* (Baton Rouge: Louisiana State University Press, 2003), 63.

92. Edward K. Spann, *Gotham at War: New York, 1860–1865* (Wilmington, DE: SR Books, 2002), 78–79.

93. J. Matthew Gallman, *Mastering Wartime: A Social History of Philadelphia during the Civil War* (Cambridge: Cambridge University Press, 1990), 130.

94. Masur, ed., *The Real War Will Never Get in the Books*, 276.

95. Mohr, ed., *The Cormany Diaries*, 290.

96. Culpepper, ed., *Trials and Triumphs*, 106.

97. Elder, ed., *Love Amid the Turmoil,* 134–36; 310–11.

98. Frances Clarke, " 'Honorable Scars': Northern Amputees and the Meaning of Civil War Injuries," in *Union Soldiers and the Northern Home Front: Wartime Experiences, Postwar Adjustments,* ed. Paul A. Cimbala and Randall M. Miller (New York: Fordham University Press, 2002), 368.

99. *Harrisburg [Pa.] Patriot and Union,* 15 April 1865.

100. Drew Gilpin Faust, "Civil War Soldier and the Art of Dying," *Journal of Southern History* 67 (February 2001): 4–8; Gary Laderman, *The Sacred Remains: American Attitudes Toward Death, 1799–1883* (New Haven, CT: Yale University Press, 1996), 22–85; Neff, *Honoring the Civil War Dead,* 22–53.

101. Laderman, *The Sacred Remains,* 113–16; Neff, *Honoring the Civil War Dead,* 46–53.

102. Stuart Murray, *A Time of War: A Northern Chronicle of the Civil War* (Lee, MA: Berkshire House Publishers, 2001), 276–77.

103. Paludan, *"A People's Contest,"* 366.

104. Mohr, ed., *The Cormany Diaries,* 256.

105. Faust, "Civil War Soldier and the Art of Dying," 13; Neff, *Honoring the Civil War Dead,* 51–52.

106. Paludan, *"A People's Contest,"* 363–64.

107. Moorhead, *American Apocalypse,* 65, 147–48; Peter J. Parish, "From Necessary Evil to National Blessing: The Northern Protestant Clergy Interpret the Civil War," in *An Uncommon Time: The Civil War and the Northern Home Front,* ed. Paul A. Cimbala and Randall M. Miller (New York: Fordham University Press, 2002), 61–89.

108. Smith and Judah, ed., *Life in the North during the Civil War,* 262–317; Daniel E. Sutherland, *The Expansion of Everyday Life, 1860–1876* (New York: Harper & Row, Publishers, 1989), 235–62; Anne C. Rose, *Victorian America and the Civil War* (Cambridge: Cambridge University Press, 1992), 109–44; Dorothy Denneen Volo and James M. Volo, *Daily Life in Civil War America* (Westport, CT: Greenwood Press, 1998), 203–23.

109. Wainwright, ed., *A Philadelphia Perspective;* Harold Earl Hammond, ed., *Diary of a Union Lady* (New York: Funk & Wagnalls Company, Inc., 1962); Allan Nevins, *The Diary of the George Templeton Strong: The Civil War, 1860–1865* (New York: The Macmillan Company, 1962).

110. Roanld J. Zboray and Mary Saracino Zboray, "Cannonballs and Books: Reading and the Disruption of Social Ties on the New England Home Front," in *The War Was You and Me: Civilians in the American Civil War,* ed. by Joan E. Cashin (Princeton, NJ: Princeton University Press, 2002), 245.

111. Kirsch, *Baseball in Blue and Gray,* 50; Smith and Judah, ed., *Life in the North during the Civil War,* 262–66.

112. Kirsch, *Baseball in Blue and Gray,* 1–27, 48–65.

113. Gallman, *Mastering Wartime,* 97–108; Doyle, *The Social Order of a Frontier Community,* 236.

114. Livermore, *My Story of the War,* 176–78.

115. Attie, *Patriotic Toil,* 95.

116. Zboray and Zboray, "Cannonballs and Books," in *The War Was You and Me: Civilians in the American Civil War,* ed. by Joan E. Cashin (Princeton, NJ: Princeton University Press, 2002), 237–61.

117. Elder, ed., *Love Amid the Turmoil,* 85.

118. Ibid., 37.

119. Louisa May Alcott, *Hospital Sketches,* ed. by Alics Fahs (Boston: Bedford/ St. Martin's, 2004); Henry Moford, *The Days of Shoddy: A Novel of the Great Rebellion in 1861* (Philadelphia: T. B. Petersom & Brothers, 1863).

120. Alice Fahs, "A Thrilling Northern War: Gender, Race, and Sensational Popular War Literature," in *An Uncommon Time: The Civil War and the Northern Home Front,* ed. Paul A. Cimbala and Randall M. Miller (New York: Fordham University Press, 2002), 27–60.

121. Alice E. Fahs, "Publishing the Civil War: The Literary Marketplace and the meaning of the Civil War in the North, 1861–1865" (Ph.D. diss., New York University, 1993).

122. Judith A. Bailey and Robert I. Cottom, eds., *After Chancellorsville: Letters from the Heart, The Civil War Letters of Private Walter G. Dunn and Emma Randolph* (Baltimore: Maryland Historical Society, 1998).

123. Ruth Douglas Currie, ed., *Emma Spaulding Bryant: Civil War Bride, Carpetbagger's Wife, Ardent Feminist, Letters and Diaries, 1860–1900* (New York: Fordham University Press, 2004).

124. Davis, ed., *Affectionately Yours,* 60.

125. Livermore, *My Story of the War,* 199–200.

126. Livermore, *My Story of the War,* 138.

127. Patricia L. Richard, *Busy Hands: Images of the Family in the Northern Civil War Effort* (New York: Fordham University, 2003), 87–175; Livermore, *My Story of the War,* 138; Elder III, ed. *Love Amid the Turmoil,* 85.

128. Davis, ed., *Affectionately Yours,* 106.

129. Johnson, *Warriors to Workers,* 247.

130. Georgeanna Woolsey Bacon and Eliza Woolsey Howland, *My Heart Toward Home: Letters of a Family during the Civil War,* ed. by Daniel John Hoisington (Roseville, MN: Edinborough Press, 2001), 34.

131. Livermore, *My Story of the War,* 129.

132. George M. Fredrickson, *The Inner Civil War: Northern Intellectuals and the Crisis of the Union* (New York: Harper & Row, Publishers, 1965; Urbana: University of Illinois Press, 1993), 98–112.

133. Michael J. Bennett, "Saving Jack: Religion, Benevolent Organizations, and Union Sailors during the Civil War"; and David A. Raney, "In the Lord's Army: The United States Christian Commission, Soldiers, and the Union War Effort" both in *Union Soldiers and the Northern Home Front: Wartime Experiences, Postwar Adjustments,* ed. Paul A. Cimbala and Randall M. Miller (New York: Fordham University Press, 2002), 253–62, 263–92.

134. Paludan, *"A People's Contest,"* 352–54; William Quentin Maxwell, *Lincoln's Fifth Wheel: The Political History of the United States Sanitary Commission* (New York: Longmans, Green & Co., 1956), 297.

135. Johnson, *Warriors into Workers,* 249; Attie, *Patriotic Toil,* 95.

136. Culpepper, ed., *Trials and Triumphs,* 252.

137. Livermore, *My Story of the War,* 144–45.

138. Attie, *Patriotic Toil,* 3.

139. Judith Ann Giesberg, *Civil War Sisterhood: The U.S. Sanitary Commission and Women's Politics in Transition* (Boston: Northeastern University Press, 2000), 71.

140. Attie, *Patriotic Toil,* 94–194, 218–19; Silber, *Daughters of the Union,* 178–93.

141. Beverly Gordon, *Bazaars and Fair Ladies: The History of the American Fund-raising Fair* (Knoxville: University of Tennessee Press, 1998), 9–11.

142. Theodore Karamanski, *Rally 'Round the Flag: Chicago and the Civil War* (Chicago: Nelson-Hall Publishers, 1993), 127–32.

143. Gordon, *Bazaars and Fair Ladies,* 66–72, for estimates of amounts raised as well as the various aspects of the more important Civil War fund raising fairs.

144. Livermore, *My Story of the War,* 435–36.

145. Giesberg, *Civil War Sisterhood,* 53–84.

146. Dorothy Sterling, ed. *We are Your Sisters: Black Women in the Nineteenth Century* (New York: W. W. Norton & Company, 1984), 250, 256–58.

147. C. Peter Ripley, et al., eds., The *Black Abolitionist Papers,* vol. 5: *The United States, 1859–1865* (Chapel Hill: University of North Carolina Press, 1992), 140–42.

148. Paul A. Cimbala, "Mary Ann Shadd Cary and Black Abolitionism," in *Against the Tide: Women Reformers in American Society,* ed. by Paul A. Cimbala and Randall M. Miller (Westport, CT: Praeger, 1997), 34–36.

149. Silber, *Daughters of the Union,* 143–60.

150. Elder, ed., *Love Amid the Turmoil,* 15, 184, 216.

151. Deanne Blanton and Lauren M. Cook, *They Fought Like Demons: Women Soldiers in the Civil War* (Baton Rouge: Louisiana State University Press, 2002; New York: Vintage Civil War Library Edition, 2002).

152. Joe M. Richardson, *Christian Reconstruction: The American Missionary Association and Southern Blacks, 1861–1890* (Athens: University of Georgia Press, 1986), 15–34; *Patricia C. Click, Time Full of Trial: The Roanoke Freedmen's Colony, 1862–1867* (Chapel Hill: University of North Carolina Press, 2001); Willie Lee Rose, *Rehearsal for Reconstruction: The Port Royal Experiment* (Indianapolis: The Bobbs-Merrill Company, Inc, 1964); Silber, *Daughters of the Union,* 236–46.

153. Sterling, ed., *We Are Your Sisters,* 261–65.

154. Sarah Emma Edmonds, *Memoirs of a Soldier, Nurse and Spy: A Woman's Adventures in the Union Army,* ed. by Elizabeth D. Leonard (DeKalb: Northern Illinois Press, 1999), 3.

155. Jane E. Schultz, *Women at the Front: Hospital Workers in Civil War America* (Chapel Hill: University of North Carolina Press, 2004); Silber, *Daughters of the Union,* 194–221; Culpepper, ed., *Trials and Triumphs,* 315–53.

156. Masur, ed., *The Real War Will Never Get in the Books,* 22–23.

157. Commager, ed., *The Civil War Archive,* 562.

158. Quoted in Silber, *Daughters of the Union,* 210.

159. Attie, *Patriotic Toil,* 240.

160. Kyle S. Sinisi, *Sacred Debts: State Civil War Claims and American Federalism, 1861–1880* (New York: Fordham University Press, 2003); Niven, *Connecticut for the Union,* 408.

161. Marshall, ed., *A War of the People,* 254–55.

162. Bray Hammond, *Sovereignty and an Empty Purse: Banks and Politics in the Civil War* (Princeton: Princeton University Press, 1970), 359.

163. Robert Franklin Bensel, *Yankee Leviathan: The Origins of Central State Authority in America, 1859–1877* (Cambridge: Cambridge University Press, 1990), 168; Leonard P. Curry, *Blueprint for Modern America: Nonmilitary Legislation of the First Civil War Congress* (Nashville: Vanderbilt University Press, 1968), 149–80; Paludan, *"A People's Contest,"* 117–21.

164. Hubert H. Wubben, *Civil War Iowa and the Copperhead Movement* (Ames: Iowa State University Press, 1980), 179–80.

165. Melinda Lawson, "Let the Nation Be Your Bank: The Civil War Bond Drives and the Construction of National Patriotism," in *An Uncommon Time: The Civil War and the Northern Home Front,* ed. Paul A. Cimbala and Randall M. Miller (New York: Fordham University Press, 2002), 90–119.

166. Mark Thornton and Robert B. Ekelund, Jr., *Tariffs, Blockades, and Inflation: The Economics of the Civil War* (Wilmington, DE: SR Books, 2004), 60–65.

167. Curry, *Blueprint for Modern America,* 181–206; Paludan, *"A People's Contest,"* 111.

168. Marshall, ed., *A War of the People,* 155, n. 2.

169. Niven, *Connecticut for the Union,* 408.

170. Robin L. Einhorn, "The Civil War and Municiple Government in Chicago," in *Toward a Social History of the American Civil War: Exploratory Essays,* ed. by Maris A. Vinovski (Cambridge: Cambridge University Press, 1990), 128–29.

171. Eugene C. Murdock, *One Million Men: The Civil War Draft in the North* (Madison: The State Historical Society of Wisconsin, 1971), 176–77.

172. George Templeton Strong, *Diary of the Civil War, 1860–1865,* ed. by Allan Nevins (New York: The McMillan Company, 1962), 201.

173. Smith and Judah, *Life in the North during the Civil War,* 198–99.

174. Elder, ed., *Love Amid the Turmoil,* 119.

175. Marshall, ed., *A War of the People,* 155.

176. Silber and Stievens, ed. *Yankee Correspondence,* 59.

177. Strong, *Diary of the Civil War,* 201.

178. Thornton and Ekelund, *Tariffs, Blockades, and Inflation,* 68–72, McPherson, *Battle Cry of Freedom,* 447.

179. William Blair, "We Are Coming, Father Abraham—Eventually: The Problem of Northern Nationalism in Pennsylvania Recruiting Drives of 1862," in *The War Was You and Me: Civilians in the American Civil War,* ed. by Joan E. Cashin (Princeton, NJ: Princeton University Press, 2002), 183–207.

180. Niven, *Connecticut for the Union,* 299–300.

181. William Gillette, *Jersey Blue: Civil War Politics in New Jersey, 1854–1865* (New Brunswick, NJ: Rutgers University Press, 1995), 143.

182. Silber and Sievens, ed., *Yankee Correspondence,* 113.

183. Allen C. Guelzo, *Lincoln's Emancipation Proclamation: The End of Slavery in America* (New York: Simon & Schuster, 2004), 167.

184. Marshall, ed., *A War of the People,* 124.

185. Wainwright, ed., *A Philadelphia Perspective,* 456.

186. James M. McPherson, *The Struggle for Equality: Abolitionists and the Negro in the Civil War and Reconstruction* (Princeton, NJ: Princeton University Press, 1964), 192–220; Noah Andre Trudeau, *Like Men of War: Black Troops in the Civil War, 1862–1865* (Boston: Little, Brown and Company).

187. James W. Geary, *We Need Men: The Union Draft and the Civil War* (DeKalb: Northern Illinois Press, 1991), 114–15, 145–46.

188. Gillette, *Jersey Blue,* 158–59.

189. Eugene C. Murdock, *One Million Men: The Civil War Draft in the North* (Madison: The State Historical Society of Wisconsin, 1971), 198.

190. Geary, *We Need Men,* 145, 154, 168.

191. Blair, "We Are Coming, Father Abraham," 187–88.

192. Geary, *We Need Men*, 39.

193. Thomas F. Curran, *Soldiers of Peace: Civil War Pacifism and the Postwar Radical Peace Movement* (New York: Fordham University Press, 2003), xiii, 65–67.

194. Jean H. Baker, *Affairs of Party: The Political Culture of Northern Democrats in the Mid-nineteenth Century* (New York: Fordham University Press, 1999), 156, 338.

195. Wubben, *Civil War Iowa and the Copperhead Movement*, 63.

196. Grace Palladino, *Another Civil War: Labor, Capital, and the State in the Anthracite Regions of Pennsylvania, 1840–68* (Urbana: University of Illinois Press, 1990), 99–103.

197. Paul A. Cimbala, "Union Corps of Honor," *Columbiad* 3 (winter 2000): 75–76; Palladino, *Another Civil War*, 104–17.

198. Karamanski, *Rally 'Round the Flag*, 198.

199. Adrian Cook, *The Armies of the Streets: The New York City Draft Riots of 1863* (Lexington: University Press of Kentucky, 1974), 52.

200. Ibid., 194, 213–18; Spann, *Gotham at War*, 95–101.

201. Palladino, *Another Civil War*, 104–17.

202. Wubben, *Civil War Iowa and the Copperhead Movement*, 123.

203. Kenneth H. Wheeler, "Local Autonomy and Civil War Draft Resistance: Holmes County, Ohio," *Civil War History* 45 (June 1999): 147–59.

204. Geary, *We Need Men*, 110–11.

205. Joan E. Cashin, "Deserters, Civilians, and Draft Resistance in the North," in *The War Was You and Me: Civilians in the American Civil War*, ed. by Joan E. Cashin (Princeton, NJ: Princeton University Press, 2002), 262–85.

206. Cimbala, "Union Corps of Honor," 76–77.

207. Gillette, *Jersey Blue*, 158.

208. Wubben, *Civil War Iowa and the Copperhead Movement*, 127.

209. Wainwright, ed., *A Philadelphia Perspective*, 445, 449.

210. Frank L. Klement, *Dark Lanterns: Secret Political Societies, Conspiracies, and Treason Trials in the Civil War* (Baton Rouge: Louisiana State University Press, 1984).

211. Stephen E. Towne, "Killing the Serpent Speedily: Governor Morton, General Hascall, and the Suppression of the Democratic Press in Indiana, 1863," *Civil War History* 52 (March 2006): 41–65; Mark E. Neely, Jr., *The Fate of Liberty: Abraham Lincoln and Civil Liberties* (New York: Oxford University Press, 1991); Frank L. Klement, *The Limits of Dissent: Clement Vallandigham and the Civil War* (New York: Fordham University Press, 1998).

212. Niven, *Connecticut for the Union*, 301.

213. Silber and Sievens, ed., *Yankee Correspondence*, 155.

214. Elder, ed., *Love Amid the Turmoil*, 142.

215. Larimer, ed., *Love and Valor*, 294.

216. Bryon C. Andreasen, "Civil War Church Trials: Repressing Dissent on the Northern Home Front," in *An Uncommon Time: The Civil War and the Northern Home Front*, ed. Paul A. Cimbala and Randall M. Miller (New York: Fordham University Press, 2002), 214–42; Andreasen discusses Blundell's case on pp. 222–24.

217. Karamanski, *Rally 'Round the Flag*, 185–223.

218. Joel H. Silbey, *A Respectable Minority: The Democratic Party in the Civil War Era, 1860–1868* (New York: W. W. Norton & Company, Inc., 1977), 137–39.

219. Baker, *Affairs of Party*, 261–316.

220. Gallman, *Mastering Wartime*, 188–89.

221. Baker, *Affairs of Party*, 261–316.

222. Harold Earl Hammond, ed., *Diary of a Union Lady, 1861–1865* (New York: Funk & Wagnalls Company, Inc., 1962), 312.

223. Gillette, *Jersey Blue*, 295–96.

224. O'Connor, *Civil War Boston*, 223–26.

225. Karamanski, *Rally 'Round the Flag*, 230.

226. Strong, *Diary of the Civil War*, 576–81.

227. Howland and Bacon, *My Heart Toward Home*, 385.

228. Edmund J. Raus, Jr., *Banners South: A Northern Community at War* (Kent, OH: Kent State University Press, 2005), 252.

229. O'Connor, *Civil War Boston*, 226–27.

230. Doyle, *The Social Order of a Frontier Community*, 239–40.

231. Karamanski, *Rally 'Round the Flag*, 234–35; Livermore, *My Story of the War*, 468–70.

232. Raus, *Banners South*, 253.

233. Gallman, *Mastering Wartime*, 189; O'Connor, *Civil War Boston*, 228.

234. Strong, *Diary of the Civil War*, 579–81; Gillette, *Jersey Blue*, 306.

235. Livermore, *My Story of the War*, 471.

236. Strong, *Diary of the Civil War*, 580.

237. Hans Trefousse makes the case that northerners considered Lincoln to be second only to Washington among their presidents and that his good reputation was quite secure before his assassination. He quotes the Cincinnati *Commercial*. Hans L. Trefousse, *"First among Equals": Abraham Lincoln's Reputation during his Administration* (New York: Fordham University, 2005), 134–35.

238. Howland and Bacon, *My Heart Toward Home*, 390.

239. Strong, *Diary of the Civil War*, 583–86.

240. Bailey and Cottom, eds., *After Chancellorsville*, 213.

241. Allen C. Guelzo, *Abraham Lincoln: Redeemer President* (Grand Rapids, MI: William B. Eerdman's Publishing Company, 1999), 439–40; Merrill D. Peterson, *Lincoln in American Memory* (New York: Oxford University Press, 1994), 6–7; Margaret Leech, *Reveille in Washington, 1860–1865* (New York: Harper & Brothers, Publishers, 1941), 399; Hammond, *Diary of a Union Lady*, 357; Wainwright, ed., *A Philadelphia Perspective*, 493–95; David D. Van Tassel, with John Vacha, *"Behind Bayonets:" The Civil War in Northern Ohio* (Kent, OH: Kent State University Press, 2006), 100, 103.

242. Ernest B. Ferguson, *Freedom Rising: Washington in the Civil War* (New York: Alfred A. Knopf, 2004), 392–94.

243. Strong, *Diary of the Civil War*, 583–86.

244. Franny Nudelman, *John's Brown Body: Slavery, Violence, and the Culture of War* (Chapel Hill: University of North Carolina Press, 2004), 88–89.

245. Wainwright, ed., *A Philadelphia Perspective*, 492–93.

246. Peterson, *Lincoln in American Memory*, 21.

247. Strong, *Diary of the Civil War*, 587.

248. Peterson, *Lincoln in American Memory*, 14–21; Bailey and Cottom, eds., *After Chancellorsville*, 213; Marshall, ed., *A War of the People*, 305; Nudelman, *John's Brown Body*, 88–89; Van Tassel with Vacha, *"Behind Bayonets,"* 104–9; Wainwright, ed., *A Philadelphia Perspective*, 493; Gillette, *Jersey Blue*, 307.

249. Peterson, *Lincoln in American Memory*, 7–8; Moorhead, *American Apocalypse*, 174–76; Lawson, *Patriot Fires*, 173–78.

250. Spann, *Gotham at War,* 188.

251. Gray, *Business of Captivity,* 148–51.

252. Spann, *Gotham at War,* 188.

253. Lois Bryan Adams, *Letter from Washington, 1863–1865,* ed. by Evelyn Lasher (Detroit: Wayne State University Press, 1999), 263–68; Leech, *Reveille in Washington,* 415–17.

254. Paul A. Cimbala, "The Veteran Reserve Corps and the Northern People," in *Union Soldiers and the Northern Home Front: Wartime Experiences, Postwar Adjustments,* ed. Paul A. Cimbala and Randall M. Miller (New York: Fordham University Press, 2002), 202–3.

255. Mohr, ed., *The Cormany Diaries,* 576.

256. Ibid., 578, 579; Spann, *Gotham at War,* 190.

257. Bailey and Cottom, eds., *After Chancellorsville,* 230.

258. Ibid., 241–42.

259. Gillette, *Jersey Blue,* 312.

260. Niven, *Connecticut for the Union,* 429–38.

261. William B. Holberton, *Homeward Bound: The Demobilization of the Union and Confederate Armies, 1865–1866* (Mechanicsburg, PA: Stackpole Books, 2001), 35.

262. Niven, *Connecticut for the Union,* 429–38.

263. Kiper, ed., *Dear Catharine, Dear Taylor,* 18, 414.

264. Spann, *Gotham at War,* 191–92; Frances Clarke, " 'Honorable Scars,' " 361–94.

265. Frisch, *Town Into City,* 117–23.

266. Niven, *Connecticut for the Union,* 442–45; Karamanski, *Rally 'Round the Flag,* 242.

267. Van Tassel, with Vacha, *"Behind Bayonets,"* 98.

268. Bee, ed., *The Boys from Rockville,* 176.

269. Mohr, ed., *The Cormany Diaries,* 571–73, 584–86.

270. Bacon and Howland, *My Heart Toward Home,* 419.

271. Ibid., 420–21.

272. Carol Faulkner, *Women's Radical Reconstruction: The Freedmen's Aid Movement* (Philadelphia: University of Pennsylvania Press, 2004); Ronald E. Butchart, *Northern Schools, Southern Blacks, and Reconstruction: Freedmen's Education, 1862–1875* (Westport, CT: Greenwood Press, 1980), 115–34.

273. Attie, *Patriotic Toil,* 268–69; Eric Foner, *Reconstruction: America's Unfinished Revolution, 1863–1877* (New York: Harper & Row, Publishers, 1988), 472–73.

274. McPherson, *The Struggle for Equality,* 287–432.

275. David W. Blight, *Frederick Douglass' Civil War: Keeping Faith in Jubilee* (Baton Rouge: Louisiana State University Press, 1989), 208–9.

276. O'Connor, *Civil War Boston,* 243–44.

277. Foner, *Reconstruction,* 462.

278. Donald R. Shaffer, *After the Glory: The Struggles of Black Civil War Veterans* (Lawrence: University Press of Kansas, 2004), 47–48.

279. David W. Blight, *Race and Reunion: The Civil War in American Memory* (Cambridge, MA: The Belknap Press of Harvard University Press, 2001); Joseph T. Galatthaar, *Forged in Battle: The Civil War Alliance of Black Soldiers and White Officers* (New York: The Free Press, 1990), 231–64.

280. David Herbert Donald, *Liberty and Union: The Crisis of Popular Government, 1830–1890* (Boston: Little, Brown and Company, 1978), 169–211.

281. Jeremiah E. Goulka, ed., *The Grand Old Man from Maine: Selected Letters of Joshua Lawrence Chamberlain, 1865–1914* (Chapel Hill: University of North Carolina Press, 2004), 253.

FURTHER READING

Cimbala, Paul A., and Randall M. Miller, eds. *An Uncommon Time: The Civil War and the Northern Home Front.* New York: Fordham University Press, 2002. This volume presents a collection of original essays dealing with a variety of topics, including the media portrayal of combat, popular war literature, religion, war bond drives, partisanship, women and dependency, the Smithsonian Institution, black suffrage, the confiscation acts, and state war claims.

Cimbala, Paul A., and Randall M. Miller, eds. *Union Soldiers and the Northern Home Front.* New York: Fordham University Press, 2002. This essay collection focuses on the interaction of northern communities and Union soldiers. Topics include mobilization, society's quest to understand the combat experience, the work of benevolent organizations, the activities of the Veteran Reserve Corps in northern communities, and the veterans' return to society.

Creighton, Margaret S. *The Colors of Courage: Gettysburg's Forgotten History, Immigrants, Women, and African Americans in the Civil War's Defining Battle.* New York: Basic Books, 2005. Creighton's work is a unique study of that famous town and its moment in history. Its focus on immigrants, women, and blacks touched by the Gettysburg campaign helps to illuminate their role not only at home in Gettysburg, but also in the greater scheme of the northern war effort.

Gallman, J. Matthew. *The North Fights the Civil War: The Home Front.* Chicago: Ivan R. Dee, 1994. Gallman's study of the northern home front is a compact look at how northerners coped with the crisis of secession and war. The author's organizing concept is "adjustment," and his topical chapters look at how northerners dealt with, among other things, race, manpower requirements, and the economy. The chapters on how northerners dealt with loss and separation and on the various civilian voluntary activities and ritual are especially revealing.

Geary, James W. *We Need Men: The Union Draft and the Civil War.* DeKalb: Northern Illinois University Press, 1991. Geary's work remains the best treatment of northern conscription.

Gray, Michael P. *The Business of Captivity: Elmira and Its Civil War.* Kent, OH: Kent State University Press, 2001. Gray's community study of Elmira, New York, home of a military depot and a prisoner of war camp, helps to develop a greater understanding of the impact of the war at the local level.

Green, Michael S. *Freedom, Union, and Power: Lincoln and his Party during the Civil War.* New York: Fordham University Press, 2004. Green traces the wartime development of the Republican party's ideology, which, he argues, changed as it attempted to deal with the responsibilities of governing a nation at war.

Hess, Earl J. *Liberty, Virtue, and Progress: Northerners and Their War for the Union.* New York: Fordham University Press, 1997. This short volume remains the clearest statement of why northerners believed the Union was worth saving.

Lawson, Melinda. *Patriotic Fires: Forging a New American Nationalism in the Civil War North.* Lawrence: University Press of Kansas, 2002. Lawson explores various aspects of northern home-front activity that helped to develop a greater nationalist spirit, including sanitary fairs, war bond drives, partisanship, and Union Leagues.

Marten, James. *Children for the Union: The War Spirit on the Northern Home Front.* Chicago: Ivan R. Dee, 2004. Marten looks at how the war affected the lives of northern children. Among his topics are family life, children, and the community, and how northern society militarized its youngest members.

Moorehead, James H. *American Apocalypse: Yankee Protestants and the Civil War, 1860–1869.* New Haven: Yale University Press, 1978. Moorehead's study remains an important treatment of how evangelical Protestants, particularly northern Baptists, Congregationalists, Methodists, and Presbyterians, interpreted the war.

Neely, Mark E., Jr. *The Fate of Liberty: Abraham Lincoln and Civil Liberties.* New York: Oxford University Press, 1991. Neely's book provides a reasonable treatment of how the Lincoln administration handled political dissent during the war.

Neely, Mark. E., Jr. *The Union Divided: Party Conflict in the Civil War North.* Cambridge, MA: Harvard University Press, 2002. Neely challenges the long-held notion that partisan politics was good for the Union war effort. Rather, it was the Constitution at work that contributed to northern victory.

Paludan, Phillip Shaw. *A People's Contest: The Union and Civil War, 1861–1865,* 2nd ed. Lawrence: University Press of Kansas, 1996. Palludan's comprehensive study is the most complete look at the northern home front. It covers topics ranging from mobilization, politics, and congressional activity to agriculture, industrial workers, and religion.

Richardson, Heather Cox. *The Greatest Nation of the Earth: Republican Economic Policies during the Civil War.* Cambridge, MA: Harvard University Press, 1997. Richardson explores how Republican ideology influenced the development of wartime economic legislation, including war bonds, paper money, agriculture, taxation, the transcontinental railroad, and slavery.

Silber, Nina. *Daughters of the Union: Northern Women Fight the Civil War.* Cambridge, MA: Harvard University Press, 2005. Silber's study is the best comprehensive treatment of women's wartime activity, from fund raising on the home front to nursing sick and wounded soldiers.

Index

About the Editors and Contributors

Richard V. Barbuto earned a doctorate in American history from the University of Kansas after serving 23 years as an Army officer. Professor Barbuto is currently the deputy director of the Department of Military History at the U.S. Army Command and General Staff College at Fort Leavenworth, Kansas. His first book, *Niagara 1814: America Invades Canada,* was published in 2000. He is currently researching his next book, which will examine the 1812 campaign in New York State.

Paul A. Cimbala earned his PhD at Emory University. He is the author of *Under the Guardianship of the Nation: The Freedmen's Bureau and the Reconstruction of Georgia, 1865–1870* (1997, 2003), which received the 1999 Malcolm and Muriel Barrow Bell Award of the Georgia Historical Society, and *The Freedmen's Bureau: Reconstructing the American South after the Civil War* (2005). He is also co-editor of seven essay collections including *An Uncommon Time: The Civil War and the Northern Home Front* (2002), *Union Soldiers and the Northern Home Front: Wartime Experiences, Postwar Adjustments* (2002), *The Freedmen's Bureau and Reconstruction: Reconsiderations* (1999) and the forthcoming *Making a New South: Race, Leadership, and Community after the Civil War.* He participated in the editing of a volume of original documents in *The Black Abolitionist Papers* series dealing with African Americans and antislavery in Canada (1986) and has published articles, book chapters, and essays on slavery, Civil War soldiers, and Reconstruction. He is now at work on a *Civil War Soldiers' Lives* and *Soldiering on the Home Front: The United States Army's Veteran Reserve Corps during the Civil War and Reconstruction.*

David S. Heidler and **Jeanne T. Heidler** met as graduate students at Auburn University and married in 1981. Jeanne is currently a professor of history at the United States Air Force Academy, where she is the senior civilian member of her department; David is associated with Colorado State University–Pueblo. Together, they have written and edited numerous books and articles on early nineteenth-century American history, including *Old Hickory's War,* and *Indian Removal.* They are the editors of two definitive encyclopedias, *Encyclopedia of the War of 1812* and the award-winning *Encyclopedia of the American Civil War: A Political, Social, and Military History.*

Gregory S. Hospodor is an assistant professor of history at Delta State University in Cleveland, Mississippi, where he teaches courses in U.S. History, the American Civil War, and Latin American History. He received his PhD in 2000 from Louisiana State University, completing a dissertation entitled, "Honor Bound: Southern Honor and the Mexican War." He is the author of numerous articles and conference presentations including, "'Bound by All the Ties of Honor': Southern Honor, the Mississippians, and the Mexican War" published in the *Journal of Mississippi History.*

Wayne E. Lee is an associate professor of history at the University of North Carolina, Chapel Hill. He has written *Crowds and Soldiers in Revolutionary North Carolina: The Culture of Violence in Riot and War* as well as a number of other articles on early American and Native American military history. He also works and publishes in the field of archaeology based on projects in Greece, Albania, and Virginia. He is currently working on a study of the structural and cultural restraints on warfare from antiquity through industrialization.

James Marten is professor and chair of the Department of History at Marquette University, where he teaches courses on the Civil War era and on children's history. He is author of *The Children's Civil War,* which was named an "outstanding academic title" by *Choice Magazine* for 1998, and of *Civil War America: Voices from the Homefront* (2003). He is editor of *Childhood and Child Welfare in the Progressive Era: A Brief History with Documents* (2004) and *Children and War: A Historical Anthology* (2002).

Armstrong Starkey is a professor of history at Adelphi University, Garden City, New York. He received his PhD from the University of Illinois. Among his many published works are *European and Native American Warfare, 1675–1815* (1998) and *Warfare in the Age of the Enlightenment, 1700–1789* (2003).